CW00449891

Dean Acheson and the
Obligations of Power

Biographies
IN AMERICAN FOREIGN POLICY

Joseph A. Fry, University of Nevada, Las Vegas
Series Editor

The Biographies in American Foreign Policy series employs the enduring medium of biography to examine the major episodes and themes in the history of U.S. foreign relations. By viewing policy formation and implementation from the perspective of influential participants, the series humanizes and makes more accessible those decisions and events that sometimes appear abstract or distant. Particular attention is devoted to those aspects of the subject's background, personality, and intellect that most influenced his or her approach to U.S. foreign policy, and each individual's role is placed in a context that takes into account domestic affairs, national interests and policies, and international and strategic considerations.

Volumes Published

Lawrence S. Kaplan, *Thomas Jefferson: Westward the Course of Empire*
Richard H. Immerman, *John Foster Dulles: Piety, Pragmatism, and Power in U.S. Foreign Policy*
Thomas W. Zeiler, *Dean Rusk: Defending the American Mission Abroad*
Edward P. Crapol, *James G. Blaine: Architect of Empire*
David F. Schmitz, *Henry L. Stimson: The First Wise Man*
Thomas M. Leonard, *James K. Polk: A Clear and Unquestionable Destiny*
James E. Lewis, Jr., *John Quincy Adams: Policymaker for the Union*
Catherine Forslund, *Anna Chennault: Informal Diplomacy and Asian Relations*
Lawrence S. Kaplan, *Alexander Hamilton: Ambivalent Anglophile*
Andrew J. DeRoche, *Andrew Young: Civil Rights Ambassador*
Jeffrey J. Matthews, *Alanson B. Houghton: Ambassador of the New Era*
Clarence E. Wunderlin, Jr., *Robert A. Taft: Ideas, Tradition, and Party in U.S. Foreign Policy*
Howard Jablon, *David M. Shoup: A Warrior against War*
Jeff Woods, *Richard B. Russell: Southern Nationalism and American Foreign Policy*
Russell D. Buhite, *Douglas MacArthur: Statecraft and Stagecraft in America's East Asian Policy*
Christopher D. O'Sullivan, *Colin Powell: American Power and Intervention from Vietnam to Iraq*
David F. Schmitz, *Brent Scowcroft: Internationalism and Post–Vietnam War American Foreign Policy*
Christopher D. O'Sullivan, *Harry Hopkins: FDR's Envoy to Churchill and Stalin*
Michael F. Hopkins, *Dean Acheson and the Obligations of Power*

Dean Acheson and the Obligations of Power

Michael F. Hopkins

ROWMAN & LITTLEFIELD
Lanham • Boulder • New York • London

Published by Rowman & Littlefield
A wholly owned subsidiary of The Rowman & Littlefield Publishing Group, Inc.
4501 Forbes Boulevard, Suite 200, Lanham, Maryland 20706
www.rowman.com

Unit A, Whitacre Mews, 26-34 Stannary Street, London SE11 4AB

British Library Cataloguing in Publication Information Available

Library of Congress Cataloging-in-Publication Data

Names: Hopkins, Michael F. (Michael Francis), 1953– author.
Title: Dean Acheson and the obligations of power / by Michael F. Hopkins.
Description: Lanham : Rowman & Littlefield, [2017] | Series: Biographies in American foreign
  policy | Includes bibliographical references and index.
Identifiers: LCCN 2016052917 (print) | LCCN 2017002524 (ebook) | ISBN 9780742544918 (cloth) |
  ISBN 9781538100028 (electronic)
Subjects: LCSH: Acheson, Dean, 1893–1971. | Acheson, Dean, 1893–1971—Political and social
  views. | Statesmen—United States—Biography. | Cabinet officers—United States—Biography. |
  United States—Foreign relations—1945–1953. | United States—Foreign relations—Philosophy.
  | BISAC: HISTORY / United States / 20th Century. | BIOGRAPHY & AUTOBIOGRAPHY /
  General. | BIOGRAPHY & AUTOBIOGRAPHY / Historical. | BIOGRAPHY & AUTOBIOG-
  RAPHY / Political. | HISTORY / Modern / 20th Century.
Classification: LCC E748.A15 H66 2017 (print) | LCC E748.A15 (ebook) | DDC 973.918092 [B]—
  dc23 LC record available at https://lccn.loc.gov/2016052917

Printed in the United States of America

Contents

Preface   vii

Introduction   ix

1   Beginnings   1
2   National Duty: Assistant Secretary of State, 1941–1945   17
3   The Obligations of Power: Under Secretary of State and After, 1945–1948   57
4   Leadership in Foreign Policy: Secretary of State, 1949–1950   97
5   Confronting Perils, 1950–1951   135
6   Global Challenges, 1951–1953   173
7   Afterlife of a Secretary   211

Conclusion   257

Bibliographical Essay   265

Index   275

About the Author   289

Preface

Dean Acheson was one of the most significant figures in twentieth century American foreign policy. His life has attracted the attention of some fine scholars, who, given his ardent advocacy of robust policies toward the Soviet Union, have understandably concentrated on his involvement in the Cold War. Indeed, the fullest (and excellent) account by Robert Beisner is subtitled, *A life in the Cold War*, devoting about 80 percent of its text to 1949–1953. Yet Acheson began working at the State Department more than five years before the East-West confrontation erupted. This study contends that Acheson's contribution touched more than Cold War policies, and that even those policies need to be understood in the context of his earlier experiences. It offers the first detailed scrutiny of the whole of Acheson's public career based on the full range of government and private papers now available. In particular, it is the first substantial analysis of Acheson's period as assistant secretary during the Second World War. His activities during the war were important in shaping him as a public official and saw the progressive emergence of his ideas about the United States' world role. My book suggests fresh perspectives on Acheson's career. It differs from previous work in giving greater emphasis to his role in articulating a vision of American engagement in the world; in stressing that, although European concerns were his priority, Asian issues were of importance to him; and in suggesting that his approach to policy on both the Soviet Union and the Chinese communists was a good deal less clear-cut, even as late as 1949, than his memoirs later claimed.

It has been a pleasure to work on the abundant sources in more than twenty archives, whose staffs have been unfailingly helpful. I welcome this opportunity to express my thanks to the professionals at the following archives: Birmingham University Library; the Bentley Library, University of

Michigan, Ann Arbor, Michigan; Bodleian Library, Oxford; British Library of Political and Economic Sciences, London; Churchill College, Cambridge; Clemson University, Clemson, South Carolina; Special Collections, Margaret King Library, University of Kentucky; Houghton Library, Harvard University; King's College, Cambridge; Manuscripts Division, Library of Congress, Washington, DC; the National Archives, College Park, Maryland; the National Archives, Kew, United Kingdom; New York Historical Society; the Public Archives of Canada, Ottawa; Franklin D. Roosevelt Library, Hyde Park, New York; Seeley G. Mudd Library, Princeton University, Princeton, New Jersey; Harry S. Truman Library, Independence, Missouri; Sterling Memorial Library, Yale University; Worcester College, Oxford; University of Virginia, Charlottesville, Virginia; Marshall Foundation Library, Lexington, Virginia.

My research was greatly facilitated by travel grants from the Franklin D. Roosevelt Library Institute and the Harry S. Truman Library Institute; a British Academy grant; a Friends of Princeton University Library fellowship; and a term as a Global Policy Scholar at the Woodrow Wilson International Center for Scholars, Washington, DC. I am also most grateful for the financial assistance I have received as a member of the department of history at the University of Liverpool; and in my previous post at Liverpool Hope University.

I have presented my ideas about Acheson to audiences across the United Kingdom and the United States, and in China, Germany, and South Korea, and have profited greatly from the astute questions and fruitful discussions. I am grateful to John Thompson of St. Catharine's College, Cambridge, for encouraging my decision to examine Acheson's wartime service in greater depth. A discussion at Boston University with Erik Goldstein, Bill Keylor, David Mayers, and Cathal Nolan was a particularly rewarding experience.

Many scholars and friends have read portions of my work, discussed issues, and offered advice. In particular, I wish to thank Bill Burr, John Young, Lloyd Ambrosius, Michael Hughes, John Kent, Mark Kramer, Fredrik Logevall, Katherine Field, and Alisa Kramer. Above all, I wish to record my deep gratitude to Andy Fry for his meticulous examination of the entire manuscript and his many sage suggestions.

I dedicate this book to my nieces, Elizabeth and Alex Hopkins.

Introduction

Washington, DC, at the time of Franklin D. Roosevelt's inauguration in March 1933 was a sleepy southern town. Even in 1940, after the expansion of government's role and the growth of federal agencies in the New Deal, the US capital was still a small-scale city. By 1942, however, it was the nerve center of a global alliance against Nazi Germany, fascist Italy, and Tojo's Japan. Unlike the American involvement in the First World War, this was the beginning of a long-term engagement in international affairs—first in waging war and planning for the peace, next in trying to settle and reconstruct the postwar world, and then in the Cold War. If Roosevelt was the principal author of the momentous change in 1941, it was his successor, Harry S. Truman, who was responsible for making it a permanent shift in peacetime. Dean Acheson's public career almost exactly coincided with these developments. After an abortive six months at the US Treasury in 1933, he returned to the Roosevelt administration in February 1941 and worked at the State Department as assistant secretary, 1941–1945, under secretary, 1945–1947, and secretary of state, 1949–1953. He was not only a member of the government, but he was also prominent in shaping the new American outlook.

EVOLUTION OF A REPUTATION

Such shifts in US foreign policy inevitably brought controversy at the time and have continued in historical assessments. Given Acheson's central role in these years, he has been the focus of much debate. He was the subject of admiring and critical comment almost from the time he entered government service—on a small scale over his resignation in 1933 and as a member of a disparaged department in 1941–1945 and, after 1945, in his own right, reaching a peak in 1950–1952. It is interesting to note that criticisms of him while in office focused mainly on his alleged failure to take a firm enough line against Soviet and Chinese communism. From the late 1950s onward there emerged a more critical assessment of the policy of containment of communism. As one of the leading exponents of this policy, Acheson then faced accusations of being too tough.

In the earliest studies to feature him Acheson figured only as one among a number of senior officials in the State Department. Robert Bendiner's *The Riddle of the State Department* spoke of the "dead weight of tradition. Other agencies of the government in varying degrees reflect the times, but the faded and moth-eaten tradition of Victorian diplomacy seeps out of every cranny in the antiquated home of the State Department."[1] A review of the book agreed that a thread of appeasement had run through the department in the preceding decade, endorsed Bendiner's injunction that it should be closer to the people and more responsive, and advised that it "should serve the great cause for which we are now at war and the material interests of the government."[2]

After the war certain writers revisited their doubts about American entry and goals during the conflict. Charles Beard identified Acheson as one of the people who advanced the capitalist economic agenda.[3] As the grand alliance gave way to the Cold War, critics turned to current developments, charging Acheson with reacting too slowly to Soviet behavior. If the administration's policy on Europe enjoyed bipartisan backing, no such concord extended to Asia. The communist victory in China in October 1949 galvanized much Republican opposition, which deepened with Senator Joseph R. McCarthy's (R-Wisconsin) claims of communist infiltration of the State Department. The outbreak of the Korean War in June 1950 saw bipartisan support for the commitment of American forces but, when US-dominated UN troops suffered defeats by the Chinese in late 1950, there were vociferous calls for the resignation of Acheson.[4] Acheson and his supporters were not idle in responding to the attacks. In 1950 the State Department published a collection of his statements in *Strengthening the Forces of Freedom*.[5] This was prepared before but appeared after the outbreak of the Korean War. In early 1952 McGeorge Bundy edited a book based on Acheson's speeches, statements, and extemporaneous remarks—*The Pattern of Responsibility*.[6] After the Truman presidency ended in January 1953, Acheson assumed the role of elder statesman and commentator, publishing four books in the next eight years. *A Democrat Looks at His Party* defended his party's twenty years in government; *A Citizen Looks at Congress* demonstrated his extensive dealings with the Hill; *Power and Diplomacy* articulated his cautious approach in the nuclear era; and *Sketches from Life of Men I Have Known* (1961) provided his first attempt to capture aspects of his period in office.[7] In 1959 the *New York Times* reevaluated Acheson a decade after he had become secretary of state. It acknowledged his substantial achievements but also noted that "he made more trouble for himself by what he said than by what he did"; his "imperious scorn" did not endear him to legislators.[8] Historical assessments also began to appear, vindicating American policy and Acheson's role.[9] But, as the 1950s gave way to the 1960s, Acheson faced a more critical scrutiny. William Appleman Williams's *The Tragedy of American Foreign Policy* appeared in 1959 and questioned whether the Soviets had been aggressive or even provocative. He argued, instead, that US policy was driven by economic goals, resulting in a more forward policy by Washington. D. F. Fleming declared in 1961: "from the first it was the West which was on the offensive, not the Soviets." In the course of the decade, there were further critiques of US foreign policy and its leading architects since 1945 from revisionist scholars, which included David Horowitz, Ronald Steel, and Richard Barnet.[10] The shadow of American failure in Vietnam, seen as a manifestation of the policy of containment devised in the Truman years, undoubtedly influenced what were increasingly tough judgments on Acheson.

It was partly to respond to these charges that he wrote his huge memoir, *Present at the Creation*.[11] The memoirs robustly defended his record and the validity of the general policy of containment and proved hugely influential in shaping our understanding of Acheson and the Truman administration's foreign policy. Both critics and admirers have utilized its invaluable details to support their arguments. But Acheson offered a more coherent account of the emergence of his responses to the Soviets and the Chinese communists than the contemporary records suggest.[12]

In the same year the first book-length (though brief) study appeared. It painted a favorable picture of a secretary whose many gifts—command of his brief, excellent working relations with members of the State Department, very good understandings with most people in other departments, and adeptness in securing congressional support—allowed him to pursue and achieve his goal of establishing the predominance of the State Department in foreign policy.[13]

Acheson's memoirs and Ronald Stupak's study did not divert the revisionists. Prominent among them was Lloyd Gardner, who suggested Acheson used "holy pretense" to secure his blinkered view of the Soviet threat: "By the time of the Korean War he was blaming the 'distant and shadowy figures in the Kremlin' for practically everything that had gone wrong since World War II."[14] Each of the revisionists developed distinctive arguments but as a group they offered some common claims. They accused Acheson (and Truman) of needlessly militarizing the confrontation between the Soviet Union and the United States, of hardening the Cold War division. They maintained that he misdiagnosed the nature of Soviet behavior and overreacted to it. His overreaction had deleterious effects not only on US foreign policy but also on US domestic life and they lasted for a generation and more. It might not have engendered McCarthy's anti-communist witch hunts but it certainly created an atmosphere that was conducive to their pursuit.

Acheson survived the appearance of his memoirs just long enough to see them receive the Pulitzer Prize. He died in October 1971. *Time* magazine, never his most devoted admirer when in office, described him as "The Diplomat Who Did Not Want to Be Liked."[15] There soon followed two impressive and favorable biographies by Gaddis Smith in 1972 and by David McLellan in 1976. Both regarded him as a man of real talent, someone who wielded influence, and did so for the benefit of the United States and the world. This was just before the release of the government documents for the period. Good though Smith and McLellan were, they needed to be supplemented with the many detailed studies, based on the newly available sources, which appeared on various aspects of Truman's presidency.

Acheson has been most fortunate in his biographers. There have been five studies since the main government sources were opened to scholars. Walter Isaacson and Evan Thomas produced a shrewd assessment of Acheson in their group biography of key figures in US foreign policy; again the verdict was favorable. Douglas Brinkley published an excellent pioneering study of Acheson's career after stepping down as secretary, demonstrating his continued importance in debates and as a presidential advisor.[16] James Chace wrote the first full biography, a clear, fluent, admiring account based on extensive use of Acheson's papers and some other private papers, but he utilized few government documents and many other relevant personal papers. Robert Beisner's huge volume of nearly 800 pages, rooted in vast reading in printed and manuscript sources, concentrated on the Cold War years and Acheson's term as secretary of state. It abounds in perceptive comments on Acheson, his policies, and his impact. A more skeptical view of postwar American foreign policy and a more critical evaluation of Acheson is evident in the most recent study, a pithy and astute assessment by Robert McMahon based on a wide range of original sources.[17]

General studies of the Truman administration have also assessed Acheson's performance. In his detailed examination of both domestic and foreign affairs, Robert J. Donovan praised the foreign policy achievements of the Truman-Acheson partnership.[18] Two major studies of Cold War policy have been less enthusiastic. Melvyn Leffler was dubious about the scale of the American commitment, which only made sense if the Soviets were bent on world domination, but Leffler doubted that was their goal. In particular, he was unconvinced by the willingness of Acheson and others to "run the risk of an escalatory cycle over much less significant interests" such as those in Southeast Asia. Arnold Offner was scathing, saying Truman "significantly contributed to and exacerbated the growing Cold War and militarization of U.S. foreign policy." And Truman's policy, according to Offner, owed a great deal to manipulation by Acheson, who presented proposals to the president in a way calculated to secure their acceptance, though Offner does not undertake a systematic examination of Acheson's influence through this technique. [19]

DEAN ACHESON AND AMERICAN FOREIGN POLICY

The debate about Acheson has been dominated by the Cold War. This is understandable because he held high office as the East-West confrontation emerged and he played a central role in framing US policy, retaining throughout his life a robust attachment to containment. But he also served in the State Department before the Cold War. Any account must look at the man and his actions in this wider setting. This study aims to explore the role of this singular individual by first understanding him as a man, his character, talents, emotional baggage, his social attitudes, and his ideas about government and foreign affairs—and especially his perspectives on America's place in the world. A second aim is to recreate some sense of the climate of opinion in which he had to work, to see Acheson's thinking in the context of other views at the time. Thirdly, this volume scrutinizes the evolving framework for foreign policymaking and, in particular, his relations with presidents, with successive secretaries of state (1941–1947), with the members of the State Department, and other government agencies, especially the military. These years marked a rise in the importance and efficiency of the State Department, a development that owed a good deal to the efforts of Dean Acheson.

Acheson's responses to international developments could not be formulated purely within the US government machine. He had to operate in a wider domestic and international context. He faced various domestic pressures—from electoral vicissitudes to the activities of pressure groups, such as neo-isolationists or the "China lobby" who blamed him for not stopping the communists from coming to power. He encountered difficult episodes, sometimes of his own making, such as his refusal to condemn a former colleague, Alger Hiss, after conviction for perjury, to congressional difficulties over legislation. There were also the shifting moods in popular and informed opinion about foreign relations and about his own performance. Acheson had to conduct American foreign policy in an atmosphere of considerable criticism for a large part of his time as secretary. These critiques were often mediated through the debates among columnists such as Walter Lippmann and the Alsop brothers and an informed reporter like James Reston. Moreover, he had to take account of international circumstances—from limitations on American influence to unexpected developments to the need to work with allies, the British especially, who had their own domestic considerations. He was astute enough to appreciate that issues often looked very different to Western Europeans, if not always so sensitive to the world beyond.

Ultimately, Acheson's time in office centered on the issue of the role of American power in the world. He entered the State Department as Roosevelt increasingly involved the nation in international developments; he rose to high office under Truman who committed the United States to continuing engagement. These decisions corresponded with his belief in the obligations of power and the verdict on his public career turns on the nature and consequences of that conception.

NOTES

1. Robert Bendiner, *The Riddle of the State Department* (New York: Farrar & Rhinehart, 1942), 109.

2. R. L. Duffus, "Diplomatic 'Riddle," *New York Times* (20 September 1942).

3. Charles Beard, *President Roosevelt and the Coming of War, 1941* (New Haven, CT: Yale University Press, 1941), 291n21.

4. See, for example, editorial, "The Case against Acheson," *The Freeman* (11 December 1950), 165–167.

5. See review by Crane Brinton in *New York Herald Tribune Book Review* (3 September 1950).

6. McGeorge Bundy, ed., *The Pattern of Responsibility* (Boston, 1952); reviewed in James R. Newman, "The Case for Acheson: A Deferential and Discreet Defense," *New Republic* 126 (Boston: Houghton Mifflin, 1952), 17–18.

7. *A Democrat Looks at His Party* (New York: Harper, 1955), *A Citizen Looks at Congress* (New York: Harper, 1957), *Power and Diplomacy* (Cambridge, MA: Harvard University Press, 1958), and *Sketches from Life of Men I Have Known* (New York: Harper, 1959).

8. Cabell Philipps, "Dean Acheson Ten Years Later," *New York Times Magazine* (18 January 1959).

9. Norman A. Graebner, "Dean G. Acheson," in Norman A. Graebner, ed., *An Uncertain Tradition: American Secretaries of State in the Twentieth Century* (New York: McGraw-Hill, 1961), 267–288. Herbert Feis, *Churchill, Roosevelt, Stalin* (Princeton, NJ: Princeton University Press, 1957); idem., *Between War and Peace: the Potsdam Conference* (Princeton, NJ: Princeton University Press, 1960).

10. William Appleman Williams, *The Tragedy of American Foreign Policy* 2nd ed. (New York: Dell, 1962); D. F. Fleming, *The Cold War and Its Origins, 1917–1960* (Garden City, NY: Doubleday, 1961), quotation at I, 31; David Horowitz, *The Free World Colossus: A Critique of American Foreign Policy in the Cold War* (New York: Hill and Wang, 1965); Ronald Steel, *Pax Americana* (New York: Viking, 1967).

11. Acheson, *Present at the Creation: My Years in the State Department* (New York: W. W. Norton, 1969).

12. On the memoirs, see Douglas Brinkley, *Dean Acheson: the Cold War Years* (New Haven, CT: Yale University Press, 1992), 275–277; and Wilson D. Miscamble, "In Retrospect: Dean G. Acheson's *Present at the Creation: My Years in the State Department,*" *Reviews in American History* 22 (1994), 544–560.

13. Ronald J. Stupak, *The Shaping of Foreign Policy: The Role of the Secretary of State as Seen by Dean Acheson* (New York: Odyssey Press, 1969).

14. Lloyd C. Gardner, *Architects of Illusion* (Chicago: Quadrangle, 1970), 202–231, quotation at 205. See also Joyce and Gabriel Kolko, *The Limits of Power* (New York: Harper & Row, 1972); Walter LaFeber, *America, Russia and the Cold War* (New York: Wiley, 1967); Stephen Ambrose, *The Rise to Globalism* (New York: Penguin, 1971).

15. *Time* (25 October 1971).

16. Brinkley, *Acheson.*

17. Walter Isaacson and Evan Thomas, *The Wise Men: Six Friends and the World They Made* (London & Boston: Faber and Faber, 1986); James Chace, *Acheson: The Secretary of*

State Who Created the American World (New York: Simon & Schuster, 1998); Robert Beisner, *Dean Acheson: A Life in the Cold War* (New York: Oxford University Press, 2006); Robert J. McMahon, *Dean Acheson and the Creation of the American World Order* (Dulles, VA: Potomac Books, 2009).

18. Robert J. Donovan, *Conflict and Crisis: The Presidency of Harry S. Truman, 1945–1948* (New York: W. W. Norton, 1977); idem., *Tumultuous Years: The Presidency of Harry S. Truman, 1949–1953* (New York: W. W. Norton, 1982).

19. Melvyn P. Leffler, *A Preponderance of Power: National Security, the Truman Administration and the Cold War* (Stanford, CA: Stanford University Press, 1992), 510–511. Arnold A. Offner, *One Such Victory: President Truman and the Cold War, 1945–1953* (Stanford, CA: Stanford University Press, 2002), 457–458 (quotation), 329–330.

Chapter One

Beginnings

The very name Dean Gooderham Acheson conjures up the image of the East Coast WASP (White Anglo-Saxon Protestant). His appearance as an adult—tall, mustachioed, dapper, assured—only added to the impression. Yet he might so easily have not been an American at all. His father was a British migrant to Canada, while his mother was the daughter of a Toronto banker and distiller. Acheson was born in Middletown, Connecticut, on 11 April 1893, the first son of Eleanor Gooderham and Edward Campion Acheson, who also had a daughter, Margaret, and another son, Edward.[1] His father had been born in England and immigrated to Canada where he served in the army and saw military action before training as an Anglican priest. He had moved to Middletown to become rector of Holy Trinity Church and, in 1915, he was appointed episcopal bishop of Connecticut. Acheson's father was a tall and imposing figure but was easygoing and able to mix easily, while his mother was elegant and well-dressed, a witty but less gregarious, rather formidable individual. Over the years, Acheson came to display many of his mother's traits from a sense of humor and penchant for witticisms to sartorial elegance; and, perhaps above all, he developed a similarly formidable character. Middletown was a small town of 20,000, about thirty miles north of New Haven. In these secure and tranquil surroundings the young Dean enjoyed a carefree childhood, roaming the fields and avoiding formal schooling while being educated by a governess. His father encouraged in him what would be a lifelong enthusiasm for fishing. He absorbed a secular version of the virtues espoused by his father but seemed untouched by his religious commitment. In particular, he applied his father's stoic code: "Much in life could not be affected or mitigated and, hence, must be borne. Borne without complaint, because complaints were a bore and nuisance to others and undermined the serenity necessary to endurance."[2] In addition, he shared the Reverend Acheson's belief that good works rather than moralizing was what counted: the less fortunate needed help not lectures.

Acheson's formal schooling began with two years at a preparatory school, Hamlet Lodge, in nearby Pomfret, followed by Groton School from 1905 to 1911, which, under the leadership of the redoubtable Endicott Peabody, encouraged its pupils to consider public service. Acheson came last in his class of twenty-four pupils. He did not appear to enjoy either the need to conform or the pervasive conservative political outlook, though he did begin a lasting friendship with Averell Harriman, who was his rowing coach.[3] In the summer between school and college, he worked on a railroad in northern Canada, where he thoroughly enjoyed the rudimentary life of a working camp. His studies at Yale University in 1911–1915 were marked by minimal scholarly achievement but great social success. Prized for his polished manner and sharp wit, he was a member of numerous student societies, in particular the secret Scroll and Key, second only to Skull and Bones in the hierarchy of status. Among his friends were the composer Cole Porter and the poet and future Librarian of Congress Archibald MacLeish. Acheson continued his education at Harvard Law School from 1915 to 1918. Modest academic performance seemed no impediment to entry into two elite schools. At Harvard, however, he became, for the first time in his life, intellectually engaged, though this did not occur immediately. "This was a tremendous discovery— the discovery of the power of thought," he told a journalist in 1949.[4] The spur to think and develop his intellect came from a number of talented professors and above all from Felix Frankfurter, who had an aptitude for spotting gifted young men. Taken by Acheson's elegance, droll demeanor, and largely untutored intelligence, Frankfurter became a mentor and thus began a lifelong friendship. Acheson later noted that Frankfurter was no secluded scholar but, rather, someone with a genius for friendship and avid for good conversation.[5] Harvard "not only afforded an intellectual challenge hitherto missing, but more importantly it provided him with a socially sanctioned mode of excelling and of achieving personal distinction which was destined to become a crucial goal in his life."[6] Acheson discovered he need not make up his mind in advance—decisions were the result of analyzing the facts.[7] He was elected to the *Harvard Law Review* and graduated fifth in his class (his friend from Yale, Archibald MacLeish, was first). On 5 May 1917 he married Alice Stanley, the daughter of a Detroit railroad lawyer, who had been his sister's roommate at Wellesley College. They were to have three children—Jane, David, and Mary.

On graduation he was commissioned into the naval auxiliary service but the war ended before he could serve. Instead, he went to Washington, where, on the recommendation of Felix Frankfurter, he served from 1919 to 1921 as law clerk to Louis Brandeis, the first Jewish Supreme Court justice.[8] Brandeis was even more demanding than Frankfurter that legal arguments should be rigorous and precise and rooted in the facts rather than abstractions. During these years Acheson learned to work hard and intensely. He later cited Brandeis's dictum that a year's work could be done in eleven months but not in twelve months: Brandeis "worked with intensity, or recharged his reserve of energy until he could."[9] This was an approach he would apply throughout his own career. Acheson wrote later of Brandeis's brilliant mind, the warmth of his interest and solicitude for his aides, and his burning faith in the eternal verities.[10] He shared many of Brandeis's views: sympathy for those suffering, recognition that the law could not be separated from social justice but skepticism about "mass salvation through universal Plumb Plans."[11] He also absorbed Brandeis's belief that an elite should take the lead, for they possessed the grander vision and intelligence that enabled them to overcome the uninformed preoccupations of the masses. By the end of his clerkship Acheson had developed the essentials of a discernible philosophy, as he melded his father's and Brandeis's examples to a commitment to integrity, loyalty, intellectual rigor, and pursuit of the truth, achieved with a stoical spirit.

As a result of working with Brandeis, Acheson met another hugely influential figure, Supreme Court justice Oliver Wendell Holmes. Acheson ranked him, alongside General George C. Marshall (Chief of Staff of the US Army, 1939–1945 and Secretary of State, 1947–1949), as the greatest man he had met—both were notable for their grandeur and presence.[12] Unlike the more austere Brandeis, Holmes combined intellect and wit in a way that appealed to Acheson.

Unsure what to do when his clerkship ended in 1921, he consulted Frankfurter and briefly considered moving to New York, before deciding to join the new Washington law firm of Covington, Burling and Rublee, where he worked for the next twelve years. In 1926 he was made a partner. By then he had acquired a house in Georgetown (2805 P Street, built in 1843) and a farm at Silver Spring, Maryland (built in 1775). He came to specialize in appellate cases, sometimes before the Supreme Court, and often on matters concerning the federal government. His legal skill in these cases brought handsome rewards—in good years he earned between $100,000 and $150,000, according to one journalist.[13] During this time, he became involved in Democratic Party politics, though he soon recognized that he did not enjoy either the need to evince enthusiasm (whether sincere or simulated) for people and policies or the rough and tumble of elective politics. He preferred campaigning for others. In 1928 he backed Al Smith for president. Then in 1930 he worked for the successful Senate campaign of Dwight Morrow, a Republican with associations with his law firm. As a lawyer at the banking firm J. P. Morgan, Morrow had helped facilitate loans to the Allies during the First World War. In his campaign he was the first federal government official to condemn Prohibition and advocate its repeal, an approach strongly encouraged by the martini-drinking Acheson.[14]

UNDER SECRETARY AT THE TREASURY, 1933

In the 1932 presidential election Acheson campaigned enthusiastically for Franklin D. Roosevelt. Not long after Roosevelt's inauguration on 4 March 1933, Acheson came to the White House for discussions on a legislative program. He had hopes of becoming solicitor general but this was thwarted by the attorney general, Homer Cummings. Acheson only discovered later that this was probably because his father had refused a church blessing for the twice-divorced Cummings's third marriage in 1929.[15] Instead, Acheson was made under secretary of the Treasury, being formally appointed on 19 May 1933. The secretary of the Treasury was William Woodin, one time president of the American Car & Foundry Company and a major donor to FDR's campaign.

Dean Acheson in March 1933 was a six-foot-two-inch tall, well-tailored, and striking figure with bushy eyebrows and military mustache. He had visible self-confidence and a sharp tongue. With his well-honed intellect, he cut to the heart of issues and rebuked challengers. He had a feel for Washington, having worked there since 1919, and a reasonable experience of the world, having toured Europe with his father in 1907 and visited Japan in 1915. He was inclined to control his feelings, though he could not always contain his disdain for ill-considered views. Although he came from a comfortable WASP background, he was receptive to the New Deal and ready to see social change, though he had a rather conservative interpretation of the new policies. In general he was dubious about panaceas, preferring to see steady advances against problems. He might have been an assured individual but he was unschooled in the ways of politics and rather rigid and legalistic in his view of legitimate governmental action.

Acheson served as under secretary for six months, or, as he put it, "more accurately as acting secretary due to secretary Woodin's fatal illness" until "a spectacular row with the President and my resignation took me back to private life."[16] His relations with the president were more respectful than enthusiastic: "He remained a formidable man, a leader who won admiration and respect. In others he inspired far more, affection and devotion."[17] He told a biographer: "I respected his ability to rule, but did not like him."[18]

At the beginning of his presidency Roosevelt wanted to reverse the worrying spiral of falling prices, and was especially keen to raise farm prices. As Acheson explained, "Rising prices, it was pretty generally believed, would increase production and payrolls in industry, and give farmers more money to spend in the market."[19] One way of doing this was to raise the rate of dollars to gold, for the value of the dollar was tied to gold. As the dollar price of gold increased, the dollar exchange rate would fall relative to other currencies on the fixed gold rate. The price of gold had been $20.67 since Congress had set it in 1900. Henry Morgenthau, leader of the Farm Credit Administration, or rather his advisor, George F. Warren, advised the president that they should purchase gold at higher prices. It was exactly the kind of device that appealed to Roosevelt. The proposal involved using the Reconstruction Finance Corporation (RFC), established by Herbert Hoover in 1932 to provide liquidity to banks, but expanded by FDR to offer loans to agriculture, for houses and for businesses, and now to purchase gold. The RFC's funds came overwhelmingly from the Treasury, though it did issue some public bonds. The Treasury, the Federal Reserve Bank of New York, and the director of the budget, Lewis Douglas, opposed this move, favoring a stable dollar tied to gold. This was also the goal of the London Economic Conference of June–July 1933, which sought coordinated international action in the face of the economic crisis. But Roosevelt withheld US support for the London Conference's declaration on currency stabilization.

Debate on the issue of buying gold continued throughout the summer, but, by September, Warren's advocacy had persuaded the president. Acheson returned from a fishing trip to discover that Morgenthau had told the president that his counsel at the Farm Credit Administration, Herman Oliphant, maintained that the RFC was legally entitled to buy gold at varying prices. Acheson, however, argued that the price of gold was set by law and the executive did not have the legal right to make purchases at whatever price it set. He was also bothered about the ethics of taking action that would devalue the dollar at the very time he was arranging the issue of government bonds. These securities would suffer immediate depreciation. Acheson sought the opinion of Brandeis who agreed with Acheson's verdict. Acheson, nevertheless, completed the issuing of the Liberty Bonds on 11 October. Meanwhile he insisted on the attorney general's written opinion in favor of RFC purchases of gold, a stance that angered Roosevelt. A meeting at the White House on 19 October approved purchases of gold. Arthur Schlesinger Jr. vividly described what followed: "Acheson arrived at the meeting of the RFC Board, his mustaches bristling, his face scarlet, his jaws clamped together, looking (according to Morgenthau) like a thunder cloud." Acheson told the meeting that FDR had "ordered me to do it. I will carry out his orders."[20] On 22 October the president announced the decision in one of his fireside chats. The next day Acheson reported to Roosevelt: "At your request I have conferred with Oliphant, [Walter] Reed [general counsel for RFC] and Walter Wyatt [of Federal Reserve] on question of whether the initiation of gold purchases by the Reconstruction Finance Corporation will cause any added legal difficulties in dealing with the problem of the profit accruing to the Federal Reserve Banks, if and when you should reduce the gold content of the dollar. It is our unanimous opinion that these legal problems attendant upon the ultimate devaluation under the Thomas Amendment will not be affected by the gold purchases made by the Reconstruction Finance

Board."[21] The price of gold thereafter rose gradually until it was fixed at $35 in January 1934.

The press soon began to report Acheson's opposition to the policy. Angry at this and wrongly assuming that Acheson had leaked the stories (it is probable that Douglas was the source), the president wanted Acheson's resignation. This coincided with Woodin's departure through ill health and his replacement by Morgenthau. On 1 November Acheson sent his handwritten letter of resignation to the president. He declared that he was "most appreciative of the opportunity . . . to have some part in your administration during these stirring times" and extended his "most sincere good wishes for the success" of the administration.[22] Morgenthau's swearing in took place on 17 November. To FDR's surprise, Acheson attended and, bidding farewell, thanked the president for the opportunity to work with him. This impressed the president who said he had been very angry with him but now admired his sportsmanship.[23] Acheson was applying the Peabody code with another former Groton pupil.

RETURN TO THE LAW, 1933–1939

Acheson now returned to Covington, Burling and Rublee (by 1936 it was Covington, Burling, Rublee, Acheson, and Shorb) and practiced law, making only occasional forays into politics, where he endorsed FDR for president in the 1936 election. All the while he was developing his ideas about government partly in the light of his experience in 1933. Acheson remained critical of aspects of New Deal economic actions. He disapproved of the activities of the Agricultural Adjustment Administration (AAA), which sought to control supply and demand of key crops by paying farmers to take land out of cultivation. He referred to the "misguided efforts of the New Deal liberals" in the National Recovery Administration (NRA), which aimed to apply a voluntary code of fair trade practices to businesses. Acheson thought that many of the changes since mid-1933 had "retarded rather than helped a liberal and lasting treatment of matters which have long been pressing for treatment." Many people were "distrustful and frightened of governmental efforts," while a larger proportion of the nation has "become increasingly impatient and reckless." Moreover, he was concerned that the president's speeches suggested that "discussion will not be on the basis of thought but on the basis of emotion."[24]

Acheson even attended a meeting voicing criticism of Roosevelt's approach—the 26 January 1936 Liberty League banquet at the Mayflower Hotel, Washington. He heard Al Smith declare that the Supreme Court had been forced to throw the alphabet out of the window three letters at a time. Smith spoke of the socialist tendency of the FDR administration. By the time of the presidential election, however, Acheson had returned to his support of FDR.[25]

For his part, Roosevelt's view of Acheson was improving. His admiration for what he saw as the sporting way he had accepted leaving the administration was reinforced when he discovered that Lewis Douglas had been the source of leaks to the press about the gold issue and not Acheson. Moreover, Acheson's handling of the confirmation hearings for the appointment of Felix Frankfurter as an associate justice of the Supreme Court in January 1939 reminded the president of his former Treasury under secretary's talents. First he had to prove Frankfurter was a citizen, which he accomplished by producing the necessary paperwork. The greater challenge was to defeat the efforts of Senator Patrick McCarran (R-Nevada), who would prove a future Acheson sparring partner, to suggest Frankfurter was a communist sympathizer or a communist by virtue of his associations. Acheson convinced Frankfurter of the need to address the issue directly and not to dwell on legal niceties, not to reply by asking what the chairman meant by "communist." When asked whether he was a communist, Frankfurter replied unequivocally that he had never been a communist "because that does not represent my way of life, nor my view of government." The answer produced loud approval from the public audience and the hearing was concluded. Frankfurter was duly confirmed.[26]

By 1939, Roosevelt was ready to ask Acheson to work for him again. He wished to make use of Acheson's considerable legal skills by nominating him as an associate justice of the US Court of Appeals. But Acheson politely turned down the offer. He noted the "honor of the confidence you expressed in me . . . [which] seems to me so fine an act of sportmanship that I shall never forget it." He did not feel he could give his "whole heart and head and soul" to such a position.[27] Undeterred by this, the president now asked Acheson to become a member of attorney general Frank Murphy's Committee on Administrative Procedure. Acheson soon made his mark. On 6 March he wrote to Committee Chairman James W. Morris: "What we want to get in as realistic a form as possible is the problem or problems faced by each agency and the methods which they actually pursue at present. Lawyers have an inevitable tendency to think about these problems in terms of court review. And I suggest that it might be most helpful to us to have the benefit of a wholly different point of view." By October Acheson had become the chairman. In an address to the American Bar Association, Section of Judicial Administration in Philadelphia he outlined the committee's progress. The final report was submitted in 1941.[28] Acheson also looked more favorably toward Roosevelt. He told a seminar in 1953: "I did not have enough consideration for the problems of the President."[29] In a memoir, published in 1965, he concluded that his actions were right but "tinged with stubbornness and lack of imaginative understanding of my own proper role and of the President's perplexities and needs."[30] But, above all, what brought Acheson and Roosevelt closer together was the outbreak of war in Europe in September 1939, when Britain and France declared war on Germany after its invasion of Poland. They held a common view of the danger and of America's need to act.

RESPONDING TO WAR, 1939–1940

In the first months of the war, Acheson made speeches and spoke in forums to articulate his view of the international situation and his recommendations about what the United States should do. Acheson's perspective was rooted in his extensive reading on Victorian Britain and, in particular, the role of the Royal Navy in controlling the oceans and the merchants banks of London in providing capital to projects around the world. On 28 November 1939 he spoke at Yale University. He talked approvingly of the stable nineteenth-century world order which comprised free trade, London as the global financial center, and the Royal Navy providing security. He then outlined the collapse of this Pax Britannica and the rise of the totalitarian dictatorships. The United States, he insisted, must respond to the threat from these powers by undertaking an immediate and major program of military preparedness. He also maintained that America should plan for the future. If the postwar era were to be prosperous and peaceful, there would need to be capital for economic reconstruction, a stable international monetary system and an end to preferential trade.[31] On 4 June 1940 he gave a speech to the International Ladies Garment Workers Union in New York City and again urged assistance for the democracies, Britain and France, against the dictatorships. He warned about the dangers of doubt. At the very time that France was facing defeat, it was important not to encourage our enemies by talking about doubts and differences. Rather, it was important to discuss building up military strength, even though this would be costly in lives and treasure.[32]

By the time of the second speech his viewpoint was winning support as Americans watched the Nazi victories in Europe. US military weakness was now a public concern. In 1939 the United States had about 100,000 troops on the American mainland, when Germany and the Soviet Union had armies in the millions, and it possessed 800 combat aircraft in the air corps and another 800 in the naval air force, when Germany had 3,600 and the Soviet Union had 10,000. When Roosevelt asked, on 16 May 1940, for $1.18 billion in defense spending, Congress not only agreed but voted for $1.5 billion, $320 million more than he had requested, and by the end of month had approved a further $1.7 billion. Obstacles to aiding the Allies were also evaporating, as the president proved able to send them World War I rifles, field pieces, machine guns, and mortars. Indeed, the nation seemed gripped by a panic about military unpreparedness. This was partly fueled by the series of Nazi victories in Norway, Holland, Denmark, Belgium, and France in late spring and early summer 1940. The successful withdrawal of British forces from Dunkirk in June, however, restored some confidence in the Allied cause: in a survey on 29 May, 47 percent backed aircraft sales to Britain and France; in a poll on 10 June support rose to 80 percent.[33]

Roosevelt sought to build on this by cultivating bipartisan support for assistance to Britain. On 19 June 1940 he appointed Henry Stimson and Frank Knox, pro-Allied Republicans, as secretary of war and secretary of the navy. They replaced the two most isolationist members of the cabinet, Harry H. Woodring and Charles Edison. Yet the summer saw much anxiety among the American public about whether Britain would survive. Even FDR was wary about sending supplies to a lost cause and thereby into Nazi hands.

Acheson was an important member of two related organizations which sought to persuade the president and the American public to overcome their reservations and back the Allies. The Committee to Defend America by Aiding the Allies (founded in May 1940 and led by the renowned newspaper editor, William Allen White) had, by July 1940, "developed a well-planned and effective propaganda in support of Britain as the first line of American defense."[34] It established a network of local chapters that concentrated on influencing newspaper editors. Another organization, known informally as the Century Group, named after the club where its members dined, was founded in July 1940 and pressed for more active intervention by the United States or, at least, much fuller aid to Britain than was possible under existing legislation. It had three goals: to persuade the US public to give "all aid short of war"—it particularly advocated the sale of the 50 overage destroyers; to assault the "fallacies" of the isolationists; and to favor various American governmental actions which would result in US involvement in the war. The Century Group was small: it comprised 28 individuals, all white and 22 of them Protestant. The members, however, were well-connected and influential. They included Admiral William H. Standley, former chief of Naval Operations, the businessmen Lewis Douglas, head of Mutual Life Assurance and former Budget Director, the Pulitzer Prize–winning playwright, Robert Sherwood, and the journalist Joseph Alsop. Its energetic executive secretary was Francis P. Miller of the Council on Foreign Relations.[35]

Pitted against these efforts in the battle for American public opinion was the America First Committee, which emerged in the summer of 1940. Mark Chadwin has accurately captured its character: "The continentalist tradition, the persistence of the conspiracy legend, the pacifist movement, the self-interest of several large ethnic minorities, Catholic and business anti-communism, and the propaganda of extremists of the left and right all interacted to resist American commitment to the Anglo-French Allies."[36] In other words, it represented that amalgam of different ideas and interests that constituted isolationism. Isolationism had become particularly powerful in the 1930s, as the long-standing tradition of isolation from world affairs and avoidance of entangling alliances was wedded to the inward-looking response to economic depression, resentment at the failure of former allies to repay their First World War debts and allegations that bankers and arms manufacturers had connived at American involvement in the First World War for financial gain. These pressures yielded Senator Gerald Nye's (R-North Dakota) investigation of arms manufacturers in 1934–1936, the Johnson Act of 1934 that prohibited loans to those who had not repaid their war debts, and the Neutrality Acts of 1935 and 1937 which placed an arms embargo on belligerents. America First's members feared that the course of events in the war and the activities of both White's committee and the Century group would erode the predominance of their outlook in Washington. Indeed, in November 1939 Roosevelt had secured a minor revision to the Neutrality Act that allowed supplies to Britain and France, though on a cash-and-carry basis. Isolationists also had to adjust their arguments from espousal of disengagement with international affairs to putting America's interests first. As the panic over military preparedness of May–June 1940 led to increased defense expenditure, isolationists now insisted that no measure be taken that endangered US security. So the National Defense Appropriation Act of June 1940 contained the clause that equipment could only be transferred if certified not to be essential for national defense.

Langer and Gleason maintain it is not possible to give an accurate estimate of the influence of the Committee to Defend America and the Century Group, but reckon "there can be little doubt that it was considerable and that it contributed substantially toward overcoming the incipient hopelessness of the American public after the fall of France." Opinion polls thereafter revealed 73 percent support for all possible assistance to Britain.[37]

DESTROYERS FOR BASES DEAL

In one particular case, Acheson gained an opportunity to wield influence. On 15 May 1940, in his first message to Roosevelt since becoming prime minister, Winston Churchill requested various armaments, in particular 40 or 50 (50 to 60 in a later message) overage destroyers.[38] In further messages Britain's other needs became more precise: twenty motor torpedo boats (MTBs), five heavy bombers, five flying boats, and 250,000 rifles with ammunition. The British need was urgent as German victories continued, but America was reluctant and Roosevelt was preoccupied with his reelection campaign.[39]

Senator Claude Pepper (D-Florida) introduced a resolution to authorize the sale of the destroyers but by early August his efforts had stalled in the face of Republican resistance. On 1 August members of the Century Group visited the White House and brought with them a memorandum arguing that the president could act without congressional authority, but Roosevelt was noncommittal. At the same time Harold Ickes, the secretary of the interior, described the situation to the president in terms that would be adopted by him by year's end: "It seems to me that we Americans are like the householder who refused to lend or sell his fire extinguisher to help put out the fire in the house that is next door, although that house is all ablaze and the wind is blowing from that direction." Ickes also drew the president's attention to a memorandum of 19 July by Benjamin V. Cohen, counsel to the National Power Policy Committee and White House confidante, that argued there was no US or international legal barrier to the president's sanctioning the sale of the ships to the British.[40] Roosevelt had previously been skeptical about Cohen's memorandum, telling Navy Secretary Frank Knox on 22 July that he was unconvinced and thought that Congress would object to such action. Yet at a cabinet meeting on 2 August there was unanimity that the survival of Britain might depend on receiving the destroyers.[41]

Meanwhile, Cohen, on the advice of Felix Frankfurter, secured the assistance of Acheson. The two men worked in the law library of the New York City Bar Association to produce a more convincing version of Cohen's case. In a carefully argued opinion they maintained that the president had the authority to approve the sale, claiming that "there is no reason for us to put a strained or unnecessary interpretation on our own statutes contrary to our national interests. There is no reason to extend the rules of international law beyond the limits generally accepted by other nations to the detriment of our country." Acheson then contacted Charles Merz, his Yale classmate, the director of the editorial pages of the *New York Times*. The Cohen-Acheson opinion appeared on 11 August as a letter to the editor and was signed by Charles C. Burlingham, Thomas D. Thatcher, George Rublee, and Dean Acheson.[42] Acheson had advised the president that he did not need to go to Congress. He would say the same to Truman in June 1950 on the issue of deploying US forces in Korea. Acheson did not expect the letter to persuade Roosevelt directly. Instead, he hoped to convince the attorney general, Robert H. Jackson, whom he tracked down from his holiday. Jackson duly supported the opinion, citing the Supreme Court judgment on the *Curtiss-Wright* case in 1936, which, while constraining the president's powers in domestic matters, suggested that in foreign affairs the president could act without recourse to legislation. A flavor of the favorable public context in which this idea was received can be seen in the 16 August edition of the *Christian Science Monitor* whose headlines placed the threat to Britain alongside the prospect of a deal on destroyers: "US-Britain Talk Trade? Destroyers for Air Bases. 2,500 Planes Strafe Britain."[43] The combination of public sympathy, Jackson's endorsement, and the willingness of Wendell Willkie, the Republican presidential candidate, not to oppose the transfer persuaded Roosevelt to apply Acheson's solution.

Although the Cohen-Acheson opinion overcame the problem of congressional assent, work was still needed on the content of an agreement. As early as May the British had explored the idea of granting the Americans certain facilities on British possessions in the Western Hemisphere. In an exchange of messages in August Churchill conceded two American demands. The first was a declaration that if the Nazis defeated Britain, they would not acquire British vessels. Churchill initially resisted, saying such an announcement would undermine morale. However, he told the House of Commons on 20 August that if the Germans seized Britain, then the Royal Navy would fight on for Canada and the Dominions. The British also agreed to offer the Americans ninety-nine-year leases for bases on land in British territories— Newfoundland and Bermuda (as outright gifts); and Antigua, Bahamas, Jamaica, St. Lucia, Trinidad, and British Guiana (in return for the destroyers). On 2 September Roosevelt concluded the deal by executive agreement, formalized in an exchange of notes with Britain.[44] It took until spring 1941 before officials from the two countries had worked out locations for the bases.[45] The deal was more symbolic than practical for Britain, since, by the end of 1940, only nine of the fifty ships were seaworthy. Moreover, in the course of the discussions, the focus fell on the destroyers and the other military requests were forgotten. The responsibility for this must be shared. In the first place, the British ambassador, Lord Lothian, had the habit of referring to the "destroyers" for convenience when addressing the issue. Then, Sumner Welles, under secretary of state, and Henry Stimson, who had led the talks, went on vacation without adequately briefing Cordell Hull, the secretary of state. Hull did not prove especially diligent in the discussions, for his papers indicate that the British were seeking more than the destroyers. Roosevelt's rather carefree approach to negotiations also contributed.[46] Although there was no serious public concern about the deal, scholars vigorously debated its legality.[47]

RETURN TO THE FOLD

Acheson's help in facilitating the destroyers agreement attracted Roosevelt's attention. So too did his public support for the president's reelection, made in an article in the *Baltimore Sun* on 3 October 1940. The *New York Times* observed: "The letter is regarded here with special interest, inasmuch as Mr. Acheson was one of those who left the Roosevelt Administration some years ago, presumably because of lack of sympathy with the Treasury program." More important was the reaction of FDR who wrote to Acheson: "I am perfectly delighted to read your letter in the paper this morning particularly since your support of me is based on consideration of world conditions and a recognition of their serious import to our American future. Quite aside from our personal friendship, I am glad that you have publicly taken this much more important view."[48] In consequence, Roosevelt asked Acheson to help him in the final days of his election campaign. A major speech of 1 November in Cleveland was heavily influenced by Acheson's thoughts on the need to be positive about the case for defending democracy against the dictators. That same day, Acheson spoke in favor of Roosevelt's reelection in a radio broadcast on station WBAL Baltimore, saying, "The President has become to millions of men and women in this country the symbol of the renewal of democratic faith in a dark and bloody time."[49]

Meanwhile, Acheson continued to advance the case for a tough response to Germany. On 6 October 1940 he joined Senators William H. King and Bennett Champ Clark and General Hugh S. Johnson in "The American Forum of the Air" radio discussion, which considered the topic: "Shall We Give Further Aid to Britain?" Acheson was direct in his identification of the problems before Americans and the solutions:

> [W]e Americans have lived so long in irresponsible security that we now wake with something of a shock to find ourselves the object of a hostile alliance which is making the greatest play in history to control all Europe and Asia and Africa, and which makes no secret of its ambitions in this hemisphere. . . . If they should conquer Great Britain there would be no question of the power with which they would speak. Their navies, leaving the British fleet out of account, would be double ours. They would control 70 per cent of the merchant tonnage of the world.

He added that US security came thanks to the Royal Navy which "controlled the Atlantic and controlled it in the interest of peace and security in this hemisphere." Continued American security depended upon preserving that control. It was therefore vital that the United States furnish the British "the planes and ships which are essential to maintain the fight, the fight which gives us time to prepare."[50] On 2 January 1941 he signed an open letter to Congress warning of the threat from Germany, Italy, and Japan.[51] A week later, he argued in the "Town Meeting of the Air" that Hitler's defeat was essential to America.[52] The discussion turned heated when Acheson's fellow debater, Verne Marshall, chairman of the No Foreign War Committee, in the words of the *New York Times*, "invited hecklers in the audience to come up on the platform to meet him in fistic debate."[53]

The United States might not have been at war but Acheson articulated a growing recognition that German behavior could not be ignored, though his inclination to do more did not yet enjoy majority support among the American public. However Acheson's advocacy of both FDR's reelection and a firm response to Hitler seems to have convinced the president that he should return to the administration. Hull called Acheson and asked him to serve as assistant secretary of state for economic affairs to replace Henry Grady, who was returning to the University of California. Acheson might have asked for time to consider but Frankfurter observed: "The heady experience of being in on big political decisions . . . Once Dean had dined on such rare meat, it was painful to return to the hard tack of the law."[54] On 1 February 1941 Acheson was sworn into office by Brandeis, with Frankfurter also present. So began Acheson's near continuous twelve years of service to US foreign policy.

NOTES

1. The account of Acheson up to 1933 is based on Dean Acheson, *Morning and Noon* (Boston: Houghton Mifflin, 1965); Philip Hamburger, "Mr. Secretary—I," The *New Yorker*, 12 November 1949, 39, 42, 44, 46, 48, 50, 52–53; idem., "Mr. Secretary—II," The *New Yorker*, November 19, 1949, 40–42, 44; Gaddis Smith, *Dean Acheson* (New York: Cooper Square Publishers, 1972), 1–10; David S. McLellan, *Dean Acheson: The State Department Years* (New York: Dodd, Mead, 1976), 1–24.

2. Acheson, *Morning and Noon*, 18.

3. At the close of Acheson's first year at Groton, Peabody told his parents that he did not think he would be able to make him a "Groton boy." Mrs. Acheson demonstrated her determined manner by telling Peabody she did not want him to make Dean a Groton boy but to educate him. In the face of her firm stance, Peabody yielded. Walter Isaacson and Evan Thomas, *The Wise Men: Six Friends and the World They Made* (London: Faber & Faber, 1986), 55.

4. Hamburger, "Mr. Secretary—I," The *New Yorker* (12 November 1949), 39.

5. Dean Acheson, *Fragments of My Fleece* (New York: W. W. Norton, 1971), 219–222.

6. McLellan, *Acheson*, 12.

7. Hamburger, "Mr. Secretary—I," The *New Yorker* (12 November 1949), 39.

8. Library of Congress [hereafter L of C], Felix Frankfurter Papers, box 19 contains Acheson's letters about his clerkship; their correspondence continued for the rest of Frankfurter's life and covered the law, their careers, politics, and literature.

9. Acheson, *Morning and Noon*, 78.

10. Acheson, *Fragments of My Fleece*, 213–215.

11. L of C, Frankfurter Papers, box 19, Acheson, Dean G. 1920 folder, Acheson to Frankfurter, 16 November 1920.

12. L of C, Frankfurter Papers, box 19, Acheson, Dean G. 1920 folder, Frankfurter to Acheson, 9 December 1920, Acheson to Frankfurter, 11 December 1920. Acheson, *Morning and Noon*, 62, 65. David S. McLellan and David Acheson, eds., *Among Friends: Personal Letters of Dean Acheson* (New York: Dodd, Mead, 1980), 182, Acheson to Michael Janeway, 24 May 1960.

13. Neal Stanford, "Who Is Acheson?," *Christian Science Monitor* (1 September 1945).

14. Acheson, *Morning and Noon*, 155–159; Harold Nicolson, *Dwight Morrow* (London: Constable, 1935).

15. Cummings was famous for his marriages—he wed for a fourth time after the death of his third wife. During his time as a state attorney in Connecticut he prevented the conviction of a vagrant for the murder of a popular local priest. Using other names, the episode was made into a film, *Boomerang* (1947) directed by Elia Kazan, with Cummings's character played heroically by Dana Andrews.

16. Dean Acheson, *Present at the Creation: My Years in the State Department* (New York: W. W. Norton, 1969), 3.

17. Acheson, *Morning and Noon*, 165.

18. Interview with David McLellan, 2 April 1963, quoted in McLellan, *Acheson*, 28.
19. Acheson, *Morning and Noon*, 166.
20. On the gold issue see Harry S. Truman Library [hereafter HSTL], *Princeton Seminars*, microfilm, roll 2, frames 108–118, 2 July 1953; and Arthur M. Schlesinger Jr., *The Coming of the New Deal* (Boston: Houghton Mifflin, 1959), 238–243, quotation at 239–240.
21. Franklin D. Roosevelt Library [hereafter FDRL], FDR Papers, Official File (OF) 229, box 2, Money (Inflation) October 8–31, 1933 folder, Acheson to FDR, 23 October 1933.
22. FDRL, President's Secretary's File (PSF), box 77, Treasury, 1933–36 folder; Acheson, *Morning and Noon*, 192.
23. Different sources offer different verbatim accounts: "I have been awfully angry with you. But you are a real sportsman" (James Chace, *Acheson: The Secretary of State Who Created the American World* (New York: Simon & Schuster, 1998), 66–67); "I'm as mad as hell with you, but for you to come here today is the best act of sportsmanship I've ever seen!" (Schlesinger, *Coming of New Deal*, 242).
24. FDRL, Alexander Sachs Papers, box 1, Acheson, Dean folder, Acheson to Sachs, 10 October 1936. See Arthur M. Schlesinger Jr., *The Politics of Upheaval* (Boston: Houghton Mifflin, 1960), 470–474, which explains the Monday 6 January 1936 Supreme Court decision to declare the interventions of the Agricultural Adjustment Administration as unconstitutional.
25. William Leuchtenburg, *Franklin D. Roosevelt and the New Deal, 1933–1945* (New York: Harper & Row, 1963), 178–179.
26. "Frankfurter Named to Supreme Court; Succeeds Cardozo," *Washington Post* (6 January 1939), 1; "Frankfurter Wins Senate Vote," *New York Times* (13 January 1939), 1; Acheson, *Morning and Noon*, 201–208.
27. FDRL, FDR Papers, PSF, box 91, Acheson, Dean folder, Acheson to FDR, 6 February 1939.
28. HSTL, Dean Acheson Papers, box 1, Attorney General's Committee on Administrative Procedure folder 1, press release 24 February 1939, Acheson to Morris, 6 March 1939, Acheson to Murphy, 20 October 1939; Manuscripts and Archives, Yale University, Acheson Private Papers, box 46, folder 3 [microfilm reel 30, 762–772]. *Administrative Procedure in Government Agencies: Report of the Committee on Administrative, Procedure, appointed by the Attorney General, at the request of the President, to investigate the need for procedural reform in various administrative tribunals and to suggest improvements therein* (Charlottesville, Virginia: University of Virginia Press, 1968). Reprint of Senate document No. 8, 77th Congress, 1st session (1941), 1–121.
29. *Princeton Seminars*, roll 2, frame 116, 2 July 1953.
30. Acheson, *Morning and Noon*, 191.
31. Acheson, *Morning and Noon*, 267–275.
32. HSTL, Acheson Papers, box 134, June 4, 1940—International Ladies Garment Workers Union—New York City folder. Extracts in Acheson, *Morning and Noon*, 218–222.
33. Robert Dallek, *Franklin D. Roosevelt and American Foreign Policy, 1932–1945* (New York: Oxford University Press, 1979, 1995), 228.
34. William L. Langer and S. Everett Gleason, *The Challenge to Isolation, 1937–1940* (New York: Harper, 1952), 710.
35. Mark Lincoln Chadwin, *The War Hawks of World War II* (Chapel Hill: University of North Carolina Press, 1968), 44–45, 54, 71; Langer and Gleason, *Challenge to Isolation*, 710–711.
36. Chadwin, *War Hawks of World War II*, 15–16.
37. Langer and Gleason, *Challenge to Isolation*, 710–711.
38. Warren F. Kimball, *Churchill and Roosevelt: The Complete Correspondence* I (Princeton, NJ: Princeton University Press, 1984), 37–38.
39. On the topic, see Philip Goodhart, *Fifty Ships that Saved the World: The Foundation of the Anglo-American Alliance* (London: Heinemann, 1965); James Leutze, *Bargaining for Supremacy* (Chapel Hill: University of North Carolina Press, 1977); David Reynolds, "Lord Lothian and Anglo-American Relations, 1939–1940," *Proceedings of the American Philosophical Society*, 73:2 (1983), 1–65; idem.; *From Munich to Pearl Harbor* (Chicago: Ivan R. Dee, 2001), 83–87.

40. Chadwin, *War Hawks of World War II*, 85–86, 89; Elliott Roosevelt, ed., *FDR: His Personal Letters: 1928–1945* II (New York: Kraus Reprint, 1970), 1053; see also Harold L. Ickes, *The Secret Diary of Harold Ickes* III (New York: Simon & Schuster, 1954), 288–294.

41. Joseph P. Lash, *Roosevelt and Churchill, 1939–1941: The Partnership that Saved the West* (New York: W.W. Norton, 1976), 198; *Foreign Relations of the United States* [hereafter *FRUS*] 1940 III, 58–59.

42. *New York Times* (11 August 1940). Lash, *Roosevelt and Churchill*, 210. See also Cohen comments in Emmet John Hughes, *The Living Presidency* (New York: Coward, McCann & Geoghegan, 1972, 1973), 324.

43. *Christian Science Monitor* (16 August 1940). Most newspapers were generally favorable but the *Chicago Daily Tribune* of 12 August, under the headline "Fear Roosevelt Will Turn Over Ships to Britain," lamented that the administration would be able to circumvent legislation and secure the sale.

44. The National Archives, Kew, United Kingdom [hereafter TNA], CAB 65/7, WM 141(40), 27 May 1940, CAB 65/9, WM 239(40), 2 September 1940; *FRUS 1940* III, 59–74.

45. See Charlie Witham, "On Dealing with Gangsters: The Limits of British 'Generosity' in the Leasing of Bases to the United States, 2 September 1940–27 March 1941," *Diplomacy & Statecraft* 7 (1996), 569–610.

46. Reynolds, "Lothian," 30–31.

47. See the special issue of *American Journal of International Law* XXXIV (October 1940); extracts are available in Armin Rappaport, ed., *Issues in American Diplomacy Vol. 2: World Power and Leadership since 1895* (New York: Macmillan, 1965), 280–295.

48. McLellan and Acheson, *Among Friends*, 40, FDR to Acheson, 2 October 1940.

49. Yale, Acheson Private Papers, box 46, folder 3 [microfilm reel 30, p. 808].

50. Yale, Acheson Private Papers, box 46, folder 3 [microfilm reel 30, pp. 776–783].

51. HSTL, Acheson Papers, box 3, National Defense activities—correspondence, 1941 folder.

52. Yale, Acheson Private Papers, box 46, folder 4 [microfilm reel 46, p. 817].

53. *New York Times* (10 January 1941).

54. Acheson, *Morning and Noon*, 226–227; David McLellan interview with Frankfurter, 17 June 1960 in McLellan, *Acheson*, 31.

Chapter Two

National Duty

Assistant Secretary of State, 1941–1945

Acheson became assistant secretary of state in February 1941 as the United States embarked on a tumultuous ten months. They witnessed the progressive breakdown in relations with Japan, culminating in the attack on Pearl Harbor on 7 December, the escalating naval confrontation with German submarines in the Atlantic, and increasing support for Britain which, by year's end, left the United States and Britain waging war against both Germany and Japan. For nearly four years Washington was at the center of a global alliance, and Acheson played a part in many important developments. Yet this is the least considered period of his public service, despite its revealing his emerging talents and his evolving ideas about foreign affairs. In these years he exercised his first real influence on US foreign policy. His contributions touched important areas of policy: economic sanctions against Japan; Lend-Lease aid for America's allies; the formation of the United Nations Relief and Rehabilitation Administration to tackle the devastation of war; and the Bretton Woods conference that created a new economic system centered on the World Bank and the International Monetary Fund. These years also saw the creation of the United Nations. Although he played no role in its formation, it featured prominently when he led State Department efforts to secure congressional and American public support for these new international organizations. [1]

Throughout this period, Acheson's ideas on America's place in the world were developing into a coherent policy vision. He came to office with the same pragmatic approach as the president and his senior adviser, Harry Hopkins. He shared their view that the United States should deepen its engagement with the world's problems, but he placed greater stress on economics.

Like Secretary of State Cordell Hull, he believed that reducing restrictions on international trade and monetary transactions was the best means of securing prosperity and achieving harmonious international economic relations, which, in turn, would reduce the risks of war. Unlike the secretary, however, he did not see free trade as a simple panacea for global ills. Acheson had a more sophisticated understanding of international economics. His thinking unfolded in policy debates within the State Department and with the Treasury and other agencies. These ideas fed into the thinking of the State Department and helped shape US policy. He became the department's preeminent speaker on these matters to Congressional committees and to the public. Indeed, Acheson was at the center of the promotion of the Roosevelt administration's ideas to the public. This was not surprising; after all, he had returned to the administration as a result of his efforts in the Century Group in Washington and the White committee's more public persuasion campaign. In the last months of Roosevelt's presidency, Acheson served as the department's liaison with Congress.

During these years the State Department expanded and evolved in response to the demands of war. It was restructured in 1944–1945 to improve operational efficiency but, above all, to raise its public profile and image. Acheson was a prominent part of the department's more public face.

FRANKLIN D. ROOSEVELT AND AMERICAN FOREIGN POLICY

Acheson was now working for a remarkable political figure. Franklin D. Roosevelt on the eve of power had been, as Arthur Schlesinger noted, "a man of charm, courage, craftiness"; experience in office had hardened and deepened him, "changing a genial and enigmatic gentleman into a tough, forceful and still profoundly enigmatic President."[2] For David Kennedy he possessed a trait common to many disabled people—he had contracted polio aged thirty-nine—"a talent for denial, a kind of forcefully willed optimism." "Sometimes this talent abetted his penchant for duplicity." Moreover, Roosevelt "was a master reconciler" who displayed "utter self-confidence and calm mastery."[3] Frederick Marks has memorably captured his political gifts: "an electricity in his voice, an intuitive brilliance about his style, that made him the salesman par excellence of domestic legislation. . . . Few presidents have been as eloquent in the cause of democracy or breathed as much optimism into a people that needed dearly to be encouraged."[4] FDR was supremely confident that he could resolve even the most intractable problems, exploring different, often inconsistent alternatives so long as he accomplished his goals. His charm and strong personality usually allowed him to surmount the doubts of his colleagues and allies; and he possessed an instinct for taking the right line on big issues. Roosevelt rarely committed his thoughts to paper.

Although he permitted his advisers to compete in arguing their cases, there was never any doubt that he was in charge—his was always the last word.[5]

Harry Hopkins, who came to Washington in 1933 and ran various government agencies, became Roosevelt's principal foreign policy advisor in May 1940, serving until the president's death in April 1945. Described as having "a mind like a razor, a tongue like a skinning knife, a temper like a Tartar and a sufficient vocabulary of parlor profanity . . . to make a muleskinner jealous,"[6] Hopkins was a clever and skilled operator, who oversaw the federal bureaucracy and appointed people at the second and third levels of government agencies who were loyal to him and the president. Serving as Roosevelt's main foreign envoy, he undertook regular trips to London and Moscow. He was entrusted with these tasks because he developed an ability to read and anticipate the president's wishes and moods. FDR particularly valued him because, unlike nearly everyone who saw him, Hopkins wanted nothing more than to serve the president.[7]

Roosevelt's relations with the State Department were mixed. On the one hand, he declared that he could not "get a damned thing through the State Department."[8] The department was often uninformed about the latest initiatives and lacked presidential direction on the policy goals to be pursued by diplomats. On the other hand, he displayed no animus to the department and gave it responsibility for oversight of postwar problems.[9] Roosevelt chose Cordell Hull as secretary of state because his high standing in the Democratic Party, in Congress, and the American South was a real political asset; but also because he was someone who would bend easily to the president's wishes. Tennessee-born Hull was the quintessential Southern gentleman in speech and appearance. He was deeply religious, indeed rather rigid in morality, disliked socializing, preferring the company of his long-established friends, and was rather provincial in outlook. Yet he was consistently voted the most popular member of the administration after the president.[10] The veteran assistant secretary Breckinridge Long observed that Hull was "*not* an administrator—nor an executive. He is indecisive" but "once he has taken a decision, he is very tenacious."[11] The cautious secretary was, in Acheson's judgment, implacable in his hatreds, which were cold and always resulted in "getting" his enemy.[12] Hull did not enjoy close relations with the president and had a limited role in policy leadership. He declared in his memoirs that he did not attend key wartime meetings at Casablanca, Cairo, or Tehran, even though the British foreign secretary was present.[13]

Decision making in foreign policy was made more difficult by the tense relations between Hull and his deputy, Sumner Welles, who became under secretary in 1937 and served until September 1943. The president frequently relied on Welles, not Hull, for advice on key questions. Welles and Roosevelt shared a similar background: each was born into a wealthy family and was educated at Groton and Harvard. They also shared a similar foreign policy outlook. In addition, Welles was much abler than Hull. He had an incisive, quick mind and the ability to get things done. The antagonism also had a personal quality, as Welles, though he could be a polished performer when he wanted, was often brusque, sharp tongued, and condescending.[14] The Hull-Welles rivalry produced administrative chaos. Acheson confronted a situation where the heads of departmental divisions were "like barons in a feudal system weakened at the top by mutual suspicion and jealousy between king and prince, [who] were constantly at odds, if not at war."[15]

WORKING IN CORDELL HULL'S STATE DEPARTMENT

When Acheson assumed his post as an assistant secretary and entered this complex world of decision making, he was a more mature political animal than the man who had resigned as under secretary of the Treasury nearly eight years earlier. He had a keener sense of how politics worked and how policy was formulated and, in particular, what was needed for a successful relationship with the president. It was not a case of developing a talent for political expediency. Rather, he had recognized his earlier failings and had learned lessons about the political process. He was less legalistic and more focused on practicalities. He already possessed considerable skills in mastering his brief and in advocacy. When he returned to government service in 1941 he brought a greater recognition of the ways of government and the bureaucracy and was developing a feel for how to operate in this environment with a focus on achieving results. His work at the State Department during the war saw him further hone these skills.

Acheson did not enjoy especially close relations with either Hull or Welles; and had few contacts with the White House. Although he often made unflattering remarks about the secretary, Acheson was loyal to Hull and shared his central conviction that a reduction in tariffs would contribute to economic prosperity and political stability and, therefore, to the promotion of a peaceful world. Acheson established good working relations with Welles, whom he described as someone who grasped ideas quickly and got things done: "His manner was formal to the point of stiffness. His voice, pitched much lower than would seem natural, though it had been so since he was a boy, lent a suggestion of pomposity. . . . Welles was not an easy man to know but I respected and liked him."[16]

Acheson admired Roosevelt's political skills and commanding presence as national leader but was uneasy at the president's caution and tendency to temporize. Roosevelt had what Schlesinger called a "weakness for postponement," though "his caution was always within an assumption of constant advance."[17] Acheson later wrote, following Schlesinger's evaluation, that though "Roosevelt lacked decisiveness . . . he had a sense of direction in which he constantly advanced. It seemed to those in the government whose views I shared that our most useful function was to increase, so far as we could, the rate of that advance." Indeed, Acheson had a clearer idea of what he wanted to do than his chief: "I did not come back to dream in a somnolent office. Plainly plenty of work was waiting to be done. The question was: Would the State Department do it? I proposed to have a shot at finding out."[18]

There was some confusion about Acheson's exact role. His formal duties entailed "coordination of commercial and economic questions with questions of major policy." Assistant secretary Adolf Berle Jr. was charged with "coordination of financial questions with questions of major policy." Herbert Feis, the department's economic adviser, took responsibility for stockpiling foreign materials for war production and other supply problems. Acheson's more detailed responsibilities involved overseeing the Division of Commercial Treaties and Agreements; Division of Controls; Treaty Division; Division of Commercial Affairs; and the Editor of Treaties. He observed that the war "had reduced to a bare minimum the usual activities of the divisions under my supervision, except for the Division of Controls, which dealt with the issuance of licenses. As may be imagined, its business had boomed."[19] Breckinridge Long was assistant secretary for special war problems and fisheries; and Leo Pasvolsky was special assistant to the secretary directing studies and postwar planning. According to a well-informed profile after the war, many of Acheson's colleagues "had the impression that their duties were identical with his; practically every fourth person considered himself an economic coordinator, or at least an economist." Acheson encountered "large amorphous, intense, prerogative-minded groups in charge of such matters as trade agreements, the gathering of vital commodities, the collation, analysis, and hashing over of economic data."[20]

Acheson described his early days as being one of a "search for a function."[21] Acheson and Berle competed for influence. By war's end Berle developed a real animus toward Acheson, partly because of their bureaucratic rivalry. At first, however, they cooperated, though Berle's diary conveys an element of intrigue and maneuver. On 11 February he recorded, "I want to navigate the Frankfurter boys into the picture and let them stand the brunt of the opposition from the Treasury. Later Feis will intrigue with Acheson, or endeavor to do so; but that will not come until a little later. Acheson seems to me like a decent chap, and he just may not lend himself to all this. We will know later."[22]

Meantime, Acheson was focused on the approach he intended to adopt: "In accepting Mr Hull's invitation to enlist, I had a much clearer idea of what I wanted to do than he had of what he wanted me to do." Before taking office the new assistant secretary had been urging US engagement in both the European and Asian struggles. "Both Mr. Hull and the President knew of my activity before I came to the State Department. They also knew me and, surely, had not asked me into the Department to perform the largely nonexistent duties defined in the *Bulletin*."[23]

Within weeks of his appointment, Acheson was active in publicizing his view of the need for American action against the threats from abroad. In an address to American farmers in Des Moines, Iowa, he stressed the seriousness of the danger that threatened the Western Hemisphere and rejected claims that the aggression in Europe and Asia need not touch them. He cleverly appealed to their patriotism and economic self-interest. The best chance of safeguarding American freedom and independence lay "in extending adequate and timely material aid to Britain and other victims of aggression." The Western Hemisphere needed unrestricted access to the British market, without which American farmers would "face severe measures of adjustment." American farmers had a material stake in the outcome of the war but also a vital interest in the preservation of American independence and liberty. If the aggressors were to triumph, then the United States would "face the necessity of maintaining vast and unprecedented armaments on a permanent basis . . . [which] must fall upon every element of our population but with crushing effect upon agriculture." The cost of doing this would force down living standards and so spending on food and clothing which came from the soil. Americans faced the responsibility of preserving themselves and their nation—"We cannot meet this responsibility unless we are willing to play our part in world affairs." He closed by invoking Lincoln's words: "The fiery trial through which we pass will light us down in honor or dishonor to the latest generation. . . . We shall nobly save or meanly lose the last, best hope of earth."[24]

Acheson's rhetoric was perfectly attuned to the circumstances, for he assumed his post in the middle of a major initiative to help Britain, which was feeling the financial strain of war: the British ambassador, Lord Lothian, told the press on 23 November 1940, "Well, boys, Britain's broke: it's your money we want." Although the president was sympathetic, there were legal obstacles: the Neutrality Acts forbade aid to belligerents; and the Johnson Act of 1934 banned loans to countries which had defaulted on their debts to the United States (which included every First World War ally except Finland). Roosevelt's solution was to remove the "silly, foolish, old dollar sign": the United States would increase its production and then lend or lease to the British the supplies they required. At war's end, the British would return, in good repair, those supplies it retained and would replace those it had used. Treasury secretary Morgenthau strongly supported the president's proposal.

Drafting of a Lend-Lease bill began on 2 January 1941 in the office of the general counsel of the Treasury. Hull and the State Department were consulted but played subsidiary roles. A talented lawyer, Oscar Cox, led the Treasury team and was ably assisted by Edward Foley. Morgenthau was keen to utilize Acheson's legal skills and so asked Foley to show him the draft. Foley met Acheson on Sunday evening 5 January. But Acheson's only response was to say that "he wished he could make a brilliant suggestion, but he had none to make."[25] Roosevelt presented his Lend-Lease idea to Congress on 6 January. Four days later a draft bill was sponsored by the majority leaders of the Senate and the House, Alben Barkley (D-Kentucky), and John McCormack (D-Massachusetts). After sometimes heated discussions, a slightly amended bill passed on 11 March and the president signed it into law on 24 March, releasing a first appropriation of $7 billion.[26]

Acheson's role in the passage of Lend-Lease was limited but he took a more active part in negotiating the detailed arrangements with Britain, talks which lasted until early 1942. While working on this, he became involved in the more pressing issue of the American response to Japanese actions in East Asia.

SANCTIONS AGAINST JAPAN

By early 1941 the Roosevelt administration was deeply disturbed by Japanese expansion. The Japanese had conquered Manchuria in 1931–1932 and launched a full-scale onslaught on China after July 1937. Worsening Japanese behavior in their war against China led to steadily escalating measures by the Americans. In July 1939 Washington abrogated the US-Japanese Commercial Treaty of 1911. Roosevelt gave credits to the Chinese in their fight against the Japanese. The president was greatly concerned about Tokyo's coercion of French Indochina. Japan was dependent on the United States for 80 percent of its oil and for a number of strategic materials. On 26 July 1940 the Americans imposed an embargo on premium grades of scrap iron and steel and on high octane gasoline. In September 1940 Germany, Italy, and Japan signed the Tripartite Pact. A clause promising aid to its signatories if involved in hostilities, except with the Soviet Union, was read by Roosevelt as aimed at the United States. In December 1940 iron ore and pig iron were added to the American embargo and in January 1941 copper and brass joined the list. But no other oil products were added, because of Hull's opposition.[27]

There was vigorous debate among the president's advisers about how to respond to Japan's actions. Morgenthau, Secretary of the Interior Harold Ickes, and War Secretary Henry Stimson favored a tough stance, while Hull, the US Navy, and the ambassador to Japan, Joseph Grew, warned against tough sanctions that might lead the Japanese to seize alternate supplies.[28] In pursuit of a diplomatic solution, Hull held a series of ultimately fruitless talks with the Japanese ambassador, Kichisaburo Nomura, between April and December 1941.[29] Hull also had reservations about the other economic tool—

freezing Japanese assets. The secretary had resisted freezing German assets and, in consequence, Roosevelt's June 1940 executive orders had only blocked the funds of those countries conquered by Germany—Denmark, Norway, Holland, Belgium, and France. For nearly a year, Morgenthau argued the case for extending controls to Germany and Italy. After February 1941 he found an ally in Acheson whose advocacy coincided with further German aggression, which combined to persuade Hull to recommend in June freezing the funds of all European countries, with certain exemptions.[30]

Acheson had departmental responsibility for what had become a significant area. His role in imposing restrictions on Germany and Italy was limited, but he quickly assumed a prominent part in shaping economic actions against Japan. Two scholars suggest Acheson's role was decisive. Jonathan Utley believes it was "more by accident than design," while Edward S. Miller contends Acheson was a "consummate opportunist" who was determined to seize his chance.[31] But they overstate his role. Acheson's influence stemmed from a combination of his mastery of his responsibilities and his effective ties with two key individuals, Welles and Morgenthau. Unusually for a member of the State Department, he enjoyed good relations with the Treasury secretary. Although Welles backed Morgenthau's proposals, the Treasury secretary felt most at ease with Acheson: he told Frankfurter that he welcomed Acheson at the State Department because he was equally loyal to the president and was someone with whom he could speak freely.[32] By March he was speaking approvingly of consulting with Acheson on Lend-Lease: "It is good to tell Dean . . . he wants to help."[33] Clearly Morgenthau had developed a more favorable opinion since his admonition to Roosevelt in September 1939 not to appoint Acheson to the War Resources Board.[34] Morgenthau and Acheson shared a desire to deny assets to the aggressor powers; and events were moving their way.

Acheson also made a positive impression in another part of the machinery of economic diplomacy. As assistant secretary he had responsibility for the division under Joseph C. Green established by the Neutrality Act of 1935 which, from July 1940 onwards, approved or rejected export licenses in cooperation with a separate agency, the Export Control Administration, supervised by Lieutenant Colonel (later Brigadier General) Russell L. Maxwell. Acheson made quite an impact on Maxwell. The American military attaché in London, Raymond Lee, noted in his journal that Maxwell "talked at length about Dean, for whom he entertains a considerable admiration." Maxwell considered Acheson "very cagey," and believed he "had been careful to look over the whole ground and move extremely cautiously until he had everything just the way he wanted it, whereupon he seized the whole area of economic warfare."[35]

Within a month of entering office, Acheson consulted the assistant attorney general, Francis M. Shea. Their talks yielded two draft executive orders for freezing assets: Shea's placed the Treasury in charge of the process, while Acheson's put the State Department in control.[36] For Miller it was a "clumsy power grab" by Acheson.[37] On 3 March Roosevelt and Morgenthau spoke on the telephone about extending freezing orders and, in particular, a memorandum prepared in attorney general Robert Jackson's office by Shea and Acheson. The record of their conversation noted: "After the [Treasury] Secretary hung up, he said that the President told him that he couldn't take a memo from Cordell Hull through HMJr [Morgenthau], and that we should give it back to Dean Acheson and tell him to give it to Hull. The President said he wants an agreement, an affirmative agreement, concurred in by the State Department."[38]

On 24 March the State Department lawyer, Carlton Savage, drafted an executive order aimed at applying severe freezing and exchange control on Japan. There would be a Cabinet-level committee to oversee this policy—the Foreign Exchanges and Foreign Owned Property Committee.[39] This draft, says Miller, was almost certainly the product of Acheson's initiative: no other figure in the department had a comparable interest in financial warfare.[40] Yet the Morgenthau-Roosevelt conversation of 3 March suggests that, while Acheson might have taken the lead, the president evidently wanted action of this kind. The pressure to complete the legislation for Lend-Lease, however, meant that the proposal went nowhere until July.

Meanwhile, Axis-controlled holdings in Europe were progressively frozen. In April 1941 Greek assets were blocked. In the same month Acheson urged Morgenthau to press Hull, but the Treasury secretary did not want his department to appear as the driving force for action. By 30 April, however, Acheson told Morgenthau that the situation had changed: "You are not pushing for something. It is we who are."[41] In June Hull accepted a freeze on all European nations. By July he joined Morgenthau and Robert Jackson in persuading the president to authorize the blocking of the assets of certain nationals. In February Roosevelt had requested that the three men form the Foreign Funds Control Committee to oversee any Treasury actions against foreigners' assets. By June 1941 the committee consisted of Edward Foley, Acheson, and assistant attorney general Francis Shea.[42]

During the summer of 1941 the international scene grew increasingly menacing. On 22 June 1941 Nazi Germany attacked the Soviet Union, which led Roosevelt to consider extending Lend-Lease aid to Moscow. Intercepted signals revealed that Japan was committed to expand southward. Welles, acting secretary while Hull was recuperating from illness between 23 June and 4 August, told the British ambassador, Lord Halifax, on 10 July, that the president had instructed him to say that if Japan took "any overt step . . . of pressure or force to acquire or conquer territories," the United States "would immediately impose various embargoes, both economic and financial."[43] American-British talks on 15 and 16 July explored possible action, which encompassed freezing Japanese assets and trade embargoes, but no decisions were made. The cabinet decided, at its meeting of 18 July, on the principle of applying further sanctions and Welles then requested on the 19th that a memorandum be drafted outlining orders for the freezing of Japanese assets.[44]

Welles gave the job of producing a draft to Acheson and asked Joseph C. Green to work out an oil export quota. Green suggested that they use the total for 1935–1936, the last full year of peace, but at only half that figure since the 1935–1936 amount was greater than that for January–July 1941. Acheson and Edward Foley of the Treasury spent several hours on Saturday 19 July discussing a memorandum produced by Acheson that proposed reducing the annual export of petroleum products from the current four million barrels to one million. Foley observed: "This is unquestionably very strong action vis-à-vis Japan, but apparently that is what is desired."[45] Acheson's draft recommended that each Japanese transaction should require a Treasury license, as Roosevelt favored. Acheson also suggested that there be a halt for a number of weeks in releasing funds. When Welles read the memorandum on Monday 21 July, he accepted the oil quota but rejected an explicit pause in trade. Yet, as Acheson told British embassy officials, the Americans expected their measures to produce a standstill in trade .[46]

Acheson might have proposed a tougher approach but he conveyed the more restrained official policy in his diplomatic conversations. He told Noel Hall of the British embassy that "my prior conversation with him was not to be interpreted as meaning that this government would put all the controls into effect simultaneously or immediately." Uncertainty ended on 24 July when it was revealed that the Vichy French authorities had given way to Japanese demands for bases in Indochina.[47] At the cabinet that same day Roosevelt responded decisively, announcing the creation of a full-scale Philippine army command, and recalling Douglas MacArthur from retirement to command it. More importantly, Roosevelt proposed freezing Japanese assets, as had been done to Germany and Italy. Japan would now require licenses for all its transactions: an export license to obtain any product related to national defense (as had been necessary since July 1940) and another license to unblock dollars for payment. Miller contends that Acheson used this decision to press for much harsher action than the president wanted. Roosevelt, it is true, did not envisage a total embargo at this stage, but he adopted a firm line, declaring that the policy "might change any day and from thereon we would refuse any and all licenses." And he did not challenge Welles's suggestion that the Foreign Funds Control Committee would determine policies from day to day. Miller underestimated the toughness of Roosevelt by late July. The president told the Japanese ambassador, Nomura, that a move against the Dutch East Indies would result in war with the British and French and a serious situation because of the American policy of aid to Britain. As Langer and Gleason observe, the president decided to "emit a loud and resounding bark, in the hope that Tokyo might yet be frightened away;" and, if this failed, "he proposed to bite, as often and as hard as the situation might require."[48]

On 25 July the Foreign Funds Control Committee agreed that export licenses for oil would continue to be "automatically granted" by the Export Control Administration and the State Department and that payment for them would have to come from blocked Japanese accounts rather than from dollars earned by Japanese exports. The committee confirmed the orders for a freeze. Welles and the committee then conferred and agreed that "the exportation to Japan of oil, gas, and petroleum products will be a matter to be dealt with on specific licenses. There will be no public announcement as to what action will be taken on such applications although for the time being such licenses will be automatically granted." So oil exports to Japan would be permitted for nonaviation petroleum up to amounts purchased during 1935–1936. The Export Control Committee would calculate how much this was and then issue a license authorizing such purchases. The Foreign Funds Control Committee would then release enough frozen dollars for the oil licensed for export. The orders for a freeze were issued on 26 July.[49]

Acheson explained these measures to Hall at the British Embassy on 24 July, saying that licenses to pay for oil would be granted but this would be left to the Japanese to discover. The aim was to keep them in "a condition of maximum uncertainty." Welles and Acheson also spoke to the Australian minister in Washington, R. G. Casey, on 25 July. In reporting Casey's meeting, the British seemed disappointed that American action was "a little less harsh" than they had expected. There would not be an embargo on petroleum products, "though it may look as if it did." Acheson believed that the procedure would result, after a little experience, in considerable confusion, meaning that a definite policy with regard to imports and exports would need to be settled. As ever, he sought a rigorous and clear approach to the question. Casey concluded that Acheson and Welles did not expect the Japanese to lie down under the economic restrictions.[50]

Acheson now addressed the practicalities of the freeze. On 29 July he told the Foreign Funds Control Committee that he had spoken to Welles who thought that "for the next week or so the happiest solution with respect to Japanese trade would be for the Foreign Funds Control [Committee] to take no action on Japanese applications."[51] After the meeting, George F. Luhringer, from the department's office of the advisor on international economic affairs, prepared a memorandum "to embody the suggestions you [Acheson] made following the meeting." It proposed that no action be taken for the next two weeks on all Japanese requests for the release of their blocked funds. The Foreign Funds Control Committee approved the memorandum. Acting secretary Welles also endorsed most of the proposals. He told Roosevelt that the Foreign Funds Control Committee would continue to hold without action applications for petroleum products and would subsequently grant licenses only in accordance with the policy initiated by Export Control. In addition, he recommended preventing the export of additional products including rubber and chemicals. The president approved the proposals with "SW OK. FDR." Roosevelt and Welles were about to travel to the Argentia conference with Churchill (9–12 August 1941), and Waldo Heinrichs thinks that they probably intended "to extend the withholding of action at least until the Roosevelt-Churchill conference." On 1 August, following the advice of Welles (reflecting the views of the Foreign Funds Control Committee) Roosevelt issued an order prohibiting the export of a range of exports to Japan, including petroleum capable of being refined into aviation gasoline. The British Ambassador, Lord Halifax, felt the American aim was to "keep the Japanese in a state of uncertainty." He discerned an "overriding wish" to prevent the Japanese from acquiring certain qualities of oil, especially California crude and blending agents.[52]

In the course of the following weeks, the freeze became a total embargo. The Japanese made repeated efforts in the coming weeks, which turned into months, to try to secure supplies, but to no avail.[53] On 1 August, the same day that Roosevelt approved tougher restrictions on oil exports, the Export Control Committee notified the Foreign Funds Control Committee that it was authorizing oil supplies to Japan in quantities laid out in petroleum schedule 10.[54] Utley says that Japan was thereby entitled to 450,000 gallons of "not so good" gasoline and issued licenses for $300,000 worth of diesel fuel.[55] A memorandum by Acheson of 16 August offered somewhat different figures.[56] But Japan never received this oil. It is clear that Acheson's tough approach was a major impediment, but he made his outlook clear in two memoranda sent to Welles on 16 August. In the first one he explained how licenses had not been granted to release frozen funds because the Japanese had sufficient money, having withdrawn between $1 million and $2 million from US banks before these accounts were blocked. In the second memorandum he argued for quotas based on 1920–1929, rather than 1935–1936, which would mean reducing the sanctioned exports of crude oil from 5,216,130 barrels to 470,000 barrels (a barrel contains 42 US gallons).[57] The British embassy clearly understood the dynamics of policymaking on the issue when it reported to London that Welles and Acheson "completely dominate the administration of economic pressure on Japan," and that they "override differences of opinion that exist inside the State Department and other United States Government Departments concerned."[58]

Officials from the Japanese embassy held talks with Acheson and Treasury officials on the question. Acheson told the Japanese in August that the petroleum products available under the three licenses could be funded from cash which had been withdrawn from US banks before 26 July or by transferring dollars deposited in South American banks.[59] Edward Miller of the State

Department told Nisiyama, financial attaché at the Japanese embassy, that they could not accept his proposal that payment come through the Yokohama Specie Bank of New York; Acheson had meant that the Japanese should use free funds available to them in South America.[60] The US Treasury, the British embassy reported, was not ready to license the release of frozen funds when the Japanese had $2 million in the United States and $6 million in South America.[61] Iguchi, counselor at the Japanese embassy, told Acheson that cash withdrawn before the freezing order had been handed to the Japanese navy; and he hinted that he could do little about this, since the navy was not subject to the civil authorities.[62]

In September Acheson told a Dutch diplomat that three export licenses for small amounts of petroleum products had been granted but the Japanese refused to pay for them with hidden currency held in the United States, so there had been no transaction.[63] In October the Americans refused to release the oil, even when the Japanese offered to pay from accounts in South American banks. This prompted the Japanese financial attaché to wonder "whether any method of payment would ever be acceptable."[64] Acheson clearly wanted to make the process difficult for the Japanese, but this had been the agreed approach since 25 July. Moreover, he offered a rationale for opposing payment from South American banks that other officials, including Welles, accepted. The South American accounts held funds moved from New York to avoid the freeze. Acheson told Iguchi that the US Treasury would not wish such funds to be used when they properly belonged to the New York branch of the bank and should be used to meet its obligations. These accounts also contained dollars earned in exports to South America. As early as 25 July the Foreign Funds Control Committee had rejected payments from export income. The Americans, at this time, were particularly concerned about Japanese (and German and Italian) hidden assets. They knew that the Japanese had withdrawn $2 million from the Yokohama Specie Bank forty-eight hours before the freezing order. As the British embassy reported, licenses under the freezing order could not be issued until this currency had been rebanked.[65] Acheson told Welles on 16 August that the Treasury calculated that the Japanese had enough money in the United States to pay for the oil, and so did not need a license to release frozen funds.[66] Utley suggests that Acheson was trying to give the impression that the Treasury was taking the lead in blocking the transaction, when he was its most enthusiastic advocate. This is not entirely convincing. Acheson's tough attitude to Japan must have been evident to Welles from their correspondence and conversations. He was now invoking Treasury support for his position, and, in particular, on the matter of hidden assets, whose importance Utley underestimates.[67]

Hull returned to office on 4 August unaware of what was happening; and his officials did not tell him about the actual situation. It seems he only discovered that no licenses had been granted from a conversation with the Japanese ambassador, Nomura, on 4 September.[68] This was not the only example of Welles's failure to keep the secretary fully informed on an issue. Hull saw Acheson the next day and decided he could hardly allow the release of supplies after they had been blocked for a month. After the tough talk in July, this would appear a climb down, which would only encourage the hardliners in Tokyo. [69] Acheson told the Foreign Funds Control Committee on 11 September that Hull "does not want any new restrictive measures to be introduced, neither does he want any relaxation of our present attitude."[70]

The situation reached by September did not result from Acheson acting beyond his instructions. Roosevelt and Welles were happy to delay a decision on how much oil to allow the Japanese until after their meeting with Churchill in August. They raised no complaint about the way the measures were applied. Acheson told the British, who sought a clear tough policy, that he regretted the "somewhat opportunistic measures" of the US government, which administrative and political circumstances in Washington obliged them to take.[71] The British were satisfied because the US freeze was applied "much more severely than foreshadowed"; the Americans clearly "intended a higher level of restrictions than now appears to be the case."[72]

The secretary assumed overall charge of policy in September and stamped it with his own approach. He strongly supported the need to be tough. He declared he was "profoundly disillusioned by the Japanese move into southern Indochina and the aggressive intent revealed in 'Magic' intercepts while he was negotiating with Nomura [Japanese ambassador] and doggedly trying to stave off sanctions." Hull felt that the United States had "reached the end of possible appeasement with Japan and there is nothing further that can be done with that country except by a firm policy."[73] Hull endorsed the general policy, and, as Acheson told Treasury officials, the Japanese should be "kept in a state of indecision and uncertainty."[74]

Hull's and Welles's readiness to deploy blocking tactics toward Japan over the three licenses that had been granted shows that they were in sympathy with Acheson's general approach. Acheson was the dominant figure in the Foreign Funds Control Committee but the records of its meetings do not reveal him as a domineering force; and, indeed, he chaired only one of more than twenty meetings between July and December.[75] He had adopted a tough attitude but had not exceeded his instructions: there is no evidence of the secretary, the under secretary, or the president, lodging complaints about developments. Acheson was able to act as he did because, as Lester H. Brune has said, "Secretary Hull and Maxwell Hamilton, chief of the Far Eastern Division, consciously established nebulous regulations as a stalling mechanism anticipating the final breach of diplomacy."[76]

In any event, the embargo did not dissuade the Japanese. Rather than give way to American pressure, they chose to prepare military action, embarking on the road to the attack on Pearl Harbor that ultimately brought the United States into the Second World War.

LEND-LEASE AGREEMENT

The United States was already indirectly involved in the war through Lend-Lease aid. After Lend-Lease was signed into law on 24 March 1941, each recipient country had to sign a formal agreement. The Treasury had overseen the drafting and passage of the legislation, but Hull argued that the State Department should take a prominent role in framing an agreement with Britain, for it had an important political dimension. Roosevelt agreed, not wanting Hull "to get his nose out of joint."[77] Hull asked Acheson to lead talks with the British. The president did not want the agreement to adopt language that would make it appear to be a treaty, for that would require two-thirds of the Senate to approve it. Acheson and Morgenthau would have preferred to offer materials to Britain as an outright gift, but they recognized this was not feasible. Acheson suggested that Britain be asked to return whatever was left at war's end and commit itself to work with the United States to free world trade by reducing tariffs and exchange controls. Morgenthau felt Congress would expect something more substantial.[78] So Acheson (and Morgenthau) pursued a more substantial quid pro quo, which came to be called the consideration. It took until February 1942 to conclude an agreement, mainly because of British hesitations, rather than because of State Department–Treasury differences. The path to agreement was eased by US entry into the war in December, which meant the British could help the American war effort through reverse Lend-Lease (aid to US forces on British territory).

State Department thinking about the content of the consideration was influenced by its views of British economic policy. Opinion was united in endorsing Hull's commitment to freeing trade by reducing tariffs. Officials regarded British imperial preference, which allowed free trade within the empire and placed tariffs on a range of goods from outside, as the principal external difficulty. The most enthusiastic opponents of imperial preference were a group that stressed the economic merits of multilateralism. It included Herbert Feis, economic advisor to the secretary, Clair Wilcox, director of international trade policy, and Harry Hawkins, chief of the division of commercial treaties and agreements. Acheson belonged to another group, which emphasized geopolitical considerations, and it included Welles, Pasvolsky, and Berle. Both groups were wary of economic nationalism in the Treasury, where Morgenthau and assistant secretary Harry Dexter White seemed more interested in undermining sterling than in building a new, more open commercial system. They were also united in their concern about the persuasive powers of the British representative, John Maynard Keynes, the exceptionally able economist who was coming to Washington to negotiate the formal Lend-Lease agreement. They feared he might avoid any commitment to end imperial preference.[79] As a result, someone in the State Department, probably Harry Hawkins, suggested linking the abolition of British imperial preference with the consideration. The department enthusiastically embraced the idea and began drafting a consideration agreement.[80]

Keynes arrived in Washington on 9 May and met Morgenthau on the 14th, noting that he "clearly wants to be helpful."[81] But he found Morgenthau was "a difficult chap to deal with. I have seldom struck anything stickier than my first interview. One seemed to be able to get no human reaction whatever, which is, I suppose, his method of protection until he is quite sure what you are after." Keynes, however, was convinced that the Treasury secretary wanted "to do his best for us."[82] He then saw Harry Hopkins, who complained that Keynes was using him to outmaneuver the Treasury. Yet Hopkins's biographer notes, "If Keynes was moving on several fronts, it was partly because of the peculiarities of Lend-Lease administration. Morgenthau might have promised the money in March, but by May Hopkins had it."[83]

Acheson held his first formal meeting with Keynes on 25 May. They developed a very good relationship, despite some very sharp exchanges in their first conversations. In his memoirs Acheson described Keynes as "delightful and engaging." He added, "His many-faceted and highly polished mind sparkled and danced with light. But not all felt his charm; to some he appeared arrogant."[84] Keynes concluded that the Americans were "anxious, I believe, to do what is most helpful to us, provided we can find a formula which looks reasonably plausible to Congress." He added that, if the indications given to him of the draft consideration were correct, then "it seems to all of us here extraordinarily satisfactory." Keynes had dined with Felix Frankfurter, Robert Brand, head of the British Food Mission, Washington, and Acheson on 24 May. The dinner conversation throws an interesting sidelight on Acheson's rather belligerent outlook at this time. Frankfurter and Acheson passionately debated Acheson's contention that Roosevelt, in his capacity as Commander in Chief, should declare war or its equivalent by "ordering the fleet to its battle stations." Frankfurter thought this would be a political mistake and "expose the President to a rebuff from Congress." Keynes observed that "Mr. Acheson had such impatience and felt so strongly to the contrary was an interesting sign of how some people in the Administration are feeling at the continued delay."[85]

Acheson met Keynes again on 11 and 20 June but they made no progress.[86] Making little headway with the State Department, Keynes and the British ambassador, Lord Halifax, met the president on 7 July. The ever astute Keynes believed that the first person to press his views on Roosevelt usually got what he wanted. At the president's request, Keynes reported the conversation to Acheson, who wryly observed in his memoirs: "Keynes did not appear to think it unusual that I should receive instructions from the President via the British Embassy."[87] Keynes had predicted such a procedure as early as 21 June: "Methods in this country are so odd that it is probably I who will have to pass on to the State Department the President's instructions on the matter!"[88] The president, Keynes reported, was not under pressure from Congress to achieve a Lend-Lease agreement with Britain, but he desired some kind of preliminary agreement; and this would only require Britain to return unused materials and indicate general "arrangements for postwar relief and reconstruction."[89]

Seeking to benefit from his meeting with the president, Keynes then presented a British draft preliminary agreement to Acheson on 15 July, suggesting it met Roosevelt's expectations. But Acheson felt it "did not provide for any obligation on the part of the British except to return 'so far as practicable' goods which might be in existence at the end of the emergency." He believed it would be "very difficult for the President to leave the matter in so vague and unsatisfactory a situation." Acheson consulted Roosevelt, who shared Acheson's reservations: he wanted the British to return all Lend-Lease goods not destroyed or consumed, if the president determined them useful for US defense, and to continue talks about aid and cooperation.[90]

Acheson quickly recovered the initiative: he devised an alternative draft, received the president's general approval of it, and submitted it to Keynes on 28 July. It embraced some of the British terminology but restated the case for multilateralism. As Theodore Wilson neatly puts it, a "gleeful Acheson then presented it to Keynes and awaited the explosion."[91] Keynes broadly accepted the first six articles. Then he read article VII: "terms and conditions upon which UK receives defense aid . . . shall be such as to not burden commerce between them and betterment of world-wide economic relations: they shall provide against discrimination in either the United States of America or the United Kingdom." He exploded with anger against this assault on imperial preference, delivering, according to Acheson's memoirs, "a speech such as only he could make." Keynes argued that "the only hope of the future was to maintain economies in balance without great excesses of either exports or imports, and that this could be only through exchange controls, which Article VII seemed to ban." Acheson retorted "as coldly as I could" that Keynes's draft was "wholly impossible." It provided merely that Lend-Lease be extended; that the British would return what was practicable; no obligation would be created but they would be ready to talk about other matters. Such a proposal could not be defended in America. Acheson declared that the aim was to provide a commitment that "should not be too hard for the British," namely a readiness not to take measures against a country that offered such vast aid. Despite the sharp exchanges, both men left the meeting with cause for hope. Acheson concluded that Keynes "seemed more reconciled to the Article, but by no means wholly so." Keynes reported that "there is a difficulty here, but I do not think it is an insuperable one."[92]

The next day Keynes wrote to Acheson saying he hoped that his "cavilling at the word 'discrimination'" would not detract from "the excellence and magnanimity of the first part of that Article VII and of the document as a whole." He would do his best to present American thinking to people at home and felt "some confidence that a right conclusion will be reached." He added that his strong response about discrimination was a consequence of his passionate desire that they should be "free to produce something new and better of the post-war world." He wished Acheson to "forgive my vehemence which has deep causes in my hopes for the future." He believed they would be able to work something out.[93] Neither man was wholly wedded to his government's position. Keynes wanted to remove barriers to trade but was conscious of how vulnerable Britain would be at the war's end. Full free trade would hinder the recovery of British exports. Acheson recognized this difficulty for Britain but was conscious of American opinion objecting to providing aid for a country that discriminated against US goods. Acheson said he had had to "obfuscate" before the House Appropriations Committee in saying what he was doing in defining compensation for Lend-Lease.[94]

On his return to London Keynes was less understanding of Acheson and the State Department than in his letter to Acheson of the 29th. He suggested that "Acheson as good as admitted" that the State Department sought to impose a more precise commitment than envisaged by Roosevelt, who "had nothing so definite in view" and expected only that "we should agree to cooperate and to do so in a certain spirit and with a general purpose." Keynes recommended that the British should respond with a willingness to see an absence of discrimination in the postwar period, but this would be "an indication of spirit and intention, not a commitment."[95]

There the matter rested until the Argentia meeting of 9–12 August between Roosevelt and Churchill when they agreed on the Atlantic Charter, a joint declaration of the eight principles they would adopt in seeking to shape the postwar world. Its fourth article read "they will endeavor, with due respect for their existing obligations, to further the enjoyment by all States, great or small, victor or vanquished, of access, on equal terms, to the trade and to the raw materials of the world which are needed for their economic prosperity." The British succeeded in resisting an American attempt to add the words "without discrimination."[96]

Further delays resulted from Acheson's preoccupation with Japanese sanctions in August and September. When talks resumed in October, Acheson conducted them with Ambassador Halifax, who submitted a redraft of article VII. Acheson was unimpressed: "the insertion of slippery words had robbed of all meaning our prohibition of discrimination against importation of American goods into Britain."[97] Fresh efforts in December were similarly unsuccessful before the issue was overtaken by the Japanese attack on Pearl Harbor on 7 December. Churchill visited Washington from 22 December 1941 to 14 January 1942 but he and Roosevelt did not pursue the matter in any detail. Acheson described what followed as "two months of blind man's bluff."[98]

On the basis of careful consultation with the president, Acheson put pressure on Halifax. At their meeting on 30 January 1942, he said that if the British still objected to the inclusion of the "discrimination clause," then the only alternative would be to strike out all of article VII and leave the British without any commitment on the final settlement. In its place there would have to be provision for negotiations without any indication of the final terms and conditions. In a further discussion on 7 February Acheson told Halifax that the president would not accept a definition of discrimination that excluded imperial preference. He also made a concession that opened the way for a solution. The Americans, he said, had always accepted that article VII did not require unilateral action and that modifications to preferential arrangements were open to discussion.[99]

It was Roosevelt's political adaptability rather than Acheson's negotiating skills that broke the deadlock. Acheson and Welles revised a draft brought to them by Hopkins, which became the president's letter to Churchill of 11 February 1942. FDR declared that, contrary to the fears of the British cabinet, article VII did not involve a commitment in advance that empire preference would be abolished. It was something he felt sure that the British government could not give; after all, he could not make any commitment relative to the vital revision of US tariff policy. So, he continued, the United States and Britain would enter into "a bold, forthright, and comprehensive discussion looking forward to the construction of what you aptly call 'a free, fertile economic policy for the post-war world.'" Churchill replied the next day, saying that he was "deeply grateful" and that Roosevelt's reassurance "entirely meets my difficulties." The British dropped their objections and on 23 February the two governments exchanged Mutual Aid Agreement documents.[100]

The Americans had also decided to extend aid to the Soviet Union after the 22 June 1941 attack by Nazi Germany. At first the administration proceeded warily, partly because there was still strong isolationist resistance to any further steps toward intervention against Germany and partly because of a dislike of communism. Acheson played a minor role in facilitating the supply of munitions to Moscow. He visited the Treasury in what Morgenthau called a hush-hush manner with a list of what the Russians wanted. He also took the lead in resolving a jurisdictional dispute between the State Department and the Treasury. Both Morgenthau and Welles wanted US munitions to go to the Soviets, but they were being delayed partly because Morgenthau insisted that, since this was principally a foreign policy issue, it was up to the

State Department to make clear that this was how they should proceed. Welles favored this course but wanted the department to take the lead in negotiations. Seeing the problem, Acheson took the initiative and secured Welles's consent to letting the Treasury handle the talks.[101] Meanwhile, officials debated whether to extend Lend-Lease to Moscow. The situation was improved by various initiatives, including Hopkins's mission to Moscow in July–August, and a Moscow Conference in September–October, when American and British delegations, led by Averell Harriman (the president's special representative in London) for the United States and Lord Beaverbrook for Britain, held talks with Stalin.[102]

Congress eventually approved aid to the Soviet Union on 24 October, which was signed into law on the 28th. On 7 November 1942, the twenty-fifth anniversary of Bolshevik Revolution, Roosevelt announced Lend-Lease to the Soviet Union. Negotiations with the Soviet Union produced an agreement in June 1942. Roosevelt and Hopkins devised an unconditional aid policy to maximize shipments to the Soviet Union. Unlike other Lend-Lease recipients, the Soviets did not have to give detailed explanations of their need for each item and how it would be used.[103]

Acheson took a leading role in arguing the administration's case for Lend-Lease in public. In a speech on 6 July 1942 he declared that even the most elementary considerations of self-preservation demanded a program for supplying the armies of our allies. Indispensable though the aid was to the allies, they must not exaggerate its extent in relation to American resources and America's own war effort or in relation to the effort of the allies. American materials formed only a small part of the vast supplies which these armies were using. The countries receiving aid had entered into agreements that would not burden commerce between the nations. The recipients of aid accepted that deals should not be exclusive, but open to all, and recognized the need to eliminate discrimination in trade and reduce tariffs. Acheson stressed how Hull had striven throughout his life to show the folly of discrimination, to break the network of restrictions which were choking world trade.[104]

UNRRA, 1942–1943

Acheson was at the center of a new initiative in economic diplomacy in late 1942. Following Soviet and British requests, he coordinated three-power meetings that established a framework for substantive talks on an international relief organization. These were conducted between January and June 1943 by the so-called four wise men—the British ambassador, Lord Halifax; the Chinese ambassador, Wei Tao-ming; the Soviet ambassador, Maxim Litvinov; and Acheson for the United States. As the official history notes, negotiations proceeded "under the able direction of Acheson."[105]

These discussions were Acheson's first sustained experience of working with Soviet diplomats (his earliest more limited contacts came in the summer of 1941 over extending Lend-Lease aid to the Soviets). He later observed in his memoirs how most of them "cultivated boorishness as a method of showing their contempt for the capitalist world," but Maxim Litvinov was "an old Bolshevik but an old-school Russian . . . [who] understood the forms and uses of courtesy."[106] Acheson concluded that "the three of us did rather better with the USSR in our negotiation than many of our successors have done since, not due, I hasten to add, to our skill but to the Soviet desire for relief assistance." A number of sticking points were overcome. Litvinov was determined that nothing should be undertaken in any country except with that country's consent. The other three argued that this would cause delay in those territories where governments were in the process of being reestablished. As Acheson later put it, "Relief, we said with righteous fervor, must be kept free from politics. The idea amused Litvinov. In the Soviet Union nothing was free of politics." So they conceded the Soviet point. Litvinov also insisted that votes in the organization's central council should be unanimous. Acheson succeeded in proposing a flexible rule: "sometimes, perhaps normally, a majority should control; sometimes, a larger proportion; on occasion, unanimity might be necessary because of the very nature of the question." Only in the final draft in September did they agree on majority voting.[107]

Acheson faced a bigger obstacle from within the United States. Although Roosevelt had spoken to various congressional figures about the talks, he had not consulted any members of either the House Foreign Affairs Committee or the Senate Foreign Relations Committee. Senator Arthur Vandenberg (R-Michigan), an influential member of the committee, erupted angrily to the draft proposal. He objected to American membership in the new organization being established by executive agreement, rather than by Congress. He also protested at the commitment of the United States to "full support" for the new agency. By "some judicious eating of crow," Acheson overcame Vandenberg's strictures. The United States would join the new agency through an authorizing act of Congress, and the American commitment would move from "full support" to the more restrained "insofar as its appropriate constitutional bodies shall authorize." The episode taught Acheson the crucial value of obtaining the support of Congress, and the Senate Foreign Relations Committee in particular, when pursuing new measures in foreign affairs.[108]

Forty-four nations signed the United Nations Relief and Rehabilitation Administration (UNRRA) Agreement at the White House on 9 November 1943. A conference at Atlantic City, held 10 November–1 December 1943, then launched UNRRA.[109] In the course of the next eighteen months, practical arrangements were made for the implementation of UNRRA when the war ended. Acheson again led for the Americans.[110] UNRRA's main activities were undertaken in Europe, though it had a worldwide remit. Most of its work took place in 1945 and 1946 and had largely ceased by early 1947. The operations were under the leadership of an American Director-General, Herbert Lehman, 1944–1946, Fiorello La Guardia, 1946, and Major-General Lowell P. Rooks, 1946–1948. The United States contributed $2.6 billion to UNRRA, 1943–1947, which amounted to 73 percent of total operating funds. Washington also gave $6.1 billion to the Government and Relief in Occupied Areas Program between 1943 and 1951.[111]

At the same time as he was coordinating talks on UNRRA, Acheson also took a leading role in the creation of a United Nations Food and Agriculture Organization. A conference at Hot Springs, Virginia, in May–June 1943 set up an Interim Committee in Washington to draft a plan for the permanent Food and Agriculture Organization (FAO).[112] Acheson enthusiastically embraced the new scheme, describing it as a "phenomenal success."[113] American participation in the new agency was secured by a joint resolution of Congress on 31 July 1945. The FAO held its first meeting in Quebec City, Canada, in October.[114]

Once again Acheson was a central figure in persuading the American public of the merits of these new international agencies. Even before the agreements on UNRRA and FAO were concluded, he was extolling the virtues of American postwar involvement in rebuilding the war-torn world.[115] On 23 November he participated in an American Forum of the Air radio discussion, inquiring "Will We Get our Money's Worth Out of UNRRA?" Asked whether the United States would get its money's worth, Acheson conceded that there would not be a specific return in dollars and cents. But, he added, "in a broader sense we shall get back more than our money's worth." No nation can live in economic isolation. "Devastation or depression in any important area is promptly felt in all other areas." The benefits of UNRRA were of many kinds. While war was continuing, it would help swell US war production. As war drew to a close, a start would already have been made toward the restoration of ordinary economic life in the liberated areas. "Instead of utterly chaotic conditions of production and trade, some of the liberated areas will be better able to resume their former position as markets for goods produced in the rest of the world and as sources of goods needed by the rest of the world."[116] The next month he asserted that the allied countries should bring the same dedication to helping the war-ravaged peoples as they had shown to fighting together against the common enemy.[117] The editor of the prestigious journal *Foreign Affairs*, Hamilton Fish Armstrong, recognizing Acheson's preeminence in the field and talent for lucid and persuasive prose, tried unsuccessfully to commission him to write an article for the periodical.[118]

CHANGES AT THE STATE DEPARTMENT

Acheson's work on UNRRA and FAO marked real achievements for the State Department's economic diplomacy in 1943, but the year ended badly for the department's reputation within the United States. Under secretary Sumner Welles was forced to resign in August. Bullitt's long animosity toward him meant that the under secretary's sexual encounter with a male railway porter would not be allowed to pass, even though it was not made public at the time.[119] This coincided with press criticism of the performance of the department. Blair Bolles spoke in *The Nation* of "Dissension, duplication, and bureaucratic rivalries hampering the development of US foreign policy."[120]

Roosevelt sought to restore confidence by appointing Edward Stettinius, the successful administrator of Lend-Lease, as the new under secretary in September. He proved himself an efficient administrator, an agreeable colleague, and loyal to the president. Acheson later noted that he "had gone far with comparatively modest equipment." Although he lacked the intellect of his predecessor, he was not the empty-headed manager suggested by some critics.[121] He was a popular choice with journalists. *Time* magazine celebrated the arrival of the "handsome, white-topped" Stettinius and emphasized how the department's "crusty old walls got a coat of paint." He would tackle what the magazine saw as its three major failings: an indifference to public opinion, poor organization, and a reactionary outlook.[122]

Stettinius instituted a reorganization of duties (he increased the number of assistant secretaries from four to six) and clearer structures (twelve line offices would replace the old system of nineteen divisions and four offices whose jurisdictions sometimes overlapped); and he placed a new emphasis on public information. In particular, he initiated a series of four NBC radio programs, titled "The State Department Speaks," which comprised interviews with senior figures in the department. The third of these involved Acheson and Adolf Berle, with most of the interview focusing on Acheson's views. Acheson outlined the economic warfare America was waging to deny supplies to Germany and Japan. He also explained postwar planning—"you just can't wait until the last gun is fired to begin preparing for the economic conditions which you know will be present when the war ends." In answer to a question, he denied that the United States was acting as Santa Claus in schemes like UNRRA.[123] Stettinius's reforms pleased Acheson, who had already suggested reorganizing the department so as to improve its ability to take a central coordinating role on economic diplomacy.[124] No one was more assiduous in asserting State Department ascendancy over the various agencies claiming jurisdiction over aspects of American international economic and financial policy—from the Administrator for Export Control to the Board of Economic Warfare to the Foreign Economic Administration (FEA).

BRETTON WOODS, JULY 1944

Although Acheson was the principal State Department representative, the Treasury coordinated the major international conference at Bretton Woods in July 1944. It was the culmination of discussions between Keynes and Harry Dexter White, assistant secretary at the Treasury and chief monetary adviser, designed to develop a new global economic order. Keynes wanted to establish a stable international monetary system that would give have-not trading nations the financial reserves to survive the multilateral era. He proposed a Clearing Union, whereby a central bank held foreign reserves and acted as an intermediary. White's plan envisaged the creation of a reconstruction bank and a stabilization fund.[125] By October 1943, they had issued a Joint Statement, which saw the British accept the US framework.[126] Having succumbed to Keynes's appeal that Morgenthau "not take us to Washington in July, which would surely be a most unfriendly act," and arranging for White and Acheson to confirm the viability of the location, Morgenthau issued invitations to forty-two countries to attend a conference in Bretton Woods, New Hampshire.[127]

Acheson joined a distinguished American delegation comprising Morgenthau as chairman and Fred Vinson, deputy chief of the Office of Economic Stabilization, as deputy chairman. Among its others members were Edward R. Brown, president of the First National Bank of Chicago, and two senators and two congressmen. Besides White, there were also various technical experts from the State Department and the Treasury.[128] With Morgenthau as chairman and Vinson as deputy chairman, the conference divided its work into three commissions: commission I, chaired by White, tackled the stabilization fund; commission II, chaired by Keynes, considered the reconstruction bank; and commission III, chaired by Eduardo Suarez of Mexico, addressed miscellaneous aspects of international cooperation.[129]

It was natural that Acheson should act as the senior State Department official. His good relations with Morgenthau continued during the conference. In his memoirs, he lavished considerable praise on the Treasury secretary for the "patience and thoroughness with which he prepared with Congress, foreign governments, and the public." This was all the more impressive because they had disagreed about including Senator Charles Tobey of New Hampshire, the ranking Republican on the Senate Banking and Currency Committee. Concerned by Tobey's isolationist views, Morgenthau wished to appoint the next Republican on the committee. Acheson, now an astute political tactician, argued that they simply could not omit Tobey from a major financial conference in his home state. Acheson also arranged (with Vinson's assistance) for Tobey to deliver an Independence Day address at the conference. Tobey never forgot Acheson's understanding attitude.[130]

During the conference, Acheson worked closely with White but their relations were far from easy. He respected White's considerable intellect, but disdained his disorganized working habits. Acheson complained about the procedural confusion arising from the way in which issues were referred to various sub-committees. "The thing is buzzing round in a perfectly nonsensical way. . . . A draft comes in from somewhere and nobody reads it, so it gets referred to somebody else; the delegates are going crazy." White conceded there were some difficulties with the Bank, but added, "I think the confusions are all in your mind so far as the Fund is concerned." To this Acheson made the telling reply, "I am sure they have been settled, but I don't think the delegates know that."[131] In his memoirs he noted that White had "served Morgenthau with complete loyalty and great skill" but Acheson had "often been outraged by White's capacity for rudeness," an interesting observation by someone renowned for his own directness of manner.[132]

Acheson played a minor role in commission I's consideration of a stabilization fund, the International Monetary Fund (IMF). But he made an important contribution to resolving a concern of the Soviet delegation, which was disappointed with its quota of $800 million for the IMF. Acheson explained that an increase in the quota might not make economic sense but it made sense from the point of view of military power. He proposed raising their quota to $900 million, though this was still lower than the $1.25 billion of the British quota. This was still too low for the Soviets but they agreed when the Americans suggested a quota of $1.2 billion, so long as Moscow increased the proportion of its subscription from 25 percent to 50 percent in gold.[133] Acheson also brokered a deal on Latin American quotas: Cuba would be third in size of quota (after Mexico and Brazil), followed by Chile, while Colombia had only slightly less than Chile.[134] On the question of the location of the Fund, Acheson was sympathetic to Keynes's claim that this was a political issue that the governments should decide. But White insisted that the United States was the financial center of the world and the headquarters of the IMF should reflect this, while Vinson maintained that this would be a condition of congressional support. Morgenthau persuaded Keynes to accept a statement saying that the IMF and the Bank would be located in the country with the largest quota.[135]

Acheson's role was more prominent in commission II's work on a reconstruction bank, what came to be called the International Bank for Reconstruction and Development, more commonly known as the World Bank. Matters did not begin well. Acheson was critical of the way Keynes chaired the commission, describing its meetings as "rushed in a perfectly impossible and outrageous way." But he expressed sympathy for Keynes, for he recognized there had been much less preparatory work on the Bank, as compared with the Fund.[136]

Acheson left the technical details of the Bank to White and the experts. The Bank's total capital would be $10 billion, one-tenth to be paid in advance, and one-tenth on call. With that 20 percent the Bank could make direct loans, while with its entire capital, including the 80 percent promised but not subscribed, it could underwrite private loans. The Americans made sure that loans would not be permitted to exceed the total subscription to the Bank of recipients; otherwise the United States would end up guaranteeing loans beyond the members' subscriptions. Acheson entered the fray when the Soviets proposed preferential treatment of loans for reconstruction, which would clearly benefit them and other countries devastated by the war. Acheson opposed the Soviet proposal, recognizing that demoting loans for undeveloped countries would hinder Latin American applications. In partnership with Keynes, he persuaded the commission to agree to treat both types of loans on an equal basis and to emphasize need as the crucial criterion.[137] Acheson was uninvolved in a final difficulty with the Soviets, who did not want their Bank subscription to exceed $900 million. Countries favored a large IMF quota, since its size determined withdrawal rights and voting power, and a small bank subscription, since its size did not influence access to loans. The Americans hoped Moscow would subscribe the same as that agreed for the IMF, namely $1.2 billion. It was not until one hour before the final plenary session that the Soviets declared that they would accept $1.2 billion. Acheson was delighted, seemingly regarding it as a triumph of the spirit of cooperation he tried to cultivate in the commission. According to Morgenthau, Acheson considered "this was almost unbelievable, and that he regards it as a great diplomatic victory . . . and as a matter of great political significance."[138]

Thanks partly to Acheson's advocacy with Congress and the American public, the Bretton Woods agreement passed the Senate 61–16 on 19 July 1945, and was signed into law by the president on 31 July. But his expectations of the Soviet Union were disappointed when Moscow failed to meet the December 1945 deadline to ratify the agreement. Even in the absence of the Soviets, Acheson had contributed to an important development in international economics. Bretton Woods' rules-based system, designed to avoid the chaos of the Great Depression, captured the "passionate and sincere belief of all participants that the postwar economic order should represent a new beginning."[139]

DUMBARTON OAKS

Acheson had no direct involvement in the second major conference of 1944, held at Dumbarton Oaks in Washington to create a new, more durable international organization than the League of Nations founded after the First

World War. President Roosevelt first used the phrase United Nations to describe the twenty-six signatories to the January 1942 declaration of war aims. Acheson played a minor role in shaping initial American thinking about the nature of the new body. Acheson joined a State Department planning group in February 1942. Its draft proposal included a United Nations Authority and an executive committee of four powers (United States, Britain, the Soviet Union, and China) and five regional powers, and a security commission. Both the president and Hull were cautious about acting in advance of American public opinion, but by 1943 attitudes were shifting. At their first summit meeting at Tehran in November–December, Roosevelt, Churchill, and Stalin agreed to an outline proposal for a new international organization.

The Dumbarton Oaks conference opened in August 1944 and by 7 October had produced a framework agreement. There would be a United Nations organization; a General Assembly of all member nations; a Security Council of five permanent members (including France) and six non-permanent members elected by the General Assembly; an Economic and Social Council; and an International Court of Justice. A Military Staff Committee, comprising officers from the five permanent members, would have command of forces made available by member states for collective UN action. There remained one major unresolved issue—the veto in the Security Council. The Soviets also raised the possibility of having all sixteen Soviet republics as members of the UN General Assembly.[140]

Acheson made a significant contribution in promoting the administration's commitment to the Dumbarton Oaks and Bretton Woods agreements. On 22 August 1944 Acheson, White, and Morgenthau, together with Senator Tobey, who again rewarded Acheson's support of his inclusion in the US delegation at Bretton Woods, all spoke on the American Forum of the Air radio program in favor of Bretton Woods.[141] On 30 November Acheson made a statement before a House of Representatives committee, stressing that the pursuit of peace abroad went hand in hand with the achievement of liberty and prosperity at home. American capital investment abroad would provide "an immediate market for United States goods" and increase the ability of foreign countries to purchase American goods. American membership in Bretton Woods and the UN would promote a stable international economy and domestic prosperity: the United States should participate in world trade and finance "in a manner commensurate with its power and responsibility."[142]

When he encountered difficulty in persuading Congress, Acheson took his case to the country with talks on the West Coast.[143] On 23 March 1945 Acheson spoke twice in San Francisco. At the Commonwealth Club, he said that each country had a clear choice between meeting postwar problems "through methods of international collaboration" and "relying upon its own resources and its own strength, and going its own way." If they were to rely on the unsuccessful methods of the past, they would "face the disintegration of the whole world system into a state of economic warfare." At the Center for International Understanding, he described the UN as an "enduring institution for winning the peace," but added that peace and security needed to be rooted in prosperity at home and abroad. The "true commercial interests of the United States are not opposed to those of foreign countries." To illustrate his point, he explained that British purchases from the United States depended on how many dollars they earned to pay for them, which required Americans to buy British products. "Trade is not as simple as a two-way street. In fact it has to be about an eight-way crossroads to be really effective."[144]

SECRETARY STETTINIUS, ACHESON, AND
CONGRESSIONAL RELATIONS

As Acheson engaged in this campaign of persuasion, the leadership in the State Department changed. Ill health forced Hull to retire, just as his long desire to establish a liberal economic order and to create the United Nations was reaching fruition. In November 1944 Stettinius succeeded him as secretary of state. Roosevelt believed that he and Stettinius had "a perfect understanding and complete harmony and work as a team, you recognizing the big things I would have to handle, at your suggestion." He added: "we will never have any misunderstanding on who carries what and we will work things out so that everything will fit in properly between the White House and the department." Stettinius, though, wanted the department to be properly informed, noting the "past record had not been too good." The president promised: "You and I are going to work out a system so we are both kept more fully informed."[145]

Joseph C. Grew became the new under secretary. In his memoirs, Acheson described the grave-faced Grew calling on him, outlining the new allocation of offices, and then offering him the post of assistant secretary for Congressional Relations: "The offer carried with it the distinct impression that it was expected to be declined." But Acheson was determined not to leave office "during a general housekeeping," and he calculated that relations with Congress would be important as the war came to a close—from Bretton Woods to the United Nations to the Trade Agreements Acts. So he accepted.[146] It is not clear why Acheson was chosen for this post, though it seems unlikely Stettinius selected him because he detected special skills in this area. It might have reflected Stettinius's lower opinion of Acheson. Yet, on 17 January 1945 Roosevelt confirmed Acheson as number three in the department: he was "hereby authorized by the President to perform the duties of the Secretary of State during the absence or illness of the Secretary of State or the Under Secretary."[147]

Stettinius's first significant activity as secretary came at the Yalta conference in February 1945 when Roosevelt, Stalin, and Churchill addressed major postwar issues.[148] Acheson had no involvement with the conference but his committee work touched a key debate. He chaired the interdepartmental Executive Committee on Foreign Economic Policy (ECEFP), which produced a memorandum that envisaged Germany retaining full economic productive power. Morgenthau advocated a much harsher approach and expressed his concern about the ECEFP report.[149] Roosevelt backed Morgenthau partly through choice and partly because such a policy would appeal to the Soviets and make them more willing to join the UN. Stettinius overcame the key stumbling block by persuading Stalin to agree that there would be a veto on enforcement of a decision but no veto on what could be discussed. Stalin then said he would seek only two extra seats, for White Russia and Ukraine. Roosevelt and Churchill accepted the implied deal. It was agreed that a formal conference should meet in San Francisco on 25 April to draw up the UN Charter.

Stettinius sought Acheson's assistance when the deal on the extra Soviet seats leaked to the press, appearing in the *New York Herald Tribune* on 29 March. It was indicative of Acheson's new closeness to legislators that he was in the office of Sol Bloom, chairman of the Senate Foreign Relations Committee, when the secretary telephoned. Acheson suggested that they should clarify "whether the president agreed that the delegates at San Francisco would unquestionably support the Russian claim." In reply Stettinius said that "the president had committed the U.S. government but not the delegates." Acheson then explained that Bloom believed that "the wisest course would be to omit any questions about the delegates supporting the Russian claim and their ability for putting forward a claim of their own." [150]

PRESIDENT HARRY TRUMAN

Roosevelt did not survive to see the creation of the UN at San Francisco. He died on 12 April and was succeeded by Harry Truman, who had been elected vice president in November 1944. Truman possessed limited experience and knowledge in foreign affairs. He assembled no foreign policy staff and he sought no briefings from either the State Department or the War Department, even though he was aware of Roosevelt's poor health. But he had served in the Senate for ten years and chaired its special committee to investigate the national defense program. His considerable reading on American history gave him an understanding of the importance of his new office. Truman was a small, honest, energetic, straight-talking individual, who was a skilled politician with a keen sense of duty and loyalty that could shade into partisanship. He possessed a considerable talent for focusing on a problem and reaching a decision—his desk contained the sign "The Buck Stops Here." He embraced Roosevelt's New Deal and supported the formation of the UN and the establishment of the Bretton Woods system. He felt the United States had a special responsibility to promote postwar economic and political cooperation.[151] Acheson's immediate reaction to the new president was positive. In a letter to his son, he wrote: "He is straight-forward, decisive, simple, entirely honest. He, of course, has the limitations upon his judgment and wisdom that the limitations of his experience produce, but I think he will learn fast and inspire confidence."[152]

Although Truman was committed to continuing Roosevelt's policies, he decided not to retain Stettinius as secretary. Unlike Roosevelt, Truman did not wish to be his own secretary of state, and sought a stronger figure than Stettinius. He turned, instead, to James F. Byrnes, a man whose wartime prominence in domestic affairs led to the epithet "assistant president." But the new president wanted Stettinius to complete his work on the founding of the United Nations Charter at the San Francisco Conference.

The conference began on 25 April with a total of 282 delegates from 46 nations attending.[153] Despite some last-minute difficulties, the Soviets agreed to the formulation of a veto on action but no veto on what could be discussed. The UN Charter was adopted on 25 June. Proceedings closed the next day with a speech by President Truman. The Senate approved the Charter on 28 July. Stettinius resigned on 30 June and, on the following day, Byrnes became secretary of state. Stettinius and Acheson exchanged warm letters of appreciation. On 3 July Stettinius thanked Acheson for his "tireless and loyal support" and "wise counsel." He added, "I am sure that to your activities on the Hill must go much of the credit" for progress in "Congress on the Reciprocal Trade Agreements Act and many other measures." In his reply on 21 July, Acheson expressed gratitude for the "kind and thoughtful note." He praised Stettinius for having discharged "the tremendous responsibilities" of his post with "such success and so much profit to the nation," especially in his leadership throughout the UN negotiations. He also spoke of "how essential" the former secretary's work would be in "the crucial task" of ensuring the success of the UN, where Stettinius would be the first US representative from December 1945 to June 1946.[154]

Acheson stressed the importance of ensuring the UN's success in powerful testimony to the Senate Banking Committee in June. He set his thoughts in a grand historical framework, painting a picture of great danger requiring US intervention: "There is a situation in the world, very clearly illustrated in Europe, and also true in the Far East, which threatens the very foundations, the whole fabric of world organization which we have known in our lifetime and which our fathers and forefathers knew." He added, not since the eighth century when Muslim conquests "split the known world completely in two" had the international outlook been so grim. Such a serious situation demanded simultaneous action on several fronts: in monetary matters, in trade and commercial policy, and in ensuring international order through the UN. He concluded, "A whole gamut of things must be done and must be done very quickly, because there isn't much time, and this thing will go to pieces."[155]

Although he made a compelling case in public, he was more wary about the UN in private. In his memoirs he confessed that he had always regarded the Charter as impracticable and expressed his concern about unrealistic expectations for the institution. In a talk in June 1946 he spoke of the limitations of speeches at the UN: "In the Arab proverb, the ass that went to Mecca remained an ass, and a policy has little added to it by its place of utterance."[156]

Acheson by then had decided to resign and return to the law. This was partly because Edward Burling and George Rublee were over seventy-five and wanted Acheson to return to the firm and assume the leading role. It was also due to his need of money: he told Frankfurter his problem was "urgently financial."[157] Perhaps he was also tired and less motivated after his demotion to oversight of congressional relations. Roosevelt had previously suggested that Acheson become solicitor general, telling Felix Frankfurter that he would "favorably compare with some of the great figures who have held that office in the past."[158] The president's death on 12 April ended the idea. Acheson also resisted an attempt by Fred Vinson, who was director of the Office of War Mobilization and Reconversion and succeeded Morgenthau as secretary of the Treasury on 5 July, to appoint him as director of the Foreign Economic Administration. Acheson offered a deft solution—including oversight of FEA in the duties of assistant secretary Clayton, which would bring the added bonus of eliminating the friction that had sometimes arisen between the two agencies.[159]

ACHESON'S WAR

Acheson's work as assistant secretary was significant in several ways: for his contribution to US wartime diplomacy; for the development of his skills as a bureaucratic operator and his understanding of the decision-making process; and for his deepening grasp of international affairs and the consequent evolution of his views on foreign affairs and America's role—all of which added to the steady rise in his authority and reputation.

He made important contributions on a number of substantive issues. He assumed a leading role in the application of sanctions to Japan in 1941 and in negotiating the consideration in the Lend-Lease agreement with Britain. He coordinated the negotiations leading to UNRRA and FAO and was the State Department representative at Bretton Woods. Through this work, he had gained a considerable understanding of the workings of government and enjoyed effective working relations with most of the key individuals. He had become a skilled bureaucratic operator with an astute appreciation of the mechanics of the decision-making process. Above all, he knew how to get things done. During the war serious bureaucratic battles had raged between the main government departments and the agencies created in wartime. The State and Treasury departments competed for control of various financial and economic foreign policies. Acheson became an adept operator in these contests. He not only developed an outlook and played a role, but he also acquired and improved skills for advancing his ideas and securing his and the State Department's goals. A profile of Acheson in 1949, when he was secretary of state, recognized the talents developed in these years: as "economic coordinator in a State Department of seven thousand employees, and while handling the subsequent hot potatoes, he had an opportunity to learn more about the intricate inner workings of the State Department than any other high Departmental officer within memory." In consequence, he was "one of the few foreign secretaries, in any country, who are not, in a sense, trapped by their departmental experts."[160]

Acheson's impact extended beyond the government machinery. In his last months he was extremely successful in handling Congress, developing highly effective relations with many key figures such as Sol Bloom. One newspaper noted, "Congressmen like him. He knows his facts. He is frank and genial. His ability to work with Congress has restored a link in the American legislative procedure that badly needed repair."[161]

He also demonstrated a sophisticated grasp of the complexities of international politics and economics. He articulated in speeches, debates, and Congressional testimony a foreign policy vision in which the United States should play a role "commensurate with its power and responsibility." Many of the fundamentals of his foreign policy outlook emerged in these years: robustly confronting threats to US national security and to Western democratic societies; demonstrating resilience in the face of such dangers; and recognizing that American steadfastness should be underpinned by substantial military strength and a vital economic framework based on free trade and a stable monetary system. Earlier than most, he identified the importance of economic foundations—and he conceived this in a more practical way than Hull and his commitment to free trade as a panacea.

Surely the new secretary of state would not want to lose so talented an individual.

NOTES

1. A rare study is Oscar William Perlmutter, "Acheson and the Diplomacy of World War II," *Western Political Quarterly* 14:4 (December 1961), 896–911. Perlmutter examines Acheson's work on economic foreign policy; on planning and study groups; as the State Department representative at conferences; as the department's liaison officer with Congress. He omits Lend-Lease and economic sanctions against Japan.

2. Arthur M. Schlesinger Jr., *The Coming of the New Deal* (Boston: Houghton Mifflin, 1959), 511.

3. David M. Kennedy, *Freedom from Fear: The American People in Depression and War, 1929–1945* (New York: Oxford University Press, 1999), 96–97, 114.

4. Frederick W. Marks III, *Wind Over Sand: The Diplomacy of Franklin Roosevelt* (Athens: University of Georgia Press, 1988), 287. Marks also highlights FDR's elusiveness, which could shade into slipperiness, but goes too far in suggesting he was undependable.

5. William D. Leahy, *I Was There* (New York: Harper, 1950); George M. Elsey, *An Unplanned Life* (Columbia, Missouri: University of Missouri Press, 2005), 18–47; Richard L. Walker, *E. R. Stettinius, Jr.* (New York: Cooper Square Publishers, 1965), 12–14; Irwin F. Gellman, *Secret Affairs: FDR, Cordell Hull, and Sumner Welles* (New York: Enigma Books, 2002), 1–30. Warren Kimball, *The Juggler: Franklin Roosevelt as Wartime Statesman* (Princeton, NJ: Princeton University Press, 1994).

6. General Hugh Johnson, quoted in Tim Tzouliadis, *The Forsaken* (Harmondsworth, UK: Penguin, 2003), 203.

7. Woods, *Changing of Guard*, 10–11; Theodore A. Wilson, *The First Summit: Roosevelt and Churchill at Placentia Bay*, revised edition (Lawrence: University Press of Kansas, 1991), 8–10; see also Robert E. Sherwood, *Roosevelt and Hopkins* (New York: Harper, 1948) and George McJimsey, *Harry Hopkins* (Cambridge, MA: Harvard University Press, 1988).

8. Quoted in Martin Weil, *A Pretty Good Club* (New York: W. W. Norton, 1978), 105.

9. Hull to Roosevelt, 22 December 1941, in Harley Notter, *Postwar Foreign Policy Preparation, 1939–1945* (Washington, DC: US GPO, 1949), 63.

10. Gellman, *Secret Affairs*, 21–30.

11. L of C, Breckinridge Long Papers, box 5, Diary 1936–1946, p. 274 (entry for 9 December 1942).

12. *Present at Creation*, 9.

13. *The Memoirs of Cordell Hull*, 2 vols (New York: Macmillan, 1948), II, 1109–1110.

14. *Present at Creation*, 12; Woods, *Changing of Guard*, 76–77.

15. *Present at Creation*, 15.

16. *Present at Creation*, 12.

17. Schlesinger, *Coming of New Deal*, 529.

18. *Present at Creation*, 18, 22.

19. "Functions of Assistant Secretaries," *Department of State Bulletin* [hereafter *DOSB*] 4:89 (8 March 1941), 271; *Present at Creation*, 16, 17.

20. Philip Hamburger, "Mr. Secretary II," *The New Yorker* (12 November 1949), 48.

21. *Present at Creation*, 16.

22. FDRL, Adolf A. Berle Jr. Papers, box 212, Diary, January–April 1941 folder, 11 February 1941 entry.

23. *Present at Creation*, 18.

24. Acheson, "World Crisis and the American Farmer," *DOSB* 4:87 (22 February 1941), 207–211.

25. FDRL, Morgenthau Diaries, 344:149–155, Memorandum for the Secretary's Desk, (Acheson quotation at 152); see also John Morton Blum, *Years of Urgency, 1938–1941* (Boston: Houghton Mifflin, 1965), 214, and Kimball, *Most Unsordid Act*, 137.

26. Kimball, *Most Unsordid Act*, 132–229; Leon Martel, *Lend-Lease, Loans and the Coming of the Cold War: A Study of the Implementation of Policy* (Boulder, CO: Westview Press, 1979), 1–5.

50   Chapter 2

27. Edward S. Miller, *Bankrupting the Enemy: the US Financial Siege of Japan before Pearl Harbor* (Annapolis, MD: Naval Institute Press, 2007), 88–89; Blum, *Years of Urgency*, 133–137, 372–373.

28. Miller, *Bankrupting the Enemy*, 109–110; Joseph Grew, *Turbulent Era : A Diplomatic Record of Forty Years, 1904–1945*, edited by Walter Johnson, 2 vols. (Boston: Houghton Mifflin, 1952), II, 1226, 1231, 1233; Waldo Heinrichs, *Threshold of War: Franklin Roosevelt and American Entry into World War II* (New York: Oxford University Press, 1988), 133–134.

29. *FRUS Japan 1931–1941* II, 387–792 (record of conversations), 325–386 (memorandum of 19 May 1942).

30. Blum, *Years of Urgency*, 326–337.

31. Jonathan Utley, "Upstairs, Downstairs at Foggy Bottom: Oil Exports and Japan, 1940–41," *Prologue*, 8:1 (Spring 1976), 28. See also Jonathan Utley, *Going to War with Japan, 1937–1941* (Knoxville: University of Tennessee Press, 1985), and Irving H. Anderson, "The 1941 De Facto Embargo on Oil to Japan: A Bureaucratic Reflex," *The Pacific Historical Review* 44:2 (May 1975), 201–231. Miller, *Bankrupting the Enemy*, 109.

32. FDRL, Morgenthau Diaries, 347: 242–251, Morgenthau-Frankfurter telephone call, 14 January 1941; Blum, *Years of Urgency*, 332.

33. FDRL, Morgenthau Diaries, 380:349–393 (meeting "Re Aid to Britain," 11 March 1941, 10:20am), quotation at 387.

34. FDRL, Morgenthau Presidential Diaries, 2:308–311, memorandum of lunch with the president, 25 September 1939.

35. James Leutze, ed., *The London Observer: The Journal of General Raymond E. Lee 1940–1941* (London: Hutchinson, 1971), 437–438 (31 October 1941 entry).

36. FDRL, Morgenthau Diaries, 372:209 (Schwarz to Morgenthau, 14 February 1941), 210 (Hull to FDR, memorandum on freezing funds, 14 February 1941), 215–230 (Treasury staff conference, 14 February 1941 am), 245–259 (Shea draft executive order, no date), 260–262 (Foley to Morgenthau, n.d.), 263–271 (amended draft executive order).

37. Miller, *Bankrupting the Enemy*, 111.

38. FDRL, Morgenthau Presidential Diaries, 4:840–841, memorandum of telephone call, 3 March 1941.

39. National Archives and Records Administration, College Park, Maryland [hereafter NARA], RG 59, State Department Central Decimal Files, 1940–1944, 894.5151/242, Savage to Welles, 24 March 1941.

40. Miller, *Bankrupting the Enemy*, 114.

41. FDRL, Morgenthau Diaries, 393:57–68, meeting re Foreign Funds, 30 April 1941, 11:10am (quotation at 59); see also Blum, *Years of Urgency*, 336.

42. FDRL, Morgenthau Diaries, 376:83, Roosevelt memorandum, 26 February 1941; Blum, *Years of Urgency*, 137, 326–328, 335–337.

43. *FRUS 1941* IV, 300–303 (quotation at 301), memorandum of conversation by Welles, 10 July 1941.

44. *FRUS 1941* V, 828–832, memorandum of conversation by Hornbeck, 16 July 1941; FDRL, Morgenthau Diaries, 423:198, memorandum by Welles, 19 July 1941; Wilson, *First Summit*, 101–102; William L. Langer and S. Everett Gleason, *The Undeclared War, 1940–1941* (New York: Harper & Brothers, 1953), 647–648.

45. NARA, RG59, State Department, Central Decimal Files, 1940–1944, box 3677, 811.20(D)Regulations/3884, memorandum by Joseph C. Green, 19 July 1941; FDRL, Morgenthau Diaries, 423:194–197, Foley to Morgenthau, 21 July 1941; see also Langer and Gleason, *Undeclared War*, 648. The National Archives, London [hereafter TNA], FO371/27972, F6472/1299/23, Halifax to FO, telegram 3392, 19 July 1941.

46. Miller, *Bankrupting the Enemy*, 176; Utley, "Upstairs, Downstairs at Foggy Bottom," 24; FDRL, Morgenthau Diaries, 423:194–197, Foley memorandum, 21 July 1941, and 424: 153–155, Foley memorandum, 24 July 1941. TNA, FO371/27972, F6588/1299/23, Halifax to FO, telegram 3409, 21 July 1941 and F6599/1299/23, Halifax to FO, telegram 3410, 21 July 1941.

47. *FRUS 1941* IV, 841–842, memorandum of conversation by Acheson, 23 July 1941.

48. FDRL, Morgenthau Diaries, 424:145–151, D. W. B[ell] memorandum for Morgenthau, 24 July 1941, and 424:153–154, Foley memorandum, 24 July 1941; Miller, *Bankrupting the Enemy*, 176; *FRUS Japan 1931–1941* II, 527–530, memorandum by Welles, 24 July 1941; Langer and Gleason, *Undeclared War*, 649.

49. FDRL, Morgenthau Diaries, 424:268–269, memorandum of policy to be carried out in administering the freezing control order for Japan and China, 25 July 1941; *FRUS 1931–1941* II, 267 (Executive Order, 26 July 1941), 267–268 (Welles to Ambassador in Japan, 29 July 1941); Langer and Gleason, *Undeclared War*, 649; Utley, *Going to War*, 154.

50. TNA, FO371/27972, F6728/1299/23, Halifax to FO, telegram 3473, 24 July 1941 and FO371/27975, F7664/1299/23, Butler to FO, 25 July 1941.

51. NARA, RG 59, Lot 1, Records of the Office of Assistant Secretary and Under Secretary Dean Acheson, 1941–48, 1950, box 9, File #3: Policy Committee—Minutes and Agenda (thru Dec 1941), memorandum for the secretary's files, 30 July 1941.

52. *FRUS 1941* IV, 844–846 (Luhringer memorandum, 30 July 1941), 846–848 (Welles to Roosevelt, 31 July 1941), 850 (1 August order); Miller, *Bankrupting the Enemy*, 195–196, Heinrichs, *Threshold of War*, 141, 246n; TNA, FO371/27974, F7213/1299/23, Halifax to FO, telegram 3639, 2 August 1941; Langer and Gleason, *Undeclared War*, 655.

53. See coverage of this in NARA, RG59, State Department Central Files 1940–1944, box 4864, 840.51 Frozen Credits/3302, memorandum of conversation, 15 August 1941, 840.51 Frozen Credits/3476, Jones to Acheson, 22 August 1941, 840.51 Frozen Credits/3336, Feis to secretary, 27 August 1941; box 4868, 840.51 Frozen Credits/4185, Miller memorandum, 24 October 1941, and 840.51 Frozen Credits/4235a, State Department to American Embassy, Tokyo, 10 November 1941; see also, *FRUS 1931–1941* II, 268–272 and *FRUS 1941* IV, 852–904. Miller, *Bankrupting the Enemy*, 204–212.

54. NARA, Record Group 169, Foreign Economic Administration, Office of Administrator of Export Control, July 1941–May 1942, Central File, box 173, 334.8 Legislation, Proclamations and Regulations folder, minutes of the subcommittee on legislation, proclamations, and regulations, 1 August 1941.

55. Utley, "Upstairs, Downstairs," 24–25; he cites minutes of the subcommittee on legislation, proclamations, and regulations, 1 August 1941, which do not contain these figures.

56. NARA, RG59, State Department, Central Decimal Files, 1940–1944, box 3678, 811.20(D)Regulations/4148 2/3, Acheson memorandum, "Export Quotas for Petroleum to Japan," 16 August 1941, which suggests a quota of 445,185 barrels of gasoline; see also NARA, RG59, General Records of the State Department, Central Decimal Files, 1940–1944, box 4863, 840.51 Frozen Credits 3220A PS/MS, Acheson memorandum, 23 August, enclosing 16 August 1941 booklet listing all licenses granted.

57. NARA, RG59, State Department, Central Decimal Files, 1940–1944, box 3678, 811.20(D)Regulations/4148 1/3, Acheson memorandum, "Status of Trade with Japan and Japanese Controlled Territory since the Freezing Order," 16 August 1941; and NARA, RG59, State Department, Central Decimal Files, 1940–1944, box 3678, 811.20(D)Regulations/4148 2/3, Acheson memorandum, "Export Quotas for Petroleum to Japan," 16 August 1941.

58. TNA, FO371/27982, F9794/1299/23, Campbell to FO, Saving 267, 13 September 1941.

59. NARA, RG59, State Department Central Files 1940–1944, box 4864, 840.51 Frozen Credits/3476, Jones to Acheson, 22 August 1941.

60. NARA, RG59, State Department Central Files 1940–1944, box 4864, 840.51 Frozen Credits/3476, A. U. Fox memorandum, 19 August 1941.

61. TNA, FO371/27982, F9795/1299/23, Washington to FO, Saving 268, 14 September 1941.

62. *FRUS 1941* IV, 857–858, memorandum of conversation, 15 August 1941.

63. *FRUS 1941* IV, 886–887, memorandum of conversation, 26 September 1941.

64. NARA, RG59, State Department Central Files 1940–1944, box 4868, 840.51 Frozen Credits/4185, Miller memorandum, 24 October 1941.

65. NARA, RG131, Records of Office of Alien Property, Foreign Funds Control Committee Files, General Correspondence, 1942–1960, box 237, Japan: Diplomatic accounts and Conferences, Commercial Attaché Reports folder, memorandum of conversation, 18 October 1941; TNA, FO371/27975, F8287/1299/23, Washington to FO, telegram 4474, 14 August 1941.

52 Chapter 2

66. *FRUS 1941* IV, 859, Acheson memorandum, 16 August 1941.
67. Utley, *Going to War*, 155–156.
68. *FRUS Japan 1931–1941* II, 595–596 (memorandum of conversation, 4 September 1941), 597–600 (statement by Japanese ambassador, 4 September 1941).
69. *FRUS 1941* IV, 869 (memorandum of conversation, 5 September 1941), 881–884 (Acheson memorandum, 22 September 1941), 884–885 (Hornbeck memorandum, 24 September 1941), 886–887 (memorandum of conversation, 26 September 1941), 887–888 (memorandum of conversation, 27 September 1941); Utley, *Going to War*, 155–156; Miller, *Bankrupting the Enemy*, 203, Heinrichs, *Threshold of War*, 177–179.
70. NARA, RG 59, Lot 1, Records of the Office of Assistant Secretary and Under Secretary Dean Acheson, 1941–48, 1950, box 9, File 3: Policy Committee—Minutes and Agenda (thru Dec 1941), memorandum for the secretary's files, 12 September 1941.
71. TNA, FO371/27980, F9322/1299/23, Washington to FO, telegram 4231, 13 September 1941, and F9324/1299/23, FO to Washington, draft telegram, [n.d., but September 1941], FO371/27982, F9966/1299/23, Washington to FO, telegram 4450, 26 September 1941 (contains quotation), F9976/1299/23, Washington to FO, telegram 4459, 27 September 1941, and F9795/1299/23, Campbell to FO, 268 Saving, 14 September 1941; *FRUS 1941* IV, 881–884 (Acheson memorandum, 22 September 1941), 886–887 (Hiss memorandum of conversation, 26 September 1941). See also, Heinrichs, *Threshold of War*, 178.
72. TNA, FO371/27973, F7153/1299/23, minute by L. H. Foulds, 1 August 1941; FO371/27980, F9324/1299/23, FO to Washington, draft telegram [n.d., but September 1941].
73. Henry L. Stimson Diary, 8 August 1941, quoted in Anderson, "The 1941 De Facto Embargo," 229. Hull told Welles in a telephone conversation on 2 August that "nothing will stop them except force"; *FRUS 1941* IV, 359. Hull also said the Japanese "would have stood for cutting off oil entirely as a deserved penalty for going into Indochina"; remarks that demonstrate that Hull was unaware of the total embargo on oil, according to Utley (*Going to War*, 155). Yet Hull was accurately describing US measures: there was not a complete embargo, which only emerged from the tough attitude of Acheson and Treasury officials about methods of payment in the course of that month.
74. NARA, RG56, Treasury, Foreign Funds Control Activities, box 57, Freezing, Japan folder, 1 October 1941 memorandum.
75. NARA, RG 59, Records of the Office of Assistant Secretary and Under Secretary Dean Acheson, 1941–48, 1950, box 9, File 3: Policy Committee—Minutes and Agenda (thru Dec 1941) contains records of the meetings, but they only begin on 29 July, the day Acheson requested copies. The final meeting on 5 December touched Acheson personally, for it saw a resurgence of Homer Cummings's feud with him. The committee rejected Cummings's claim that Acheson had a conflict of interest because his law firm had written an opinion saying that General Aniline & Film Corporation, whose finances were under close scrutiny by the committee, could be trusted and need not be put under an alien property custodian.
76. Lester H. Brune, "Considerations of Force in Cordell Hull's Diplomacy, July 26 to November 26, 1941," *Diplomatic History* 2:4 (October 1978), 398.
77. FDRL, Morgenthau Diaries, 382:80 (memorandum for Secretary's Diary, 14 March 1941); see also Blum, *Years of Urgency*, 243.
78. FDRL, Morgenthau Diaries, 382:77–81 (memorandum for Secretary's Diary, 14 March 1941), 382:82 (Morgenthau to FDR, 14 March 1941), 382:103–106 (Morgenthau-Acheson telephone conversation, 14 March 1941); 386:230–236 (Acheson-Morgenthau telephone call, 7 April 1941); 404:269 (meeting, 4 June 1941), 406:157–165 (meeting, "Re Aid to Britain," 9 June 1941), 406:165–171 (memorandum for the President, 5 May 1941). See also, Blum, *Years of Urgency*, 242–244.
79. On opinion within the State Department, see Woods, *Changing the Guard*, 16–24, and Wilson, *First Summit*, 155–156.
80. Wilson, *First Summit*, 155, 272–273n26.
81. Donald Moggridge, ed., *The Collected Writings of John Maynard Keynes Volume XXIII: Activities 1940–1943 External War Finance* (London and New York: Macmillan and Cambridge University Press, 1979), 81, Keynes, "Course of My Negotiations I," 20 May 1941.
82. Moggridge, ed., *Keynes XXIII*, 87–91, Keynes, "Mr. Morgenthau," May 1941.

83. McJimsey, *Hopkins*, 159. Hopkins was executive secretary of the Lend-Lease advisory committee.

84. *Present at Creation*, 29.

85. Moggridge, ed., *Keynes XXIII*, 94–97 (Keynes to Sir Horace Wilson, 25 May 1941), 97–101, ("Course of My Negotiations II," 26 May 1941), 101–102 (cable, 25 May 1941), quotation at 95–96.

86. Moggridge, ed., *Keynes XXIII*, 127–129, Keynes to Halifax, 12 June 1941. NARA, RG 59, Department of State, Lot 1, Records of Assistant Secretary and Under Secretary Dean Acheson, 1941–48, 1950, box 3, Acheson memorandum of conversation, 20 June 1941.

87. *Present at Creation*, 29.

88. Moggridge, ed., *Keynes XXIII*, 134, Keynes to Wood, 21 June 1941.

89. *FRUS 1941* III, 6–7, Acheson memorandum of conversation, 7 July 1941.

90. FDRL, PSF, box 77, Welles, Sumner June–December 1941 folder, Acheson memorandum of conversation, 15 July 1941, memorandum for the acting secretary of state and assistant secretary of state by Franklin D. Roosevelt, 18 July 1941.

91. Wilson, *The First Summit*, 157.

92. *FRUS 1941* III, 10–13 (memorandum of conversation, 28 July 1941), 13–15 (Acheson draft of Temporary Lend-Lease Agreement); *Present at Creation*, 29–30; Moggridge, ed., *Keynes XXIII*, 172; Keynes, "Consideration" memorandum of conversation with Acheson, 28 July 1941.

93. *FRUS 1941* III, 16–17, Keynes to Acheson, 29 July 1941.

94. Randall Bennett Woods, *A Changing of the Guard* (Chapel Hill: University of North Carolina Press, 1990), 54.

95. Moggridge, ed., *Keynes XXIII*, 202.

96. "Atlantic Charter, 14 August 1941, available at http://avalon.law.yale.edu/wwii/atlantic.asp (viewed 20 January 2017); Moggridge, ed., *Keynes XXIII*, 202. See also Wilson, *First Summit*, 172–174, 178.

97. *FRUS 1941* III, 38–40 (Acheson memorandum of conversation, 3 October 1941), 40–41 (Acheson memorandum of conversation, 17 October 1941), 41–42 (British draft of Temporary Lend-Lease Agreement), 42–43 (draft letter, Halifax to Acheson). *Present at Creation*, 31.

98. *FRUS 1941* III, 43–45 (Acheson memorandum of conversation, 2 December 1941); *Present at Creation*, 32; Wilson, *First Summit*, 213.

99. NARA, RG 59, Department of State, Lot 1, Records of Assistant Secretary and Under Secretary Dean Acheson, 1941–48, 1950, box 3, Temporary British-American Lend-Lease Agreement, 29 January 1942, Acheson memorandum of conversation, 30 January 1942, Acheson memorandum of conversation, 2 February 1942, Acheson memorandum of conversation, 7 February 1942.

100. *FRUS 1942* I, 535–536; Warren Kimball, ed., *Churchill and Roosevelt: The Complete Correspondence* 3 vols (Princeton, NJ: Princeton University Press, 1984), I, 357–358 (FDR to Churchill, 11 February 1942), 360 (Churchill to FDR, 12 February 1942). Anglo-American Mutual Aid Agreement, 23 February 1942; Master Lend-Lease Agreement, 1942; both available at http://avalon.law.yale.edu/wwii/angam42.asp and http://avalon.law.yale.edu/20th_century/decade04.asp (viewed 20 January 2017).

101. FDRL, Morgenthau Diaries, 418:15–18, 21–25 (meeting "Re Aid to Russia," 3 July 1941, 10:00am), 418:19–20 (Morgenthau-Welles telephone conversation, 3 July 1941); see also Blum, *Years of Urgency, 1938–1941*, 261–262.

102. Averell Harriman, with Elie Abel, *Special Envoy to Churchill and Stalin 1941–1946* (London: Hutchinson, 1976), 76–105; Blum, *Years of Urgency, 1938–1941*, 256–271.

103. Mutual Aid Agreement Between the United States and the Union of Soviet Socialist Republics, 11 June 1942, available at http://avalon.law.yale.edu/wwii/amsov42.asp (viewed 20 January 2017); George C. Herring, *Aid to Russia, 1941–1946* (New York: Columbia University Press, 1973), 2–21, 34–35, 38–39.

104. FDRL, Lowell Mellett Papers, box 2, Acheson, Dean folder, "Building in War for Peace," speech to the Institute of Public Affairs, University of Virginia, 6 July 1942.

105. Martel, *Lend-Lease, Loans and Cold War*, 8; George Woodbridge, *The History of the United Nations Relief and Rehabilitation Administration*, 3 vols (New York: Columbia University Press, 1950), I, 12.

106. *Present at Creation*, 34, 68. For an example of their cool but effective working relationship, see *FRUS 1942* I, 160–162, memorandum of conversation, 20 December 1943.

107. *Present at Creation*, 69.

108. *Present at Creation*, 71–72; Arthur H. Vandenberg Jr., ed., *The Private Papers of Senator Arthur Vandenberg* (Boston: Houghton Mifflin, 1952), 67–74.

109. *FRUS 1942* I, 89–162; *FRUS 1943* I, 851–1028; *Present at Creation*, 68–79; E. F. Penrose, *Economic Planning for the Peace* (Princeton, NJ: Princeton University Press, 1957), 120, 132–145, 146–167; Woodbridge, *UNRRA*, I, 3–32.

110. See FDRL, FDR Papers, PSF, box 71, State: July–Dec 1943 folder, Acheson memorandum for Hull, "Future United States Representation on United Nations Relief and Rehabilitation Administration and its Standing Committee," 13 December 1943; and FDRL, FDR Papers, OF 4966, box 2, UNRRA 1944 folder, correspondence on US membership of UNRRA committees, January–April 1944.

111. Woodbridge, *UNRRA* I, 108; Katherine Sibley, "Foreign Aid," in Alexander DeConde, Richard Dean Burns, and Fredrik Logevall, eds., *Encyclopedia of American Foreign Policy*, 2nd edition (New York: Scribner's and Sons, 2002), 94.

112. *FRUS 1943* I, 820–850; *Present at Creation*, 73–75; Penrose, *Economic Planning*, 116–131.

113. FDRL, FDR Papers, OF 50F, box 18, Receptions and Social affairs 1943–45 folder, S.T.E[early] memorandum, 6 June 1944.

114. *FRUS 1945* II, 1117.

115. Acheson, "Post-War Economic Policy," address to New York Chamber of Commerce, 29 April 1943, in *DOSB* 7:201 (1 May 1943), 378–381; FDRL, Oscar S. Cox Papers, box 1, Acheson, Dean folder, Cox to Acheson, 6 May 1943, Acheson to Cox, 18 May 1943.

116. Yale, Acheson Private Papers, box 46, folder 5, microfilm reel 30, pp. 956–961.

117. Acheson, "War, Rehabilitation and Lasting Peace," *DOSB* 9:234 (18 December 1943), 421–422.

118. Princeton, Hamilton Fish Armstrong Papers, box 1, Acheson, Dean 1941–1954 folder. Armstrong to Acheson, 14 April 1944, Acheson to Armstrong [no date, but late April 1944], Armstrong to Acheson, 16 June 1944, Acheson to Armstrong, 30 June 1944.

119. FDRL, FDR Papers, PSF, box 77, Welles, Sumner 1943–44 folder, Welles to Roosevelt, 16 August 1943.

120. John H. Crider, "Conflicts Impair State Department, President Is Told," *New York Times* (4 August 1943); Drew Pearson, "The Washington Merry-Go-Round" and editorial "Sumner Welles," *Washington Post* (26 August 1943); Arthur Krock, "Sumner Welles' Passing Ends a Long Disagreement," *New York Times* (29 August 1943). Blair Bolles, "Foreign Policy Wanted," *The Nation* (14 August 1943), 174–175.

121. Walker, *Stettinius*, 1–26; Woods, *Changing of Guard*, 154–155, 210; *Present at Creation*, 88.

122. "State's Shake-Up," *Time* (24 January 1944). See also, Ernest K. Lindley, "New Undersecretary. Stettinius Natural Diplomat," *Washington Post* (29 September 1943).

123. On the reorganization, see *DOSB* 10:238 (15 January 1944), 43–67. The texts of "The State Department Speaks" are at *DOSB* 10:237 (8 January 1944), 30–37; *DOSB* 10:238 (15 January 1944), 68–75; *DOSB* 10:239 (22 January 1944), 100–107; *DOSB* 10:240 (29 January 1944), 117–129. See *Present at Creation*, 39–47 for his account of the bureaucratic warfare; and note his claim that reorganization mattered less than having good leadership (47).

124. L of C, Cordell Hull Papers, box 51, June–Aug 10, 1943 folder, microfilm reel 23, frames 311–315, Acheson memorandum for Hull, 9 July 1943.

125. For Keynes's ideas, see Donald Moggridge, ed., *Collected Writings of John Maynard Keynes XXV: Shaping the Post-War World: The Clearing Union* (London and New York: Macmillan and Cambridge University Press, 1980). For White's thinking, see Princeton, Harry Dexter White Papers, boxes 8 and 9. See *FRUS 1942* I, 163–242, *FRUS 1943* I, 1054–1098, and *FRUS 1944* II, 1–135 for talks up to June 1944.

126. *FRUS 1943* I, 1084–1090.
127. Donald Moggridge, ed., *Collected Writings of John Maynard Keynes XXVI: Activities, 1941–1946: Shaping the Post-War World: Bretton Woods and Reparations* (London and New York: Macmillan and Cambridge University Press, 1980), [26–28] 27–28, Keynes to White, 24 May 1944.
128. John Morton Blum, *Years of War, 1941–1945* (Boston: Houghton Mifflin, 1967), 251–252.
129. For a record of conference discussions, see *Proceedings and Documents of the United Nations Monetary and Financial Conference, Bretton Woods, New Hampshire, July 1–22, 1944*, 2 volumes (Washington, DC: USGPO, 1948). Important studies include: Armand Van Dormael, *Bretton Woods: Birth of a Monetary System* (London: Macmillan, 1978); Georg Schild, *Bretton Woods and Dumbarton Oaks: American Economic and Political Postwar Planning in the Summer of 1944* (New York: St. Martin's Press, 1995); Harold James, *International Monetary Cooperation Since Bretton Woods* (Washington, DC/New York: IMF/Oxford University Press, 1996); Benn Steil, *The Battle of Bretton Woods* (Princeton, NJ: Princeton University Press, 2013).
130. *Present at Creation*, 81–82; Moggridge, ed., *Keynes XXVI*, 82, Keynes to Catto, 4 July 1944.
131. FDRL, Morgenthau Diary, 753:133–164 (quotations at 135–136), Steering Committee Minutes, 13 July 1944, 8:30pm. Steil says White deliberately aimed at confusion to retain control; *Battle of Bretton Woods*, 220.
132. *Present at Creation*, 81.
133. Blum, *Years of War*, 259–265, Schild, *Bretton Woods and Dumbarton Oaks*, 119.
134. FDRL, Morgenthau Diary, 752:48, Steering Committee, 10 July 1944, 4:30pm; Blum, *Years of War*, 265–266.
135. FDRL, Morgenthau Diary, 753:122–129 (Steering Committee, 13 July 1944, 5:30pm), 753:159–163 (Steering Committee, 13 July 1944, 8:30pm), 754:3–6 (Steering Committee, 14 July 1944, 9:30am); Blum, *Years of War*, 268–270; Moggridge, ed., *Keynes XXVI*, 88–90 (Keynes to Morgenthau, 13 July 1944), 90–92 (Keynes to Anderson, 14 July 1944).
136. FDRL, Morgenthau Diary, 753:133–164, Steering Committee, 13 July 1944, 8:30pm (quotation at 143); see also Van Dormael, *Bretton Woods*, 198.
137. Blum, *Years of War*, 271, 274–275; *Present at Creation*, 84; Schild, *Bretton Woods and Dumbarton Oaks*, 127.
138. Blum, *Years of War*, 275, 277; Schild, *Bretton Woods and Dumbarton Oaks*, 122n43, 113; FDRL, Morgenthau Diaries, 757:15–16, Morgenthau to Roosevelt, 22 July 1944; *Present at Creation*, 83.
139. James, *International Monetary Cooperation*, 56, 57.
140. This account is based on *FRUS 1943* I, 1–38; *FRUS: Conferences at Washington and Quebec*, 389–1340; *FRUS: Conferences at Cairo and Tehran*, 457–652; *FRUS 1944* I, 614–959. See also Townsend Hoopes and Douglas Brinkley, *FDR and the Creation of the UN* (New Haven, CT: Yale University Press, 1997) and Stephen C. Schlesinger, *Act of Creation: The Founding of the United Nations* (Boulder, CO: Westview Press, 2003).
141. Yale, Acheson Private Papers, box 46, folder 5, microfilm reel 30, pp. 996–1005.
142. FDRL, Cox Papers, box 1, Acheson, Dean folder, Sub-Committee on Foreign Trade and Shipping of the House Special Committee on Postwar Economic Policy and Planning, 30 November 1944.
143. *Among Friends*, 50, Acheson to David C. Acheson, 2 April 1945.
144. FDRL, Cox Papers, box 129, Acheson, "The Place of Bretton Woods in Economic Collective Security; Acheson, "An Economic Policy for Peace," *DOSB* 12:300 (25 March 1945), 507–512.
145. Thomas M. Campbell and George C. Herring, eds., *The Diaries of Edward R. Stettinius, Jr., 1943–1946* (New York: New Viewpoints, 1975), 184–185 (entry for 27 November 1944).
146. *Present at Creation*, 89.
147. FDRL, FDR Papers, President's Personal File, 6906, Acheson, Dean folder.
148. See the record at *FRUS: Conferences at Malta and Yalta, 1945*, 547–996.

149. *FRUS 1945* III, 389–392, memorandum, 17 January 1945; *FRUS 1944* I, 287–299, ECEFP memorandum, 12 August 1944.

150. Campbell and Herring, *Diaries of Stettinius*, 305–308.

151. On Truman, see Alonzo L. Hamby, *Man of the People: A Life of Harry Truman* (New York: Oxford University Press, 1995); Robert H. Ferrell, *Harry S. Truman: A Life* (Columbia: University of Missouri Press, 1994); and David McCullough, *Truman* (New York: Simon & Schuster, 1992). On Truman's outlook in April 1945, see Wilson D. Miscamble, *From Roosevelt to Truman: Potsdam, Hiroshima, and the Cold War* (New York: Cambridge University Press, 2007), 1–33.

152. Acheson to David Acheson, 30 April 1945, quoted in *Present at Creation*, 104.

153. See the record of proceedings at *FRUS 1945* I, 1–1432.

154. University of Virginia, Stettinius Papers, box 675, Acheson, Dean G. folder (2 of 2).

155. 79th Congress, 1st Session, Senate Committee on Banking and Currency, *Bretton Woods Agreements Act* (Washington, DC: USGPO, 1945), 19, 21, 49, Acheson testimony, 13 June 1945.

156. *Present at Creation*, 111; "Random Harvest," in McGeorge Bundy, *The Pattern of Responsibility* (Boston: Houghton Mifflin, 1952), 17.

157. *Among Friends*, 63, Acheson to Frankfurter, 5 August 1945.

158. *Roosevelt and Frankfurter: Their Correspondence, 1928–1945* annotated by Max Friedman (London: Bodley Head, 1967), 743, Roosevelt to Frankfurter, 17 March 1945.

159. *Among Friends*, 55, 56, Acheson to Mary A. Bundy, 3 June 1945 and 10 June 1945; see also *Present at Creation*, 81.

160. Philip Hamburger, "Mr. Secretary II," *The New Yorker* (12 November 1949), 48.

161. Neal Stanford, "Who Is Dean Acheson?," *Christian Science Monitor* (1 September 1945).

Chapter Three

The Obligations of Power

Under Secretary of State and After, 1945–1948

August 1945 seemed full of the promise of new opportunities for Acheson. It appeared the war with Japan was about to end, after the atomic bombs dropped on Hiroshima on the 6th and on Nagasaki on the 9th. The imminent end of hostilities only confirmed his decision in July to resign, despite Byrnes's attempts to convince him to remain in the department.[1] Acheson agreed not to act until after Truman and Byrnes returned from the Potsdam conference with Stalin and Churchill (replaced halfway through the meeting by the new prime minister, Clement Attlee). The president and secretary came back on 7 August and a day later Acheson saw Byrnes and submitted his letter of resignation, which received the president's assent the following day. At a dinner that evening, hosted by Eugene Meyer, the publisher of the *Washington Post*, Fred Vinson, newly appointed as Morgenthau's successor as secretary of the Treasury, tried to persuade Acheson to change his mind. Acheson, instead, left with his wife for Saranac Lake in upstate New York to be with their daughter Mary Bundy, who was recovering from tuberculosis.[2]

No sooner had Acheson arrived in Saranac Lake than his daughter told him that Byrnes had been trying to reach him on the telephone. In his memoirs, he said that he did not feel any sense of urgency. So they only spoke when Byrnes rang again on the evening of the 11th. The secretary said that accepting his resignation had been a mistake. Indeed, he and the president wanted Acheson to return as under secretary. Acheson was "dumbfounded and appreciative" but resisted accepting. Byrnes, however, was insistent, saying he would send an army plane to bring him back to Washington to discuss the appointment. Because the next day, 12 August, was his wife's and daughter's joint birthday, he arranged to return on the 15th. He met

57

Byrnes that afternoon for what he called a "rambling talk." He discovered
that Will Clayton would remain in his post and that Benjamin V.
Cohen would be counselor, an appointment Acheson felt comfortable with, given
their "long friendship." Acheson tried to arrange for Julius Holmes to remain
as assistant secretary for administration but Byrnes preferred "his former law
partner, Donald Russell of South Carolina (later named as the Secretary's
choice)." Acheson decided to reflect on the offer overnight, then, after a
further talk the next morning, he accepted.[3] Acheson told Frankfurter: "The
Hon. Jimmy brought me back to Washington by air and told me I had caught
him in a weak moment and he didn't mean any of it. I had not escaped. I was
not to be allowed to and that the President would draft me by virtue of the
Title something Section something if I resisted."

Acheson was at first uncertain. As Walter Isaacson and Evan Thomas
explain, he was fifty-two years old and "had cultivated a gracious style and
longed to become accustomed to the manner in which he was living." Promotion to under secretary would increase his salary from nine thousand dollars a
year to ten thousand, but this was insignificant when compared with the
earnings of a senior partner at Covington & Burling. He did not warm to the
idea of working with Byrnes, but a combination of the prospect of playing a
role in important events and Byrnes's flattery seems to have tilted the balance. As he told Frankfurter, "I have no strength of character anyway and
certainly not when anyone is as charming as His Honor was."[4]

The reasons behind Acheson's appointment are not entirely clear.
Byrnes's first choice seemed to be James Dunn, even though Byrnes's two
earlier appointees, Benjamin Cohen, made a counselor, and Donald Russell,
made an assistant secretary for administration, preferred Acheson. The new
secretary appears to have wanted to persevere with Dunn. So he accepted
Acheson's resignation before changing his mind, and declaring that pressure
of work had caused him to err. Byrnes seems to have been persuaded to
choose Acheson after the intervention of Fred Vinson, who had worked with
Byrnes in the Office of War Mobilization. Vinson was on good terms with
Truman, who described him as a "devoted and undemonstrative patriot,"
someone with "a sense of personal and political loyalty seldom found among
the top men in Washington."[5] Truman wrote in his diary that Vinson was "a
straight shooter, knows Congress, and how they think, a man to trust."[6] In
any event, Acheson had made a favorable impression on the president during
his time as the department's liaison with Congress. Aware that Vinson had
regular conversations with Truman, Acheson later concluded: "I always
thought that Fred Vinson had got in there." Vinson also warmed to liberal
Acheson's belief that a sterner line should be taken with Japan; that the
Americans should not follow what appeared the too accommodating approach proposed by Supreme Commander Allied Powers (SCAP), General
Douglas MacArthur.[7]

The response to Acheson's appointment was generally favorable. The *New York Times* noted how Byrnes had been impressed by Acheson's work as the department's liaison with Congress, resulting in the passage of legislation on the UN, Bretton Woods, and the Export-Import Bank.[8] Even the radical journalist, I. F. Stone, who had earlier remarked on Acheson's liberal outlook, welcomed the appointment.[9] In an article in *The Nation* he declared: "Of all the men now in the department Acheson was by far the best choice for Under-Secretary." Stone praised him for his effective relations with Congress, aiding the passage of legislation for the Bretton Woods schemes and the UNO and his "knowledge and experience in handling foreign economic problems," which were of such current importance.[10]

His confirmation was a recess appointment, because Congress was not sitting, and so required a vote of the whole Senate. It encountered some difficulties from Senator Kenneth Wherry (R-Nebraska), who objected to Acheson's challenge to MacArthur's view that there could be a reduction in the planned scale of the US occupation force in Japan. As he did so often in his career, the general made his view public: he argued that there were so few risks of Japanese resistance that American forces could be reduced to 200,000. This appealed to many in Congress under pressure to bring US troops home as soon as possible. But it was not official policy. Acheson firmly rejected MacArthur's idea in a press conference, saying policy was made in Washington, not in the field.[11] This was an early intimation of future duels with Wherry. The vote on Acheson's confirmation was 69 to 1 in favor, with Wherry alone opposing.

JAMES BYRNES

Acheson was deputy to a very different figure from his predecessor, Edward Stettinius, or indeed Cordell Hull before him. James F. Byrnes was a political operator whose talents had been deployed on various domestic issues during the war. The importance of his contribution meant he joined the small band of Roosevelt advisors who were called "assistant president." Born in Charleston, South Carolina, in 1882, Byrnes left school at fourteen to work in a law office and became a court stenographer, before putting himself through law school. He served as a senator between 1931 and 1941, as an Associate Justice of the Supreme Court in 1941–1942, and then took up Roosevelt's offer to coordinate the work of all the war agencies and federal departments. Byrnes was a small, personable figure, alive with energy, described in a journalistic profile in 1940 as someone "whom enemies call the slyest, and friends the ablest, member of the Senate."[12] As his biographer notes, "Byrnes had always exuded confidence in his own abilities to solve any negotiable problem, including those of foreign diplomacy."[13] This was rooted in his considerable grasp of Congress and the federal bureaucracy and his talent for making political deals. But by 1945, maybe through overwork during the war, there seemed to be two Byrnes: the public one was "easygoing, courtly, always ready to assuage politicians' bruised egos with a bourbon"; and the more private "snappish, wounded, self-protective one."[14]

Byrnes met Truman's need for a strong and capable figure to lead the department and to continue Roosevelt's policies. Byrnes's presence at Yalta as one of Roosevelt's advisers seemed especially valuable. In addition, the president was conscious of Byrnes's disappointment at not being chosen as vice presidential candidate for the 1944 election: Truman thought his appointment as secretary "might help balance things up." However, Byrnes came to feel that he should lead the nation (partly because he regarded himself as abler than Truman and partly because he considered himself better suited to continuing FDR's policies). Truman might have underestimated Byrnes's independent streak but he admired the skills of his new secretary, calling him "my able and conniving Secretary of State."[15] Veteran assistant secretary Breckinridge Long approved, describing Byrnes as "capable, experienced, erudite," someone who could "make a great Secretary of State." His lack of "previous history in foreign affairs is immaterial," since "very few . . . who have become Secretary of State have had any extensive experience of that kind. . . . But most of them had had political experience and were men of sound judgment and character."[16]

The State Department soon bore Byrnes's imprint. It witnessed significant changes—in the role of the secretary, in personnel, and in atmosphere. Byrnes needed to attend numerous conferences overseas as the wartime allies sought to remake the world after the war. His memoirs record his 77,000 miles of foreign travel and his absences from Washington for 350 days out of his 562 in office.[17] This amounted to 62 percent of his time abroad. Hull had been abroad for 22 percent of his time, while the figures for George Marshall (1947–1949) and Acheson (1949–1953) were 47 percent and 25 percent.[18] Such absences meant that much work, outside the topics covered in Byrnes's conference meetings with the Soviets, British, and French, fell on the shoulders of his second-in-command, under secretary Dean Acheson.[19]

Although he lacked any detailed grasp or experience in handling foreign affairs, Byrnes was disinclined to seek the assistance of his departmental officials. Instead, he worked with a small group led by Benjamin Cohen. The British ambassador, Lord Halifax, noted that "Mr. Byrnes is known to regard the State Department with a highly critical eye and to be irritated by the manner and outlook of the typical career man." Byrnes told one State Department member, Theodore Achilles: "Hell, I might tell the president sometime what happened . . . but I'm never going to tell those little bastards at the State Department anything about it."[20] Charles Bohlen, one of the few members of the State Department to work closely with him, remarked: "Byrnes's personal style was to operate as a loner, keeping matters restricted to a small circle of advisers . . . Thus he failed to get the most out of the talent and expertise of the State Department," though he praised his use of humor to remove strains.[21] In oral testimony, shortly after leaving office, Acheson said that Byrnes thought the State Department was only six people.[22] Acheson later wrote feelingly about how the secretary needed the assistance of the whole department "from which flow his [the secretary's] information and his initial analysis of problems and recommendations for dealing with them."[23]

Nevertheless, the State Department became more efficient during his term of office. Byrnes's memoirs stressed passage of the Kee-Connally Act, signed into law on 13 August 1946, which was the first legislation on the Foreign Service since the Rogers Act of 1924 and brought improved salaries but also placed "more rigid requirements on training and promotion."[24] He might also have acknowledged the benefits of the reorganization begun by Stettinius, which restructured the department into a series of "offices," each containing different geographical and topical "divisions." Stettinius also contributed to the department's effectiveness with his emphasis on public relations, partly to persuade people of the merits of policies but also to recognize the shifting arena for the conduct of foreign relations. Byrnes, however, was not as accommodating to the press, refusing to yield to requests for more than one press conference a week. Acheson as under secretary held one per week when Byrnes was away.[25]

ACHESON AND BYRNES

Byrnes appreciated that structural and procedural changes would only be effective if the right personnel were in place: "The best planned organization, however, depends for its strength on the calibre of its people." He readily appreciated the talents of his deputy, describing Acheson as a man of "unusual ability and energy."[26] Acheson, however, was more restrained in his regard for Byrnes. In a letter to his daughter, he wrote that Frankfurter "thinks well of him and, I am sure, rightly in the light of his experience on the Court. But in this field of foreign policy, I have seen several problems put up to Byrnes and he never seemed to understand the criteria for judgment." He added (and this was when he expected to leave), "I think however, he will do his wowing without me—which is probably in accord with his wishes."[27] Acheson commented unfavorably on Byrnes's organizational methods in an oral testimony in 1955. He observed that "although I was second in command, things didn't flow through me. When he went off, I had to find out what was happening, to pick it up and run it."[28]

Byrnes began his duties with much promise. He enjoyed the full confidence of Truman who held him in high regard. Unfortunately, this did not last much beyond the end of the year. The new secretary did not feel the need to keep the president fully informed. Perhaps the decision to abandon Stettinius's wise initiative to appoint Charles Bohlen as liaison with the White House was an indication of how Byrnes intended to proceed. As Acheson's biographer says, "Byrnes never did acquire the loyalty which every President deserves from his Secretary of State."[29] Byrnes's first major task as secretary came at the Potsdam conference of July–August 1945 and he secured an agreement known as the "Byrnes Package Deal," which confirmed the occupation zones in Germany, the arrangements for German reparations, and the German-Polish frontier. Truman, Stalin, and Attlee also agreed to establish a Council of Foreign Ministers (CFM) to continue the work on a postwar settlement.[30] Byrnes returned to Washington on 7 August but remained preoccupied with continuing this work. To this end, he was frequently in Europe for meetings of the CFM, which met in London, September–October 1945, in Moscow, December 1945 and in Paris, April–May and June–July 1946.

Meanwhile, Acheson focused on running the department in Washington, trying to bring orderly practices to its functioning. In Byrnes's absence Acheson was acting secretary, holding regular meetings with the president, attending cabinet meetings, testifying before Congress, and delivering major speeches. Acheson was at the peak of his powers and in excellent health: he relished the work he was doing. He developed a routine of walking to the department from his Georgetown home in the company of Felix Frankfurter and working from 9:00am until about 7:00pm. As acting secretary Acheson was punctilious in keeping Byrnes informed of issues and events. He introduced a regular 9:30am meeting of the secretary's staff committee, which became an important part of departmental practice. It usually lasted no more than half an hour but allowed Acheson "some measure of control or, at least, knowledge" of activities in the department.[31] When Byrnes was back in Washington he showed little desire to attend this committee. Indeed, the return of the secretary often hindered the smooth running of the department, as Byrnes and his closest advisers ignored the procedures and lines of authority and responsibility Acheson was trying to create.

Acheson also had to cope with growing problems between Byrnes and the president. He showed a deftness of touch in remaining on good terms with both Truman and Byrnes: he sought to mollify the president's aspersions, even though he sympathized with them, while trying to remain loyal to the secretary. In trying to accomplish this, he displayed "a patience and control that he had not always previously exercised . . . he showed more willingness to suffer fools if not gladly then at least patiently." According to Archibald MacLeish, Acheson underwent during this period a "remarkable personal growth." He "took on a style and a stature I had not expected." He was more even tempered in working with others.[32]

Acheson enjoyed being at the center of power and, as a result, was more at ease and less prone to explosions of temper, though he could still deliver sharp remarks, as some of the exchanges in congressional committees reveal. On one occasion he observed: "If you didn't talk so much and listened more I think you would understand better what this is all about."[33] He was beginning to have an influence. This was in part a product of his talent for producing powerful and lucid analysis and policy recommendations. It was also due to the special circumstances of the time. Truman had the self-confidence to make decisions, but unlike Roosevelt who was comfortable making personal decisions, he preferred to seek the informed advice of the secretary of state. Byrnes, however, did not always fully consult the president, and he was frequently away. As a result, Acheson saw a good deal of the president, as well as other senior figures in Washington, and his stature with the president, Congress, and the public steadily grew: "Never in American history has a second-ranking officer of the Department of State exerted as much influence on foreign policy. . . . He was the balance wheel, the coordinator, the provider of continuity and sense of direction during an extraordinarily baffling time."[34]

Byrnes tackled the larger questions of policy for Germany, political arrangements in the liberated countries, and cooperation with Britain and the Soviet Union; and took the lead in tense US-Soviet exchanges over Iran. Acheson concentrated on three main areas: atomic energy, financial talks with Britain, and US policy in Asia. He also assumed a prominent role in a crisis over Turkey.

ATOMIC ENERGY

One of the first issues to engage Acheson was atomic energy. As he left the post of secretary of war, Henry Stimson wrote a paper on 11 September 1945, which was discussed at a cabinet luncheon on the 18th and at a full cabinet on the 21st. Stimson favored approaching the Soviets, after discussing this with the British, to seek an agreement to control and limit the use of the atomic bomb. He said: "If we fail to approach them now and merely continue to negotiate with them, having the weapon rather ostentatiously on our hip, their suspicions and their distrust of our purposes and motives will increase."[35] Acheson attended cabinet as acting secretary while Byrnes was at the inaugural conference of the Council of Foreign Ministers in London. Acheson observed in his memoirs: "The discussion was unworthy of the subject. No one had had a chance to prepare for its complexities." Nevertheless, he backed Stimson. Treasury Secretary Fred Vinson and Attorney General Tom Clark opposed Stimson's suggestion. The Joint Chiefs of Staff (JCS) also were reticent, wanting to retain the secrets of atomic weapons.[36]

When the cabinet did not decide on Stimson's proposal, Acheson wrote to Truman on 25 September recommending that they approach the Soviets to seek an agreement. He also suggested that the president inform Congress of this initiative, urge its members to pursue their own consideration of atomic energy and indicate to them the type of legislation he was likely to favor.[37] Truman largely followed this advice. On 3 October he sent a message to Congress outlining his desire to create an atomic energy commission.[38]

Meanwhile, British anxieties about atomic collaboration caused Prime Minister Attlee to visit Washington in November. Talks with Truman and the Canadian prime minister, Mackenzie King, produced three agreements. The first was the Tripartite Washington Declaration, which proposed a UN commission to investigate atomic energy. It favored the exchange of basic information with any nation for peaceful ends but it opposed the release of specialized information until enforceable safeguards acceptable to all nations were devised. The second agreement reaffirmed the commitment in the Quebec Agreement of 1943 to "full and effective co-operation" between the three countries. The third document was a memorandum of intention between General Leslie Groves, army commander of the Manhattan Project to build the atomic bomb, and Sir John Anderson, chairman of the British Cabinet Committee on atomic energy, promising they "will not use atomic weapons against other parties without prior consultation with each other." It also specified full cooperation but only on basic research.[39] In his memoirs Acheson observed: "If I was consulted at all about the discussions, I have forgotten it."[40]

The November Tripartite Declaration proposing a UN commission for the control of atomic energy ran counter to Acheson's advice that the issue only be put to the UN after agreement with the Soviets. But this did not deter Byrnes as he pursued Stimson's ideas at the next meeting of the CFM at Moscow in December. He spoke to both the Senate Foreign Relations Committee and the House Foreign Affairs Committee about the intention to explore the exchange of atomic information with the Soviets.[41] At a meeting on 14 December Senator Arthur Vandenberg pressed the president to tell Byrnes only to open the topic of exchanges and not go any further. Acheson attended this meeting.[42] Byrnes then traveled to Moscow and secured Soviet approval. Truman seemed at this stage happy to continue these exploratory talks, as Acheson told the US ambassador in Moscow, Averell Harriman, on 21 December.[43]

The Moscow CFM, however, was also the setting for a major disagreement between the secretary and the president. Harriman claimed that Byrnes refused to cable Truman to keep him informed of developments at Moscow, declaring that he could not trust leaks from the White House. Byrnes's release of the Moscow conference communiqué before consulting Truman confirms Harriman's judgment.[44] Byrnes worsened the situation by asking

Acheson to organize for him a radio broadcast on his return when he would report to the American people. Acheson felt that this "was not in accordance with etiquette"—the secretary should see the president first and then, with Truman's approval, make his speech. Acheson informed the president, who was furious, calling Byrnes to see him. In his memoirs Truman described a robust dressing down, while Byrnes's memoirs spoke of an agreeable exchange of views. The president gave Acheson an account that was "even more vivid," and it included the letter-memorandum that Truman said he had read out to the secretary. Acheson assessed the rival versions in a judicious manner. "On most occasions Mr. Truman's report of his bark vastly exaggerated it," for he was a personally kindly man. Byrnes was "accustomed to the lusty exchanges of South Carolina politics" and so would not have been offended by the president's insistence on being informed. Whatever the exact nature of the conversation, Byrnes thereafter was better at notifying Truman of his initiatives. Acheson learned important lessons from this episode about the proper relationship between the president and secretary: "The Secretary cannot be the President. However much freedom he may properly be given for operation and maneuver, he cannot be given or take over the ultimate presidential responsibility."[45] For all the incident's difficulties, it led to a deepening of relations between Acheson and the president.

ACHESON-LILIENTHAL PLAN

Meanwhile, Acheson wanted to bring order to US atomic policy. He told David Lilienthal, the former head of the Tennessee Valley Authority, that commitments had been made "without knowledge of what the hell it was all about," and explained how he had persuaded the secretary and president to act. On 7 January 1946 Byrnes asked Acheson to chair the committee that would draw up the US plan for international control of atomic energy. The committee consisted of James B. Conant, Dr. Vannevar Bush, General Leslie Groves, and John J. McCloy. The committee would study atomic energy security and safeguards, and offer guidance for those selected to represent the United States on the UN Commission. The ever-shrewd under secretary then approached Lilienthal on 16 January and asked him to become a member and chairman of the board of consultants to assist with the work of the committee. Acheson wanted the committee to "have the benefit of the judgment and insight of especially qualified consultants."[46] An impressive team was recruited, including Robert Oppenheimer, scientific leader of the Manhattan Project. In talks at Dumbarton Oaks in Washington, where the UN charter had been devised, Lilienthal's creativity and Acheson's coordinating skills combined to produce a proposal, which came to be known as the Acheson-Lilienthal Plan.[47]

Acheson submitted the "Report on International Control of Atomic Energy" on 16 March. In the foreword he explained that the report was primarily "the work of a Board of Consultants to the Department of State." It was released to the public on 28 March.[48] Unfortunately, Byrnes then made a terrible decision about how to respond to the report. He sought out the views of the financier, Bernard Baruch. In a letter to him on 19 April 1946 he declared: "I am favorably impressed by the report . . . [but] I am not of the opinion that it is the last word on the subject." He invited Baruch to offer his views informally, which he would consider carefully.[49] Following these exchanges, Byrnes recommended that Truman appoint Baruch as the American representative on the UN commission. Roger Makins at the British embassy in Washington reported on 30 March that Acheson "confessed as much astonishment as I did at Baruch's appointment, about which, I need hardly add, he was not consulted."[50] Baruch wanted to include sanctions in the scheme to punish violations. Acheson felt that the best mechanism was for the commission to reveal any violations and then for the other nations of the world to decide how to respond.

Lilienthal called this a "crazy kind of finale," adding that the news of Baruch's appointment made him "quite sick." "We need a man who is young, vigorous, not vain, and whom the Russians would feel isn't out simply to put them in a hole," and Baruch had none of these qualities.[51] Acheson was convinced that Baruch's plan was "almost certain to wreck any possibility of Russian acceptance."[52] He observed in an interview in 1955 that his view was "don't let us get into a straight-jacket."[53] Acheson enlisted the support of Lilienthal in May to try and dissuade Baruch from this approach, but to no avail.[54]

The Acheson-Lilienthal Plan was wrecked by a "pompous egotist" who "distrusted Acheson, probably because he [Baruch] wanted all the glory for creating the American plan for himself." It is doubtful whether Baruch "ever thought it would be accepted. Perhaps he intended the Soviet Union to reject it all along."[55] Acheson drew a larger lesson from the episode: he "was again reconfirmed in his conviction that a Secretary of State must plan carefully and brief the President fully. His obsession for administrative order arose out of demonstrations of dramatic disorder."[56]

LIMITING COOPERATION: THE MCMAHON ACT

At the same time as Byrnes and Baruch were mangling the Acheson-Lilienthal plan, the British were trying to improve atomic collaboration. Congress, however, was very anxious about protecting atomic secrets, especially after the Ottawa communist spy ring was revealed in February 1946. Many in Congress were unaware of the secret understandings with Britain in November 1945. Even Truman was reconsidering his pledges. The Americans sought to enshrine the more restricted cooperation in the Groves-Anderson memorandum: in return for rather limited information from the Americans the British would provide raw materials to the United States. At the 15 February 1946 meeting of the Anglo-American-Canadian Combined Policy Committee (CPC), the first that Acheson attended, Byrnes and War Secretary Robert Patterson appeared unenthusiastic about confidential cooperation.[57] Truman told Attlee on 20 April that he believed the Quebec Agreement allowed the United States to block certain information.[58]

Acheson remarked in his memoirs that he discovered in winter 1945–1946 something that was "to disturb me for some years to come." The US government had made an agreement but "was not keeping its word and performing its obligations."[59] The more restricted interpretation of collaboration was partially overturned through conversations with Acheson, who accepted that the administration was not honoring its Quebec commitments. General Groves, in administrative charge of American atomic work until the creation of the Atomic Energy Commission in August 1946, wanted all materials to go to US plants, arguing that they were most acutely needed there, and that they would be vulnerable if sent to British plants. In discussion with Halifax on 30 April Acheson was, according to the British, "visibly embarrassed" by Groves's proposal.[60] In May 1946 the under secretary brokered an understanding by which materials already in America would go to the American program but the remaining materials would be shared equally between the two countries. He informed the American members of the CPC of the compromise on 7 May.[61] Acheson told an official at the British embassy in June, "Although we made the agreement, we simply could not carry it out . . . things like that happen in the Government of the United States due to the loose ways things are handled."[62]

James Byrnes acted less honorably in his pursuit of an end to cooperation with the British. At a CPC meeting in April 1946 he denied having seen either the Washington agreement or the Groves-Anderson memorandum, despite having chaired the CPC meeting in December 1945 which considered both documents.[63] In an attempt to overcome the growing difficulty, Attlee wrote to Truman three times, only to receive one rather brief reply. Attlee wrote a long letter, full of feeling, to Truman, saying that "our three governments stand on a special relationship to one another . . . we believe we are entitled [to full information], both by the documents, and by the history of our common efforts in the past."[64] British appeals were to no avail. The president had decided against further collaboration. Congress passed the McMahon Act in July and Truman signed it into law on 1 August 1946. It established the American Atomic Energy Commission and restricted the release of atomic information to third parties, including the British.

LOAN TO BRITAIN

Acheson was also at the center of financial assistance to Britain, another major Anglo-American issue that carried over from the war. He had taken a leading role on financial relations with Britain since his work on the Lend-Lease "consideration" in 1941 and subsequent talks on Lend-Lease matters. Nearly simultaneously with the Bretton Woods conference in 1944, and partly overlapping in subject matter, were Anglo-American discussions on the next phase of Lend-Lease—Stage II, which would cover the period from the end of war with Germany to the end of war with Japan. Britain achieved a good deal: seeking $3 billion on the military side, Britain secured $2.838 billion; and hoping for a further $3 billion on the civilian side, Britain had gained $2.569 billion.[65] Then in 1945 came the more difficult task—Stage III, which concerned the transition to peace after all hostilities had ended. E. F. Penrose, economic adviser to John Winant, the US ambassador in London, thought there should be retroactive Lend-Lease, to reimburse the British for the investments liquidated in the US to meet war purchases before Lend-Lease. Penrose regretted the failure to tackle Britain's specific difficulties, in particular how it had used up its investments because of the Neutrality legislation and the Johnson Act.[66] However, as the war came to an end in August, Truman ended Lend-Lease aid to Britain.[67] Keynes laid out the problem in a paper for the government. The country would need to spend more on food and raw materials and other imports than it could expect to earn. Britain could no longer rely on Lend-Lease to meet the shortfall and confronted over the next three years a "deficit of the order of $5 billion which can be met from no other source but the United States."[68]

Keynes led a delegation to North America in search of funds to solve this problem. He traveled first to Canada on 2 September to discuss how British "ideas and points of view are likely to impinge on the Americans," and the Canadians were "on the whole encouraging." [69] The British then went to Washington. At a dinner at the British embassy on 9 October various congressmen cross-examined the British and did so, according to the diary of Keynes's aide, Freddy Harmer, "on whole intelligently and good-humouredly." He added astutely: "The pro-British line always needs defending in this country: the anti-British one never."[70]

William Clayton, under secretary for economic affairs at the State Department, and Treasury Secretary Fred Vinson led the American negotiating team. Both men were pro-British but Clayton's forceful commitment to free trade was less welcome to the British, who wanted time to move from imperial preference.[71] Busy with other matters until November, Acheson played a lesser role. Halifax and Keynes led for the British. The discussions lasted from 22 September until the agreement of 6 December. [72] Keynes noted in one message that Acheson "can be relied upon to take a friendly and reasonable line toward us."[73] The talks began with Keynes asking for $5 billion plus whatever was needed to settle Lend-Lease, hoping for a grant-in-aid or, at the very least, an interest free loan.

Hard bargaining resulted in an American offer of $3.75 billion at 2 percent interest repayable over fifty years from December 1951 with a provision for waiver of interest (but not capital repayments) in years when British overseas earnings fell below certain levels. The second part of the agreement was a generous settlement of Lend-Lease. The net debit of $20 billion was canceled and $650 million was charged for American property and goods in transit which author Robert Hathaway has estimated were worth more than $6 billion.[74] Canada provided a loan of $1.25 billion. A grand total of $5.65 billion was being lent to Britain.

Once the agreement was signed, Acheson assumed the lead in persuading the American public and Congress to support it. He took the case to a wide variety of forums. He addressed expert audiences: on 18 March he spoke to the Economic Club of Detroit on "Mutual Advantages of the British Loan."[75] He appeared on the radio: he and Fred Vinson took part in an NBC radio discussion of the loan, arguing that it was good for the United States and not just for Britain.[76] From the beginning he was sure that the agreement would be approved by Congress. He told the British ambassador, Lord Halifax, in January that he was "very confident that the loan would go through Congress all right, but with a good deal of disagreeable yapping."[77]

Acheson also delivered numerous speeches, such as his 25 January address, "Why a loan to England?" He rejected claims that it was a gift or a precedent for similar loans to other countries. He declared: "This loan is unique. It is made to the one country in the world which is absolutely essential to the restoration of world trade. It is made under conditions which make possible, and indeed inevitable, the restoration of world trade."[78] On 13 March 1946 Acheson testified before the Senate Committee on Banking and Currency on the Anglo-American Financial Agreement. He stressed the importance of Britain to the world economy. Before the war the dollar and the pound had provided the currency for one-half of global trade; after the war, with the elimination of Germany and Japan, two-thirds or three-quarters of that trade would be conducted in those currencies. To fight the war, Britain had accumulated massive debts. Unlike the United States, British debts were to other countries: Britain had purchased goods in return for sterling credits, which could be used to buy British goods after the war. This meant that Britain's exports after the war must go to repay debts, rather than to generate income. This dynamic would lead to closed trading blocs. To avoid this outcome, the United States needed to loan money to the British so they could buy goods in the United States and anyone who sold goods in Britain would secure funds that could be used in the United States. The loan, then, was the best means of restoring world trade.[79] There was some resistance, especially among those in Congress who disliked funding Britain's newly socialist government, but Acheson's arguments proved very persuasive and were reinforced by Vinson and Assistant Secretary of the Treasury Harry Dexter White, and many others in politics and business. The loan passed Congress and was signed into law by Truman on 15 July 1946.

THE MARSHALL MISSION TO CHINA

At the same time as he was tackling atomic and financial matters, Acheson also took the lead in addressing various aspects of American policy in Asia, while Byrnes remained focused on Europe. Three countries were at the center of American concerns in late 1945—Japan, Korea, and China. Apart from the episode in September 1945 when Acheson publicly asserted presidential authority over General MacArthur's occupation regime, Japan was not a prominent issue for the under secretary. He favored cooperation with the Soviets to try and establish a unified government for the Korean Peninsula; and even after the failure of efforts in 1946, he oversaw a further attempt in 1947. By this time he was a leading advocate of aid to Korea, especially because of its importance to the Japanese economy.[80] China was the most pressing Asian problem and the one that most engaged Acheson in 1945–1946.

Americans since the late nineteenth century had felt a particular attachment to the fate of China. During the Second World War American forces under General Stilwell had fought the Japanese, enjoying variable support from Chiang Kai-shek's nationalists and Mao Zedong's communists. Both the communists and the nationalists retained a very large part of their forces in reserve for their coming struggle for power. After the defeat of Japan, China lacked a government in charge of the whole country. Soviet forces controlled Manchuria to the north. In the northern parts of central China and in the southeast the Japanese occupied the main cities, while the communists were in power in the surrounding areas. There were 1,235,000 Japanese troops and 1,700,000 Japanese civilians in China. They could not be simply shipped out of the country, otherwise the communists would seize control of the cities. So the Americans sent 50,000 Marines to occupy key seaports, guard principal rail lines, and assume control of coal supplies on the eastern coast. Meanwhile, the Americans evacuated the Japanese and airlifted nationalist forces into these areas. By late 1946, nearly three million Japanese had been removed.[81]

Acheson sent a message to Truman on 13 September 1945 explaining that the United States should aid the Chinese in "the development of armed forces for the maintenance of internal peace and security, and the assumption of adequate control over liberated areas of China, including Manchuria and

Formosa." The United States should avoid furnishing "military equipment to China for use in fratricidal war or for the support by force of an undemocratic administration."[82] As events were to reveal, Acheson's aspirations were unachievable, since the nationalists believed that routing the communists was the best guarantee of "internal peace" and "adequate control."

The Americans tried to bring the two sides together. Patrick J. Hurley went to China, first as the president's personal representative and then as US ambassador, and helped to produce an agreement on 11 October 1945. This committed the parties to calling a National Assembly, holding a consultative meeting of all political leaders, creating a joint committee to reorganize the armed forces, and introducing constitutional government. But the fighting soon resumed.

As critical voices began to be raised about the effectiveness of the US Marines in China, Acheson attended a meeting of the secretaries of state, war, and Navy on 27 November, and suggested a four-part approach. The Marines should stay; they should move Chinese government forces north by water; they should explore the possibility of a truce in areas evacuated when Japanese troops were removed; and they should encourage efforts at a political settlement between the nationalists and communists. He also recommended that they pressure Chiang to be more serious in pursuing a settlement.[83] On the very same day, Hurley added to the administration's difficulties by complaining that Foreign Service staff in China sided with the communists. Hurley requested and secured the removal of these Foreign Service officials but they were then appointed to the Chinese and far eastern sections of the State Department and ended up as Hurley's supervisors. Hurley declared that there was a "wide discrepancy between our announced policies and our conduct of international relations."[84] Truman now asked George C. Marshall, recently retired as Army chief of staff, to undertake a mission to China to try and find a solution. On 9 December Marshall met Byrnes, Acheson, and John Carter Vincent, director of the Office of Far Eastern Affairs, to agree upon his instructions. He received his formal commission from the president on 15 December.[85]

Acheson played a vital role in Washington by acting as the general's "rear echelon." He would coordinate contacts between Marshall and the president, which involved frequently bypassing the secretary.[86] The experience deepened his relationship with Marshall and educated him in the complexities and frustrations of framing a policy for China. Marshall's mission proved an exasperating affair. He enjoyed a temporary success when he helped to arrange a ceasefire between the two sides but successive attempts to build on this were followed by disappointment when it proved impossible for them to reach an agreement.[87]

All the while, Acheson tried to gain congressional support for these endeavors in China. He spoke to the House Foreign Affairs Committee on 19

June 1946, arguing in favor of a bill that would provide military advice and assistance to the Chinese nationalists. The Americans had already given much—between VJ Day and February 1946 they had furnished $600 million worth of supplies. They had extended Lend-Lease aid first until 31 March and then to 30 June 1946, but they were fast approaching the termination date. Acheson argued that new arrangements were needed. Marshall had made a great deal of progress and so it was urgently necessary that the United States was able to provide any additional aid that the general required. In particular, Marshall wanted the creation of a 1,000-strong military advisory group to help in reorganizing the Chinese military and integrating communists into the national army.[88] At Truman's request, Acheson spoke to the cabinet about China on 2 August. He explained that the US Marines had helped facilitate the evacuation of Japanese forces, and, although that task was now completed, they were still needed to support Marshall's efforts. He added that the nationalist government was not all that could be desired and Marshall was not getting any help in his efforts to secure peace. Nevertheless, he felt they "should back Marshall up to the limit until he himself has said that there is no longer any hope of gaining his objective and that it is time to come out and reconsider our position in China and our general policy in the Far East."[89] The situation in China deteriorated. As Acheson told the Senate in June 1951, "One side or another would believe that it could gain an advantage by capturing this or that city or area, and believed it could strengthen itself in the negotiations."[90]

Acheson always seemed less hopeful than Marshall. In his memoirs he said: "As the mission straggled to a discouraged and discouraging end in December, almost a year from its inception, it seemed to me that its whole conception and General Marshall's heroic efforts to achieve it were not understood at home. . . . Would it not be helpful, I asked him, to prepare and submit a comprehensive paper for public information of what we had tried to do in the past year, what we had done and left undone, and why?" Here, perhaps, were the seeds of the *China White Paper* issued in 1949 by Acheson when he was secretary of state. Marshall, however, opposed such a statement, still confident he "could destroy the power of the reactionaries and bring a liberal element into control of the government" while exposing communist "misrepresentation and vicious propaganda."[91]

Marshall submitted his report to the president and made a public statement on 7 January 1947.[92] He concluded there was little point in further US aid, for the nationalists were losing and were doing so because of poor performance. As Acheson informed the Senate in June 1951, "the effort to mediate came to an end with his departure." There followed "the military period of the struggle between the two governments."[93]

The so-called China lobby, which favored support for Chiang, soon grew critical of Truman and Acheson. Shortly afterward, therefore, Truman asked

General Albert C. Wedemeyer, Army chief of plans and operations and former commander of US forces in China from October 1944 to May 1946, to
investigate. He reported to the president on 19 September 1947. Wedemeyer
recommended significant American assistance to the nationalists. But Truman was unconvinced.[94]

ACHESON AND THE SOVIETS

While Acheson tackled atomic energy, the loan to Britain, and China, Byrnes
attended the CFMs to address various facets of the postwar settlement in
Europe. After deadlock at London in October, he managed to settle many
issues at Moscow in December 1945. By his return to Washington in January
1946, however, the climate of opinion was turning against deals with Moscow. Given his later reputation for being an unyielding advocate of a tough
attitude toward the Soviet Union, it is interesting to note that Acheson took a
hopeful view of working with the Soviets at this time. In a memorandum on
atomic energy, he counseled against exclusive American control of the new
technology. "I cannot see why the basic interests of the two countries should
conflict. Any long range understanding based on firmness and frankness and
mutual recognition of the other's basic interests seems to me impossible
under a policy of Anglo-American exclusion of Russia from atomic development." He recommended that the United States approach Moscow with a
view to developing a program of mutual cooperation on atomic energy, but to
do so gradually.[95] The Acheson-Lilienthal Plan aimed at cooperation without
the unworkable and heavy-handed sanctions suggested by Baruch. Acheson
also embraced collaboration with the Soviets in Korea. Furthermore, he
agreed to give a speech on 14 November 1945 titled "American-Soviet
Friendship" to the National Council of American-Soviet Friendship, New
York. Although he offered forthright disapproval of Soviet actions in eastern
Europe, occasioning booing from his pro-Soviet audience, he also declared
that the two countries could pursue peaceful development and trade without
the need for aggression.[96] In a speech in January 1946 he declared "it is
absolutely unthinkable that we should fight Russia." He also told the Soviets
in May that Washington had not abandoned the possibility that the Export-
Import Bank would make a $1 billion loan to the Soviets to assist their
postwar reconstruction.[97]

Still, Acheson could be bluntly critical over particular matters. During the
New York speech, he pointedly criticized events in Czechoslovakia.[98] But he
viewed these as individual problems that needed to be addressed and not yet
as components of a larger pattern of behavior. His response to Stalin's speech
of 9 February 1946 illustrates his perspective at this time. Stalin spoke about
the capitalist-imperialist roots of the Second World War and the need to be

prepared in what was a hostile international system. Paul Nitze in the State Department regarded this as the declaration of an offensive against the West. Acheson was much less worried and told Nitze that his fears "were all nonsense," that he was seeing "hobgoblins under the bed," yet Acheson sought assessments from Charles Bohlen and the other major Soviet expert, George Kennan at the Moscow embassy. Kennan drafted a lengthy evaluation, which became known as the Long Telegram, advocating containment of Soviet ambitions.[99]

Less than two weeks after Kennan's dispatch, Winston Churchill gave a speech in Fulton, Missouri, on 5 March 1946, in which he popularized the phrase "iron curtain" to describe what he regarded as the growing divide between East and West; and advocated the formation of an Anglo-American alliance. Byrnes read and approved it when he saw Churchill in Florida before the former prime minister traveled to Fulton. On the day of the speech the secretary sent three telegrams. According to Fraser Harbutt, there were separate reasons for sending each of them, but the decision to send them on the same day "is consistent with the administration's determination to convey an impression of complete solidarity with Churchill."[100] Many writers regard this as a further indication of a toughening American attitude to the Soviets. Acheson wrote in his memoirs about "Stalin's offensive against the United States and the West" in spring 1946.[101] But at the time he did not think this way. Just as he had doubts about Nitze's reading of Stalin's February speech, so he did not accept the claim in the Fulton address that cooperation between the three wartime allies was no longer possible. He was due to host a dinner in New York in honor of Churchill, but he canceled it, at Byrnes's request, who appears to have wanted to avoid trouble from the Soviets over what might have been seen as endorsement of Churchill's anti-Soviet outlook. At a dinner party Acheson gave to replace the Churchill reception, he spoke strongly in favor of the former prime minister's belief that it was necessary to be firm with the Soviets but he did not support the idea of an anti-Soviet partnership with Britain.[102]

Nor did Acheson adopt an aggressive tone in the same month when there arose the first serious US-Soviet confrontation—a crisis over Iran. Byrnes took the lead in framing an American response. At war's end in 1945 there were American, British, and Soviet troops in Iran. In September they agreed to leave by 2 March 1946. But the Soviets prevaricated and seemed to be encouraging separatists in Azerbaijan. Acheson recommended a firm response. A message went to Moscow questioning Soviet commitment to the territorial integrity of Iran.[103] Byrnes was convinced that his decision to attend the UN Security Council and challenge the Soviets forced them to back down. American pressure helped but mainly to strengthen the hand of the Iranian prime minister, Ahmad Qavam, in his skillful negotiations with the Soviets. He promised Moscow control of a joint oil company if the troops were removed. Once Soviet forces departed, however, Iranian troops suppressed the separatist movement and the Iranian parliament canceled the oil deal.

GERMANY

American relations with the Soviet Union were also deteriorating over Germany, even though Truman and Byrnes still sought a deal. The secretary made a further effort to negotiate with the Soviets in the spring and summer of 1946 at the Paris CFM. He tabled a proposal for a twenty-five-year treaty between the four main powers that would demilitarize Germany. The Soviets initially agreed to consider the suggestion but insisted on reparations first. This stalled the American offer and persuaded Byrnes that he could no longer reach an agreement with the Soviets on Germany.[104] The CFM, sitting as a peace conference in a series of sessions until November, did manage, however, to produce peace treaties with Bulgaria, Romania, Hungary, Italy, and Finland.[105]

The failure to make progress in reaching a settlement on Germany highlighted the daily troubles of administering the separate zones and of cooperation between the different zonal authorities. General Lucius D. Clay, the military governor of the American zone, halted shipments of reparations from the US zone until agreement was reached on economic unification. His action was aimed more at the French, who wanted control of the Saar coal mines, detachment of the Ruhr, a separate Rhineland and administrative decentralization of Germany. Contrary to many accounts, he did not blame the Soviets for delays in sending reciprocal supplies of food and raw materials stipulated at Potsdam. He said that Potsdam allowed two years for delivery of reparations and five years for return items.[106] Inability to agree on a framework for German economic unity led the Americans and British, in July, to agree to the economic merger of their occupation zones—the Bizone came into effect in January 1947.

AUGUST CRISES—TURKEY AND YUGOSLAVIA

As cooperation proved increasingly difficult over Germany, a war scare arose over Turkey. On 1 August 1946 the American ambassador in Turkey, Edwin Wilson, cabled that the Turkish ambassador to the Soviet Union told him that the reported assignment of the most distinguished Soviet general, Georgi Zhukov, as commander of the Odessa military district indicated possible preparation for a Soviet military assault, since a number of Soviet leaders wanted direct action if diplomacy did not work.[107] Then on 7 August the Soviets sent a note to the Turkish government insisting on the ending of the Montreux Convention of 1936 which had given control of the Straits to Turkey.[108] The Americans believed that the issue should be settled through the UN and not by intimidatory notes.[109]

Acheson feared the Soviets were trying to make Turkey a satellite and advocated a firm response to Moscow's note. He went to the White House on 15 August to report to the president, who had also called secretary of the Navy James Forrestal and under secretary of war Kenneth Royall and the JCS. Acheson drafted a strong American reply, which Truman endorsed. He also persuaded the president to send a naval task force to Istanbul, consisting of an aircraft carrier, the USS *Franklin D. Roosevelt*, two cruisers, and five destroyers to join the USS *Missouri*, already in the Dardanelles, to demonstrate American determination. Their ostensible function was to return the body of the Turkish ambassador to Washington.[110] When the 24 September Soviet response was unsatisfactory, Washington maintained the diplomatic pressure.[111] In October the Soviets eased their pressure on Ankara, and Washington again concluded that a firm response had yielded dividends.[112] In the same month the Turks sought American assistance in obtaining military supplies, which Byrnes approved in December.[113] Acheson proposed that the British should provide arms to Turkey and, if they could not do so, then the Americans should give the British the arms needed to transfer them to the Turks.[114]

As the crisis over Turkey was beginning, Acheson had to handle another tense issue. On 9 August the Yugoslavs forced down an American Army transport plane; and ten days later, they shot down another plane. The Americans adopted the same approach that they had applied to Turkey: a tough note, backed up with the movement of the US military to the scene. Acheson penned a message demanding the release of both aircrews, not knowing at the time that all of the second crew were dead. The president also "ordered our troops along the Morgan Line and the reinforcement of our air forces in northern Italy." Acheson was triumphant in his memoirs: "Tito got the point and backed down."[115]

COLD WAR ATTITUDES

Byrnes responded to the August crises and the failure of progress on Germany with a speech that pointed to a sharpening of the administration's attitudes toward the Soviet Union. His carefully publicized address in Stuttgart on 6 September committed the United States to help rebuild the western zones of Germany whether or not the Soviets agreed. American troops would remain in Germany beyond the eighteen months originally envisaged. He added, "The United States favors the early establishment of a provisional Government for Germany." He concluded: "If complete unification cannot be secured, we shall do everything in our power to secure maximum possible unification."[116] Six days later Henry Wallace, the secretary of commerce and Roosevelt's vice president, 1941–1944, gave a speech in New York criticizing the increasingly tough attitude to the Soviet Union adopted by Byrnes.[117] Truman had originally approved the speech, without reading it carefully. But Byrnes was furious at its criticism of his policies and threatened to resign. Not wanting to lose his secretary of state, he decided instead to force Wallace to resign on 20 September. Although the decision was partly political, it also reflected the shift from the cooperation with Moscow that Wallace advocated.

In that same month Clark Clifford, special counsel to the president, submitted to Truman an alarmist assessment of the Soviet threat and recommended an aggressive military response. In July Truman had become concerned about Soviet behavior and had asked Clifford to prepare a record of Soviet violations of international agreements.[118] Clifford and his assistant George Elsey consulted a range of senior officials, including George Kennan and Charles Bohlen. When they approached Byrnes he reacted somewhat sharply to their enquiries, feeling the task should have been given to the State Department.[119] Clifford asked Acheson to provide him with details of US agreements with the Soviet Union, which he did in a four-page memorandum, "Comments on Soviet Compliance with International Agreements Undertaken since January 1941."[120]

It is not clear whether Acheson knew about the Clifford-Elsey report. Many years later Acheson denied any knowledge of the report in answer to a question from an academic. Acheson said he had never heard of Clifford's "'Report to the President,' now published in Krock's memoirs, so I see no way of helping you."[121] Moreover, it certainly did not capture his outlook at this time. In replying to Clifford's request, he observed: "Much of the difficulty regarding the implementation of agreements to which the United States and the U.S.S.R. are signatories results from the divergence of objective with which the two countries approach postwar problems."[122]

BYRNES'S RESIGNATION

Byrnes and Truman might have been in harmony in their increasingly firm approach to the Soviet Union but their personal relationship had not improved since their disagreements in January. In April Byrnes had been wrongly diagnosed with a heart condition and submitted his first resignation letter, to become effective on 1 July 1946.[123] The day before, Acheson had also submitted a resignation letter. He was not enjoying working with the secretary, feeling lines of command were not clear. Matters came to a head over the issue of the intelligence and research sections, transferred from the wartime Office of Strategic Services to the State Department in October 1945. In his memoirs, Acheson explained that he and the man he persuaded Byrnes to appoint as director of intelligence, Colonel Alfred McCormack of Army Intelligence, faced three sources of difficulty as they tried to ensure the department retained its central coordinating role: "congressional opposition to professional intelligence work, civil disobedience in the State Department, and indecision in high places brought on by military opposition to both unification of the services and civilian control of intelligence." Congress cut funding for intelligence work. Members of the department's geographical divisions claimed they already collected such intelligence as was needed. In January 1946 Truman accepted a directive shifting primacy in intelligence from the State Department to the Executive Office of the President. In April Byrnes agreed to a recommendation from assistant secretary Donald Russell that yielded to the pressure from the geographical divisions and ordered the transfer of units (the majority of the staff) working on specific areas to geographical divisions. McCormack resigned. Acheson also tendered his resignation, dismayed by Byrnes's decision and feeling he could not continue to work in a department lacking clear organization.[124]

Truman did not want to accept either resignation but he was already thinking ahead and had sought a replacement for Byrnes. He sent a message through General Dwight D. Eisenhower, Army Chief of Staff, to General Marshall asking him to consider becoming secretary of state when he had completed his work in China. Eisenhower reported back Marshall's readiness to serve wherever the president directed. Acheson discovered this from references to it in his communications with Marshall, a discovery which "left me dissatisfied."[125] By December circumstances favored a change of secretary; Marshall was coming to the end of his mission, Byrnes had just ended work on the peace treaties in the Paris and the New York meetings of the CFM. Byrnes sent his second resignation on 19 December.[126] The president accepted the secretary's resignation, which became effective on 20 January 1947. Acheson expected he would also depart but Truman wanted him to remain.

By the end of 1946 Acheson and President Truman had developed a relationship of considerable mutual respect. The under secretary had never warmed to Roosevelt's style of governing, but welcomed Truman's direct and decisive approach. At a time when the secretary of state did not always accord due respect to the chief executive, the president valued Acheson's loyalty. This was demonstrated in November 1946 when he alone met the returning president after the mid-term election defeats. Truman also greatly valued Acheson's command of the issues and his habit of always consulting him about policy. Acheson had confirmed his loyalty by revealing the more tentative allegiance of James Forrestal. The secretary of the Navy held lunches with other members of the cabinet to consider policies without informing the president. Truman quickly halted the practice.[127]

UNDER SECRETARY TO GEORGE C. MARSHALL, JANUARY–JUNE 1947

Acheson agreed to remain as under secretary until 30 June 1947, partly out of growing respect for the president.[128] Even more influential was his high regard for the new secretary: he declared on many occasions that he admired George Marshall more than any other living person.[129] The new secretary was a very different individual from his predecessor. He was a figure of enormous integrity with a deep sense of duty. He had presence and a serenity rooted in self-knowledge, self-discipline, and indifference to reputation, although he could occasionally give way to explosions of temper. James Reston offered a perceptive comparison of the characters of Byrnes and Marshall: while Byrnes was a "warm, happy man, with a rare capacity for political manipulation and a wonderful stock of illustrative anecdotes," Marshall evinced "moral grandeur," and was "[s]evere and aloof, with none of the Virginian's love of people and capacity for humor."[130]

Acheson was delighted to be working for Marshall. Lilienthal's diary records the enthusiasm with which he approached his duties.

> [To] work with him is such a joy that he can hardly talk about anything else. I am delighted about this, for Jimmy Byrnes' erratic and often thoughtless (as well as sometimes plain inept) administrative and other ideas had about driven Dean crazy. Marshall has put great responsibility upon Dean. Partly because he trusts him, I have no doubt, partly because Marshall would have been completely sunk if he had done anything else, and partly because Marshall has neither the excess of energy nor the interest in detail that would permit him to get into administration of the department. But it has made a new man of Dean, and this is a good thing for the country right now.[131]

Acheson now had a chief who valued orderly procedures. He asked what Marshall expected of him. "I was to be his chief of staff, he explained, and run the Department, coming to him only when I needed help (and his look indicated that that had better not be often); he wished matters for his decision to come to him through me. And so it was."[132]

Acheson was able to build on his introduction of the 9:30 secretary's staff meeting, because Marshall created a central secretariat, which "served his office and mine and through which we kept track of everything coming in or going out of the Department, and the progress, or lack of it, being made on each matter." Marshall and Acheson kept the head of the secretariat informed of all policy decisions. It was now possible for the work of the department to be "under the direction of a chief executive officer." The central purpose of the meeting was not to frame policies. Rather, it was to assign responsibility for new matters as they arose, to oversee and ensure progress on current work, and to "present proposals to the President for necessary decisions, authority, and means."[133]

Reflecting in his memoirs on his thinking in 1946, Acheson observed that for five years he had become increasingly convinced that proper control should reside "in the Secretary of State as the President's chief secretary." Lines of command were not clear under either Hull or Byrnes. The latter was "an individual operator using half a dozen close associates upon those problems that engaged his attention. For him the four or five thousand other people in the Department and any other problems on which he was not working hardly existed. It was not strange, then, that ideas of reorganization were not congenial to him."[134]

Although he served as Marshall's deputy for only six months, Acheson was involved in work of pivotal significance. Like Byrnes before him, Marshall was often away from Washington. A particular priority was the Moscow CFM in March–April. Acheson helped shape a response to the problems in Greece and Turkey that led to the formulation of the Truman Doctrine in March. He also took the lead in developing ideas about economic aid to Western Europe that resulted in the creation of the Marshall Plan. In pursuing these goals, he emerged as a much harsher critic of Soviet behavior than had been evident in late 1946. Indeed, he made the first public reference by an American official to Soviet aggression in a congressional hearing on 10 February 1947, when he suggested that the foreign policy of Russia was "aggressive and expansionary." This drew a strong Soviet protest.[135]

THE ASSISTANCE PROGRAM FOR GREECE AND TURKEY

By late 1946 American officials were increasingly worried about both Greece and Turkey. Acheson had proposed in November that the Americans should provide arms for Turkey if the British were unable to furnish them. The American ambassador in Athens, Lincoln MacVeagh, sent reports to Washington of the mounting difficulties facing the Greek government in its fight with the communists. Earlier fighting had ended in a fragile stalemate in February 1945 but a communist guerrilla campaign began in summer 1946.[136] In January 1947 an economic mission led by Paul A. Porter, former administrator of the Office of Price Administration, visited Greece.[137]

On 21 February the British sent two notes through their ambassador, Lord Inverchapel, saying that they could no longer finance their troops in support of the government in the Greek civil war nor provide funds for the Turkish government.[138] This was part of a British policy of major disengagement. In the face of economic difficulties and depletion of the American loan, London decided to reduce overseas costs by ending aid to Greece and Turkey and by quitting Palestine and India. The Americans, and Acheson in particular, had already anticipated the need to become involved. Mark Etheridge, US representative on the UN Commission of Investigation into Greek frontier incidents, cabled on 17 February to say the Soviets viewed Greece as a "ripe plum."[139] On Thursday 20 February Acheson reworded a memorandum evaluating the situation by Loy Henderson, director of the Office of Near Eastern and African Affairs, giving it a much stronger import. The next day he informed Marshall, "unless urgent and immediate support is given, it seems probable that the Greek government will be overthrown," which could lead to the "loss of the whole Near and Middle East." Marshall directed Acheson to "prepare the necessary steps for sending economic and military aid."[140]

When the British aide-memoire arrived on Friday the 21st, it merely hastened the US reaction. Although Marshall had by then left to deliver a speech at Princeton University, Acheson called his staff together and instructed them to prepare papers for the secretary on implementing aid for Greece and Turkey. He then contacted Truman and Marshall to tell them of the British note and his response; both swiftly approved his action. On Monday the 24th, the papers arrived for Marshall's scrutiny. After a few queries, he delegated responsibility for action to Acheson. Preoccupied with the Moscow CFM, Marshall left Acheson to deal with the question. On 26 February Marshall and Acheson briefed the president but the under secretary took the lead, presenting the recommendations of the State-War-Navy Coordinating Committee (SWNCC) held earlier that day. Truman agreed that the Americans should replace the British commitment, lest Greece and Turkey fall under Soviet influence or control. However, he knew that he must persuade Congress, a task made more difficult by the Republican victories in the November 1946 mid-term elections.[141]

Marshall and Acheson, together with the president, met congressional leaders on 27 February. Although he did not relish the work, Acheson had proved adept at the arts of persuading legislators since 1945, helping to ensure the passage of the UN, the Bretton Woods agreements, and the loan to Britain. Acheson observed in his memoirs how he felt as the meeting began: "we were met at Armageddon."[142] Marshall delivered a rather dry strategic assessment that did not make a strong impression. Joseph Jones, a State Department official involved in drafting Truman's subsequent speech to Congress, recalled that Marshall "conveyed the overall impression that aid should be extended on the grounds of loyalty and humanitarianism."[143] The congressmen seemed underwhelmed, wondering why they should pull British chestnuts out of the fire. Fearful that Marshall had "flubbed" his statement, Acheson asked the secretary's permission to speak. He then presented his case for aid in a much more dramatic fashion. The world was witnessing a conflict unequalled since that between Rome and Carthage. If the United States remained idle, the situation would deteriorate. The congressional leaders were impressed, supported the administration's intention to commit $400 million in aid to Greece and Turkey, and advised the president to speak to Congress in powerful terms so as to guarantee its approval.[144]

The State Department immediately began drafting a speech for the president. Acheson told the drafters that they should stress that the goal was the protection of democracy and avoid language likely to provoke the Soviets.[145] State Department officials prepared a first draft, which Acheson amended before sending it to Truman's aides at the White House, who were led by Clark Clifford in the task of preparing a text. Clifford felt the State Department draft was "not crisp or tough enough for a Presidential speech" and so set about "Trumanizing" it with the aid of Joseph Jones and Carl Humelsine of the State Department. As the drafting proceeded, Jones became concerned that its language was becoming ever more sweeping, giving the impression that the goal was authorization for aid to any country deemed at risk. It is interesting to note that Acheson invoked Franklin Roosevelt to solve the problem: "If F.D.R. were alive, I think I know what he would do. He would make a statement of global policy, but confine his request for money right now to Greece and Turkey." This was readily adopted. Acheson also made an important alteration, inserting a clear, forward-looking phrase: "I believe it must be the policy of the United States to give support to free peoples who are attempting to resist subjugation by armed minorities and outside forces."[146]

Marshall left for the Moscow CFM, which began on 10 March. On 12 March Truman spoke to a joint session of Congress and delivered his speech, enunciating what became known as the Truman Doctrine, offering help to those nations in danger of internal or external subjugation. He declared, in a sentence almost identical to Acheson's recommendation: "I believe it must be the policy of the United States to support free peoples who are resisting attempted subjugation by armed minorities and external pressure." He added: "If we falter in our leadership, we may endanger the peace of the world—and we shall surely endanger the welfare of our own nation."[147]

Within a few days, Acheson was engaged in selling the program to Congress. He gave testimony on 20 March, arguing powerfully for the assistance. He soothed worries that the policy might heighten the risk of war, maintaining that by "strengthening the forces of democracy and individual freedom . . . you do a great deal to eliminate the sort of situation which would produce friction between the powers." But he sometimes found it difficult to suppress his irritation with some of the questioning. Witness his sharp reply to Congressman James P. Richards's request for clarification: "Perhaps saying something two or three times does clarify it."[148] Congress accepted Truman's request for $400 million and the president signed it into law on 22 May.

Most scholars see the Truman Doctrine as a decisive shift in American foreign policy. Certainly the whole episode made clear that Acheson had now embraced a very tough attitude to dealing with Moscow. Yet it is wrong to suggest that he saw the Truman Doctrine as universal in scope. Senator Tom Connally (described by Acheson as "a good friend in a free-for-all") asked the under secretary: "This is not a pattern out of a tailor's shop to fit everybody in the world." Acheson agreed, saying that requests would have to be judged "according to the circumstances of each specific case."[149]

EUROPEAN RECOVERY: LAYING THE GROUNDWORK FOR THE MARSHALL PLAN

Even before Truman had delivered his speech, Acheson was contemplating further American action. On 5 March 1947 he noted that Greece and Turkey were "only part of a much larger problem growing out of the change in Great Britain's strength." He then proposed that the department study "situations elsewhere in the world which may require analogous financial, technical and military aid on our part."[150] On his return from the Moscow CFM, Marshall was frustrated at continued Soviet reluctance to allow economic recovery in Germany. On 28 April he declared in a radio address "the patient is sinking while the doctors deliberate."[151] Meanwhile, George F. Kennan, head of the newly formed Policy Planning Staff of the State Department, recommended in a 16 May memorandum that a program "be designed to encourage and contribute to some form of regional political association of Western European States," which would aid the economic restoration of Western Europe. He wanted the plan to be agreed on in advance with Britain.[152] On 8 May Acheson gave a speech in Cleveland, Mississippi, on Europe's dollar shortage and the need for reconstruction. He emphasized that Americans were concerned not with ideology or armies but with food and fuel.[153]

Acheson convinced Marshall that he should use his forthcoming speech at Harvard University to highlight the economic problems and suggest that American assistance was likely if the Europeans took the initiative. He lunched with three British reporters to stress the significance of what Marshall would be saying:

> I explained the full import of the Harvard [speech] . . . asking that they cable or telephone the full text and have their editors send a copy to Ernest Bevin [British foreign secretary] with my estimate of its importance. This they did while Miall broadcast the story to Britain from Washington.[154]

On 5 June Marshall spoke at Harvard and proposed that the European nations prepare a joint plan for their own recovery and reconstruction which the United States would help to finance.[155]

Bevin's response was immediate. He and French foreign minister Georges Bidault invited Vyacheslav Molotov, the Soviet foreign minister, to a meeting in Paris to consider Marshall's offer. Bevin envisioned an Anglo-American partnership but Washington rejected this, saying it would "violate the principle that no piecemeal approach to the European problem would be undertaken." Bevin yielded to the American position.[156] Talks in Paris among Bidault, Bevin, and Molotov began on 27 June but had broken down by 2 July, because the Soviets would not enter into any program requiring the disclosure of their production plans. Bidault and Bevin assembled the representatives of sixteen nations to form the Committee of European Economic Co-operation (CEEC). By an Anglo-French compromise the CEEC met in Paris but had a British chairman, Sir Oliver Franks. The CEEC worked through the summer identifying the main economic needs of the participating nations and estimating the amount of necessary aid from the United States.[157] The negotiations proceeded without Acheson's oversight. He left office on 30 June, after completing the six months he had agreed to serve as Marshall's under secretary.

WASHINGTON ATTORNEY AND ENGAGED CITIZEN, JULY 1947–DECEMBER 1948

Acheson had mixed feelings about leaving the department and returning to his old law firm. On the one hand, he wished to start earning enough to finance his way of life—a Georgetown house, a farm in Maryland, and regular social engagements. After six years' service, he was tired and needed a break. On the other hand, he greatly enjoyed working for Marshall and admitted to his daughter in May to being "very sad and somewhat panic stricken" about returning to his law firm. He added: "I like what I am doing and have some sense of sureness of touch and a willingness on the part of others to let me drive." After more time to reflect, he wrote in his memoirs that he suffered some of the anguish and unhappiness of an addict: "Public life is not only a powerful stimulant but a habit-forming drug."[158]

As he surrendered his responsibilities, Acheson made arrangements for a smooth transition. His successor was Robert A. Lovett, graduate of Harvard Law School and Wall Street banker, who had served in the War Department during the war. Acheson briefed him on issues and procedures. He was also sensitive to the needs of his State Department colleagues. He told William Clayton: "I have discussed with Bob Lovett the desirability of relieving you of some of your load." Acheson did not make a complete break, for he came into the department two days each week to help with anything that arose. Still, adjusting to private life was not easy, as he explained to Clayton: "I . . . find it very strange not to have pressure on me every moment." He now did "a good deal of work around the farm, which gets me physically tired so that I can get some sleep which I have not been doing." He then took a two-week holiday fishing in British Columbia.[159]

On his return from Canada, Acheson began his work as a Washington attorney. He worked principally on two cases: one before the Supreme Court concerning a group of poor California farmers and fishers of Japanese origin; the other involved a dispute between two large industrial companies.[160] He also remained busy on behalf of American foreign policy. He joined the Citizens' Committee for the Marshall Plan, making frequent speeches and arguing that Europe's economic health was a vital protection for the United States against communist advances from within or without.

Between July and September the CEEC met in Paris, submitting on 22 September a report recommending $22.4 billion of dollar aid over four years.[161] President Truman sent a European Recovery Plan (ERP) Bill to Congress on 19 December proposing aid of $17 billion over four years—less than the $22.4 billion of the CEEC report, but still a considerable achievement.

Acheson simultaneously undertook extensive travel across the country arguing the case for the Marshall Plan, or the European Recovery Program as it was officially known. As he told Lilienthal on 31 October: "The State Department has mapped out a speaking program for me which no human being could survive."[162] He had a particularly demanding schedule in November and December. He spoke at small informal lunches and at large gatherings across the country.[163] In San Francisco he warned that a failure to help return West Europeans to self-support might result in their turning to the East for assistance; and their probable incorporation into the communist political and economic system. This would have an impact on American security and well-being. He regarded the Soviets as "primarily realists, not mere ideologists" looking for opportunities. In Portland, Oregon, he explained that the Soviets were not seeking "real trouble with anyone at present."[164] He knew that resistance to the aid would be strong in the Midwest but was surprised by the enthusiastic reception to his talks in Minneapolis and Duluth. As he told the president, he had found his speaking tour "an exceedingly interesting one," revealing a "great desire to know about the problems which call for the Marshall Plan and about the Plan." He was especially encouraged by the response of a 3,000-strong meeting of mainly miners and labor leaders in Duluth. "I had been warned that these would be particularly hostile, but found them eager for information and encouragingly open-minded."[165] Acheson's campaign of persuasion made a great impression. For example, Robert Butler, US ambassador to Australia, attended the lunch in Minneapolis when Acheson addressed approximately 1,000 people. He told the president: "It was masterful. What we need is more Dean Achesons. I was extremely proud of him."[166]

Acheson also worked with a non-governmental organization to advance the case. In November he agreed to serve on the executive committee of the Committee on the Marshall Plan to Aid the European Economies, which launched a nationwide campaign of persuasion.[167] As he continued his activities in support of Marshall Aid in 1948 in public addresses and through testimony before Congress, he did so as a prominent member of this organization. He spoke on 28 and 29 January 1948 to the House Committee on Foreign Affairs. He described European recovery as "the front line of American security," which was enhanced if other nations were not vulnerable to internal subversion or external pressure. The Soviet Union was doing its best to prevent European recovery, but it always adjusted in the face of strong and stable positions. Therefore, the recovery of Western Europe would improve relations with the Soviet Union.[168]

Congress was persuaded and passed the Economic Cooperation Act, which became law in April 1948. That same month Truman attempted to persuade Acheson to take charge of the aid program, but Acheson knew that Senator Vandenberg would oppose this, partly because he did not warm to Acheson and partly because 1948 was an election year during which the Republican senator did not want another Democrat in a prominent position. Acheson suggested to the president that he ask Vandenberg about the appointment, saying he thought the senator would want Paul Hoffman, president of the Studebaker automobile company. He was, indeed, the senator's choice; and Hoffman was duly appointed Administrator of the European Cooperation Administration.[169]

HOOVER COMMISSION

Acheson was already involved in another demanding public duty. He was a member of the Hoover Commission on the Organization of the Executive Branch of the United States Government, which was created in the summer of 1947. Members were appointed in equal numbers by the Speaker of the House, the President Pro Tempore of the Senate, and the President of the United States, who selected Acheson as a member and vice chairman. He chaired the sub-committee on the State Department. Much to his surprise, he enjoyed working with the former Republican president, Herbert Hoover. He "had a sense of humor . . . [h]e did not like to lose; but when he did, he did not sulk . . . when he asked for advice, he wanted it straight and did not get angry when it was not what he hoped for."[170] Acheson told James H. Rowe on 6 November 1947: "I think our chief usefulness can be more in recommendations for continuing leadership, appraisal and control of administration than in specific regrouping of functions." Any structural changes the committee suggested were bound to become obsolete as circumstances changed. So "we should give substantial if not primary attention to those problems associated with dynamic administration."[171] The report was completed in late December 1948 but not forwarded to Congress until January 1949, one week before Marshall left office on 20 January.[172]

APPOINTMENT AS SECRETARY OF STATE

By late 1948, failing health prevented George Marshall from continuing as secretary. After securing reelection in November, Truman invited Acheson to Blair House, the president's official residence while the White House underwent repairs, and asked him to become secretary of state. After some protestations of not being qualified "to meet the demands of the office in that unprecedented time," Acheson accepted.[173]

As incoming secretary, Acheson could build on considerable development as an individual and an impressive performance in office as under secretary. He had grown into the post, enjoying the work and the opportunity to take the lead. This was possible because Truman was willing to allow the secretary and the department to take the initiative, which often fell to Acheson because of Byrnes's frequent foreign trips and Marshall's readiness to devolve authority to his deputy. Acheson's contentment showed in his temperament. He was still sharp tongued but more capable of restraint than hitherto. He displayed an adept approach in his relations with politicians and in his public engagements. He skillfully navigated the tensions between Byrnes and Truman, remaining on good terms with the secretary while displaying loyalty to the president. His relations with Marshall were excellent, though formal. Above all, he was establishing a relationship of mutual respect and real trust with Truman. He had learned what should be the proper relationship between president and secretary.

His talents were deployed on important work. Even though not the secretary, he was a vital figure in this period. His contribution included the abortive Acheson-Lilienthal Plan and Marshall's fruitless mission to China; and the successful promotion of the British loan. He provided an important impetus to both the Truman Doctrine and the Marshall Plan. His introduction of clear, orderly procedures improved the running of the department. He was the main public advocate of the administration's foreign policy. He was not at this stage the fully-fledged cold warrior of many accounts—including his own memoirs. During his time as under secretary he adopted a robust approach but also a readiness to work with Moscow. This is evident from the March 1946 proposal on nuclear cooperation and his response to Clifford's request about Soviet behavior. Nor did he share the misgivings of many about Stalin's speech in February 1946. Even in 1947 he was not the unrelenting advocate of containment. But by late 1948 his hopes of effective relations with the Soviets were disappearing.[174]

Acheson faced a daunting list of challenges. US-Soviet cooperation had broken down at the December 1947 CFM meeting in London. A communist takeover in Czechoslovakia in spring 1948 led the West Europeans, and Britain in particular, to seek a security arrangement with the United States. This resulted in the North Atlantic Pact talks, which were continuing in December 1948. In addition, there was a full-scale crisis over Berlin: the Soviets had been blockading the western sectors of the city since June 1948 while the British, French, and Americans had been organizing an airlift of essential supplies.

NOTES

1. See Acheson to his daughter, Mary Bundy, 5 July 1945 and 30 July 1945, in *Among Friends*, 58, 61–62.

2. *Present at Creation*, 113–115.

3. *Present at Creation*, 113–115, 119–120.

4. *Among Friends*, 64, Acheson to Frankfurter, 20 August 1945; Isaacson and Thomas, *Wise Men*, 322.

5. McCullough, *Truman*, 404, 507.

6. Robert H. Ferrell, ed., *Off the Record: The Private Papers of Harry S. Truman* (New York: Penguin, 1980), 46 (entry for 17 June 1945).

7. Marc Gallicchio, *The Cold War Begins in Asia* (New York: Columbia University Press, 1988), 94–95; *Present at the Creation*, 119–121; Weil, *A Pretty Good Club*, 236–237; HSTL, Truman Papers, box 641, Acheson interview, 6 February 1955. Gallicchio thinks that McLellan, *Acheson*, 57, is probably wrong to say the Acheson appointment was Byrnes's idea.

8. Lansing Warren, "Grew Resigns as Under-Secretary; Acheson Is Named as Successor. . . ," *New York Times* (17 August 1945), which described Acheson as "a proponent of close cooperation with Russia and Great Britain." Lansing Warren, "More Changes Likely at State Department," *New York Times* (18 August 1945), which notes how Acheson's career in the department had been closely allied with Byrnes's rise; Acheson was "a man whom the new Secretary trusts fully."

9. Isaacson and Thomas, *Wise Men*, 322; FDRL, FDR Papers, Official File, [OF 5152–5176 box], OF5175, Lehman, Herbert (Director of UNRRA) folder, I. F. Stone, "Hull Wins Power Over Foreign Relief From Lehman," *PM*, [8?] June 1943.

10. I. F. Stone, "Shake-up in the State Department, *The Nation* (25 August 1945), 171–172.

11. "US Initial Post-Surrender Policy for Japan," 22 September, and Acheson's comments at press conference, 19 September, *DOSB* 13:326 (23 September 1945), 423–427; "Concerning Policy Toward Japan: Exchange of Letters Between Senator Wherry and Acting Secretary Acheson," *DOSB* 13:327 (30 September 1945), 479–480; "Acheson Sets Path: Government and Not MacArthur Force Will Decide, He Says," *New York Times* (20 September 1945); Arthur Krock, "Acheson-M'Arthur Tilt Raises Disunity Issue," *New York Times* (23 September 1945); *Present at Creation*, 126–127. See also, McLellan, *Acheson*, 58.

12. Joseph Alsop and Robert Kintner, "Sly and Able," *Saturday Evening Post* (20 July 1940); Robertson, *Sly and Able*, 447.

13. David Robertson, *Sly and Able: A Political Biography of James F. Byrnes* (New York: W. W. Norton, 1994), 15–363 covers Byrnes's life from 1882 to July 1944, quotation at 446.

14. Robertson, *Sly and Able*, 7.

15. Robert L. Messer, *The End of an Alliance: James F. Byrnes, Roosevelt, and the Origins of the Cold War* (Chapel Hill: University of North Carolina Press, 1982), 31–70, quotation at 67; Harry S. Truman, *Memoirs I: Year of Decisions* (New York: Signet edition, 1965), 34–35. Ferrell, ed., *Off the Record*, 49 (entry for 7 July 1945).

16. L of C, Long Papers, box 5, Diary 1936–1946, 1945 folder, entry for 1 July 1945.

17. James F. Byrnes, *Speaking Frankly* (New York: Harper, 1947), 245.

18. Barry Rubin, *Secrets of State* (New York: Oxford University Press, 1985); Henry Wriston, "The Secretary of State Abroad," *Foreign Affairs* 34:4 (July 1956), 523 [523–540].

19. Robertson, *Sly and Able*, 443. *Present at Creation*, 122 speaks of Byrnes's "many and often protracted absences."

20. Robertson, *Sly and Able*, 446; Messer, *End of Alliance*, 126. Achilles made the claim in his oral history interview for the Dulles Oral History Project but omitted it in his Truman Library Oral History.

21. Charles Bohlen, *Witness to History 1929–1969* (New York: W. W. Norton, 1973), 256–257.

22. *Princeton Seminars*, 2 July 1953, roll 2, frame 0134.

23. Acheson, *A Democrat Looks at His Party* (New York: Harper, 1955), 160.

24. Byrnes, *Speaking Frankly*, 246–247. HSTL, Acheson Papers, box 27, Foreign Service Act of 1946 folder, Harold Stein to Acheson, 1 November 1948, enclosing a memorandum by John Meck.

25. Clemson University, Byrnes Papers, box 17, folder 1 Press Conferences August 1945 and folder 2 Press Conferences September 1945.

26. Byrnes, *Speaking Frankly*, 245–246.

27. *Among Friends*, 58, Acheson to Mary Bundy, 1 July 1945.

28. HSTL, Truman Papers, box 641, Acheson interview, 18 February 1955 a.m., p. 24; see also *Present at Creation*, 163.

29. Smith, *Acheson*, 26.

30. *FRUS: The Conference of Berlin, 1945*, 2 vols; the protocol summarizing the main conference agreements is in vol. II, 1478–98.

31. *Present at Creation*, 129.

32. McLellan, *Acheson*, 59.

33. Chace, *Acheson*, 183.

34. Smith, *Acheson*, 25.

35. Henry L. Stimson and McGeorge Bundy, *On Active Service in Peace and War* (New York: Harper & Bros., 1948), 642–646.

36. Truman, *Year of Decisions*, 576–579; *Present at Creation*, 123–125, quotation at 123.

37. *FRUS 1945* II, 48–50, Acheson to Truman, 25 September 1945.

38. Truman, *Year of Decisions*, 581–584.

39. *Documents on British Policy Overseas* [hereafter *DBPO*] Series I, Volume IV (London: HMSO, 1987), 618–620, 630–632; Gowing, *Independence and Deterrence* I, 76.

40. *Present at Creation*, 131.

41. Vandenberg, ed., *Private Papers of Vandenberg*, 227–230.

42. *FRUS 1945* II, 609–610, acting secretary to secretary of state, 15 December 1945.

43. *FRUS 1945* II, 709–710, acting secretary to ambassador in the Soviet Union, 21 December 1945.

44. W. Averell Harriman and Elie Abel, *Special Envoy to Churchill and Stalin 1941–1946* (London: Hutchinson, 1976), 524. Messer, *End of Alliance*, 259n32 claims that Byrnes communicated regularly with Washington, citing *FRUS 1945* II, 609–610, 760, 815–824.

45. *Present at Creation*, 136–137; Truman to Byrnes letter-memorandum, 5 January 1946 is in Truman, *Year of Decisions*, 604–606. See the excellent analysis in Alonzo L. Hamby, "An American Democrat: A Reevaluation of the Personality of Harry S. Truman," *Political Science Quarterly* 106:1 (Spring 1991), 33–35. "His need to demonstrate mastery over Byrnes, with whom he had a difficult personal and political relationship, had become so great that he allowed his mind to refashion reality" (48).

46. Princeton, David E. Lilienthal Papers, box 112, Acheson, Dean 1946 folder. Acheson to Lilienthal, 16 January 1946. David E. Lilienthal, *Journals of David E. Lilienthal Volume II: Atomic Energy Years, 1948–1950* (New York: Harper & Row, 1969), 10–12.

47. *FRUS 1946* I, 761–764, Secretary's Committee on Atomic Energy to Secretary of State, 17 March 1946; Smith, *Acheson*, 41.

48. Princeton, Lilienthal Papers, box 112, Atomic Energy: International Control 1946 folder (1 of 3), *Report on International Control of Atomic Energy* by Board of Consultants (chaired by Lilienthal).

49. Clemson University, Byrnes Papers, box 1, folder 5, Byrnes to Baruch, 19 April 1946.

50. *DBPO*, 1st, IV, 233n8. See Acheson's account at *FRUS 1946* I, 768.

51. Lilienthal, *Journals II*, 30.

52. *Present at Creation*, 155.

53. HSTL, Harry Truman Papers, box 641, Acheson interview, 16 February 1955.

54. Princeton, Lilienthal Papers, box 112, Acheson, Dean 1946 folder. Acheson to Lilienthal, 9 May 1946. Acheson's account of these developments is in *Present at Creation*, 151–156.

55. Smith, *Acheson*, 42–43.

56. McLellan, *Acheson*, 84.

57. *DBPO*, 1st, IV, 117–120, Joint Staff Mission to Cabinet Office, 17 February 1946; *FRUS 1946* I, 1213–1215.

58. *FRUS 1946* I, 1235–1237.

59. *Present at Creation*, 164.

60. *DBPO*, 1st, IV, 271–272, Joint Staff Mission to Cabinet Office, 2 May 1946.

61. *DBPO*, 1st, IV, No 86, microfiche; *FRUS 1946* I, 1245–1246, (memorandum by Acheson, Vannevar Bush and L. R. Groves, 7 May 1946), 1246–1247 (memorandum by subcommittee of CPC, 13 May 1946).

62. Quoted in James Gormley, "The Washington Declaration and the 'Poor Relation': Anglo-American atomic diplomacy, 1945–1946," *Diplomatic History* 8:2 (Spring 1984), 143. Acheson made the same point in March; see Lilienthal, *Journals II*, 26.

63. John Baylis, *Anglo-American Defence Relations 1939–1984: The Special Relationship*. (London: Macmillan, 2nd ed. 1984), 238n.

64. Quoted in Francis Williams, *A Prime Minister Remembers* (London: Heinemann, 1961), 117.

65. On these negotiations, see Skidelsky, *Keynes III*, 361–371.

66. Penrose, *Economic Planning*, 13–31.

67. FDRL, Cox Papers, box 98, Lend-Lease, Termination of folder.

68. TNA, CAB 129/1, CP(45)112, Appreciation by Lord Keynes of "Our Overseas Financial Prospects," 13 August 1945. *House of Commons Debates*, vol. 413, col. 956 (24 August 1945).

69. King's, Cambridge, Harmer Diary 1945, p. 9, entry for 3 September 1945.

70. King's, Cambridge, Harmer Diary 1945, p. 38, entry for 9 October 1945.

71. Skidelsky, *Keynes III*, 409.

72. The US record is at *FRUS 1945* VI, 122–194; the British record is at *DBPO*, 1st, III (London: HMSO, 1986), 255–444.

73. *DBPO*, 1st, III, 388, British Missions to Cabinet Offices, 29 November 1945.

74. Robert M. Hathaway, *Ambiguous Partnership: Britain and America, 1944–1947* (New York: Columbia University Press, 1981), 196; the agreement is in *DOSB* 13:337 (9 December 1945), 907; *FRUS 1945* VI, 194.

75. HSTL, Acheson Papers, box 152, Mutual Advantages of the British Loan—March 18, 1946 folder.

76. HSTL, Acheson Papers, box 27, British loan—1946 folder.

77. King's, Cambridge, Keynes Papers, Letters, chronological, JMK/L/46/65, Halifax to Keynes, 25 January 1946.

78. Yale, Acheson Private Papers, box 46, folder 8, microfilm reel 30, pp. 1274–1275. See also Acheson's address to the National Convention of Women's Action Committee, Louisville,

Kentucky, 25 April 1946; published as "The British Loan and Foreign Trade," *DOSB* 14:357 (5 May 1946), 759–760.

79. FDRL, Cox Papers, box 133, Baruch, Bernard M.—re British Loan (1946) folder.

80. For Acheson's outlook on Korea in this period, see Michael F. Hopkins, "Dean Acheson and the place of Korea in American foreign and security policy, 1945–1950," *American Studies* 35:2 (November 2012), 89–117.

81. *FRUS 1945* VII, 527–721 on the situation in China following Japanese surrender; HSTL, Acheson Papers, box 152, "American Policy toward China," June 4, 1951 folder, *American Policy Toward China* [Acheson's testimony to the Senate, 4 June 1951].

82. *FRUS 1945* VII, 559, acting secretary to President Truman, 13 September 1945.

83. *FRUS 1945* VII, 684–686, minutes of meeting of secretaries of war, state, and Navy, 27 November 1945; *Present at Creation*, 140.

84. State Department, *United States Relations with China: With Special Reference to the Period 1944–1949* [hereafter *China White Paper*] (Washington, DC: USGPO, 1949), 581–584; *FRUS 1945* VII, 722–726, Hurley to Truman, 26 November 1945.

85. *FRUS 1945* VII, 754–763; HSTL, Acheson Papers, box 152, *American Policy Toward China*, 25–28; Clemson University, Byrnes Papers, box 2, folder 5, Byrnes to Joseph Alsop, 18 December 1954; *China White Paper*, 605–606 (Truman to Marshall, 15 December 1945), 607–609 (Truman statement on US policy, 15 December 1945). See also Byrnes, *Speaking Frankly*, 226.

86. Acheson, *Sketches from Life* (London: Hamish Hamilton, 1961), 144–145.

87. For full details of Marshall's efforts, see *China White Paper*, 605–695, *FRUS 1946* IX (January–August 1946) and *FRUS 1946* X, 1–723 (August 1946–March 1947). See also the firsthand account, sympathetic to the nationalists, by an American journalist appointed to the Chinese government to advise them on US government thinking and American public opinion: John Robinson Beal, *Marshall in China* (New York: Doubleday, 1970).

88. 79th Congress, 2nd Session, Hearings before the Committee on Foreign Affairs, House of Representatives, *Military Advice and Assistance to the Republic of China, H. R. 6795* (Washington, DC: USGPO, 1946), 115–137, Acheson testimony, 19 June 1946.

89. Walter Millis, ed., *The Forrestal Diaries* (New York: Viking Press, 1951), 189–190 (entry for 2 August 1946).

90. HSTL, Acheson Papers, box 152, *American Policy Toward China*, 32.

91. *Present at Creation*, 209–210; *FRUS 1946* X, 595–596 (Marshall S. Carter to Marshall, 6 December 1946), 598 (Marshall to Acting Secretary, 8 December 1946).

92. *China White Paper*, 686–687, Marshall statement, 7 January 1947.

93. HSTL, Acheson Papers, box 152, *American Policy Toward China*, 34.

94. *China White Paper*, 766–775. Wedemeyer later wrote a memoir, which was heavily critical of Truman and Acheson: *Wedemeyer Reports* (New York: Holt, 1958).

95. *FRUS 1945* II, 48–50, memorandum by acting secretary of state to President Truman, 25 September 1945.

96. HSTL, Acheson Papers, box 152, National Council of American-Soviet Friendship folder.

97. Quoted in Robert Beisner, "Patterns of Peril: Dean Acheson Joins the Cold Warriors, 1945–1946," *Diplomatic History* 20:3 (Summer 1996), 324; Robert Beisner, *Dean Acheson: A Life in the Cold War* (New York: Oxford University Press, 2006), 29; Robert A. Pollard, *Economic Security and the Origins of the Cold War, 1945–1950* (New York: Columbia University Press, 1985), 52–53. *FRUS 1946* VI, 838–839, memorandum of conversation by Acheson, 14 May 1946.

98. See *FRUS 1945* IV, 485–508. In July 1945 the Czechoslovak premier, seemingly under Soviet pressure, requested the removal of US troops from the country. US Ambassador Laurence Steinhardt advised against conceding this request. In August the American military sought to withdraw its forces from the area, because they were needed in Germany. Acheson joined Steinhardt in arguing against unilateral withdrawal. Truman suggested, and achieved, a simultaneous joint US-Soviet withdrawal in November.

99. Stalin's speech, Moscow, 9 February 1946, in Joseph Siracusa, ed., *The American Diplomatic Revolution* (Milton Keynes, UK: Open University Press, 1978), 179–186. *FRUS 1946*

VI, 696–709, Kennan to secretary of state, 22 February 1946. *Present at Creation*, 150–151. George F. Kennan, *Memoirs, 1925–1950* (Boston: Little, Brown, 1967), 549–551. Isaacson and Thomas, *Wise Men*, 350–355; Beisner, *Acheson*, 36–37. Kennan first described the strategy as containment in "Sources of Soviet Conduct," *Foreign Affairs* 25 (July 1947), 566–582.

100. Fraser Harbutt, *The Iron Curtain Speech* (New York: Oxford University Press, 1986), 188.

101. *Present at Creation*, 194.

102. Beisner, *Acheson*, 37–38, Chace, *Acheson*, 147, Isaacson and Thomas, *Wise Men*, 363. Bohlen, *Witness to History*, 252, John Morton Blum, ed., *The Price of Vision: The Diary of Henry A. Wallace* (Boston: Houghton Mifflin, 1973), 556–557 (entry for 5 March 1946).

103. *FRUS 1946 VII*, 340.

104. *FRUS 1946* III (Paris CFM, April–July 1946).

105. *FRUS 1946* III and IV (Peace Conference, July–October 1946).

106. Jean Edward Smith, ed., *The Papers of Lucius D. Clay, 1945–1949*, 2 volumes (Bloomington: Indiana University Press, 1974), I, 218–223. On this issue, see the account by two US officials: B. U. Ratchford and Wm. D. Ross, *Berlin Reparations Assignment: Round One of the German Peace Settlement* (Chapel Hill: University of North Carolina Press, 1947). Melvyn P. Leffler, *A Preponderance of Power* (Stanford, CA: Stanford University Press, 1992), 118–119.

107. NARA, RG 59, State Department, Central Decimal Files, 1945–1949, box 3835, 740.00119Council/8-146, State Department to Paris, 1 August 1946. On the other hand, see *FRUS 1946* VI, 768 (Smith to secretary of state, 15 July 1946), which said Zhukov's move might have come because of disagreement with a senior Soviet official; and FRUS *1946* VI, 780 (Durbrow to secretary of state, 30 August 1946), which suggested Zhukov's move might have resulted from disagreement with the more aggressive line being adopted.

108. *FRUS 1946* VII, 827–828, Soviet Note to Turkey, 7 August 1946.

109. *FRUS 1946* VII, 830–833, Jones to Henderson, 8 August 1946.

110. *FRUS 1946* VII, 840–842 (Acheson to President, 15 August 1946), 843 (Acheson to President, 16 August 1946); *FRUS 1946* VII, 847–848 (Acheson to Soviet Government, 19 August 1946); *Present at the Creation*, 195; Millis, ed., *Forrestal Diaries*, 192 (entry for 15 August 1946).

111. *FRUS 1946* VII, 860–866, charge in Turkey to secretary of state, 26 September 1946, enclosing translation of Soviet reply of 24 September. NARA, RG 59, State Department, Central Decimal Files, 1945–1949, box 3837, 740.00119Council/10–746, State Department to Paris, telegram 5380, 8 October 1946; *FRUS 1946* VII, 872–873 (Acheson to Charge in Turkey, 5 October 1946), 873–874 (Acheson to Truman, 8 October 1946), 874–875 (Acheson to Smith [Moscow] enclosing US reply to Soviets).

112. Chace, *Acheson*, 152–154; Randall Bennett Woods and Howard Jones, *Dawning of the Cold War* (Atlanta: University of Georgia Press, 1991), 136.

113. NARA, RG 59, State Department, Central Decimal Files, 1945–1949, 867.24/10-1546, Turkish ambassador to State Department, 15 October 1946; RG 59, State Department, Central Decimal Files, 1945–1949, 867.24/12-1346, State Department to Turkish ambassador, 13 December 1946.

114. Millis, ed., *Forrestal Diaries*, 216 (entry for 6 November 1946).

115. NARA, RG 59, State Department, Central Decimal Files, 1945–1949, box 3836, 740.00119Council/8-2246, State Department to secretary of state (Paris), 22 August 1946. *FRUS 1946* VI, 915–931, 934–937/947. Acheson note to Yugoslav charge, 21 August 1946 in *DOSB* 15:374 (1 September 1946), 417. *Present at Creation*, 195–196.

116. For the text of the speech see *DOSB* 15:376 (15 September 1946), 496–501.

117. Clemson University, Byrnes Papers, box 13, folders 1, 8, and 11.

118. "American Relations with the Soviet Union," 24 September 1946, in Arthur Krock, *Memoirs: Sixty Years on the Firing Line* (New York: Funk & Wagnalls, 1968), 421–482.

119. Clark Clifford with Richard Holbrooke, *Counsel to the President: A Memoir* (New York: Anchor Books, 1991), 110–112; George M. Elsey, *An Unplanned Life* (Columbia: University of Missouri Press, 138–144; John Acacia, *Clark Clifford* (Lawrence: University Press of Kansas, 2009), 38–49.

120. HSTL, Clark M. Clifford Papers, box 15, folder 7, Acheson to Clifford, 6 August 1946 and attached memorandum, replying to Clifford to Acheson, 18 July 1946.

121. Yale, Acheson Private Papers, box 18, folder 225, Acheson to James E. King, 4 May 1970.

122. HSTL, Clifford Papers, box 15, folder 7, Acheson to Clifford, 6 August 1946. The memorandum was written by others but captured Acheson's outlook. Beisner, *Acheson*, 29, follows Deborah Welch Larson, *Origins of Containment* (Princeton, NJ: Princeton University Press, 1985), 278–279, in wrongly attributing the words to Acheson.

123. Clemson University, Byrnes Papers, box 19, folder 19, Byrnes to Truman 16 April 1946.

124. *Present at Creation*, 157–163, 746 (Acheson to Byrnes, 17 April 1946, Acheson to Truman, 17 April 1946).

125. Acheson, *Sketches*, 146–147. See also Truman, *Year of Decisions*, 607.

126. Clemson University, Byrnes Papers, box 19, folder 19, Byrnes to Truman, 19 December 1946.

127. *Present at Creation*, 200; Joseph Lash, ed., *From the Diaries of Felix Frankfurter* (New York: W.W. Norton, 1975), 293 (entry for 7 November 1946); HSTL, *Princeton Seminars*, roll 2, frames 133–136, 2 July 1953. Beisner, *Acheson*, 27; Isaacson and Thomas, *Wise Men*, 392.

128. *Present at Creation*, 210–211.

129. *Among Friends*, 182, Acheson to Michael Janeway, 24 May 1960. Truman also described Marshall in the same way; see HSTL, Oral History Interview with Charles Murphy, Special Counsel to the President, p. 27; Truman "thought General Marshall was . . . the greatest man he ever knew."

130. Clemson University, Byrnes Papers, box 20, folder 3, James Reston, "Marshall Held Too Aloof at Conference in Moscow," *New York Times* (29 April 1947).

131. Lilienthal, *Journal II*, 158–159 (entry for 9 March 1947).

132. Acheson, *Sketches*, 154.

133. *Present at Creation*, 129.

134. *Present at Creation*, 162–163.

135. *FRUS 1947* IV, 531, ambassador in the Soviet Union (Smith) to secretary of state, 15 February 1947. The exchange of messages about this was published at the time in *DOSB* 16:400 (2 March 1947), 392–394. See also William O. McCagg, *Stalin Embattled, 1943–1948* (Detroit, MI: Wayne State University Press, 1978), 391n82.

136. *FRUS 1946* VII, 91–92 (MacVeagh to secretary of state, 11 January 1946), 226–227 (MacVeagh to Secretary of State, 30 September 1946), 240–245 (memorandum by the director of the Office of Near Eastern and African Affairs (Henderson), 21 October 1946, attaching memorandum regarding Greece, 21 October 1946). On Greek developments, see John O. Iatrides, ed., *Greece in the 1940s: A Nation in Crisis* (Hanover, NH: University Press of New England, 1981).

137. *FRUS 1946* VII, 278, acting secretary to MacVeagh, 12 December 1946; *DOSB* 15:390 (22 December 1946), 1151.

138. *FRUS 1947* V, 29–31 (memorandum by Acheson to Marshall, 21 February 1947 on deteriorating conditions in Greece), 32–35 (British aide-memoire [re Greece], 21 February 1947), 35–37 (British aide-memoire [re Turkey], 21 February 1947); *Present at Creation*, 219.

139. *FRUS 1947 V*, 24, Etheridge to secretary of state, 17 February 1947; but see *FRUS 1947 V*, 26, charge in London (Gallman) to secretary of state, 19 February 1947, who reported that the British on the spot did not feel Greece was a ripe plum.

140. *FRUS 1947* V, 16–17, 24–26, 28–31, 38–40, 820–821; Isaacson and Thomas, *Wise Men*, 389.

141. *FRUS 1947 V*, 41–62; Truman, *Memoirs II*, 122–126; Isaacson and Thomas, *Wise Men*, 389, 393.

142. *Present at Creation*, 219.

143. Joseph M. Jones, *The Fifteen Weeks, February 21–June 5, 1947* (New York: The Viking Press, 1955), 139.

144. Vandenberg, ed., *Private Papers of Vandenberg*, 337–352; *Present at Creation*, 217–221; Jones, *Fifteen Weeks*, 138–142. See also, Isaacson and Thomas, *Wise Men*, 394. Robert Frazier, "Acheson and the Truman Doctrine," *Journal of Modern Greek Studies* 17

(1999), 235, says that Acheson's address was different from Marshall's only in being more dramatic.

145. Isaacson and Thomas, *Wise Men*, 395.

146. Clifford, *Counsel to President*, 133–137. On the drafting process, see HSTL, Joseph M. Jones Papers, Subject File, Joseph Jones, "Memorandum for the File: Drafting of the President's Message to Congress on the Greek Situation," 12 March 1947, available at www.trumanlibrary.org/whistlestop/study_collections/doctrine/large/documents/index.php?documentdate=1947-03-12&documentid=7-2&pagenumber=1 (viewed 20 January 2017).

147. Harry Truman to Joint Session of Congress, 12 March 1947, available at www.presidency.ucsb.edu/ws/index.php?pid=12846&st=truman&st1= (viewed 20 January 2017).

148. 80th Congress, 1st Session, Hearings before the Committee on Foreign Affairs, House of Representatives, *H. R. 2616 A Bill to Provide for Assistance to Greece and Turkey* (Washington, DC: USGPO, 1947), 1–25 (Acheson testimony, 20 March 1947), 27–62 (Acheson testimony, 21 March 1947), quotations at 19, 11.

149. *Present at the Creation*, 225. My treatment of the Truman Doctrine has benefited from the work of my student, Katherine Field, in her dissertation, "'Present at the Creation': Dean Acheson and the Formulation of the Truman Doctrine" (University of Liverpool, 2013).

150. *FRUS 1947* V, 94–95.

151. Marshall, "Moscow Meeting of the Council of Foreign Ministers, March 24–April 10, 1947," *DOSB* 16:410 (11 May 1947), 919–924, quotation at 924.

152. *FRUS 1947* III, 221.

153. Jones, *Fifteen Weeks*, 274–281. Acheson, "The Requirements of Reconstruction," *DOSB* 16:411 (18 May 1947), 991–994.

154. *Present at Creation*, 234. See also Rene MacColl, *Deadline and Dateline* (London: Oldbourne Press, 1956), 173–175 and Leonard Miall, "How the Marshall Plan Started," *The Listener* (4 May 1961).

155. Marshall, "European Initiative Essential to European Recovery," *DOSB* 16:415 (16 June 1947), 1159–1160.

156. *FRUS 1947* III, 272, 284–288.

157. *FRUS 1947* III, 331–470.

158. *Among Friends*, 65–66, Acheson to Jane Brown, 3 May 1947; *Present at Creation*, 239.

159. HSTL, William L. Clayton Papers, box 61, Acheson folder, Acheson to Clayton, 11 July 1947.

160. *Present at Creation*, 239; Chace, *Acheson*, 183.

161. CEEC, *Report of Committee of European Economic Cooperation, July–September 1947* (London: HMSO, 1947).

162. Princeton, Lilienthal Papers, box 118, Acheson, Dean 1947 folder.

163. HSTL, Acheson Papers, box 3, Marshall Plan talks-Calif, Wash, Minn trip, 1947 folders 1–2 contain details and texts of Acheson's talks.

164. Lawrence E. Davies, "Acheson opposes Foreign Aid Cuts," *New York Times* (29 November 1947), 3; McMahon, *Acheson*, 65.

165. HSTL, Acheson Papers, box 3, Marshall Plan talks-Calif, Wash, Minn trip, 1947 folder 2, talks in Duluth and Minneapolis, 3 December 1947, Acheson to Truman, 16 December 1947.

166. HSTL, Acheson Papers, box 3, Marshall Plan talks-Calif, Wash, Minn trip, 1947 folder 2, Butler to Truman, 3 December 1947.

167. L of C, Robert Patterson Papers, box 41, Marshall Plan April–September 1948 folder, "Report on the Activities of the Committee on the Marshall Plan to Aid the European Economies," n.d., no author.

168. 80th Congress, 1st and 2nd Sessions, Hearings before the Committee on Foreign Affairs, House of Representatives, *United States Policy for a Post-War Recovery Program* (Washington, DC: USGPO, 1948), 687–711 (28 January 1948), 713–751 (29 January 1948), see especially 694–695.

169. HSTL, Truman Papers, box 641, Acheson interview, 18 February 1955 am, pp. 46–47; *Present at Creation*, 241–242.

170. *Present at Creation*, 242. Herbert Hoover Presidential Library, West Branch, Iowa, Hoover Commission Papers, box 31, Acheson correspondence.

171. FDRL, James H. Rowe Jr. Papers, box 47, Acheson, Dean COEBG folder, Acheson to James H. Rowe on 6 November 1947.

172. HSTL, James E. Webb Papers, box 20, first draft of "Commission Report on the Organization of the Government for the Conduct of Foreign Affairs," 29 December 1948; and box 24, Department of State: Reorganization Task Force #1 (Department of State) Report, May 1949.

173. *Present at Creation*, 249–250.

174. HSTL, Acheson Papers, box 4, remarks at Oberlin, Ohio, 9 April 1948; cited by Beisner, *Acheson*, 81–82. *Princeton Seminars*, roll 2, frames 159–165, Lansing, Michigan speech, 30 September 1948.

Chapter Four

Leadership in Foreign Policy

Secretary of State, 1949–1950

On 7 January 1949 President Truman announced his nomination of Dean Acheson as the fifty-first US secretary of state. Acheson's candidacy elicited claims in the press that this marked a shift from Marshall's tough line toward Moscow to Acheson's more accommodating attitude. An editorial in the *Saturday Evening Post* announced: "We aren't accepting sight unseen the prevailing view" that Acheson's appointment "indicates no change at all in the policy of this country toward Russia"; since this was a man who "was for several years associated with the policy of buttering up Russia." The magazine intended to keep a close eye on Acheson's performance and choice of associates in the department.[1] In addition, most of the letters to the president on the appointment were unfavorable. One correspondent wondered whether it was not possible to find someone without the "tinge of communism."[2]

NOMINATION

As Acheson prepared to appear before the Senate Foreign Relations Committee, his former colleague Adolf Berle cabled the committee chairman, Tom Connally, charging Acheson with complacency toward Moscow. Berle said he had warned about Soviet expansionism in 1944 but Acheson, like others in the department, had dismissed his concerns.[3] Acheson testified before the committee on 13 January. He began by outlining his experience in government and in foreign affairs, his outlook on international affairs, and his view of the relationship between president and secretary of state. He easily refuted accusations that his law firm had an improper involvement with the Polish government. More challenging was his relationship with Alger Hiss. The committee wanted him to respond to the August 1948 testimony of Adolf Berle, Acheson's former colleague as assistant secretary of state, before a sub-committee of the House Un-American Activities Committee. Berle asserted that Whittaker Chambers, an editor at *Time* magazine and former communist, told him secretly in 1939 that Alger and Donald Hiss were Soviet sympathizers and so Berle checked with Acheson, because Alger Hiss had become his executive assistant, and Acheson vouched for them. Berle was worried because Hiss was the "principal assistant of Mr Acheson's group" in the State Department, which adopted a "pro-Russian point of view." Acheson convinced the nomination committee that Alger Hiss had not been his assistant and not worked in the same section of the department. Donald Hiss had been his assistant for a short time but, when questioned by Acheson, had said there was nothing in his background that would disqualify him from taking the post.[4]

The questioning on Hiss indicated how important the committee regarded a tough attitude toward communism at home and abroad. Acheson had to demonstrate that the State Department under his leadership would have effective security mechanisms. He told the senators how he had recommended to Marshall that assistant secretary John E. Peurifoy be appointed to oversee this work and that he and Peurifoy devised the policies together. In order to drive home his outlook, Acheson also made a statement to the committee in executive session on 14 January, drafted by Vandenberg, who aided Acheson throughout the hearings. It read: "It is my view that communism as a doctrine is economically fatal to a free society and to human rights and fundamental freedom. Communism as an aggressive factor in the world conquest is fatal to independent governments and to free peoples."[5] As Smith noted of this "ritualistic affirmation," the "style was clumsy, but . . . [it] was a small price to pay for Vandenberg's blessing."[6]

On 17 January the committee recommended that the Senate take "prompt action on the nomination." The following day the Senate approved the appointment 83–6. Just as with Acheson's nomination for under secretary, Senator Wherry of Nebraska voted against the appointment.[7] Acheson took the oath of office on 21 January, the day after Truman's second inauguration.

ACHESON, TRUMAN, AND THE STATE DEPARTMENT

From the very beginning of his term Acheson was most skillful in building on the good relationship he had developed with the president during his time as under secretary. This was helped by his acceptance of Truman's candidate to succeed Robert Lovett as under secretary. The president wanted someone he knew and trusted and suggested James E. Webb, director of the budget.

Acheson knew him to be an able and loyal individual. Although he lacked expertise in foreign affairs, he possessed impressive skills in administration, and Acheson realized that these would be beneficial to the department. Acheson also recognized that presidents tended to be uneasy about the State Department: Webb's appointment might lessen that unease.[8] Webb might also prove valuable in the bureaucratic battles with the National Security Council (NSC) and the Pentagon for preeminence in the making of foreign policy. Acheson and Webb soon created clearer lines of communication and effective working practices within the department. Acheson's experience with Byrnes had taught him the importance of ensuring that the president was properly informed. Acheson realized that Truman did not want to make foreign policy from the White House; rather, he wanted close consultation and the right to veto final decisions. So he and Webb held regular meetings with Truman, often submitting short memoranda encapsulating the State Department's positions. If he was away, Acheson sent a report to the president at the close of each day. Acheson was also sensitive to the domestic concerns of the president.[9] While very different in experience and talents, Acheson "possessed a temperament so similar to that of his chief that he easily functioned as an alter ego in charge of foreign policy."[10]

Although Acheson welcomed the greater administrative order that Webb brought to the department, he also needed sound advice on the issues of the day. He appointed his friend Philip C. Jessup, deputy US representative at the UN and professor of international law at Columbia University, as an ambassador-at-large. Jessup's wife observed: "Such a position would also entail a share in the framing of foreign policy. *This* is the part that 'sold' the idea to Phil."[11] Standing six feet tall with bushy eyebrows, Jessup had an imposing presence: his secretary called him "the large ambassador." In January 1949 Acheson told Jessup: "I am going to lean on you so heavily that you should brace yourself."[12] He later described Jessup's "irrepressible humor . . . courage [and] ingenuity . . . to meet the most novel demands."[13] According to Beisner, relations between them deteriorated over Jessup's readiness to testify to Alger Hiss's probity in Hiss's trial for perjury in 1949–1950.[14]

Acheson also promoted assistant secretary Dean Rusk to the new post of deputy under secretary for substantive matters. Rusk had earned a degree from Oxford University, where one of his tutors was Oliver Franks, who had been the British ambassador in Washington since June 1948. During the war, he was in army intelligence, seeing service in Burma and China. After 1945 he worked in the War Office and then the State Department, overseeing UN affairs. Hard working, loyal, patient, unpretentious, intelligent, and resourceful, he proved himself an excellent mid-level bureaucrat. His readiness to work behind the scenes and without any desire to sing his own praises appealed to both Acheson and Truman. He saw the law as the fundamental ingredient in setting international standards and campaigned for the independence of European colonies. Kennan "thought Rusk a moralist who supported UN activities even when they were contrary to the interests of the United States."[15]

Rusk was called on to perform three main tasks as deputy under secretary. He was a key liaison with Congress and with the Department of Defense, an assignment ideally suited to someone with experience of working at the Pentagon. Finally, he had responsibility for solving bureaucratic rivalries. Acheson shared Marshall's desire that disagreements between the different parts of the department should be resolved, so that clear recommendations could be presented to him, which he could then take to the president. Unfortunately, this frequently failed to happen. Acheson utilized Rusk to solve the problem he had identified as chairman of the Hoover Commission's Task Force on Foreign Affairs. The deputy under secretary would work with the assistant secretaries to overcome difficulties and then inform Acheson of the problem and its solution.[16]

Both Rusk and Jessup also served as useful sources of ideas about policy and tactics. They helped Acheson cut to the heart of problems. As Wilson Miscamble says, Acheson's "confidence resided in his belief that he could develop appropriate policies and did not rest on any delusion about himself as an oracle"; what he sought was "to debate the strengths and weaknesses of various positions and to forge the best course for the United States." He recognized that this could only be done with the assistance of others.[17]

ACHESON'S OUTLOOK

By early 1949 Acheson had developed a sophisticated understanding of how to address international issues. In a speech in June 1946 he addressed the difficulty of framing policy and the need to avoid using what Lincoln called "pernicious abstractions." He preferred concrete ideas to vague words like sovereignty, security, interdependence, and international. He also declared: "It is evil for shrewd men to play on the minds and loyalties and fears of their fellows as an instrument." The aim, instead, should be to tackle issues through "hard and intelligent work" in order to reduce them to "manageable dimensions." This was a long and difficult task and one for which Americans were not so well-suited, for they "believe any problem can be solved with a little ingenuity and without inconvenience to the folks at large." The country had to grasp that "all our lives the danger, uncertainty, the need for alertness, for effort, for discipline, will be upon us." This was new and would prove difficult.[18] As he further explained in an essay in 1948, this was particularly challenging because Americans were a "people of impatient and energetic nature. We tend toward belief in solution by convulsion, toward belief that a situation which plagues us can be resolved by some single, all-out effort." He accepted that the Soviet Union was a central concern but he believed that the country faced not one problem but "many and varied problems" and ones that were not problems of one year but of many years. These were challenges that "exist in other parts of the world as well as in Europe." Central to these were "understandable and proper demands for higher standards of living."[19]

In a September 1948 speech he reiterated his belief that there was "no formula that will remove the difficulties which confront us." The idea of such a formula was rooted in the mistaken assumption that Americans could control international developments. It led to the belief that difficulties came only from errors. Acheson also added a note of optimism. The events of 1940–1942 had demonstrated that the nation must meet disaster and defeats with steadiness, resolution, and fortitude. Current American policies were working but even successful policies had encountered difficulties, dangers, and crises. These must be met with calm, steadiness, resolution, and fortitude. Once that was understood, Americans need not be disappointed that the dangers continued. If the Western powers were not having difficulties with the Soviets over Berlin, they would be having difficulties over some other issue. Instead of trying to eliminate problems, the country should seek "to meet the problems with even greater coolness and determination." Acheson took a tough line with Moscow, saying Stalin's speech of February 1946 had dashed hopes of cooperation. Yet he maintained that "the door must be left open—and hospitably open—for a reconsideration by the Soviet Union of its present course." For one writer this speech demonstrated Acheson's "deepening . . . pessimism." This overstates the secretary's doubts. Certainly he was becoming less hopeful, but he also declared: "It may be, and probably is, highly unlikely that any such reconsideration will soon be made by the Soviet Union, but no impediment should be placed in the way . . . despite the vilification, insults and misrepresentations of Soviet spokesmen."[20]

THE TASKS AHEAD

As Acheson assumed his post on 21 January, he had two main issues before him: the completion of negotiations for a North Atlantic pact and the continuing crisis over the Soviet blockade of the western sectors of Berlin. A third problem, not prominent in Acheson's mind at the start of the year, became a major concern by the summer: the deteriorating position of Chiang Kai-shek's Kuomintang (KMT) in their struggle for power with the Chinese communists (CCP). For all his assured manner before Congress and the press, Acheson's views were still evolving in early 1949. There were more uncertainties in his outlook than he later suggested. He understated them in his memoirs.[21] But on one matter he was unequivocal: he firmly endorsed

Marshall's commitment to negotiating a security pact with the West Europeans. Not surprisingly, he turned first to this issue.

THE NORTH ATLANTIC TREATY

In the wake of the breakdown in cooperation with the Soviet Union on Germany at the London CFM in December 1947 and the communist seizure of power in Czechoslovakia in February–March 1948, the British and the French sought some form of security guarantees from the United States. As proof of their readiness to organize themselves militarily, Britain and France signed the Brussels Treaty of Self-Defense with Belgium, the Netherlands, and Luxembourg in March 1948. Marshall was sympathetic to the Europeans' request but was careful to secure congressional approval. Under secretary Lovett persuaded Arthur Vandenberg, chairman of the Senate Foreign Relations Committee, to sponsor a resolution backing the idea of American support for European defense. The Vandenberg Resolution received the unanimous backing of the Senate Foreign Relations Committee on 19 May and was passed by the full Senate by a 64–6 vote on 11 June. Talks were then held in Washington from July to September between Lovett, or more usually John D. Hickerson, director of the Office of European Affairs, and the ambassadors of Britain, Canada, France, Belgium, the Netherlands, and Luxembourg. Following Truman's reelection on 2 November, there was a further series of discussions, which produced a draft treaty on 24 December.[22]

The draft envisaged a collective defense pact comprising the seven powers at the talks and any other states bordering the North Atlantic who were willing to commit themselves. Norway, Denmark, Portugal, Iceland, and Ireland were considered desirable additions. It included a clause encouraging economic, social, and cultural collaboration. In addition, there would be arrangements for mutual assistance and for setting up machinery to implement the treaty. The core of the proposed treaty was its obligation clause. Article 5 declared an armed attack on one or more members would be considered an attack on all, who would offer "forthwith such military or other action, individually and in concert with the other Parties, as may be necessary to restore and assure the security of the North Atlantic area." The December draft treaty left a number of issues unresolved. These included duration, agencies for consultation, the form of protection for Greece, Turkey, and Iran, and which other countries should join the seven powers as founder members of the pact.

Such was the state of negotiations when Acheson became secretary of state. He soon demonstrated not only his considerable ability to master his brief, but also his talent for identifying and tackling what was crucial to the success of the security talks. In addition, he showed a deftness of touch in working with all the key parties—the president, the six powers negotiating with the United States, and Congress. Continuing the practice developed as under secretary, he kept Truman informed and also occasionally persuaded him to utilize the prestige of his office to press the case for the pact. He adopted a confident tone with the ambassadors but showed understanding of their positions. Indeed, he and the British ambassador, Sir Oliver Franks, established an excellent, indeed extraordinary, relationship of confidential consultation. At Acheson's suggestion, they began to have regular confidential talks about a range of issues. As Acheson later observed:

> We met alone, usually at his residence or mine, at the end of the day before or after dinner. No one was informed even of the fact of the meeting. We discussed situations already emerging or likely to do so, the attitudes that various people in both countries would be likely to take, what courses of action were possible and their merits, the chief problems that could arise. If either thought that his department should be alerted to the other's apprehension and thoughts, we would work out an acceptable text setting out the problem and suggested approaches.[23]

Acheson's appointment books reveal that he held more talks with Franks than with all the other ambassadors combined.[24] Right up to Franks's departure in November 1952, they discussed issues that ranged across the globe from Marshall Aid and Berlin to the North Atlantic Treaty, from the communist victory in China and the Korean War to Middle East oil and security.

There was little immediate progress on the treaty until Acheson mastered details of the negotiations. Meanwhile, he issued a statement on 26 January saying US "national security" was "vitally affected by the security of the North Atlantic area." Recognizing the vital importance of congressional support, he stressed that American involvement in the proposed treaty would be "strictly in accordance with our constitutional processes."[25] Nicholas Henderson of the British embassy told the Foreign Office that one of the reasons for the break in the negotiations was Acheson's belief that further groundwork on Capitol Hill was necessary. Acheson told Franks that, while he accepted the need for the early resumption of discussions, he wanted to study the topic further, discuss it with the president and have additional talks with Senators Connally and Vandenberg, respectively the chairman and former chairman of the Senate Foreign Relations Committee.[26] Franks wrote later, "I think Acheson was almost certainly taken aback that not more preliminary work had been done with the Senate."[27]

Acheson spoke on 3 and 5 February to Connally and Vandenberg, who expressed their concern at the draft of article 5, which they felt virtually amounted to an automatic American commitment to go to war. Connally wanted the removal of "forthwith," "military" action, and "as may be necessary." The State Department communicated these comments to the British embassy.[28] So the problem was known to the ambassadors when Acheson met them on 8 February, but they were surprised to find that the secretary appeared to accept the points made by the senators. Acheson suggested that they try to find "more neutral language than that contained in the present draft," for the phrase "military or other action" was "an unnecessary embellishment."[29] Escott Reid of the Canadian Department of External Affairs speculated in his later assessment of the negotiations that this might have been partly tactical:

> Acheson was the new boy at the negotiating table . . . it was only 10 days since
> he had been able to look at any of the papers . . . Yet he spoke to the ambassa-
> dors not as a neophyte but as a teacher lecturing not very intelligent stu-
> dents . . . Acheson may, of course, have decided that the more arrogant the
> language he used . . . the more likely he was to break down the opposition of
> the ambassadors and their governments.[30]

In his memoirs Acheson declared: "Safety required the use of the ambassadors to urge on the senators, and the senators to hold back the ambassadors."[31]

Initially, the momentum seemed to be with the senators. In a Senate debate on 14 February many speakers expressed isolationist opinions, while Connally voiced his own reservations.[32] Acheson handled this adeptly. First, he worked closely with Franks, telling him that he shared the Europeans' desire for a strong commitment in article 5. The ambassador then reassured his fellow ambassadors. He urged the Foreign Office in London to be patient and to restrain critical reports in the British press. It was, after all, to be expected that there would be a major debate on a radical reversal of traditional US foreign policy. Franks was sympathetic to Acheson's problem, for it was only when the new secretary held talks with Connally and Vandenberg that the objections to the text of article 5 were revealed.[33] Acheson then tried to persuade Connally and Vandenberg to soften their tough stance in a meeting with them immediately after the debate.[34] He also secured the assistance of the president, who succeeded in convincing Connally to adopt a more cooperative attitude.[35]

Acheson assigned Charles Bohlen, counselor in the department, the task of finding suitable wording for article 5. Bohlen's draft read: "The Parties . . . will take, forthwith, individually and in concert with the other Parties, the measures it deems necessary to restore and maintain the security of the North Atlantic area."[36] Acheson and Bohlen discussed this language with Franks on 16 February. Franks preferred "as it may deem necessary" but had no great objection to "as may be necessary," provided it would not preclude joint consultations, military staff talks, and advance planning. He added that he could not agree to the revised wording unless "military or other" be reinserted before "measures," because to omit them would have an unfortunate effect on public opinion in Europe where it was now known that it had originally been intended to include these words. Acheson asked if the reinsertion of "forthwith" would make matters easier. Franks said he would welcome this but it would not make up for the omission of "military or other."[37]

Bohlen prepared three drafts of the article. All omitted "forthwith," but the first two included "military or other action" while the third referred only to "action."[38] Acheson discussed them with Truman on 17 February. They agreed on a revised version of the first of these new drafts but with "forthwith" added and "action including the use of armed force" to replace "military and other action." The president said he would recommend it to Senator Connally,[39] and it proved to be the breakthrough.

On the afternoon of 18 February Acheson appeared before the full Senate Foreign Relations Committee, which accepted "action including the use of armed force" to replace "military and other action," and "as it deems necessary" to replace "as may be necessary," while "forthwith" was retained.[40] At its meeting on 25 February the ambassadors' committee agreed to the new version of article 5.[41]

The second major issue to settle in the talks was the question of membership. The December 1948 draft treaty spoke of an association of states bordering the North Atlantic, which meant extending membership to Norway, Denmark, Portugal, and Iceland. In January the French pressed first for the inclusion of all French North Africa and then for just Algeria. After some reluctance from under secretary Lovett, this was accepted at the ambassadors' committee on 14 January.[42] A bigger problem arose over French advocacy of Italian membership, when French ambassador Henri Bonnet threatened to block admission of Norway, if Italy were not allowed to join. The British opposed Italian inclusion, because of the implied exclusion of Greece, Turkey, and Iran. When Acheson spoke to Senators Connally, Vandenberg, and Walter George (D-Georgia), they all opposed Italian membership. This left the secretary in a quandary: should he block Italy, upset France, and lose Norwegian membership or should he accept Italy, thereby offending the Senate and facing complaints from Greece and Turkey as excluded Mediterranean powers? His initial reluctance to back Italian membership weakened when Canada, Belgium, and the Netherlands supported Italian membership. Acheson decided to back the French because the issue seemed to matter so much to them. He spoke to Truman on 2 March saying they should accept the inclusion of Italy, because to do otherwise might cause serious problems with France, delay conclusion of the negotiations, and reveal divisions among the Western powers at the very time they sought to demonstrate unity of purpose. The president endorsed Acheson's recommendation.[43] During the remainder of the year, Acheson proved solicitous of the French position on Germany and on plans for closer European cooperation.

Despite some residual resistance by Britain, the ambassadors' committee agreed to Italian membership. This opened the way for Norway to join the envoys at their meeting on 4 March. The committee agreed at its next meeting on the 7th to invite not only Italy but also Denmark, Iceland, and Portugal to be original signatories.[44] Final details were settled at two further meetings on 11 and 15 March and the text of the treaty was published on 18 March. At the same time, Britain and the United States released declarations affirming their interest in the security of Greece, Turkey, and Iran.[45] The formal signature of the treaty took place in Washington on 4 April.

During the final stages of the negotiations and in the immediate aftermath of the formal signature of the treaty, Acheson argued the case for the North Atlantic Treaty in informal conversations with politicians, before congressional committees, and through radio addresses and speeches. He testified before the Senate Foreign Relations Committee on 8 March.[46] His radio address of 18 March captured the essentials of his case. He stressed that the treaty was a means of ensuring peace by reassuring the peoples of the world that they would not be subjected to unprovoked attack, coercion, or intimidation. The planned self-defense pact would conform to the principles of the UN Charter. Indeed, its members constituted a North Atlantic community dedicated to the common values of democracy, individual liberty, and the rule of law.[47] He told the Senate Foreign Relations Committee on 27 April: "Congress alone has the power to declare war" and if the country were "confronted again by an all-out armed attack . . . I do not believe that any action other than the use of armed force could be effective. The decision, however, would naturally rest where the Constitution has placed it."[48] The treaty was ratified by the Senate on 21 July by 82 votes to 13 and signed into law by Truman on 25 July. It came into effect on 24 August after all twelve members had ratified it.

Acheson's next task was congressional support for military aid to the members of the pact. On the day he signed the treaty into law Truman sent a bill to Congress to approve a package of $1.4 billion of military assistance.[49] The Mutual Defense Assistance Program faced various obstacles but was eventually signed into law on 6 October.[50]

GERMANY

If completing the negotiations for the North Atlantic Treaty was Acheson's primary concern in his first months in office, resolving the future of Germany was only slightly less important. He recognized that a stable and prosperous Germany was vital to a stable and prosperous Europe. In January 1949 he addressed two related German issues—the immediate problem of the continuing Soviet blockade of Berlin and the longer-term question of the future political shape of Germany.

After the collapse of four-power cooperation over Germany at the London CFM of November–December 1947, the three Western powers moved to establish a separate West German state. Talks were held in London between February and June 1948 and produced an agreement known as the London Program, which included the integration of West Germany into the European economy; an international authority, with German representation, to control the Ruhr which would remain part of Germany; the continued presence of British, French, and American troops; and the establishment of a constituent assembly to draft a constitution for a federal government.[51] The adoption of the London accords signaled the effective end of four-power cooperation on Germany. Events thereafter moved rapidly to a crisis over Berlin, the one part of Germany where the four powers were in direct contact and where the Western powers were vulnerable to Soviet pressure. On 18 June the three Western military governors informed the Soviet military government that on 20 June a new currency would replace the Reichsmark in the Western zones, except for Berlin. The next day the Russians introduced new travel restrictions for Berlin. On the 23rd they distributed their own currency in their zone, as well as Berlin. Lucius D. Clay, US military governor, without consulting Washington, but after talking to the British military governor, Brian Robertson, who fully agreed, and to the French deputy military governor, Roger Noiret, who reluctantly acquiesced, announced that West marks would now be circulated in Berlin on 24 June. The Soviet response was a complete surface blockade—road, railway, and water—of Berlin beginning at 6am on the 24th.[52]

The Western powers had no clear, immediate response. According to one scholar, "Washington seemed almost paralysed by crisis-induced stress," while France exercised "virtually no influence over American policy"; it was Britain who "moved with greater speed and decisiveness in making its basic choice to stay in Berlin." From the beginning foreign secretary Ernest Bevin advocated a firm stance, advising that Berlin be supplied by air. He established a special committee of ministers, the Berlin Committee, to oversee the problem. On 6 July the British, Americans, and French sent a joint note largely along the lines recommended by Bevin.[53] It declared that the Berlin agreements were being violated; that the Western Allies would not surrender their rights; but that they were ready to enter talks to solve difficulties, provided the transport routes were reopened. On 26 June Bevin proposed to the American ambassador, Lewis Douglas, that London be the center for discussions (by the Allied ambassadors) rather than using "the circuitous method of communicating directly with the British Embassy in Washington which in turn communicates with US."[54] Marshall agreed to the procedures the next day.[55] National pride almost certainly motivated Bevin, but he could also argue that using the British capital was more practical. Marshall accepted Bevin's judgment on the practicality of London as the location for coordination, for he agreed that handling the question both in Washington and London would produce confusion.[56]

The Western powers responded to the blockade with a round-the-clock airlift of supplies to Berlin and a counterblockade. As the blockade and airlift continued into July and August, efforts were made to talk with the Soviets. Charles Bohlen, head of the Berlin group in the State Department, visited Britain and France to investigate the possibility of conversations with Stalin. It was agreed that the three powers' ambassadors should make a coordinated approach to Moscow.[57] Their two conversations with Stalin in August offered a glint of hope but their difficult discussions with Molotov in August and meetings of the four military governors in August–September made no progress.[58] The deadlock continued, despite submission of the issue to the UN Security Council in October.[59]

Acheson assumed office in January 1949 in more propitious circumstances. The initial months of the blockade saw real hardship in Berlin, but by December 1948 the airlift was proving effective, aided by a mild winter. This made the Soviets rethink their strategy. An influential American journalist, Kingsbury Smith, interviewed Stalin and asked him if the Soviet Union would end the blockade if the West postponed the establishment of a West German state until there had been another meeting of the Council of Foreign Ministers. Stalin answered that he would remove the blockade if the West also lifted its counterblockade. No reference was made to the currency question, which had triggered the crisis.[60] Acheson deftly exploited this opportunity. He spoke to the president, who agreed that the secretary alone would present the administration's response. In his press conference on 2 February Acheson downplayed the significance of Stalin's comments, thereby restraining public expectations of a breakthrough. Indeed, he deliberately avoided any reference to Stalin's failure to mention the currency issue.[61] Truman's own press conference the next day made no mention of Stalin's remarks. Meanwhile, Acheson instructed Philip Jessup, in his capacity as deputy chief of the US delegation to the UN, to ask Jacob Malik, the Soviet UN representative, if this omission had been significant.[62] A month later, on 15 March, in Jessup's Park Avenue office, Malik replied that the answer was "not accidental." On 20 March the three Western powers declared that West German marks would be the only legal tender in West Berlin, thereby indicating that there was no room for negotiation on the issue. The next day, Malik told Jessup that if they could decide a definite date for the CFM, there could be a simultaneous lifting of the blockade and the counter restrictions before the CFM met. Cadogan, the British UN representative, and Chauvel, the French one, were then informed of the secret talks.[63]

As these talks proceeded, Acheson spoke to the British and French foreign ministers, prior to the signature of the North Atlantic Treaty by the twelve founding members. In the meetings Acheson developed highly effective and friendly relations with these two very different individuals: the short, stocky, with a rollicking sense of humor and demotic bluntness of Britain's Ernest Bevin and the spare, serious, and formal Robert Schuman of France. The three men quickly discovered an attachment to common principles, a determination to work together, and an enjoyment of each other's company.[64] Acheson reported on the Jessup-Malik confidential exchanges to Bevin and Schuman, who agreed that their ambassadors, Oliver Franks and Couve de Murville, should join Jessup in drafting a statement to send to Malik.[65] Acheson especially admired Franks's talent for devising a suitable form of words. According to Bevin's private secretary, "Even Dean Acheson, who was not lacking in intellectual clarity, used to listen admiringly to these Franks interventions."[66] In his memoirs, Acheson described Franks as possessing "one of the most creative minds I have worked with."[67]

Jessup submitted his statement to Malik on 5 April. It made clear that the Western governments would not accept the suspension or postponement of preparations for a West German government as a condition for ending the blockade.[68] While they awaited a reply from Moscow, the three Western foreign ministers discussed Germany in talks on 6–8 April. The Western powers would no longer seek to govern Germany, but would allow the Germans to run their own political and economic affairs, subject to certain provisos.[69] By 5 May an unconditional agreement about the blockade had been reached with Malik, and the restrictions ended at one minute past midnight on 12 May.

While Jessup was negotiating an end to the Berlin blockade, Acheson explored the larger question of the future of the Western zones in Germany. He discovered that opinion within the State Department was divided: some favored a continued tough approach, others wanted a more accommodating attitude, while a third group advocated a combination of both approaches.[70] In March George Kennan, director of the Policy Planning Staff, outlined his thoughts in what came to be known as program or plan A: the forces of all the occupying powers would withdraw from a reunified Germany. This he regarded as the best means of securing the removal of the Soviet military from central Europe.[71] Kennan was sent on a fact-finding mission to Germany.[72] On the other hand, Robert Murphy, acting director of the department's Office of German and Austrian Affairs, argued for the creation of a separate West German state.[73]

Acheson found merit in the recommendation for the creation of a provisional German administration in lieu of a formal governmental structure. Acheson at this stage had no settled views on Germany. He wished to keep his options open, refusing to be hurried into a decision to divide Germany.

Certainly, he did not advocate a separate West German state and could "not understand either how we ever arrived at the decision to see established a Western German government or State."[74] After discussing Kennan's paper, he told members of the 9:30am meeting that he wanted to correct the false impression that he was well-informed on Germany. Rather, he "knew very little about Germany" and wanted to be thoroughly briefed.[75] Meanwhile Acheson saw the president and persuaded him to replace the Pentagon with the State Department as the government department responsible for Germany. Instead of a military governor, there would be a high commissioner.[76]

The work already undertaken on a West German state by the Americans, British, and French had created a momentum of its own, leaving Acheson little choice but to continue with the process. At the same time, he asked Jessup to brief Bevin and Schuman on Kennan's program A. Time was short, as the CFM would meet in May. Meanwhile, Acheson, Bevin, and Schuman agreed on an occupation statute on 8 April that would grant sovereignty to the Germans on domestic matters but would retain oversight of military and foreign affairs by the occupying powers. On 8 May the Parliamentary Council in Bonn approved a Basic Law for West Germany. To all intents and purposes it was a federal constitution, but the Germans would not sign up to a constitution that applied only to part of Germany. The three Western military governors approved the Basic Law and the blockade ended on 12 May. That same day there was a press leak of Kennan's plan A for a unified but demilitarized Germany. Accusations of American abandonment of the Europeans meant the one alternative to two Germanies was dead. [77]

Adapting quickly to the changed circumstances, Acheson now advocated the creation of a West German state when he attended the sixth CFM at the Palais Rose in Paris on 23 May. Although the meeting lasted until 20 June, it only produced an impasse on Germany, but it cemented Acheson's cordial relations with Bevin and Schuman. Smith argues that Acheson "anticipated a propaganda ritual in which both sides would try to score points."[78] On his return to Washington, Acheson spoke in a press conference of such meetings acting "like the steam gauge on a boiler . . . They indicate the pressure which has built up." He added in a confident manner that the "position of the West has grown greatly in strength" while the Soviet position had "changed from the offensive to the defensive."[79] Meantime, the West Germans held elections and formed their first government in September. Konrad Adenauer became the country's first chancellor. Although in March–April he had been more flexible, May 1949 marked a hardening of Acheson's attitude toward the Soviets and Germany and the first step toward his later strategy of negotiating from strength.[80]

ACHESON AND ASIA

Acheson's concentration on negotiating the North Atlantic Treaty, which linked North America and Western Europe, and on finding a solution for Germany confirms for many writers Acheson's preoccupation with Europe. Certainly, Acheson's intellectual outlook was dominated by American and European, especially British, culture and values, as absorbed by East Coast Americans of his generation. Rusk wrote in his memoirs that Acheson "did not give a damn about the brown, yellow, black and red people in various parts of the world."[81] This oversimplifies his outlook, certainly while he was secretary, and he did not view Asians, Africans, and Arabs as inferiors. Acheson spoke approvingly of efforts by third world nations to escape poverty and hunger, and to secure independence—in a speech in October 1949 he called this a "great awakening." He did, however, express doubts about the ability of largely illiterate peoples to achieve the necessary social organization. As with many of his views, his outlook on this topic hardened as he grew older. In 1961 he declared that Latin American, Asian, and African revolutionary leaders were "wholly incompetent to manage their own affairs."[82] Rusk's verdict is almost certainly based more on these later views than on his attitudes while secretary.

It would be a mistake to think that Acheson paid little attention to the world beyond Europe and then only when crises arose in these areas. Asia figured more prominently in his thinking during his period as under secretary and as secretary than many writers allow. Contrary to some claims, Acheson had visited Asia,[83] and, as under secretary, he devoted a good deal of time to three Asian countries—Japan, Korea, and China.

During his time as assistant secretary Acheson had taken an uncompromising attitude to the imposition of sanctions on Japan in 1941. In 1945 his similarly stern position on the need to remove the emperor brought him into conflict with under secretary Joseph Grew, whom he dubbed the "Prince of Appeasers." Acheson later concluded that he had got this wrong and was glad Grew's view had prevailed.[84] In his early days as under secretary this same tough attitude was evident. He contested the claim by General MacArthur, who was in charge of the occupation regime in Japan, that there could be a reduction in the planned scale of US forces in Japan. With James Byrnes busy trying to frame a postwar settlement in the meetings of the CFM, Acheson assumed a leading role in articulating US policy on Japan. In September he held a press conference and declared that MacArthur's suggestion was not officially approved, adding policy was made in Washington not in the field.[85] At the Moscow CFM in December Byrnes reached agreement on the framework for Japan. There would be a general advisory body, the Far Eastern Commission, made up of 11 (later 13) powers, and a smaller Allied Council of four countries (British Commonwealth, China, Soviet Union, and

United States). MacArthur would largely run the occupation regime, not having to take the advice of the Allied Council. For most of 1946 Acheson kept out of Japanese affairs, allowing MacArthur a free hand in running the country, and only becoming involved to facilitate the schemes for Japanese reparations.[86] But by October Acheson decided more should be done in reaching a postwar settlement with Japan. He initiated work on a draft peace treaty with Japan in October.[87]

As the occupation regime took shape in Japan, Acheson also oversaw arrangements for the former Japanese colony of Korea. Following agreement at the Potsdam conference, the Soviet Union had declared war on Japan in August 1945 and its forces moved into Korea on 10 August, while the first Americans arrived on 4 September. The two allies agreed to divide Korea at the 38th parallel, with Soviet forces in the north and American troops in the south. Acheson displayed no distinctive outlook on Korea in the first months after the war's end. He shared the consensus view of the State Department's Asian experts led by John Carter Vincent, director of the Office of Far Eastern Affairs, who argued in favor of cooperation with the Soviet Union.[88] Efforts were made to form a provisional government for the whole peninsula but they failed in the face of the Soviets' insistence that only what they deemed "democratic" politicians should be included in the interim government. This meant the exclusion of Syngman Rhee and Kim Ku, who had been working with the Americans in the south. Although talks broke down in May 1946, Acheson continued to support efforts to negotiate with Moscow and issued public statements saying this in August and October. He declared the United States wanted to see "a united, independent, and democratic Korean government established as early as possible." He stressed the need to solve social and economic problems in the country, and he emphasized that the United States intended to stay and carry out its duties.[89]

By early 1947 Acheson grew increasingly concerned about both Korea and Japan. Officials in the State Department had been working steadily on a draft Japanese treaty since late October 1946. Then, in March 1947, MacArthur declared that he had achieved his main tasks—the country had been demilitarized and was on course to becoming a democracy. He recommended that US troops should leave and a peace treaty should be negotiated.[90] The general's pronouncements hastened efforts in the State Department toward a draft treaty. Officials, under the guidance of Hugh Borton, chief of the Office of Northeast Asian Affairs, consulted the ambassadors of nine members of the Far Eastern Commission on 1 July 1947 and submitted a draft treaty on 5 August 1947. By this time Acheson had left the department. The draft treaty encountered opposition from John Paton Davies, Far Eastern specialist on the Policy Planning Staff (PPS). The director of the PPS, George Kennan, shared this view: he believed that Japan was not ready to be "left to its own devices," fearing it would be vulnerable to "communist penetration."[91] Kennan and the PPS won the argument and the draft treaty went no further.[92] That was where the issue remained until Acheson became secretary in January 1949.

Acheson's main concern in early 1947 had not been a peace treaty. He was increasingly apprehensive about the continuing weakness of the Japanese economy. He joined Secretary of War Robert Patterson, Agriculture Secretary Clinton Anderson and former president Herbert Hoover in expressing anxieties about the economic consequences of occupation policies in both Germany and Japan.[93] Japan's economy was vital to the whole of East Asia and it was in trouble—its exports in 1947 were only one-tenth of the 1934 level. This was partly due to the failure of world trade to recover: most countries needed US products but failed to earn sufficient dollars to pay for them. This dollar gap amounted to $7.1 billion in 1945 but by 1947 it had increased to $11 billion. The Americans had to meet this shortfall. The traditional exporting countries of Germany and Japan (25 percent of its industry depended on foreign sales) needed to boost their economies. But this would only be possible if the economic policies of the occupation regimes were altered. In addition, Acheson and others argued that weakened economies, like Japan's, were vulnerable to communist infiltration. Acheson and Kennan, together with Defense Secretary Forrestal and Army under secretary William Draper, proposed a scheme that envisioned three major economic zones: one centered on the United States, one based in Europe, and a third grouped around Japan.[94] This ran counter to MacArthur's policy of limited heavy industry in Japan. The new initiative also came as MacArthur introduced a plan in January 1947 that would have removed businessmen involved in wartime aggression or with ties to ultranationalist organizations—a measure also likely to stifle economic growth.[95]

Acheson also spoke to the Senate Foreign Relations Committee on 13 March during its hearings on Truman's proposed aid package of $400 million to Greece and Turkey. He rejected the suggestion that the Truman Doctrine could be applied universally, but there were "places where we can be effective. One of them is Korea."[96] In a speech in Cleveland, Ohio, in May he argued for the need to rebuild both Germany *and* Japan.[97] Acheson feared that the Japanese economy might collapse, if the United States did not do more to promote the country's economic growth. Although Acheson did not succeed in changing the American strategy in Japan while under secretary, he contributed significantly to the pressure for a shift in policy. As a result, in January 1948 the State-War-Navy Coordinating Committee (SWNCC), which addressed issues that crossed traditional departmental boundaries, recommended a new approach, which was immediately adopted as policy by the Truman administration and communicated to the Far Eastern Commission. Industrial growth and foreign trade would be encouraged so that Japan could make its "proper contribution to the economic rehabilitation of the world economy." The Japanese government, under the supervision of SCAP, should act "energetically and effectively" to make Japan "economically self-supporting at the earliest possible time."[98]

Policy on Korea was influenced by the desire to encourage Japanese recovery. The State Department, and Acheson in particular, wanted a Korean assistance program that enhanced the country's value as a source of food and as a market for Japanese exports. There was countervailing pressure from the War Department, which faced budget cuts and concluded that withdrawal from Korea would be a good way of trimming expenditure. So SWNCC set up an inter-departmental committee to examine Korea and concluded that withdrawal would mean "complete defeat" by the Russians. It supported Acheson's proposal that there should be a three-year program of aid totaling $600 million. Under this scheme there would be $250 million for fiscal year 1948, rather than the $137 million the War Department was proposing.[99] When Acheson brought the Korea aid bill to Congress, he reduced the three-year figure for Korea to $540 million, and the amount for 1948 to $215 million.[100] Acheson left office in June 1947, having failed to secure passage of the bill. The military also questioned the strategic value of assistance for Korea. Secretary of War Robert Patterson was convinced the United States should "get out of Korea at an early date," since the US occupation of Korea was a "drain upon Army resources."[101]

While Acheson was out of office, the failure of US-Soviet cooperation led to the emergence of two separate regimes in Korea. UN supervised elections took place in May 1948, but only in the south, because the Soviets denied UN observers access to the north. Rhee's victory led to the creation in the south of the Republic of Korea, which was recognized by the UN in December. Meanwhile, in September the Democratic People's Republic of Korea, led by Kim Il Sung, was created in the north and recognized by the Soviet Union in October.

American policy on Korea shifted to withdrawal of forces and more limited aid. In Acheson's absence the military arguments proved persuasive. The Joint Chiefs of Staff (JCS) argued, in September 1947, that "from the standpoint of military security, the United States has little strategic interest in maintaining the present troops and bases in Korea."[102] By February 1948 the JCS declared that "eventual domination of Korea by the USSR will have to be accepted as a probability if US troops are withdrawn."[103] By September the War Department view prevailed when even George Kennan adopted their perspective. He asserted American policy should be "to cut our losses and get out of there as gracefully as we can."[104] The Policy Planning Staff then reported: "Since the territory is not of decisive strategic importance to us, our main task is to extricate ourselves without too great a loss of prestige."[105] On 8 April Truman approved NSC 8, which proposed US military withdrawal and sufficient American military assistance to repulse internal threats.[106]

When Acheson became secretary of state in January 1949, he inherited this policy of military withdrawal. He immediately lobbied for greater engagement with Korea. A State Department policy statement highlighted the "political and psychological repercussions throughout the Far East, as well as the strategic implications of a withdrawal which might lead directly or indirectly to Soviet domination of the entire Korean peninsula."[107] Acheson also oversaw the reconsideration of NSC 8. In NSC 8/2 the military withdrawal would still proceed. By 30 June 1949 American troops left South Korea, leaving an advisory group of about 500. But the NSC directive also contained a commitment to continued political, economic, technical, and military assistance for South Korea.[108]

Acheson took the lead in securing legislation for this assistance. He obtained the backing of the president to endorse his proposal and began a campaign to win the approval of Congress, despite Republican attacks on the administration's alleged "inaction" in China. They charged Truman and Acheson with failure to give sufficient help to Chiang's KMT in their fight with Mao Zedong's communists and dismissed the Korea aid program as "too little and too late." Acheson's testimony managed to gain the backing of the committee when he warned that inaction would send "shivers of fear" around East Asia and declared that departing "without giving these fellows who have trusted in us any possible chance to survive" was un-American.[109] Although Acheson's 25 July request for $150 million in aid to South Korea was reduced by the Republicans, Congress also passed deficiency appropriations of approximately $30 million every three months, thereby providing $120 million a year to Korea.[110]

CHINA

The Chinese civil war became Acheson's most important Asian problem in 1949, although he had not regarded it as urgent when he took office. His view of the situation had not changed much since he ended his work as coordinator for Marshall, who had reported on his mission in January 1947. Much as he disliked the prospect of a communist victory, he disdained the KMT. Events in the succeeding two years had only confirmed his low expectations. On becoming secretary, he quickly agreed with State Department officials that further aid to the KMT was pointless. Acheson's evaluation of this foreign policy problem was sound but he failed to appreciate its significance in domestic politics. Republicans abandoned bipartisanship on China and blamed the Truman administration for the failure of the KMT. In mid-November 1947 General David Barr, head of the American military mission to China said "the military position has deteriorated to such a position where only the active participation of United States troops could effect a remedy."[111] This was confirmed when the communists took control of Beijing in January 1949. On 3 February the NSC recommended that American military aid to the KMT should be ended—$60 million of the $125 million appropriated by the China Act of 1948 remained unspent. The next day Acheson attended the cabinet, which accepted the NSC's proposal.[112] On 7 February Acheson joined the president and Vice President Alben Barkley to explain the policy to Senators Connally and Vandenberg and Representatives Sol Bloom (D-New York) and Charles Eaton (R-New Jersey), all of whom opposed an end to the assistance. Vandenberg encapsulated the unreal nature of congressional opinion on China when he argued the KMT could not win but did not want to halt the aid. Truman gave way to their pressure, recognizing the weight of domestic opposition.[113]

China revealed the limits of bipartisanship in foreign policy. The Republicans, even Vandenberg, who supported the North Atlantic Treaty, were highly critical of the administration. On the same day as the president's meeting with Connally and Vandenberg, 51 House Republicans wrote to Truman bemoaning the China policy and suggesting that the KMT was losing because of the administration's failure to give them sufficient help. Acheson decided to speak directly to the signatories, 31 of whom met him on 24 February. He presented powerful arguments demonstrating that little more could have been done to prevent the KMT's defeat. Nor should a communist victory cause them to exaggerate the dangers: China was a poor country lacking economic resources and in no position to launch an assault on its neighbors. He then added: "We cannot tell what the next step is until some of the dust and smoke of the disaster clears away."[114] Unfortunately for Acheson, the phrase about letting the dust settle and not his compelling explanation stuck in the public mind. Republican congressmen leaked the words to the press, arguing that they proved Acheson and Truman were committed to a do-nothing policy.[115]

The Republicans might have been even more concerned by Acheson's exploration of the possibility of trade with the communists. In a memorandum for consideration by the NSC he argued that China was almost completely under communist control, so the main task should be to ensure that the country did not become an "adjunct of Soviet power." This outcome could best be averted by American trade with the new regime. The development of normal economic relations might help push Moscow and Beijing apart. On 3 March Truman authorized US economic agencies to implement Acheson's suggestions.[116]

Meanwhile, the pressure continued. Senator Pat McCarran, a conservative Democrat from Nevada, introduced a bill on 24 February that proposed extending a credit of $1.5 billion to the nationalists.[117] Acheson explained the US policy to Connally. Despite aid now totaling $2 billion, the position of the nationalist government had significantly deteriorated. If the United States were to offer military aid, "it would require the use of an unpredictably large American force in actual combat." He also warned against extending the credit of $1.5 billion, for the eventual cost would be "unpredictable" and "the outcome would almost surely be catastrophic."[118] McCarran's bill failed but the criticisms continued, leading Acheson and his advisers to decide on action to counter these charges. In March the department began compiling what became *The China White Paper*, a detailed collection of documents demonstrating the lengths to which the administration had gone to help the nationalists. In the final stages of the work, Philip Jessup assumed the role of editor-in-chief.[119] On his return from the Paris CFM on 21 June, Acheson was pressed by Truman to hasten the completion of *The China White Paper*. As the secretary worked throughout July on the task, he sent Jessup on a final mission to China: his instructions were to make sure that they were not neglecting any opportunity to halt the spread of totalitarian communism.[120] Acheson wrote a letter of transmittal on 30 July, saying that the leaders of the KMT government "had proved incapable of meeting the crisis confronting them" and that their failure did not "stem from any inadequacy of American aid." There was no realistic military option, for any large scale American military intervention "would have been resented by the mass of the Chinese people." *The China White Paper* appeared on 5 August 1949.[121]

The report failed miserably as a persuasive tool. Instead, it "poured gasoline, not water, on the fires of controversy."[122] Meanwhile the nationalists' position continued to collapse. On 1 October Mao's communists established the People's Republic of China and Republicans firmly placed the blame on Acheson and Truman for "losing" China.

RE-EVALUATING AMERICAN FOREIGN POLICY

The growing criticism of the administration's failed China policy came principally from partisan Republicans and others committed to aiding the nationalists, but also from a disgruntled American public, disillusioned that the world's greatest power seemed impotent in the face of the Chinese communists. Accusations about the "loss" of China compounded the anxieties caused by the successful Soviet detonation of an atomic bomb on 29 August, publicly confirmed by Truman on 23 September.[123] The combined impact of these two setbacks intensified domestic pressure to adopt a tough attitude toward Chinese and Soviet communism abroad and alleged communist activities at home. In response to these circumstances, Acheson turned his mind to reevaluating American foreign policy. Contrary to many accounts, this did not simply amount to the staged development of his notion of building "situations of strength," an approach first publicly articulated in February 1950.

His thinking was more subtle and sensitive to the complex and more challenging international scene now facing the country.

Acheson first addressed the country's nuclear policy. The Soviet atomic bomb prompted Lewis L. Strauss, one of the commissioners of the American Atomic Energy Commission (AEC), to suggest on 5 October that the United States should develop the "super," now known as the hydrogen bomb. Acheson took no immediate position, preferring to hear first from the experts. On 1 November he spoke to David Lilienthal, chairman of the AEC, and Robert Oppenheimer, head of the Manhattan Project that developed the American bomb and chairman of the general advisory committee. Lilienthal felt the issue was not one for the AEC but rather a matter of foreign policy that should be decided by Acheson and the president. Even though he did not rule out its development, it is clear that Acheson shared Oppenheimer's and Lilienthal's sense of the destructive awfulness of a hydrogen bomb: "What a depressing world it is, said Dean. . . . He said he didn't see how I had stood it as long as I have, 'living with this grim thing all the time.'"[124]

Truman asked Acheson, Lilienthal, and Louis Johnson, who had succeeded Forrestal as secretary of defense in March, to form a special committee of the NSC to investigate the case for the weapon.[125] Its first meeting was held on 22 December. The discussions mainly consisted of a battle between Johnson's advocacy of the weapon and Lilienthal's opposition, while Acheson observed. The secretary later noted that "due to the acerbity of Louis Johnson's nature" there were only two meetings of the committee.[126] Acheson began his work on the committee with an open mind about the issue, seeking advice from the PPS staff. He received opinions from Kennan and from Paul Nitze, who succeeded Kennan as PPS director on 1 January 1950. Kennan opposed building the "super," arguing that the United States should reject first use of atomic weapons and deploy other weapons for deterrence, while doing all it could to secure international control of such weapons.[127] Nitze recommended testing the possibility of a thermonuclear weapon, but reserving the decision on whether to build more bombs than those required for testing. He also proposed that they should institute a full review of US national security in the light of Soviet capability to develop a hydrogen bomb.[128] Nitze's confident, direct approach proved more appealing to Acheson. This was partly a matter of personalities, but was also a product of a shared outlook. Kennan had been arguing for a readiness to recognize Soviet security worries and the consequent need to reach compromises. Nitze favored a tough attitude to the Soviets, which Acheson increasingly embraced in January–February 1950. So he welcomed Nitze's proposed review. Work began on it in the NSC in January 1950. Meanwhile, the special committee held its second meeting on 31 January 1950 and decided in favor of developing the superbomb. Acheson, Lilienthal, and Johnson then saw the president, who asked, "Can the Russians do it?" When told that they had the necessary capabilities, Truman gave the formal go ahead.[129]

As discussions proceeded on the hydrogen bomb, Acheson took a more active role in trying to resurrect Anglo-American nuclear cooperation. His efforts as under secretary had been thwarted by the McMahon Act, which largely ended nuclear cooperation and had led the British to develop their own program in January 1947. A Cabinet committee declared: "We could not afford to acquiesce in an American monopoly of this development."[130] The British ambassador, Oliver Franks, encapsulated the British thinking behind this decision:

> The whole question of our relations with the Americans on atomic energy questions seems to me to be increasingly bound up with the larger issue of the extent to which the Americans are prepared to treat us on more or less equal terms as a first class power.[131]

Although the institutions of wartime atomic cooperation—the Combined Policy Committee (CPC) and the Combined Development Trust of Britain, Canada, and the United States—continued to operate in Washington, the British were hindered by the restrictions of the McMahon Act. In addition, the Americans feared that, if "the Soviets overrun Western Europe during 1948," they could seize British materials, laboratories, and industrial plants. A variety of solutions were advanced: locating British sites in Canada, an exchange of plutonium by the British for completed bombs by the Americans. Such ideas, however, were unattractive to the British.[132]

Anglo-American talks continued throughout 1947 and produced the January 1948 *modus vivendi*. The Americans were keen to obtain British supplies of scarce raw materials as inexpensively as possible, for they expected their own stocks to be exhausted by the end of 1949.[133] Acheson and the State Department were also under pressure from Bourke Hickenlooper (R-Iowa) and Vandenberg of the Joint Congressional Committee on Atomic Energy to remove the British veto. They managed to devise a strategy that the two senators endorsed.[134] By not signing the agreement, they avoided the need to register it with the UN or to inform Congress. Instead, the representatives of the three member-countries of the CPC declared, at the 7 January meeting, their intention to proceed on the lines of the document. It superseded all previous agreements, with certain exceptions.[135] The CPC and the Combined Development Trust (now known as the Combined Development Agency) continued to operate in Washington. The first annex practically ensured that the United States would receive all uranium supplies from the Belgium Congo in 1948 and 1949, and specified a formula for providing a proportion of British stocks, when required.[136]

Although the Americans honored the spirit of cooperation after January 1948, difficulties soon arose. Throughout 1948 the British continued to pursue the possibility of help over plutonium metallurgy. In June they formally requested the exchange of information on atomic weapons. (The *modus vivendi* did not cover information exchanges on the military applications of atomic energy.)[137] The Americans, however, refused to discuss this issue, on the grounds that no provision was made for this topic in the *modus vivendi*.

When Acheson became secretary he sought to revive Anglo-American cooperation. He persuaded the president to authorize the creation of a special committee of the NSC, chaired by the secretary, to explore how this might be done. Its report on 2 March recommended full cooperation, which Truman approved on 31 March.[138] But the Joint Congressional Committee on Atomic Energy and Defense Secretary Johnson expressed reservations. At discussions in September, and again in November, the central issue was whether nuclear components should be stored in Britain, or only in the United States and Canada. A compromise was reached whereby Britain would reduce its program from three to two piles. Bevin feared placing Britain too much in the power of the Americans. The United States proposed integrated Anglo-American weapons work in America with the Americans giving the bombs to the British.[139] The British government was willing to consider this but wondered whether the US could constitutionally deliver this. On 29 December 1949 Franks submitted a draft proposal to the State Department for "complete collaboration" in nuclear matters between the two countries. Its essential feature was that a stockpile of bombs in the UK was a *sine qua non* of any agreement.[140] But in January 1950 Klaus Fuchs, the British atomic scientist who had worked on the Manhattan Project, was arrested as a Soviet agent. The British embassy in Washington reported that the talks had been "completely wrecked."[141] There was no further progress on the issue for the remainder of the Truman presidency, except for an exchange of letters between Acheson and Franks on an "interim allocation of raw materials."[142]

Acheson's attempts to resuscitate nuclear collaboration with Britain pointed to the second area of reappraisal: deepening the relationship with West European allies. The secretary understood the value of allies and regarded Britain as the United States' main partner, an outlook reinforced by the growing intimacy of relations with the British ambassador, Oliver Franks. Britain was facing a financial crisis in 1949 that led it to devalue sterling by 30 percent (from $4.03 to $2.80) on 18 September. Acheson was sympathetic to the British position, and worked closely and successfully with Franks to find a solution.[143] Seeing the issue purely in financial terms, the Treasury secretary, John W. Snyder, believed the British should solve their own problems and not simply turn to the Americans for help.[144] Acheson took a larger view of Britain's predicament. He observed, "Britain and the sterling countries of which she is the center are . . . our partners in the great co-ordinated effort to build a secure and prosperous world. They are indispensable to us, and we are indispensable to them."[145] Acheson also demonstrated a deft touch in working with the Treasury. Although the approach favored by the State Department won the day, he conceded the leading role in the discussions to Snyder and the Treasury.[146]

Despite his Anglophile outlook, he never lost sight of American interests. One involved further progress in European cooperation. British reticence led him to turn more to the French. During his NATO discussions with Bevin and Schuman, Acheson urged Schuman to seize this "rare opportunity" of cooperating with the Germans.[147] In a message to a meeting of American ambassadors in Europe in October, the secretary declared the "key to progress towards integration" lay "in French hands." France "needs to take the initiative promptly and decisively."[148] Here was an interesting premonition of the Schuman Plan of May 1950. When the three foreign ministers met again in November, they agreed to the secretary's call for the integration of Germany into Western Europe.[149] Acheson told Franks that the United States would do all it could to advance Franco-German rapprochement, both political and economic, since it offered the best prospect of keeping Germany aligned with the West and giving her an economic outlet.[150] Acheson also urged British acceptance of the idea that Paul-Henri Spaak, the former prime minister of Belgium, be a politically authoritative director-general of the Organization of European Economic Cooperation (OEEC), what was dubbed the OEEC "Superman." The OEEC had succeeded the CEEC as the body overseeing the Marshall Aid program and as a mechanism for further economic cooperation. Britain was completely opposed to the idea of giving the OEEC political powers.[151] The Americans felt that their continent-wide market and federal system of government had benefited them and would do the same for the Europeans. The British were ready to pursue inter-governmental cooperation but did not want to surrender sovereignty. In addition, they felt schemes for European integration would diminish Britain's global status: the country was more than just another European power. As a result, Spaak operated only as a coordinator for inter-governmental cooperation.[152]

China was the third and most prominent topic for reconsideration. Acheson sought to downplay the threat posed by the new communist regime. In July he expressed his desire to work with the British and Canadians on China and have a "more positive approach."[153] He shared the thinking of Ernest Bevin, who told the American ambassador in London, Lewis Douglas, that the Chinese communists were first and foremost Chinese and were not capable of becoming Russians overnight. During talks with Acheson in New York in September, Bevin warned against being too inflexible with Mao's regime, lest this drive them into the arms of the Soviets.[154] Acheson, however, faced continuous pressure from the China lobby to aid the nationalist government that established itself on the island of Taiwan. This brought him once more into conflict with the military, which favored such aid, and Louis Johnson in particular.[155] Acheson refused to extend major assistance. In a speech in October he explained how the country needed to recognize the limitations of its power: "American assistance to other nations is always marginal."[156] At a meeting on 2 November State Department officials agreed that the United States should not detach Taiwan from the communist-controlled Chinese mainland; nor should it seek jurisdiction over the island through a UN trusteeship. If another country brought the issue of Taiwan to the UN, the Americans might support a ceasefire and the application of the principle of self-determination.[157]

Acheson also explored the possibility of recognizing Mao's government. The president proved to be an obstacle. In June the US ambassador in China, John Leighton Stuart, reported a promising conversation with his former student, Huang Hua, now a senior official in the Chinese communist party, who offered the prospect of a meeting between the ambassador and Mao, but Truman did not want to pursue this opening.[158] Assistant secretary Walton Butterworth summarized Acheson's goal as "formal regularized relations with them [the Chinese communists]; not intimate but proper."[159] On 1 October Truman "indicated strongly" to under secretary Webb that they should do nothing to undermine the KMT's blockade of major Chinese ports.[160]

Given these circumstances, it was not surprising that Acheson failed to respond more positively to Chinese interest in recognition. But he deserved credit for restraining the more aggressive attitudes of the president and departmental colleagues such as Rusk. Acheson continued throughout 1949 and in the first half of 1950 to try to convince Truman that detaching "the Peking regime from Moscow did not constitute appeasement, that harassment would be a mistake."[161] The secretary's cutting comments about Chinese communists in the *China White Paper* might suggest he had a less open outlook. But John Melby, who helped to draft Acheson's letter of transmittal, said that the secretary "didn't believe a word" of its contents about Soviet domination of the Chinese communists. Rather, as he explained in October 1949, Washington should avoid acting in ways that could be portrayed as US aggression, which would push the Chinese closer to Moscow. He also observed in March 1950: "The Chinese . . . will come into conflict with Moscow because the basic objectives of Moscow are hostile to the very basic objectives of China."[162]

Meanwhile, the British decided to grant *de facto* recognition to the Chinese communist regime on 6 January 1950. The regular confidential discussion between Acheson and Franks ensured that the administration knew about British plans. When he met the ambassador on 8 December, Acheson asked only that "if this decision were taken, I hope we would at least be given as much advance notice as possible so as to minimize the effects that misunderstanding might well create."[163] After the British cabinet decided in favor of recognition on 15 December, Acheson's response displayed what James Tang called "understanding rather than resentment."[164]

On the day before the British announcement, Truman released a statement on Taiwan. Acheson also spoke at length to the press to expand on the president's remarks. The burden of their message was that the United States would not use its armed forces to aid the nationalists, would not provide them with military assistance, but would continue to extend economic aid. Franks wondered whether "Acheson's strong statement on Formosa was designedly made on the day preceding British recognition in order to lessen the reaction against us." H. A. Graves of the embassy reported to London that it was a very astute move by Acheson to arrange for the president to make a statement about Taiwan on the 5th and to follow it up with some well-chosen "extemporaneous" remarks of his own.[165] The initiative did not deter the Republican critics. On 11 January Robert Taft (R-Ohio) declared that the State Department had "been guided by a left-wing group who have obviously wanted to get rid of Chiang and were willing at least to turn China over to the Communists for that purpose."[166]

Acheson aimed to draw together the various strands of the administration's Asian policy in a speech to the National Press Club on 12 January 1950. Rather than read what he regarded as the dull draft prepared by the department, he delivered the speech from notes in the way he would have argued a case in court, adjusting his approach according to how his audience was reacting.[167] He sought to place American policy in the framework of two central notions. First, he cited Asian "revulsion against the acceptance of misery and poverty as the normal condition of life." Here he was repeating a point made in his introductory remarks to *The United States in World Affairs, 1947–1948*. Second, he emphasized Asian "revulsion against foreign domination." He reiterated the refusal to extend military aid to Taiwan, despite the clamor of Republicans. In defining US strategic commitments in the region, the secretary excluded Korea from the area within the American defensive perimeter. Here he was only enunciating official policy. General Douglas MacArthur first delineated this concept in 1948, before expressing it to a journalist in March 1949. He said the American defense line ran "from the Philippines and continues through the Ryukyu Archipelago. . . . Then it bends back through Japan and the Aleutian Island chain to Alaska." This outlook was endorsed in December 1948 in NSC 41/1 and NSC 48/2. A policy paper of 14 November 1949 declared that the United States would deal with any aggression against Asian states through the United Nations, except where there was an American occupation.[168] Franks noted "Acheson's advocacy that the United States disembarrass itself of its contact with Chiang Kai-shek;" and "the State Department" had "gone as far as they can towards dropping the Nationalist Government short of withdrawing from it their recognition."[169]

In the immediate aftermath of the speech, no commentator or politician criticized Acheson's outlook, not even Senator Taft, who only described the speech as an "invitation to attack," after North Korea's invasion in June.[170] When Franks reported on the speech to London a few days afterward, he did not even mention the exclusion of Korea from the American defensive perimeter, focusing instead on Acheson's attempt to distance the administration from the Chinese nationalists.[171]

Various subsequent writers have been more critical. Bruce Cumings emerges in a number of studies as a leading skeptic. In his most recent book he declares that Acheson secretly committed the United States to Korea; after all, the early drafts of his speech included the country within the defensive perimeter. Acheson was obliged to be ambiguous, lest he encourage Rhee to action. Moreover, because the official text was unavailable for weeks, Cumings argues that the North Koreans and even the *New York Times* thought that Korea had been included within the defensive perimeter.[172] The text appeared in the *Department of State Bulletin* on 23 January, 11 days later. The speech was reported in the *New York Times* on 13 January and focused on Acheson's remarks about China. It reported Acheson as saying that, contrary to the claims of Republicans, the KMT had not lost because of inadequate US military assistance but because "its forces melted away"; its government had not been overthrown because "there was nothing to overthrow." Accurately reporting Acheson's key points about US strategy in the region, the *Times* did not mention the omission of Korea from the defensive perimeter. Rather, it recorded Acheson as saying that the defensive perimeter that ran from the Ryukyu Islands and Aleutians off Alaska to the Philippines continued to be upheld. It included his further remarks: "It must be clear that no person can guarantee these areas against military attack"; and "[s]hould such an attack occur . . . [init]ial reliance must be upon the people attacked to resist it and then upon . . . the United Nations which so far has not proved a weak reed to lean on."[173]

Meanwhile, there remained a chance that the United States might recognize the new regime in Beijing. Franks reported to London that immediately after Britain's recognition the American government went out of its way to be helpful.[174] Dean Rusk claimed in his memoirs that he and Franks "speculated privately that our policies would come together, depending upon the behaviour of Peking. If China entered the world community and acted reasonably in foreign affairs, American policy would move toward Britain's. But if China acted aggressively, Britain might move toward the United States and break with China."[175] Reading the American press at that time Franks had the impression that US recognition might not be more than about three months off. This optimism was short-lived.

Misunderstanding arose over American consular offices in Beijing. Under a protocol of 1901 all the powers which had suppressed the Boxer Rebellion were entitled to barracks in Beijing. By this time there were only consular officials in the American buildings, but the Chinese communists wanted to remove this symbol of foreign degradation. They threatened to seize the properties of governments which had not recognized the new government. Acheson proposed a compromise: the communists could take over most of the estate, but not the main building which would become the United States' chancellery. This would allow the Chinese to save face without causing outrage in the United States. The Americans warned the communists that seizing the building would be totally unacceptable and would result in the withdrawal of American officials from the country. Undeterred, the new government seized the property on 13 January, thinking the US warning was a bluff. Acheson treated this move as a humiliation, and on the 14th he ordered the withdrawal of all US official representatives from China. According to Cohen, neither Edmund Clubb, consul-general in Beijing, nor Acheson felt this marked a final break. He adds that Jessup and other members of the department had favored the removal to lessen the risk of incidents.[176]

On the other hand, Franks thought the prospects for US recognition were now increasingly remote. American diplomats had been withdrawn and would only return as part of a significant new initiative. This was unlikely to occur until US opinion had settled down and this would probably not happen until after congressional elections in November.[177] Hume Wrong, the Canadian ambassador in Washington, shared this perspective. A month earlier, he had felt that American "public opinion could have been conditioned to accept recognition within a period of three to six months." But the seizure of the buildings made recognition "a dead issue."[178] Perhaps Acheson and the ambassadors were over-optimistic, underestimating the intensity of US public opinion against the new regime in Beijing. After years of support for the KMT, it was improbable that Americans would easily accept recognition of their conquerors, especially when they were so vociferously communist and anti-American. Opinion polls at the time confirm this opposition: they gave two to one margins against recognition, an outlook undoubtedly encouraged by *Time* and *Life* which regularly criticized the administration for having "lost" China.[179]

January 1950 marked the first anniversary of Acheson's term as secretary. The first six months had brought success in the negotiations for the North Atlantic treaty, an end to the Berlin blockade, and the creation of a West German state. The second half of the year had been more troubled and closed without signal achievements. Acheson had brought a calm incisiveness to his reevaluation of policy, but his more imaginative ideas about Taiwan and the communist regime yielded little. The main results were the hydrogen bomb decision and the review of national security that would lead to NSC 68. Both pointed to an American foreign policy more rooted in power politics than his

thinking in late 1949 would have suggested. The year had begun with his
testimony about Alger Hiss. It ended with his response to Hiss's being found
guilty of perjury—in testimony to a congressional committee Hiss had denied passing government documents to the Soviet Union. When questioned
by the press, Acheson chose not to be non-committal but to declare that he
"would not turn his back on Alger Hiss."[180] Lilienthal captured Acheson's
thinking: "After a while you get tired of the curs yiping, and you have to
have your say."[181] The reactions to Acheson's comments on the verdict were
symptomatic of the increasingly embattled atmosphere for the secretary. As
early as May 1949, the Partisan Republicans of California had submitted
their "Petition to the United States Congress to Impeach Dean Acheson for
Conspiracy against the United States."[182] In January 1950 he was attacked in
the Catholic magazine, *The Sign*, for failing to resist communism.[183] It was
in this atmosphere that Acheson began to develop a much more resolute
foreign policy outlook.

NOTES

1. Editorial, "Dean Acheson '49 Must Improve on Dean Acheson '45," *Saturday Evening Post* (12 February 1949), 10. Smith, *Acheson*, 55; citing *US News and World Report* (14 January 1949).
2. Smith, *Acheson*, 57–58; citing HSTL, Truman Papers, OF20, Miscellaneous, Acheson, Dora E. Anderson to Truman, 7 January 1949.
3. FDRL, Berle Papers, box 97, US Committee on Un-American Activities (1948–49) folder, Berle telegram to Connally, 12 January 1949. See also FDRL, Berle Papers, box 217, Diary 1949–1950 folder, entry for 12 January 1949: "Acheson is not the kind of man whom I could regard as a friend now or later and certainly would not be my first choice as Secretary of State."
4. 81st Congress, 1st Session, Hearings Before the Senate Foreign Relations Committee, *Nomination of Dean G. Acheson* (Washington, DC: USGPO, 1949), 13 January 1949 (Hearing), 17 January 1949 (Report).
5. Vandenberg, ed., *Private Papers*, 470; "Committee Backs Acheson; Senate Approval is Forecast," *New York Times* (15 January 1949).
6. Smith, *Acheson*, 58.
7. *Nomination of Acheson*, Report, 17 January 1949, 2; C. P. Trussell, "Senate, By 83 To 6, Confirms Acheson; Debate Vigorous," *New York Times* (19 January 1949).
8. *Present at Creation*, 249–250.
9. Melvyn Leffler, *A Preponderance of Power* (Stanford, CA: Stanford University Press, 1992), 268; Wilson D. Miscamble, *George F. Kennan and the Making of American Foreign Policy* (Princeton, NJ: Princeton University Press, 1992), 154–157.
10. Alonzo L. Hamby, *Man of the People: A Life of Harry Truman* (New York: Oxford University Press, 1995), 510.
11. Miscamble, *Kennan*, 157; L of C, Philip C. Jessup Papers, box II:1, Family letters edited by Lois Walcott Kellogg Jessup, "At Large with My Ambassador; Notes from the Diplomatic Sidelines," September 1948–June 1949 folder.
12. L of C, Jessup Papers, box I: 50, Aca-AID (personal) folder, Acheson to Jessup, 19 January 1949.
13. Acheson, "Philip C. Jessup, Diplomatist," in Wolfgang Friedman, Louis Henkin and Oliver Lissitzyn, eds, *Transnational Law in a Changing Society* (New York: Columbia University Press, 1972), 6.

14. Beisner, *Acheson*, 120. On Jessup's involvement in the two trials, see L of C, Jessup Papers, 1: 213, Alger Hiss folder, Jessup's deposition, 1 June 1949, and Jessup's testimony, US District Court, Southern District of New York, 8 December 1949.

15. Thomas W. Zeiler, *Dean Rusk: Defending the American Mission Abroad* (Wilmington, DE: Scholarly Resources, 1999), 15–16, 19–20; Warren I. Cohen, *Dean Rusk* (Totowa, NJ: Cooper Square Publishers, 1980), 4–5, 7; Dean Rusk, *As I Saw It* (New York: Penguin, 1991),

16. Cohen, *Rusk*, 31.

17. Miscamble, *Kennan*, 156.

18. Acheson, "Random Harvest," in Acheson, *Fragments of My Fleece* (New York: W. W. Norton, 1971), 17–26.

19. Acheson "Introduction," *The United States in World Affairs, 1947–1948* (New York: Harper & Brothers, 1948), vii–xiv.

20. McLellan, *Acheson*, 144. *Princeton Seminars*, 2 July 1953, roll 2, frames 159–165, Acheson, "Success has Its Problems," address to State Bar of Michigan, Lansing, Michigan, 30 September 1948.

21. Wilson D. Miscamble, "Dean G. Acheson," *Reviews in American History* 22:3 (September 1994), 550 [544–560].

22. See *FRUS 1948* III, 148–250 (records of the talks), 333–343 (draft treaty).

23. *Present at Creation*, 323.

24. Smith, *Acheson*, 194–195.

25. Acheson, "Purpose of Proposed North Atlantic Treaty," *DOSB* 20:501 (6 February 1949), 160.

26. TNA, FO 371/79223, Z962, Franks to FO, Tel. No. 942, 1 February 1949.

27. TNA, FO 115/4429, Gl/141/49, Franks to Bevin, 17 February 1949.

28. NARA, RG 59, State Department Decimal Files, 1945–1949, 840.20/2-349 and 840.20/2-549, box 5661, Memoranda of Conversation, 3 and 5 February 1949; TNA, FO 371/79224, Z1053, Franks to FO, Tel. No. 692, 3 February 1949.

29. *FRUS 1949* IV, 74 and 85 [73–88].

30. Escott Reid, *Time of Fear and Hope: The Making of the North Atlantic Treaty 1947–1949* (Toronto: McClelland and Stewart, 1977), 150.

31. *Present at Creation*, 277.

32. *Congressional Record, Senate*, p. 1165 (14 February 1949); see also *Present at Creation*, 281.

33. TNA, FO 371/79225, Z1416, and Z1418, Franks to FO, Tel. Nos. 938 and 939, 15 February 1949.

34. *FRUS 1949* IV, 109, memorandum of conversation, 14 February 1949.

35. Smith, *Acheson*, 71; *Princeton Seminars*, roll 2, 15 July 1953.

36. *FRUS 1949* IV, 114–115, enclosure in Bohlen to Acheson and Webb, 16 February 1949.

37. TNA, FO 371/79226, Z1463, Franks to FO, Tel. No. 965, 16 February 1949; FO 115/4429, Gl/141/49, Franks to FO, 17 February 1949.

38. *FRUS 1949*, IV, 115–116.

39. *FRUS 1949*, IV, 117.

40. TNA, FO 371/79226, Z1544, Franks to FO, Tel. No. 1022, 19 February 1949; Public Archives of Canada, Department of External Relations, File 283(s), North Atlantic Security Pact, Vol. 7, Wrong to DEA, Tel. No. WA 446, 19 February 1949; and Wrong to DEA, Tel. No. WA 450, 21 February 1949.

41. TNA, FO 800/455, minutes of Thirteenth Meeting of Washington Exploratory Talks on Security, 25 February 1949; on 23 February the Brussels Permanent Commission had accepted the text of article 5, FO 371/79228, Z1718, FO to Washington, Tel. No. 2155, 23 February 1949.

42. *FRUS 1949* IV, 32, minutes of Eleventh Meeting of the Washington Exploratory Talks on Security, 14 January 1949.

43. Memorandum of Conversation with President, 2 March 1949, available at www.trumanlibrary.org/whistlestop/study_collections/achesonmemos/view.php?documentid=65-02_07&documentYear=1949&documentVersion=both (viewed 23 January 2017).

44. *FRUS 1949* IV, 126–135 (minutes of ambassadors' committee, 1 March 1949), 151–163 (minutes of ambassadors' committee, 4 March 1949), 166–174 (minutes of ambassadors' committee, 7 March 1949).

45. See Nicholas Henderson, *The Birth of NATO* (London: Weidenfeld & Nicolson, 1982), 119–121, for Treaty text, and 106–107 for the British and American declarations on Greece, Turkey, and Iran. This book is the published version of the author's contemporary (May 1949) account; see TNA, FO 115/4430, GI/395/49 for the original text. See also HSTL, Acheson Papers, box 64, Memorandum of Conversation with Franks, 15 March 1949.

46. Senate Foreign Relations Committee, Historical Series, *Vandenberg Resolution and the North Atlantic Treaty* (New York: Garland, 1979), 129–168 (8 March 1949), 212–249 (21 April 1949).

47. Acheson, "The Meaning of the North Atlantic Pact," *DOSB* 20:508 (27 March 1949), 384–388.

48. Smith, *Acheson*, 76; McLellan, *Acheson*, 153; 81st Congress, 1st Session, Senate Foreign Relations Committee, *North Atlantic Treaty Hearings*, 27–29 April, 2–3 May 1949, p. 11 (27 April).

49. Senate Foreign Relations Committee, Historical Series, *Military Assistance Program 1949* (New York: Garland, 1979) contains hearings on the initial bill, S.2341, and on the revised bill, S.2388, which passed in October.

50. *Present at Creation*, 309–313. On this issue, see Chester Pach, *Arming the Free World: The Origins of the United States Military Assistance Program, 1945–1950* (Chapel Hill: University of North Carolina Press, 1991), 198–226.

51. *FRUS 1947* II, 728–772 (London CFM) and 811–830 (post-CFM talks). *FRUS 1948* II, 141–143, 313–317, and 883–887; TNA, CAB 129/27, CP(48)138, Bevin, "Talks on Germany: Resumed Session," 4 June 1948.

52. *FRUS, 1948*, II, 908–909; L. D. Clay, *Decision in Germany* (London: Heinemann, 1950), 362–365; TNA, CAB 128/13, CM 42(48), 24 June 1948.

53. Avi Shlaim, *The United States and the Berlin Blockade, 1948–1949* (Berkeley: University of California Press, 1983), 198; TNA, FO 800/467, Ger/48/37 to 39; M. Carlyle, ed., *Documents on International Affairs 1947–1949* (London: Oxford University Press for RIIA, 1952), 568–588.

54. *FRUS 1948* II, 921–926, Douglas to Secretary of State, 26 June 1948.

55. *FRUS 1948* II, 926–928, Secretary of State to London Embassy, 27 June 1948. See also TNA, CAB 128/13 CM 46(48), 1 July 1948, when Bevin reported creation of a committee of Strang of the Foreign Office, Douglas, and Massigli, the French Ambassador, to review the Berlin situation.

56. Shlaim, *US and Berlin Blockade*, 310.

57. TNA, CAB 128/13, CM 53(48), 22 July 1948 and CM 54(48), 26 July 1948; *FRUS 1948* II, 968–988, 989–993; Bohlen, *Witness to History*, 178–279. Walter Bedell Smith, *Moscow Mission 1946–1949* (London: Heinemann, 1950), 229–232

58. See *FRUS 1948* III, 999–1014, 1065–1097, and 1099–1140; Millis, ed., *Forrestal Diaries*, 480–481, 485–486; TNA, CAB 128/13, CM 59(48), 10 September 1948, and CM 61(48), 22 September 1948, Bevin's reports on the progress of the talks.

59. See *FRUS 1948* II, 1212–1281.

60. See the interview in *New York Times* (31 January 1949).

61. Memorandum of conversation with the president, 31 January 1949, available at www.trumanlibrary.org/whistlestop/study_collections/achesonmemos/view.php?documentid=65-01_18&documentYear=1949&documentVersion=both (viewed 23 January 2017); Acheson, "Comments on Premier Stalin's Answers to Questions Submitted by Kingsbury Smith," *DOSB* 20:502 (13 February 1949), 192–194; James Reston, "Acheson Press Conference Reveals Impressive Skills," *New York Times* (3 February 1949). See also, Smith, *Acheson*, 84.

62. *FRUS 1949* III, 696, 697–700.

63. *Present at the Creation*, 267–270; Shlaim, *US and the Berlin Blockade*, 380–383; Philip C. Jessup, "Park Avenue Diplomacy—Ending the Berlin Blockade," *Political Science Quarterly* 87:3 (September 1972), 377–400; *DOSB* 20:514 (8 May 1949), 585–586, 590–591.

64. See Acheson's insightful and warm portraits in his *Sketches*, 11–36 (Bevin), 37–62 (Schuman).

65. *FRUS 1949* III, 156–158, 709–712; TNA, FO 800/483, NA/49/10, Acheson-Bevin meeting, 31 March 1949, Acheson-Bevin-Schuman meeting, 1 April 1949.

66. Sir R. Barclay, *Ernest Bevin and the Foreign Office 1932–1969* (London: published by the author, 1975), 56.

67. *Present at Creation*, 288.

68. *FRUS 1949* III, 712–716.

69. *FRUS 1949* III, 162–171, meetings of 6–8 April 1949; see British record at TNA, FO 800/483, NA/49/10.

70. Beisner, *Acheson*, 136; James Reston, "Secretary Acheson: A First Year Audit," *New York Times Magazine* (22 January 1950), 36.

71. *FRUS 1949* III, 96–102, paper by Kennan, 8 March 1949.

72. *FRUS 1949* III, 137–138.

73. *FRUS 1949* III, 118–137, Murphy paper, 23 March 1949.

74. *FRUS 1949* III, 102–105, memorandum of conversation, 9 March 1949, quotation at 102.

75. NARA, RG 59, State Department, General Records of the Office of the Executive Secretariat, Summaries of Daily Meetings, 1949–1952, box 1, Secretary's Daily Meeting, 23 March 1949.

76. Beisner, *Acheson*, 138–139; *FRUS 1949* III, 140–142.

77. *FRUS 1949* III, 859–862; Clay, *Decision in Germany*, 428–436; Beate Ruhme von Oppen, ed., *Documents on Germany Under Occupation, 1945–1954* (London: Oxford University Press, 1955), 374–377; Smith, *Acheson*, 93; George F. Kennan, *Memoirs, 1925–1950* (Boston: Atlantic-Little, Brown, 1967), 442–446; John Lewis Gaddis, *George F. Kennan* (New York: Penguin Press, 2011), 347–451.

78. Smith, *Acheson*, 95.

79. Acheson, "Extemporaneous remarks," *DOSB* 21:522 (4 July 1949), 860. See also, Senate Foreign Relations Committee, Historical Series, *Reviews of the World Situation, 1949–1950* (New York: Garland, 1979), 1–22 (Acheson's consultation prior to the CFM, 19 May 1949) and 23–49 (Acheson's report on the results of CFM, 22 June 1949).

80. Miscamble, *Kennan*, 173.

81. Rusk, *As I Saw It*, 422.

82. Acheson, "Problems in American Foreign Policy," *DOSB* 21:539 (31 October 1949), 668–669. Beisner, *Acheson*, 211; citing *Selected Executive Session Hearings of Foreign Relations Committee, 1943–1950*, 41–42 and Acheson, "Fifty Years Later," *Yale Review* 51 (October 1961), 7.

83. McMahon, *Acheson*, 95; Chace, *Acheson*, 35–36 outlines Acheson's visit to Japan in 1915 with a group of fellow Yale graduates.

84. *Among Friends*, 55, Acheson to Mary Bundy, 28 May 1945; Gallicchio, *Cold War Begins in Asia*, 15; *Present at Creation*, 112–113.

85. "US Initial Post-Surrender Policy for Japan," 22 September, and Acheson's comments at press conference, 19 September *DOSB* 13:326 (23 September 1945), 423–427; "Concerning Policy Toward Japan: Exchange of Letters Between Senator Wherry and Acting Secretary Acheson," *DOSB* 13:327 (30 September 1945), 479–480; "Acheson Sets Path: Government and Not MacArthur Force Will Decide, He Says," *New York Times* (20 September 1945); Arthur Krock, "Acheson-M'Arthur Tilt Raises Disunity Issue," *New York Times* (23 September 1945); *Present at Creation*, 126–127.

86. See *DOSB* 14:358 (12 May 1946), 821 and *DOSB* 15:386 (24 November 1946), 670.

87. *FRUS 1946* VIII, 348–349, first meeting of peace treaty working group, 25 October 1946.

88. *FRUS 1945* VI, 1114 [1113–1114], (Vincent to Vittrup, War Department, 7 November 1945), 1122–1124, (McCoy to Acheson, 13 November 1945), 1127–1128 (Vincent to Acheson, 16 November 1945), 1137–1138 (Byrnes to Langdon, 29 November 1945); see also Dobbs, *The Unwanted Symbol*, 53–54.

89. Acheson, "US Objectives in Policy Toward Korea," *DOSB* 15:375 (8 September 1946), 462; Acheson, "US Policy in Korea," *DOSB* 15:380 (13 October 1946), 670.

90. *FRUS 1947* VI, 450; Miscamble, *Kennan*, 250.

91. *FRUS 1947* VI, 463–464 (Braden to Acheson, 17 June 1947), 467–469 (meeting with ambassadors, 1 July 1947), 478–479 (Borton to Bohlen, 6 August 1947), 485–486 (Davies to Kennan, 11 August 1947), 537–543 (Kennan, PPS 10, 14 October 1947).

92. *FRUS 1947* VI, 463–464 (Braden to Acheson, 17 June 1947), 467–469 (meeting with ambassadors, 1 July 1947), 478–479 (Borton to Bohlen, 6 August 1947), 485–486 (Davies to Kennan, 11 August 1947), 537–543 (Kennan, PPS 10, 14 October 1947); *FRUS 1948* VI, 858 (NSC 13/2, 7 October 1948). See also, Ronald McGlothlen, *Controlling the Waves: Dean Acheson and US Foreign Policy in Asia* (New York: W. W. Norton, 1993), 40–41.

93. Millis, ed., *Forrestal Diaries*, 255–256 (entry for 13 March 1947).

94. Michael Schaller, *The American Occupation of Japan: The Origins of the Cold War in Asia* (New York: Oxford University Press, 1985), 80, 85; *FRUS 1947* VI, 696–706.

95. Schaller, *American Occupation*, 85.

96. Senate Committee on Foreign Relations, Historical Series, *Legislative Origins of the Truman Doctrine* (New York: Garland, 1979), 17, 21–22.

97. Acheson, "The Requirements of Reconstruction," *DOSB* 16:411 (18 May 1947), 991–994.

98. Schaller, *American Occupation of Japan*, 72–120; *FRUS 1948* VI, 654–656, Statement to Far Eastern Commission, 21 January 1948.

99. *FRUS 1947* VI, 608–616, Memorandum by the Special Inter-Departmental Committee on Korea, 25 February 1947.

100. *FRUS 1947* VI, 621–623, Acheson to Patterson, 28 March 1947.

101. *FRUS 1947* VI, 625–628, Patterson to Acheson, 4 April 1947; Walter Millis, ed., *The Forrestal Diaries* (New York: Viking Press, 1951), 265.

102. *FRUS 1947* VI, 817, Secretary of Defense Forrestal to Marshall, 26 [29] September 1947.

103. Quoted in Robert Ferrell, *Truman* (Columbia: University of Missouri Press, 1994), 318.

104. *FRUS 1947* VI, 784–785 (Stevens memorandum, 9 September 1947), 814 (Kennan to Butterworth, 24 September 1947).

105. *FRUS 1947* I, 776 [770–777], Report by Policy Planning Staff, Resume of World Situation, PPS/13, 6 November 1947.

106. *FRUS 1948* VI, 1164–1169, Report by the National Security Council on the Position of the United States with Respect to Korea, NSC 8, 2 April 1948.

107. NARA, RG59, State Department, Central Decimal Files, 1945–1949, 711.95/1–3149, box 3441, Policy Statement, "Korea," 31 January 1949.

108. *FRUS 1948* VI, 1337–1340, memorandum by Butterworth, 17 December 1948; *FRUS 1949* VII Part 2, 969–978, Report by the National Security Council to the President, Position of the United States with Respect to Korea, NSC 8/2, 22 March 1949.

109. William S. White, "Korea Aid Program Draws GOP Attack," *New York Times* (9 June 1949); "$150,000,000 Aid to South Korea Gets Backing of House Committee," *New York Times* (25 June 1949); William S. White, "Vote Aid or Korea Will Fall in Three Months, Acheson Says," *New York Times* (2 July 1949).

110. *Present at Creation*, 309–310.

111. HSTL, Acheson Papers, box 152, Publications File, Speeches and articles, "American Policy toward China" June 4, 1951 folder, State Department publication 4255, Acheson, *American Policy Toward China*, 44.

112. *FRUS 1949* IX, 482–483; Smith, *Acheson*, 110. William Whitney Stueck, *The Road to Confrontation: American Policy toward China and Korea, 1947–1950* (Chapel Hill: University of North Carolina Press, 1981), 116.

113. *FRUS 1949* IX, 485–486, Vandenberg, ed., *Private Papers*, 530–531.

114. *Present at Creation*, 377; Smith, *Acheson*, 112–113.

115. *New York Times* (25 February 1949); Smith, *Acheson*, 113.

116. *FRUS 1949* IX, 826–834, Note by Executive Secretary of NSC, 28 February 1949; *FRUS 1949* IX, 834, Memorandum by Executive Secretary of NSC, 3 March 1949, approving Acheson's suggestions. See also, Stueck, *Road to Confrontation*, 120–123.

117. See the hearings in US Senate Foreign Relations Committee, Historical Series, *China and Korea Assistance Acts, 1949–1950* (New York: Garland, 1979).

118. State Department, *United States Relations with China with special reference to the period 1944–1949* [hereafter *China White Paper*] (Washington, DC: USGPO, 1949), 1053–1054, Acheson to Connally, 15 March 1949. See also HSTL, Acheson Papers, box 152, "American Policy toward China" June 4, 1951 folder, State Department publication 4255, *American Policy Toward China*, 39–49 (Acheson's testimony to the Senate, 4 June 1951); and *Present at Creation*, 302–307, 749–750.

119. L of C, Jessup Papers, box I:45, "Evolution of letter of transmittal in China White Paper," 26 September 1949. See also NARA, RG 59, State Department, General Records of the Office of the Executive Secretariat, Summaries of Daily Meetings, 1949–1952, box 1, Secretary's Daily Meeting, 7 July 1949.

120. 82nd Congress 1st Session, Hearings before a Sub-Committee of the Senate Committee on Foreign Relations, *Nomination of Philip Jessup* (Washington, DC: USGPO, 1951), 603 (text of Acheson to Jessup, 18 July 1949).

121. *China White Paper*, xiv, xvi, Acheson's letter of transmittal, 30 July 1949.

122. Smith, *Acheson*, 120.

123. Statement by the President, *DOSB* 21:535 (3 October 1949), 487.

124. David E. Lilienthal, *Journals of David E. Lilienthal Volume II: Atomic Energy Years, 1948–1950* (New York: Harper & Row, 1969), 580–585, quotation at 584. See also Richard G. Hewlett and Francis Duncan, *Atomic Shield, 1947–1952: Volume II of A History of the United States Atomic Energy Commission* (University Park: Pennsylvania State University Press, 1969), 374, 381, 385, 391.

125. *FRUS 1949* I, 587–588, Truman to executive secretary of NSC (Admiral Souers), 19 November 1949.

126. *Present at Creation*, 346.

127. *FRUS 1950* I, 22–24, memorandum by the Counselor (Kennan), 20 January 1950; Kennan, *Memoirs, 1925–1950*, 471–475.

128. *FRUS 1949* I, 610–611, Nitze memorandum, 19 December 1950; Paul H. Nitze, with Ann M. Smith and Steven L. Rearden, *From Hiroshima to Glasnost* (New York: Grove Weidenfeld, 1989), 87–91. See also Nitze's response to a draft of Kennan's 20 January memorandum: *FRUS 1950* I, 13–17, Nitze memorandum, 17 January 1950.

129. Lilienthal, *Journals II*, 587–602 (3–27 November 1949), 613–615 (22–30 December 1949), 623–633 (31 January 1950). Nitze, *Hiroshima to Glasnost*, 91. See also Hewlett and Duncan, *Atomic Shield*, 394–395, 398, 406, and *Present at Creation*, 346–347.

130. TNA, CAB 130/18, GEN 163, 1st Meeting, 8 January 1947; cited in Geoffrey Warner, "The Anglo-American Special Relationship," *Diplomatic History* vol. 13:4 (Fall 1989), 481.

131. TNA, FO 115/4423, 10/183/48, Oliver Franks to Roger Makins, 29 November 1948; Gowing, *Independence and Deterrence: Britain and Atomic Energy, 1945–1952*, 2 vols. (New York: St. Martin's Press, 1974) I, 265.

132. Duncan Campbell, *The Unsinkable Aircraft Carrier: American Military Power in Britain* (London: Paladin, new ed., 1986), 98.

133. Robin Edmonds, *Setting the Mould: The United States and Britain 1945–1950* (Oxford: Clarendon Press, 1986), 89.

134. *FRUS 1947* I, [781–908], 833–834 (Hickenlooper, chairman of Joint Congressional Committee on Atomic Energy, to secretary of state, 29 August 1947), 852–860 (minutes of the meeting of the American members of the CPC, 5 November 1947), 885–886 (acting secretary of state to secretary of state, 6 December 1947). See also *FRUS 1950* VII, 1463, Truman-Attlee meeting, 8 December 1950.

135. These were the Tripartite Washington Declaration of 15 December 1945; the Declaration of Trust of 13 June 1944; and the exchange of letters between the acting secretary of state and the British ambassador of 19 and 24 September 1945, concerning Brazil: the Patent Memo-

randum of 1 October 1943, as modified by subsequent agreement on 19 September 1944 and 8 March 1945.

136. See TNA, FO 115/4421, Nos. 11, 14, 16, 18; *FRUS 1948* I, Part 2, 677–682.

137. TNA, FO 115/4469, No. 24, notes by J. N. Henderson, n.d. but probably February 1949.

138. *FRUS 1949* I, 429–430 (appointment of special committee, 10 February 1949), 443–461 (report of special committee of NSC, 2 March 1949). See also, *Present at Creation*, 314–321.

139. *FRUS 1949* I, 476–506, 585, 601–603; TNA, FO 115/4472; Gowing, *Independence and Deterrence* I, 283, 286, 291–292.

140. *FRUS 1949* I, 620–622; TNA, FO 115/4514, No. 2. See also Gowing, *Independence and Deterrence* I, 296.

141. TNA, FO 115/4514; FO 371/81611, AU1013/7, Hoyer Millar (for Franks) to FO, Tel. No. 86(S), 11 February. See also Robert Chadwell Williams, *Klaus Fuchs, Atom Spy* (Cambridge, MA: Harvard University Press, 1987), 100.

142. *FRUS 1950* I, 547–550 (minutes of meeting of American members of CPC, 25 April 1950), 551–558 (annexes, including memorandum, 18 April 1950); *Present at Creation*, 321. Even before Fuchs' arrest, Acheson felt a new agreement was impossible and suggested they seek continuation of the *modus vivendi* for another year; NARA, RG 59, State Department, General Records of the Office of the Executive Secretariat, Summaries of Daily Meetings, 1949–1952, box 1, Secretary's Daily Meeting, 1 December 1949.

143. On the devaluation of sterling, see Hopkins, *Oliver Franks*, 119–138.

144. HSTL, John W. Snyder Papers, box 32, European Trip of the Secretary of the Treasury, July 2 through July 25, 1949 Report, n. d.

145. HSTL, Webb Papers, box 25, Department of State file—Secretary of State, Notes for speech to Business Advisory Council, September 14, 1949.

146. NARA, RG 59, State Department, General Records of the Office of the Executive Secretariat, Summaries of Daily Meetings, 1949–1952, box 1, Secretary's Daily Meetings, 15 and 17 August 1949.

147. *FRUS 1949* III, 599–603, memorandum of conversation by secretary of state, 15 September 1949; quotation at 600.

148. *FRUS 1949* IV, 470, Acheson to Paris embassy, 19 October 1949.

149. *FRUS 1949* III, 635, secretary of state to president and acting secretary, 11 November 1949.

150. TNA, FO 371/81637, AU1053/1, Franks to Strang, 17 November 1949.

151. On this issue see *FRUS 1949* IV, 425–426, 429–431, 435–437.

152. Dimbleby and Reynolds, *Ocean Apart*, 207–208.

153. NARA, RG 59, State Department, General Records of the Office of the Executive Secretariat, Summaries of Daily Meetings, 1949–1952, box 1, Secretary's Daily Meeting, 18 July 1949.

154. TNA, FO 371/75814, F12843/1023/10, Bevin to Franks, 26 August 1949, and FO 800/462, FE/49/21, Bevin-Acheson meeting, 13 September 1949. Zhong-ping Feng, *The British Government's China Policy, 1945–1950* (Keele: Keele University Press, 1994). *Present at Creation*, 328. TNA, FO 371/74183, AN2868/1053/45, Franks to FO, 13 September 1949.

155. Acheson encountered major problems working with Louis Johnson. This was partly a clash of personalities. Robert Donovan accurately describes Johnson as "abrasive, cocksure, hyper-ambitious" (Robert J. Donovan, *Tumultuous Years: The Presidency of Harry S. Truman, 1949–1953* [New York: W. W. Norton, 1982], 62). Acheson concluded that Johnson was mentally ill (*Present at Creation*, 374). There were also important differences of substance. Truman sought a balanced budget, reducing military expenditure from $15 billion to $13 billion; and he chose Johnson partly because he would be determined in controlling defense spending. They also disagreed on Japan: MacArthur and Acheson sought a peace treaty; Johnson wanted to retain American forces in Japan following Mao's victory in China. Their bitter personal dispute ended with Johnson's dismissal in September 1950 when he was discovered to have been scheming with Senator Taft to secure Acheson's dismissal from office.

156. Acheson, "Problems in America Foreign Policy," in *DOSB* 21:539 (31 October 1949), 668–669.

157. *FRUS 1949* IX, 160–162, memorandum by Ogden (Bureau of Far Eastern Affairs), 2 November 1949.

158. *FRUS 1949* IX, 766–769, Stuart to secretary of state, 30 June 1949; memorandum of conversation between Truman and Acheson, 18 July 1949, *FRUS 1949* IX, 780–781, 791, 793–794.

159. HSTL, Oral History Interview with W. Walton Butterworth, 6 July 1871, p. 57, available at www.trumanlibrary.org/oralhist/butter.htm (viewed 20 January 2017).

160. *FRUS 1949* IX, 1141, memorandum of conversation by acting secretary of state, 1 October 1949.

161. Warren I. Cohen, "Acheson, His Advisers and China, 1949–1950," in Dorothy Borg and Waldo Heinrichs, eds., *Uncertain Years: Chinese American Relations, 1947–1950* (New York: Columbia University Press, 1980), 40.

162. HSTL Oral History Interview with John F. Melby, 14 November 1986, p. 167, available at www.trumanlibrary.org/oralhist/melby.htm (viewed 20 January 2017). Senate Foreign Relations Committee, *Reviews of the World Situation, 1949–1950*, 97 (Acheson testimony, 12 October 1949), 273 (Acheson testimony, 29 March 1950).

163. *FRUS 1949* IX, 219–220, memorandum of conversation by the secretary of state, 8 December 1949; TNA, FO 371/75826, F18481/1023/10, Washington to FO, 8 December 1949.

164. James Tang, *Britain's Encounter with Revolutionary China, 1949–1954* (London: Macmillan, 1992), 58. *FRUS 1949* IX, 241–242, secretary of state to ambassador in the UK, 23 December 1949.

165. Truman statement and extemporaneous remarks by Acheson in *DOSB* 22:550 (16 January 1950), 79–81. TNA, FO 371/83281, FC1022/72, Franks to Bevin, Dispatch No. 15, 7 January 1950; *ibid.*, FC1022/108, H.A Graves to P. W. Y. S. Scarlett (FO), 9 January 1950.

166. 81st Congress, 2nd Session, *Congressional Record*, volume 96, p. 298, 11 January 1950; *Present at Creation*, 355.

167. HSTL, Truman Papers, box 641, Memoirs-Post-Presidential Papers, Memoirs File, Acheson interview, 18 February 1955 am, pp. 45–46; *Present at Creation*, 354.

168. Acheson, "Crisis in Asia—An Examination of U.S. Policy," *DOSB* 22:551 (23 January 1950), 111–118; *Present at Creation*, 410; "M'Arthur Pledges Defense of Japan," *New York Times* (2 March 1949), 22; Thomas H. Etzold and John Lewis Gaddis, *Containment: Documents on American Foreign Policy and Strategy, 1945–1950* (New York: Columbia University Press, 1978), 252–276; *FRUS 1949* VII Part 2, 1212, Outline of Far Eastern Asian Policy for Review with the President, 14 November 1949.

169. TNA, FO 371/ 83013, F1022/5, Franks to Bevin, Dispatch No. 37, 16 January 1950.

170. Taft speech, 28 June 1950, in Barton J. Bernstein and Allen J. Matusov, *Truman Administration: A Documentary History* (New York: Harper & Row, 1966), 439–442.

171. TNA, FO 371/ 83013, F1022/5, Franks to Bevin, Dispatch No. 37, 16 January 1950.

172. Cumings, *Korean War*, 72. For a critique of Cummings's earlier studies, see John Edward Wilz, "The Making of Mr Truman's War," in Korean War Conference Committee, *The Historical Reillumination on the Korean War* (Seoul: War Memorial Service, 1990), [81–108], 93–94. Wilz finds Cumings's claim wholly unconvincing: had Acheson been baiting the communists to attack, then US forces would have been prepared, but these "troops were woefully unprepared."

173. Walter Waggoner, "Four Areas Listed. 'Attacking' Manchuria, Inner, Outer Mongolia, Sinkiang Cited," *New York Times* (13 January 1950).

174. TNA, FO 371/84528, FZ10345/3, Notes of a Discussion, 8 February 1950.

175. Rusk, *As I Saw It*, 158.

176. McGlothlen, *Controlling the Waves*, 154; HSTL, Oral History Interview with W. Walton Butterworth, 6 July 1971, pp. 56–57, available at www.trumanlibrary.org/oralhist/butter.htm (viewed 12 June 2014); *FRUS 1950* VI, 286–289, Clubb to secretary of state, 20 January 1950; Cohen, "Acheson, His Advisers," 40–41, citing Senate Foreign Relations Committee Executive Session, "Situation in Far East," 24 January 1950; NARA, RG59, State Department, PPS Records, box 13, Jessup for Acheson, 28 July 1949.

177. TNA, FO 371/84528, FZ10345/3, notes of a discussion, 8 February 1950.

178. Greg Donachy, ed., *Documents on Canadian External Relations Volume 16: 1950* (Ottawa: Department of Foreign Affairs and International Trade, 1996), 1176, Wrong to acting secretary of state for external affairs, 4 February 1950.

179. Hamby, *Truman*, 520.

180. *Present at Creation*, 359–360; William R. Conklin, "Hiss Is Sentenced to Five-Year Term; Acheson Backs Him," *New York Times* (26 January 1950).

181. Lilienthal, *Journals* II, 620 (26 June 1950 entry).

182. L of C, Joseph E. Davies Papers, box 23, February–May 1949 folder.

183. HSTL, Acheson Papers, box 28, folder 1, Richard L. Stokes, "Defeat for 5 Years," *Sign* (February 1950), 11–14.

Chapter Five

Confronting Perils, 1950–1951

In February and March 1950 Acheson deployed notably tougher rhetoric as he explained what he saw as the fundamental features of American foreign policy. These more robust attitudes were undoubtedly a product of his evaluation of changing international circumstances, but they were also a response to American domestic opinion. Many loyal Democrats expressed reservations about the decision to build the hydrogen bomb. Liberal misgivings about the increased focus on military strength found expression in a Senate debate on 2 February. Senator Brien McMahon, chairman of the joint Congressional Committee on Atomic Energy, declared: "if we should fail in the business of working in a crusade for peace, we would deal a severe blow both to our moral position and to our fervent hopes for a secure future. The people of the United States want harmony among nations infinitely more than they want a new bomb. A fresh proposal for atomic peace, as dramatic as it is sincere, impresses me as urgently desirable." Senator Millard Tydings (D-Maryland), chairman of the Senate Armed Services Committee, delivered what an Acheson biographer called a "more emotional" speech. Tydings proposed a resolution asking Truman to summon a world conference "charged with the single duty of entering into an understanding and an agreement to achieve world disarmament . . . by January 1, 1954."[1]

Acheson decided to respond directly to these visions of American diplomatic strategy. In a press conference and then in a speech in February he articulated his belief that a willingness to negotiate was insufficient. Agreements could only be reached by building up "situations of strength" such as those secured for Greece and Turkey and for Berlin, which would then be recognized by Moscow. He also spoke of the necessity for total diplomacy involving all the agencies of government.[2]

MCCARTHY AND THE "PRIMITIVES"

These tougher attitudes, however, did little to satisfy the much fiercer criticisms from right-wing politicians and journalists, which he characterized as the "attack of the primitives," adopting a phrase first used by John Miller of the *Times* of London. Already under fire for having "lost" China, the administration, and Acheson in particular, faced pressure to demonstrate its resolve in the fight against communism at home and abroad. Senator Joseph McCarthy delivered a speech in Wheeling, West Virginia, on 9 February claiming that the State Department was hesitant in its anti-communism: "I have here in my hand a list of 205 . . . a list of names that were made known to the secretary of state as being members of the Communist Party and who nevertheless are still working and shaping policy in the state department." The next day, he told a radio interviewer in Salt Lake City: "Last night I discussed communists in the State Department. I stated that I had the names of 57 card-carrying members of the Communist Party."[3] Assistant secretary John E. Peurifoy assumed responsibility for responding to the charges, which were an important topic at the 9:30 meetings in February and March. On 12 February McCarthy repeated his general charges in the Senate, where Senator Henry Cabot Lodge (R-Massachusetts) proposed a resolution setting up a subcommittee to investigate the claims, something Peurifoy supported. The Tydings subcommittee began its hearings on 21 February. Meanwhile, McCarthy's supporters released a pamphlet containing 100 names of alleged communists who were or had been in the State Department.[4] Acheson wanted to appear before the subcommittee but Truman refused to let him do so.[5]

At the same time, another pamphlet appeared: Joseph P. Kamp's *America Betrayed* claimed that during the war "Acheson's was one of the strongest voices for 'working with Stalin' and appeasing his demands." Kamp added that Acheson was one of the architects of the UN, which "served Russian ends by diverting American attention from the post-war Russian territorial grabs." Moreover, the "great monument" of his term as under secretary was the "abandonment of China to Russia."[6] This assault was made more serious by the readiness of the leading Republican politician to endorse it. Senator Robert Taft did not care for McCarthy or his approach but welcomed the pressure it put on the Truman administration. Taft strongly disapproved of the direction of postwar American foreign and domestic policy, was dismayed by the Democrats' victory in 1948, and disliked Acheson personally. The senator "longed to embarrass and defeat" the Democrats, but in doing so he adopted an "irresponsible position."[7]

Acheson showed real strength of character in facing the onslaught of criticism against him and his staff. Coping with it called for resilience: although the attacks' intensity varied over the months and years, they continued unabated for the remainder of the Truman administration. The secretary revealed his stoical readiness to endure tribulations as he pursued what he regarded as the right policies for the nation. In this endeavor, he was sustained by the unswerving loyalty of the president. He also received many declarations of support. White House special counsel Clark Clifford wrote an effusive letter: "I think you are doing wonderfully well, and that your enemies are in the process of being confounded . . . You will come out of this period as the greatest Secretary of State this country has ever had." He concluded: "The statements of McCarthy and his ilk remind me of curs snapping at the heels of a thoroughbred."[8] Former secretary of war Henry Stimson wrote to the *New York Times* saying, "The man who seeks to gain political advantage from personal attack on a Secretary of State is a man who seeks political advantage from damage to his country." This outlook was admirably captured in a cartoon by Herblock that appeared in the same newspaper. It depicted a McCarthy supporter and Stalin jointly holding a banner reading "Down with Acheson" and contained the cartoonist's caption "Somebody around here is helping the Communists!"[9]

Support for the secretary came also from the British ambassador, who was anxious to encourage British officials to share his sympathetic understanding of Acheson's difficulties. In April Oliver Franks sent a handwritten letter to Foreign Secretary Bevin, enclosing the secretary's off-the-record answers to questions following a speech, which revealed the secretary having "to defend himself & [*sic*] his Department . . . before in effect a public audience."[10] Acheson was most gratified to receive a message from Bevin, who described how the secretary's prestige was higher than ever in Britain.[11] Franks might have done his best to bolster Acheson's standing, but he was also an astute observer. He reported how the secretary lacked a political following; Democrats in Congress were reluctant to help him lest this damage their prospects for reelection.[12]

NSC 68

It seems probable that Acheson's embattled circumstances encouraged a hardening of his foreign policy outlook. His belief in the imperative need for greater military strength found fuller expression in April when director of the policy planning staff Paul Nitze completed his review of national security policy. The final stages of the preparation of the study witnessed another rift with the defense secretary. Defense Secretary Louis Johnson had been suspicious of the review from its inception, believing that Acheson, through Nitze, was seeking to undermine his efforts to keep defense expenditure at $13.5 billion; and was protective of his department's prerogatives in framing national security strategy. Matters came to a head in a meeting on 22 March.

Following a short summary of the draft paper by Nitze, Johnson exploded in anger. As Acheson later reported: "No one, he shouted, was going to make arrangements for him to meet with another Cabinet officer and a roomful of people and be told what he was going to report to the President. Who authorized these meetings contrary to his orders?" Acheson explained to him that the president had ordered the review and that General James Burns had served as the Department of Defense's representative. Acheson reported this episode to Admiral Sydney Souers, the former executive secretary of the NSC and recently appointed consultant to the president on national security affairs, and James Lay, Souers's successor as executive secretary; and they promptly informed Truman. Less than an hour later, the president telephoned Acheson, "expressing his outrage and telling me to carry on exactly as we had been doing."[13] Johnson's intervention was highly emotional and rather illogical at this stage in the process of review, yet his two substantive points were accurate. The study was overwhelmingly dominated by the State Department, and Acheson's strategic vision; and it visualized a defense posture that would shatter the $13.5 billion budget for fiscal year 1950 and the $13.9 billion envisaged for fiscal 1951.[14]

The drafting of Nitze's report continued and was submitted to the president in April. NSC 68 identified the Soviet Union as inherently expansionist and called on the United States to resist communism everywhere. It proposed large-scale rearmament by the US and its allies to meet the threat, but did not specify the amount of spending required for this program.[15] This was a deliberate move on Acheson's part, for he did not want to give any easy ammunition to those committed to tight control of expenditure. Nitze had offered him a rough estimate of $50 billion, but he was told not to include this figure in the report.[16] Meanwhile, the president received the memorandum but did not endorse it, asking, instead, for further information. He was still determined to try to restrain government spending and achieve a balanced budget, and continued to hold this view as late as a few days before the outbreak of the Korean War in June.[17]

This firmer line required what Acheson called total diplomacy. A robust approach to negotiations, backed by military might, should be supplemented with schemes of public persuasion. Acheson always appreciated the importance of public diplomacy to secure popular support for policies. When out of office, he joined groups seeking to influence national policy. In 1940 he was a prominent member of both the Committee to Defend America by Aiding the Allies and the Century Group, which lobbied for assistance to Britain and greater US engagement in world affairs. In 1947–1948 he was a senior figure in the Citizens' Committee for the Marshall Plan, which aimed to persuade the American people and Congress to approve economic relief to Western Europe. When he became secretary of state in 1949, he faced serious criticisms of his policy toward China, leading him to commission the *China*

White Paper to defend administration policies, something it signally failed to achieve. Undeterred by this setback, Acheson and Webb recognized the importance of public support. In February 1950 assistant secretary Edward W. Barratt helped to unveil the "Campaign of Truth," which Truman formally launched in April.[18]

INDOCHINA

The tougher anti-communist strategy, if not the increased defense expenditure, envisaged in NSC 68 and enunciated in the campaign of persuasion, also found its way into policy. This became evident first in Asia. Roosevelt had opposed European imperialism, hoping that the end of the Second World War might bring the dissolution of the colonial regimes of British Hong Kong, French Indochina, and the Dutch East Indies.[19] Truman was probably unaware of Roosevelt's views and Byrnes showed little interest in colonial nationalism. In consequence, the president told the French in May 1945 that he did not oppose French control of Indochina but, to French chagrin, he was unwilling to offer them any US aid.[20] The British also continued to rule Hong Kong, and, indeed, gained Washington's sympathy when they faced a communist insurgency in Malaya in 1948. Acheson adopted a cautious approach during his time as under secretary, offering American "good offices" to help the French reach an accommodation in their war with the Viet Minh.[21] He clearly preferred to see the colonial powers progressively moving toward granting independence to the indigenous populations and took the same view in his first months as secretary by pursuing this line resolutely with the Dutch. Although he displayed some understanding of the situation confronting the Dutch government, its rather brutal "police action" in March 1949 ended any sympathy. Thereafter Acheson pressured the Netherlands to grant independence to the Dutch East Indies, suggesting that failure to do so might jeopardize Marshall Aid to the country. The new state of Indonesia emerged in December 1949.[22] In October Acheson told the Senate Foreign Relations Committee that the United States would get nowhere by supporting French colonial power in Indochina.[23]

The French were much less susceptible, or willing to yield, to American pressure. In any case, during 1949 Acheson became increasingly concerned about the risk of Indochina falling under communist control if the French lost their fight with the Viet Minh. In June 1949 France established a new regime in Indochina under the leadership of Emperor Bao Dai of Annam. Even though Bao Dai was an uninspiring figure and given very limited power, his appointment was sufficient to satisfy American desires for devolution of power to the local population. Moreover, Truman's inaugural address in January 1949 included a commitment to extend aid to underdeveloped areas, which became known as the Point 4 Program, because it constituted the president's fourth pledge in the speech. It made it easier to contemplate assistance to French Indochina. In late 1949 Acheson abandoned his hostile attitude toward French colonial control of Indochina. He indicated a change of view in his talks with Schuman in September, when he spoke sympathetically of French efforts against communist guerrillas. He now regarded the French campaign against the Viet Minh as part of the West's fight against communism, an opinion confirmed by the January 1950 recognition of the Viet Minh regime by the Soviet Union and the People's Republic of China. But Acheson also stressed that the French could do more to prevent communist domination if they were "to satisfy the truly nationalist aspirations of the inhabitants."[24]

This change of view was part of his generally more anti-communist stance. But it was also rooted in more specific economic concerns about Asia. Acheson saw Japan as a potential bastion against the spread of communism but only if its economy were to recover,[25] and this recovery was dependent on trade with Southeast Asia. Moreover, the costs of fighting its war against the Viet Minh were becoming burdensome to France. Finally, the war in Indochina and the communist emergency in British Malaya were hampering economic growth in the region. In particular, there was a downturn in the production of tin, rubber, and other commodities, vital sources of dollar earnings for European producers. If this trend were not halted, then there might be a return of the dollar gap that the Marshall Plan sought to remove. Both Schuman and Bevin urged Acheson to act to alleviate the situation.[26] By December 1949 officials in Washington were also pushing Acheson in this direction. NSC 48/2 recommended "providing political, economic and military assistance and advice" to the French in Indochina, and suggested drawing on the $75 million assigned to the general area of China through the Mutual Defense Assistance Act of 1949.[27]

American commitments to the French in Indochina grew steadily in the spring and early summer of 1950. On 7 February Acheson announced US recognition of the Bao Dai regime, which the British also recognized.[28] Both David Bruce, the US ambassador in Paris, and Henri Bonnet, the French ambassador in Washington, lobbied for aid to the French.[29] The State Department undertook an assessment of Indochina and concluded that the United States should aid the French and the Bao Dai regime.[30] Acheson remained reticent but increasingly accepted the need for American assistance, partly because of Jessup's report on his tour of Asia which stressed the communist credentials of the Viet Minh, but mainly because of the French threat to quit Indochina if aid did not arrive. When Jessup and Acheson testified before the Senate in late March, the secretary appeared to concede the case for assistance. He also observed: "We want more effort but not additional responsibility. We do not want to get into a position where the French say, 'You take over; we aren't able to go ahead on this.'"[31]

By 9 March Acheson had received Truman's general approval of aid.[32] NSC 64 encapsulated a new policy of economic and military assistance, which Truman approved on 24 April.[33] On 8 May the secretary told the French that Washington could give up to $20 million in fiscal year 1950.[34] Acheson explained his thinking to a meeting with Bevin and Schuman three days later: "from our standpoint, the Soviet Union possesses [a] position of domination in China which it is using to threaten Indochina, push in Malaya, stir up trouble in the Philippines, and now start trouble in Indonesia."[35] Despite his clear drift toward supporting the French, Acheson was still pressing the case for French concessions to Bao Dai in spring 1950. He well understood that Washington appeared to be supporting "old-fashioned colonial attitudes," but it could not push the French too hard, lest they declare "All right, take over the damn country. We don't want it."[36] So the trend was set for steadily escalating US aid, and by the close of the Truman administration the Americans were funding approximately 40 percent of the French military effort.[37]

Acheson became progressively more committed. All his senior advisers, except George Kennan, embraced the case for assisting the French. Due to depart for sabbatical leave at Princeton in June 1950, but delayed until late August by the outbreak of the Korean War, he expressed doubts about supporting the French in one of his final memorandums. The United States, he said, was in danger of "guaranteeing the French in an undertaking which neither they nor we, nor both of us together, can win."[38] Kennan's warning went unheeded: the Korean War seemed to reinforce Acheson's commitment. In the MacArthur hearings in June 1951 Acheson declared that the French "have had this fight pretty much ever since the end of World War II."[39] By spring 1952 the French were in difficulty, leading Acheson to ask the NSC on 5 March what should be the response to a French request for direct American involvement. The JCS replied that they could only calculate the military costs once its political importance had been determined. This infuriated Acheson who felt the political decision could only be taken when they had some idea of the costs and likelihood of success.[40]

Acheson considered the view of one analyst, Allen Griffin, who argued that a military solution was not possible, and the United States should pursue a political and economic solution,[41] but there is no evidence that this proposal was pursued. Indeed, Acheson developed a strategy of military support in May and June 1952. It was entrenched in NSC 124/2, which Truman endorsed on 25 June 1952. This emphasized the importance of defending Indochina against communist aggression, since its fall or that of any other country in Southeast Asia would have dire consequences for the rest of the region. In effect, it articulated the domino theory two years ahead of Eisenhower's coinage in April 1954. The paper also identified the Chinese communists, rather than the Soviets, as the principal threat. In the event of Chinese intervention, NSC 124/2 ruled out deploying American ground troops, but recommended that the United States should, in collaboration with France and Britain, use its navy and air force against the Chinese. Acheson encountered limited enthusiasm for his ideas when he disclosed them at meetings in Paris and London. The French welcomed US aid to build up a national Vietnamese army to support French forces, but disliked his proposal that Americans assist in the training of these forces. The British were wary about military action against China, feeling it might risk war with the Soviet Union.[42]

In the final weeks of the Truman administration, Acheson met Schuman in Paris. He was critical of French failure to keep the Americans properly informed but his overarching aim was to improve cooperation rather than challenge the basic strategy.[43] This was partly because Acheson did not want Indochina to "fall into the hands of the Communists like a ripe plum." United States aid to the French could prevent this. By the late 1960s he had clearly changed his mind. When asked by his biographer to respond to the French claim that they were part of the global fight against communist aggression, Acheson replied, "As the song says, 'It ain't necessarily so.'" Instead, he cited French "blackmail."[44] As George Herring observes, American policy on Indochina was "a hostage to its policy in Europe." Acheson wanted Franco-German cooperation on the Schuman Plan, and, after 1951, on the formation of a European Defense Community which would integrate French and German troops into a European army. The French claimed they would only provide forces for a European army if they received US help in Indochina.[45] In consequence, there was no substantive change to policy by the end of the Truman administration. The legacy was an ever-deepening monetary commitment to failing French efforts to defeat the well-organized and Chinese-aided Viet Minh.

MEETINGS IN PARIS AND LONDON, MAY 1950

The American commitment of military and economic assistance to Indochina was made during Acheson's visit to Europe in May 1949. He visited Paris on 7–8 May and then traveled to London where he held conversations with the British on 9–10 May and talks with the British and French on 11–12 May. His trip ended with a meeting of the Atlantic Council, which brought together the foreign ministers of all 12 members of NATO on 15–18 May. The Americans, British, and French each came to the meetings with their own distinct priorities. Acheson was especially anxious for an improvement in the organization of the alliance, and to see a stronger military stance. He talked about how the alliance might serve as "a sort of international headquarters for the cold war."[46] Bevin and his senior officials wanted to build on the successful diplomacy of the devaluation of sterling in September 1949. The French were ready to unveil their new initiative for a better relationship with Germany.

When Acheson arrived in Paris he was surprised to hear that Schuman would be coming to see him at the US embassy. Only Acheson, Ambassador Bruce, Schuman, and his interpreter attended the meeting. Schuman explained the French decision to form a supranational authority to control the coal and steel production of its member countries. Schuman requested, and Acheson agreed, to keep the matter secret.[47] It was clearly designed to draw West Germany into the West, while ensuring its war-making industries were under international control. Acheson traveled to London, and during a meeting with Bevin, the French ambassador, René Massigli, contacted the foreign secretary to tell him of their intention of announcing the scheme. The French formally launched the European Coal and Steel Community, soon known as the Schuman Plan, on 9 May.[48] When it became clear that the secretary already knew about the plan, Bevin and his officials were irritated. Acheson later described Bevin as being "in a towering rage."[49] The British were distressed that the French and Americans had connived to present a *fait accompli*. Acheson responded that sometimes circumstances led to one country initially revealing its plans to only one of the three powers, just as the Americans had endorsed the British decision to devalue the pound in September 1949.[50] In his memoirs, Acheson acknowledged that he "had been stupid in not foreseeing Bevin's rage" at being excluded.[51]

The British ambassador to the United States, Oliver Franks, grasped the significance of the Schuman Plan much more clearly than politicians and officials in London. He maintained that it had "struck the American imagination and is widely regarded as the most hopeful development in the direction of European cooperation." He tried, without success, to persuade London to take the scheme more seriously. The Plan, he argued, was "essentially a major political question" rather than an economic one, and it might prove to be a stabilizing influence, what Franks called an anchorman, over 90 million Europeans.[52]

If the British were unhappy at the Schuman Plan, their dismay deepened when their expectations of Anglo-American talks proved to be over-optimistic. A British briefing paper declared: "It is the first time since the war that they have approached us as a partner on the most general issues of policy."[53] British optimism was boosted by the scale of arrangements for discussions: the Acheson-Bevin talks would be preceded by detailed conversations between US and British officials.

The American position was more cautious. Acheson received advice acknowledging the importance of ties with Britain but recommending he not yield to the British desire for more explicit understandings. A briefing paper maintained that "No other country has the same qualifications for being our principal ally and partner as the UK." Any "serious impairment" of Anglo-American relations "would require a whole reorientation of US foreign policy, since the achievement of many of our objectives . . . depends upon the British agreeing with those objectives and taking the necessary action to accomplish them." The memorandum acknowledged the "special close relation" of the two countries but concluded that the British "will have to recognize that in the European context, we must deal with them as a European country."[54] The American ambassador in London, Lewis Douglas, endorsed this outlook. Britain, he argued, had an incomparable range of global interests and pursued policies and had interests in common with the United States, making a special relationship "inescapable." But he cautioned against openly conceding these special relations, lest the British were to lean too heavily on the relationship.[55]

Given this advice, it is hardly surprising that Acheson was reluctant to approve overt expressions of closeness. He was anxious to avoid any undue attention to a special relationship. When he arrived in London on 9 May he discovered that a paper on Anglo-American relations had emerged from talks between State Department and Foreign Office staff while he was in Paris. At a meeting with Bevin on 10 May, Acheson responded to the paper, titled "Continued Consultation and Co-ordination of Policy," by saying he agreed with "its exposition of the need for close and continued consultation on all the parallel interests of the United States and United Kingdom." However, he felt it was "quite impossible to allow it to be known that any such paper had been drawn up or that it had been agreed to." So he could not admit to any knowledge of such a paper. He accepted the unique nature of Anglo-American relations but he feared that, in the hands of troublemakers, the paper "could stir up no end of hullabaloo, both domestic and international." He ordered that all copies be destroyed.[56] That was as far as acknowledgment of the special relationship went.

Acheson's main aim for the London meetings was to bring greater vigor and a sense of purpose to the alliance. He felt he could achieve this by persuading its members to commit themselves to clearer and more robust organizational arrangements and to pledge more funds for defense. His advocacy was effective. Although Bevin told his colleagues that the secretary was not very precise, he clearly grasped his point that the Western powers were not sufficiently organized and that they needed to increase military expenditure.[57] By the final meeting the NATO members had agreed to set up a body of deputies which would remain in continuous session in London and was directed to begin work on organizing personnel, money, and matériel.[58] As Averell Harriman, European administrator of the Marshall Plan, told the president, these agreements helped put the "O" into NATO.[59] There followed the establishment of NATO's political headquarters. The May decisions also began the process of creating a supreme commander for NATO and the integration of the national forces into a coherent command—supreme headquarters allied powers in Europe (SHAPE).

Acheson regarded the May gatherings as a great success. The new determination to give shape to the alliance and the announcement of the Schuman Plan meant his wishes were met. The French were satisfied with the American enthusiasm for the Coal and Steel Community. Although the British were disappointed at American reticence on the closeness of relations, Bevin remained committed to maintaining a friendly relationship with Acheson and the United States.

THE MIDDLE EAST

This readiness to work together found expression in agreement on a common approach to the Middle East in May 1950. This was an important step forward, for there had been Anglo-American friction since 1945 over the Palestine question. Under British control since the end of the First World War, Palestine became increasingly ungovernable in the face of large-scale illegal Jewish immigration and terrorism from Zionist groups trying to drive out the British and establish the state of Israel. In February 1947 the British decided to refer the issue to the United Nations.[60] Acheson was not a Zionist and took limited interest in the region, but he recognized the significance of the British decision and worried that it would be "hard to see how" the United States could "escape the responsibility for leadership."[61] Still, the issue was not a priority during the remaining months of his term as under secretary. During Acheson's absence from office, there were various failed attempts by the UN to broker a solution that envisioned the creation of a partitioned Palestine, one part Arab, one part Jewish. Seeing no other way forward, the British quit Palestine in May 1948.

In the face of the obvious intention of the Jews to declare the creation of the state of Israel, the United States had to decide how to respond. Clark Clifford, special counsel to the president, persuaded Truman to grant recognition immediately following the planned Jewish declaration. In a heated meeting with the president and Clifford on 12 May, Marshall argued strongly against this option and vented his anger against Clifford, accusing him of trying to win Jewish votes. So intense was Marshall's reaction, he never spoke to Clifford again. Yet it is far from clear that politics dominated Clifford's thinking. His advice, rather, stressed that the emergence of the new state was inevitable, that other powers would recognize it, and that the State Department's strategy offered no effective alternative. The secretary said that if Truman followed Clifford's proposal, then he would vote against him in the forthcoming presidential election. Truman knew he could not afford to break with so revered a figure. Talks between Clifford and under secretary Lovett managed to secure an undertaking that Marshall would not oppose recognition. American recognition of Israel was granted on 15 May, only hours after its creation.[62] The new state of Israel confronted attacks from the Arab states of Egypt, Lebanon, Syria, and Jordan. Marshall turned the department's energies to helping to secure ceasefires, to finding solutions to various problems, and to trying, in particular, to address the issue of Jerusalem.

When he became secretary of state in 1949, Acheson did his best to advance these efforts. A particular American concern was the plight of refugees. Truman appointed Mark Ethridge, editor of the *Louisville Courier-Journal*, as the US representative on the Palestine Conciliation Commission that sought a solution. Ethridge found it difficult to secure Israeli cooperation and asked Acheson for help in pressuring them.[63] Acheson informed the Israeli ambassador that the United States was ready to back Israeli membership in the UN if they were more conciliatory on refugees, borders, and Jerusalem.[64] But Chaim Weizmann, president of the provisional Israeli government, was unaccommodating, opposing repatriation and favoring resettlement of Arab refugees. This produced a strong response from Truman, who declared he was "disgusted with the manner in which the Jews are approaching the refugee problem."[65] Nevertheless, the president endorsed Israel's membership in the UN, arguing it would lead them to cooperate better on Arab refugees and Jerusalem." But, as John Judis points out, this was rationalization by the president, who had succumbed to Israeli lobbying.[66] Acheson was furious at Israeli intransigence over refugees and their territorial demands. He persuaded Truman to send a tough note to the Israelis.[67] But adept lobbying by friends of Israel ensured that Truman never applied any real pressure. By August 1949, Acheson abandoned efforts at a solution. The United States contented itself with the ceasefire settlements between Israel and its Arab foes that UN mediator Ralph Bunche negotiated. Despite this, Acheson spoke of developing a positive relationship with Israel.[68]

Meanwhile, the issue of arms supplies arose. During the Arab war with Israel the Americans supported a UN embargo on arms, but by July 1949 hostilities ended and on 11 August the UN ended the embargo. The British wanted to resume supplies to Jordan and Iraq, but especially to Egypt, with whom they were trying to negotiate a defense pact. In February 1950 London agreed to sell military equipment to Egypt. Israel sought supplies from the United States, which Acheson backed as a balance to the British arms to Egypt. The Pentagon opposed supplies to Israel, while American pro-Zionists and Israeli officials lobbied against the British deal. Truman was annoyed at Zionist pressure on him, but questioned Egypt's need of armaments while favoring help for the Israelis. Acheson solved the problem by pursuing a scheme suggested by representative Franklin D. Roosevelt Jr. and developed by George McGhee and Raymond Hare, director and deputy director of the Bureau of Near East, South Asian and African Affairs of the State Department. The idea of a joint American-British-French declaration to avoid a Middle East arms race gained Truman's support when Acheson said it would be accompanied by public commitments of nonaggression by Arab states.

Acheson presented the proposal at the London meetings in May 1950. He recognized the obstacles to a total embargo, because the British provided munitions to Jordan, Iraq, and Egypt, and he understood their value to the area's security. But he proposed a declaration that did not envisage ending these supplies. Rather, they would be kept to a level that would not lead the Israelis to say that the West was building up the aggressive potential of the Arab states. The Tripartite Declaration was issued on 25 May. It accepted the need for a certain level of arms for internal security and national self-defense; declared a regional arms race undesirable; permitted Western arms supplies only to those who renounced aggression; and warned that the three powers would take action both within and outside the UN against violations of borders or ceasefire lines. The declaration proved a useful and workable arrangement. The State Department felt it had reduced tensions. It removed American domestic criticisms of British policy and thereby allowed Acheson space to cooperate with the British in the region.[69]

ATTEMPTING TO REPAIR/RESTORE BIPARTISANSHIP

Despite some tribulations with Bevin, May and June 1950 saw harmonious relations between Acheson and his two main Western allies. Domestic politics were much less agreeable. Conscious of the problems, he sought to rebuild bipartisanship in the spring and early summer of 1950. He took John Sherman Cooper (former Republican senator from Kentucky, 1946–1948) to the London meetings, hoping to promote strong interparty cooperation. In his memoirs Acheson described Cooper as sound, loyal, wise, and delightful company.[70] The move produced an encouraging message from John Foster Dulles, the leading Republican authority on foreign policy. In reply, Acheson declared his firm desire to strive ceaselessly for unity on foreign policy in the nation and in Congress.[71]

Acheson enjoyed a reasonable working relationship with Dulles but did not like him. He had a deep aversion toward the "psalm-singing Presbyterian" whom he deemed politically devious.[72] Nevertheless, the secretary decided to take advantage of signals from friends of Dulles about a role for him with the administration. Carl McCardle of the *Philadelphia Bulletin* approached Lucius Battle, Acheson's personal assistant. Senator Vandenberg urged the appointment of Dulles to some position, describing him as very able, equipped with experience and capacity in foreign policy. He added, "I deeply feel that it is acutely advisable to bring him back into active and important cooperation with the State Department." Dulles had already volunteered the previous August to be helpful on the Far East. Although Acheson and Truman were mindful of Dulles's sharp criticisms of the administration during his failed attempt to win the Senate seat for New York in November 1949, they recognized his value as an emblem of bipartisanship. On 6 April the State Department announced Dulles's appointment to serve as a consultant to the secretary on broad problems of foreign affairs.[73]

Another decision also proved helpful to Acheson. Harriman, always keen to be at the center of affairs, wanted to return to Washington and let this be known through Lovett, who spoke to Acheson. At ease with the overture, Acheson suggested that Harriman assume the position of White House adviser on national security issues, a role informally held by Clark Clifford, but no one had performed these duties after Clifford had departed to resume his legal practice in January 1950. Truman agreed but warned the secretary that the appointment might be taken to indicate Acheson's imminent departure and replacement by Harriman. The president's prediction was all too accurate. Harriman's new post was announced on 16 June and rumors immediately began circulating that he would soon succeed Acheson as secretary. Acheson was unworried, knowing Harriman was loyal and saw more specific benefits in having Harriman at the White House. Harriman supported the increased military spending envisaged in NSC 68 and would argue the case with a still reticent Truman. He also wanted Harriman to serve as an ally against Defense Secretary Johnson, who was conspiring against Acheson.[74]

The appointment proved a success. Harriman became a valued adviser, regularly attending the 9:30 meetings.[75] Their good relationship was based on long association, a common outlook on the country's role in the world, mutual respect, and, above all, their high regard for the office of the presidency. Acheson valued Harriman's integrity, energy, and tenacity. Harriman overcame his rivalry—he had been disappointed when the president appointed Acheson over him as secretary of state. Though both men were East Coast WASPs, who had known each other at Groton school and Yale University, they were personally different. The stolid and dependable Harriman lacked Acheson's incisive intellect and quick wit, but he brought sound judgment and a forceful manner; he relished dinner parties, while Acheson enjoyed retreating to his Maryland farm and the opportunity to spend an evening alone with a book.

THE KOREAN WAR

It was at his Maryland farm that Acheson heard the news heralding the biggest crisis of the Truman presidency. Having retired to bed after several hours gardening and a good dinner, he was reading himself to sleep when he received a telephone call at 10:00pm. In the early hours of Sunday 25 June (early evening of Saturday 24 June in Washington) North Korean forces had launched a major attack against South Korea. In the course of the week that followed Acheson assumed a commanding role in shaping the American response. He always deferred to Truman, but it was the secretary's counsel that dominated discussions. From the outset, Acheson acted decisively, but with restraint. He endorsed the recommendation of John Hickerson, assistant secretary for UN affairs, proposing a meeting the next day of the UN Security Council, which the Americans would call to ask for a ceasefire. He then telephoned the president, who was away for the weekend at his home in Independence, Missouri, to brief him on the situation. Truman backed Acheson's decisions and wanted to return to Washington immediately, but the secretary persuaded him not to take a hastily arranged night flight. Acheson assured him that he would be kept fully informed of developments.[76]

Acheson drove to the State Department on Sunday morning and held discussions with his staff to draw up a draft resolution for the Security Council. Having secured the president's approval of the text in a telephone call, the resolution was put to the Security Council on Sunday afternoon. It noted with grave concern the armed attack by the North Koreans and called on them to cease hostilities immediately. The resolution passed 9–0, with one abstention (Yugoslavia) and one absence (the Soviet Union was boycotting the UN in protest at Nationalist China taking the seat it felt should be occupied by the communist government in Beijing).[77] Acheson met Truman's plane when it arrived in Washington at 6:30, giving him the latest news as they traveled together to Blair House, the president's temporary residence while the White House was being refurbished. There followed a long meeting at Blair House, where Truman and Acheson were joined by under secretary James Webb, assistant secretaries Hickerson and Dean Rusk, ambassador-at-large Philip Jessup, secretary of defense Johnson, chairman of the Joint Chiefs of Staff General Omar N. Bradley and the other chiefs of staff, and the service secretaries. During the afternoon, Acheson had dismissed his aides to reflect for an hour or two on the issues. As a result, he had some clear ideas about how to proceed. He recommended that General MacArthur be instructed to send arms to Korea; that the US Air Force should protect Kimpo airport as Americans were evacuated; and that the Seventh Fleet should be ordered north to prevent hostilities between China and Taiwan. He also proposed increased military aid to Indochina. Truman approved each of

Acheson's recommendations, and asked him to draft a statement that he would deliver on Tuesday (perhaps to Congress).[78]

On Monday the 26th, as news came in of the steadily deteriorating military situation in Korea, Acheson spoke on the telephone to senators Tom Connally (D-Texas), Alexander Wiley (R-Wisconsin), and to John Kee (D-West Virginia) of the House Foreign Affairs Committee; and sent Jack McFall, assistant secretary for congressional relations, to brief the chairmen of the Senate and House committees. Meanwhile, he concentrated on drafting the presidential statement. After consulting various officials, he again worked alone for a couple of hours to think things through, producing a draft by about 6:30pm. As George Kennan's diary explains, when the president's statement was released the next day, it was not significantly different from Acheson's text. Kennan believed this was of historical significance, for it demonstrated that the action taken by the United States was not a result of pressure from the military, but, rather, the product of the secretary's "solitary deliberation."[79] Because Acheson warned that the situation was becoming desperate and might require further action, Truman called another meeting at Blair House at 9:00pm. The secretary recommended that the US Air Force and Navy should give full support to the South Koreans; the Seventh Fleet should position itself to prevent attacks by either the Chinese communists or the Taiwanese on the other's territory; aid to Indochina be increased; and a second resolution should be put before the Security Council asking UN members to provide assistance to the South Koreans. Acheson sought approval of these proposals, which he had included in the draft presidential statement as American commitments. They enjoyed general consent, even from Johnson, and were endorsed by Truman.[80]

The Blair House meeting also agreed that the president, Acheson, and Johnson should brief congressional leaders, which they did on the morning of 27 June. Acheson summarized circumstances and Truman read his statement of the orders he had already given—in particular the commitment of US air and sea forces to aid South Korea and the submission of a second resolution to the Security Council urging UN members to lend aid. His action received general approval from the politicians. However, the second resolution to the UN Security Council encompassed language that disturbed the British. It declared that the attack "makes amply clear centrally directed Communist Imperialism has passed beyond subversion in seeking to conquer independent nations."[81] The British ambassador, Oliver Franks, persuaded the Americans to remove the phrase. The amended resolution passed the Security Council 7–1, with Yugoslavia opposing, Egypt and India abstaining, and the Soviet Union still absent.[82]

Acheson's readiness to omit the passage arose partly from reflection on its value, but more importantly from his recognition of the need to take account of the British outlook. America wanted allies. He told Lester B.

Pearson, the Canadian secretary of state for External Affairs: "if the United States had to do all the fighting in Korea there was a real danger that public opinion [at home] . . . would favour preparing in isolation for the larger conflict ahead and writing its allies off." [83] The pursuit of allies paid off when the British and thirteen other countries joined the United States in sending military forces of various sizes and India dispatched an ambulance unit. [84]

But the war was still running against the South Koreans, with the capital, Seoul, falling on 28 June. As a result, on the next day Truman sanctioned direct air attacks on the North. In the early hours of the 30th MacArthur reported on his visit to the front in Korea, saying the southern forces were in headlong retreat. He urged the immediate dispatch of US ground troops, first with a regimental combat team but then to be quickly followed with two divisions. Truman sanctioned the sending of the regimental team. He then presided over a meeting at the White House with Acheson, Johnson, the Joint Chiefs of Staff, and the service secretaries, all of whom agreed that the two divisions should be sent immediately. The first troops landed the next day. The Americans also imposed a naval blockade of North Korea. [85]

Later that morning the president and Acheson again reported to congressional leaders. Acheson recalled that the decision to commit ground troops received a "general chorus of approval." But this was interrupted by the secretary's old adversary, Senator Kenneth Wherry (R-Nebraska), who questioned whether the president had the authority to take this action. Senator Alexander Smith (R-New Jersey) then proposed that they might seek a congressional resolution approving the president's actions. Truman asked Acheson to prepare a recommendation. Wherry's dissentient note was clearly a minority view, for the meeting closed with Representative Dewey Short (R-Missouri) asserting the near unanimous support of Congress for the president's leadership. [86]

Acheson presented his recommendation to a meeting at Blair House on 3 July. [87] He suggested that Truman should give a full report on Korea to a joint session of Congress. In his memoirs, he added that he did not think that the president needed to seek a resolution approving his actions but should rather "rest on his constitutional authority as Commander-in-Chief of the armed forces." [88] The official minutes, however, recorded him as saying something slightly different. Acheson proposed that the president's report should be followed by the introduction of a joint resolution approving action in Korea, and the initiative for this should come from Congress, not from Truman. So, Acheson's later account is right in saying that he did not suggest that Truman should seek a congressional resolution, but it misleads by implying that he never favored one if it came as a result of congressional initiative. This difference is important because *Present at the Creation* has been the main source for many accounts of this episode and has led critics to say that

Acheson never wanted congressional approval. However, he did not persevere with this view. In the subsequent discussion the prevailing view was that neither of these suggestions should be adopted. General Bradley, chairman of the JCS, and Senator Scott Lucas (Illinois), the Democratic majority leader, were in the forefront of opposition to Acheson's two points. Congress had just recessed for a week and the president was reluctant to recall them. In his memoirs, Acheson added that it was unlikely that a resolution would have softened the criticism of opponents but pursuit of the resolution might have done harm by offering the opportunity for criticism at a time of military defeats. He also told the Princeton seminar of former officials in 1954 that efforts to secure the resolution would have immobilized the administration.[89] A State Department memorandum of 3 July, published on 31 July, presented the detailed case for the legal authority of the president to commit US forces to war without the need to seek congressional authority, citing eighty-five occasions when the United States had used its armed forces overseas during peacetime.[90] The memorandum was not very convincing, as these were hardly precedents for involvement in a major war.

Nevertheless, Truman and Acheson believed that the president had the authority. They were also convinced that they enjoyed overwhelming support from Congress. This was certainly true in June and July, but the lack of a formal commitment by the politicians meant their support could easily melt away in the face of battlefield failures. The president and the secretary feared that a formal declaration of war by Congress might lead to an all-out war. Later, they worried that the Korean conflict was a deliberate distraction, drawing US forces into the peninsula while the Soviets took action in the strategically more important areas of Europe and the Middle East. They also believed that the rush of events required swift responses that could not wait on the slower processes of Congress. It proved politically unwise. The lack of formal endorsement by Congress meant this became Truman's and Acheson's war, and they could be blamed if things went wrong.[91]

The American commitment to Korea reflected Truman's and Acheson's desire to send a strong message of US resolve. Acheson believed that North Korea's blatant aggression required decisive action "as [a] symbol [of the] strength and determination of [the] west." Doing anything less would encourage "new aggressive action elsewhere" and demoralize "countries adjacent to [the] Soviet orbit." He sought to reassure allies, maintain the credibility of the UN, and demonstrate the administration's strong anti-communist credentials.[92] The president and the secretary also made clear their limited war aims. In a press conference on 29 June Truman called the North Korean attack a bandit raid and agreed with a reporter that the United States was undertaking a police action under the UN. The next day Acheson spoke to the American Newspaper Guild and declared that American action was "solely for the purpose of restoring the Republic of Korea to its status prior to the invasion."[93]

Acheson wanted the United States to demonstrate firm support for the South Koreans, but he heeded Kennan's advice not to allow U.S. intervention to escalate into a direct conflict with the Soviet Union. In a draft note on 28 June he declared that the commitment of US air and naval forces did not constitute a decision to engage in a major war with the Soviet Union, if the Soviets intervened.[94] At a meeting of the National Security Council on 29 June the president declared "we did not want any suggestion that we anticipate war with the Soviet Union" and added that he "wanted to be sure that we are not committed in Korea in such a way" that precluded meeting "threats elsewhere if they developed."[95]

Acheson encouraged a firm stance over Taiwan. He told the Norwegian ambassador that if Taiwan fell, then Japan and the Philippines would panic, that Asia might fall apart. Yet he also persuaded the president to avoid any escalation with Mao's China over the island. The administration wanted to secure Taiwan against any assault from the mainland but did not want to become embroiled in the question of Chinese administration of the island.[96] Truman was initially sympathetic to the offer of 33,000 Taiwanese troops to fight in Korea, but he turned it down in the face of Acheson's emphatic opposition.[97] In a special message to Congress on 19 July, the president explained the military neutralization of Taiwan. He did not want the island to "become embroiled in hostilities" and wanted Taiwanese issues to "be settled by peaceful means as envisaged in the Charter of the United Nations."[98]

There can be little doubt that Acheson was the dominant figure in shaping the American response to the assault by North Korea in the hectic first week of the conflict. The president acknowledged this in a personally written note: "Your initiative in immediately calling the Security Council of the UN on Saturday night and notifying me was the key to what followed afterwards. Had you not acted promptly in that direction we would have had to go into Korea alone."[99]

Acheson might not have been a great enthusiast for the UN, but he and the president ensured that each move they made enjoyed the backing of the Security Council. Indeed, American troops formed part of a UN force, though this was in name only at first, for no other power made a significant contribution during the first two months. On 7 July the Security Council created the Unified Command and gave the United States the right to select its supreme commander. On 10 July General Douglas MacArthur, Supreme Commander Allied Powers Japan, assumed responsibilities.[100] The appointment proved to be another hostage to fortune for Acheson and Truman. MacArthur was a vainglorious individual with an elevated sense of his own destiny, a talent for dramatic eloquence, and a magnetic personality. He was a "rabid Asia-firster," who felt thwarted by the European focus of the Truman administration, and seized the opportunity provided by the outbreak of war in Korea to try to reorientate national policy toward Asia. He attracted around him what amounted to a court of sycophants, something that encouraged his tendency to pursue his own line and feel unconstrained by political guidance. The general's high prestige with the JCS, significant figures in the Republican Party and with the American public "made him difficult to control."[101] Acheson and Truman were likely to face difficulties in giving direction to US policy.

As early as 25 August a problem arose when Acheson heard about the release to the press of MacArthur's message to the annual convention of the Veterans of Foreign Wars due to meet on the 28th. The general advocated an aggressive defense of Taiwan that clearly contradicted Truman's and Acheson's stated policy. The secretary and Harriman met the president the next day and agreed that this "insubordination could not be tolerated." Johnson was instructed to tell MacArthur to withdraw the statement. The defense secretary demurred, hesitating to cause embarrassment. It seems Acheson informed the president of Johnson's reticence. As a result Truman telephoned Johnson and dictated a message he should send to MacArthur directing him to withdraw his message. MacArthur duly complied with the instruction. Although the episode caused the president to consider relieving MacArthur as supreme commander, Acheson did not raise this possibility. Both men seem to have believed that the offense was not serious enough to merit such action.[102]

Meanwhile July and August saw South Korean and American forces pushed steadily backward, until they were confined to a small area around Pusan in the southeastern portion of the peninsula. But the growing presence of US forces—65,000 troops had arrived by early August—and their accompanying firepower meant this advance was slowed then stopped. The situation was sufficiently reassuring for Acheson that he began a week's holiday with his wife in the Adirondacks on 11 August.

BUILDING WESTERN DEFENSES

The North Korean attack in June 1950 led not only to American military intervention, but also to a dramatic reevaluation of defense expenditure in the United States and among NATO allies. Acheson took the lead in arguing for significant increases. Aggression in Korea seemed to confirm the dire predictions of NSC 68 and the need for much more substantial military spending. On 14 July he suggested that the president should "ask for money and if it is a question of asking for too little or too much, he should ask for too much."[103] Truman asked Congress for a $10 billion increase in military expenditure.[104] Some scholars believe that NSC 68 would have been implemented even without the Korean War, for the logic of American thinking, and Acheson's conception of situations of strength in particular, pushed policy in this direction. On the other hand, the president had resisted increased defense spending right up to the eve of North Korean assault, and only abandoned this position in July. By September NSC 68 was formally adopted.[105]

Acheson also leaned on the other members of NATO to spend more on defense. On 22 July he sent a message to American diplomats around the world saying that the president proposed a large increase in the US military effort and hoped that "other free nations will also undoubtedly want to increase their defenses."[106] Charles Spofford, the US deputy on the North Atlantic Council and who also chaired its meetings, assumed responsibility for coordinating these efforts. He found a favorable response in Britain, which agreed on 1 August to increase defense expenditure for the period April 1951 to April 1954 by £800 million to a total of £3.4 billion.[107] But Spofford and other State Department officials made clear that Acheson felt this was not sufficient, prompting the British to the raise the figure to £3.6 billion in September.[108]

Such was the concern to bolster Western defenses that Acheson broached the idea of allowing the Germans to rearm. In the May meetings he had urged his NATO allies to augment their defense spending, and had raised the prospect of a German military contribution, but had not pressed the case because it made "the French very nervous."[109] By September he overcame his reticence, following advice from Ambassadors Douglas in London and Bruce in Paris, and from John McCloy, US high commissioner in West Germany, all of whom were trusted counselors and friends.[110] So Acheson put the case for German rearmament to a meeting of the North Atlantic Council in New York in September. His proposal, which became known as the "one package," comprised four inseparable elements: substantial increases in US forces in Europe; an integrated NATO command; the creation of a supreme commander; and the inclusion of German units in a European force under the auspices of NATO. He spoke to Bevin and Schuman beforehand to tell them of his intentions. Bevin was enthusiastic about the unified force and the supreme commander. He was less keen on German rearmament, yet he had already received advice from his military chiefs that the involvement of German forces would be needed.[111] Schuman, however, declared France's "very strong and firm opposition."[112] At the council Acheson deployed all his great skills in presenting the US proposal: he was logical and clear in explaining its content, he placed it in a larger geopolitical context, and he argued his case with passion.[113] Still, he could not convince the French. In the following month, sensitive no doubt to their seemingly wholly negative attitude, the French put forward an alternative proposal. It suggested that a German battalion (a unit of between 300 and 1,000 men) should join a European army. But the so-called Pleven Plan, named after the French defense minister, René Pleven, was unlikely to work, given its insistence that the Germans take menial roles in the new army. As Acheson testified before the Senate, the French "continually put forward proposals that humiliate the Germans."[114]

FROM VICTORY AT INCHON TO CHINESE INTERVENTION

As Acheson pressed the case for the defense mobilization of the West, the Korean battlefield changed dramatically. On 15 September MacArthur launched a daring amphibious assault on Inchon behind the North Korean lines. The pincer movement by UN forces from Inchon and Pusan led to the wholesale defeat of the invaders, pushing them back across the frontier at the 38th parallel.[115] Under the original war aims of late June the UN forces would have halted at the border. The United States was wary of allowing the Korean War to widen into a conflict with the Soviet Union and China. So its forces were under strict orders not to pursue their assaults across the borders into these two countries.[116]

The restraint of June–July gave way to overexuberance at military success in September–October. Charles Bohlen and George Kennan, the State Department's leading experts on the Soviet Union, argued against the advance, but Acheson was bullish. Indeed the State Department had told the British on 4 July that it was thinking of going beyond the parallel.[117] That same month, George Elsey, administrative assistant to the president, 1949–1951, observed that "the Pentagon was making plans without knowing whether our forces are to stop at the 38th parallel or continue north to the Manchurian border."[118] On 17 July Truman ordered the NSC to consider what to do when UN forces reached the parallel. On 11 September he approved NSC 81/1, which sanctioned crossing the parallel, provided no major Soviet or Chinese forces had entered the peninsula.[119] The British prime minister, Clement Attlee, and his military chiefs, had doubts about this move, but Bevin's strong support for it and the desire to avoid charges of appeasement led the British cabinet to back the decision. Indeed, Britain sponsored the UN resolution proposing the move.[120] Because the Soviet representative had returned to the Security Council and could veto it, the Americans ensured the resolution went to the General Assembly where it passed on 7 October.

Even before passage of the resolution, fighting spread across the border. On 1 October South Korean forces crossed the parallel, with US and other UN troops following a week later. This deeply disturbed the Chinese communist government, which voiced blunt warnings to K. M. Panikkar, the Indian ambassador in Beijing: if US troops crossed the parallel, China would intervene.[121] The British received these messages with great concern. Bevin warned Acheson that Chinese intervention would be a catastrophe and pro-posed inviting Beijing to speak at the General Assembly debate on Korea.[122] Acheson and Truman remained remarkably unperturbed. When the president met MacArthur at Wake Island on 15 October, he appeared principally inter-ested in associating himself with the Korean victories before the impending congressional elections. MacArthur offered the reassurances that Truman wished to hear. Chinese intervention was unlikely; but if they attacked, they would suffer the "greatest slaughter."[123] Acheson was similarly unconcerned and hawkish, dismissing the dangers of Chinese intervention as no more than a bluff. By the end of October, however, the State Department confirmed that large numbers of Chinese forces had entered battle in the region just south of the Korean-Chinese border.[124]

Decisions on the 38th parallel and the Chinese warnings were made in collaboration with a new defense secretary. Truman asked Johnson to resign on 12 September after Harriman reported his intrigues with Robert Taft against Acheson. The president persuaded George Marshall to come out of retirement to replace Johnson. The president recorded in his diary that John-son displayed an "egotistical desire to run the whole government and had offended every member of the cabinet."[125] This brought a double success for Acheson: he escaped the tensions in working with Johnson and renewed his excellent relationship with Marshall. For all his eminence, Marshall deferred to Acheson as the senior cabinet officer and accepted that the key voice, below the president, should be that of the secretary of state. At the new defense secretary's request, Robert Lovett was appointed as deputy secretary of defense. Relations between the two departments improved markedly.[126]

Acheson undoubtedly interpreted the initial Chinese incursions through the filter of his preconceptions, while Marshall followed his lead, as he sought to familiarize himself with the situation. The secretary asked the UN to call on the Chinese to withdraw their troops, while, at the same time, reassuring Beijing that the UN forces would respect the Chinese frontier. This approach was undermined by MacArthur's plan to bomb a series of bridges on the Yalu River that marked the Korean-Chinese border. Acheson and Lovett only heard of this scheme three hours before it was scheduled to begin. The secretary telephoned Truman, who was visiting Kansas City, and persuaded him to halt the raids. Acheson was worried that they might cause the Soviets to intervene to aid the Chinese under the terms of the February 1950 Sino-Soviet treaty; and that they might cause a breech with the British, whom he had promised to consult before any attacks against Manchuria. The president agreed that the bombing should only proceed if it was vital to the safety of US forces. He ordered MacArthur to suspend the raids.[127]

The task of framing a response to the Chinese intervention was hindered by a lack of clarity about Beijing's intentions. MacArthur's reports to Wash-ington only added to the confusion. Acheson later wrote of the general's "mercurial temperament," of how between 4 and 7 November messages moved from a tone of calm confidence to alarmist warnings about men and material pouring over the Chinese border and then back to confidence about the military prospects.[128] After their initial intervention, Chinese forces withdrew from the battlefield between about 4 and 24 November.[129] Uncertainty about the Chinese produced caution in the British, who sought to stabilize the front. They suggested a buffer zone roughly along the 40th parallel. Acheson was sympathetic but unwilling to halt military operations.[130] The British did not press their case. Acheson and George Marshall wished to avoid confrontation with China. Yet they underestimated the danger, partly because they had not yet abandoned their hopes of success and partly because of the need to appear tough in the face of growing criticisms of the administration's Korean strategy. Although a CIA report of 8 November warned that Beijing could probably put 350,000 troops into the field within sixty days, it did not sway them.

Omar Bradley, chairman of the JCS, encapsulated Washington's thinking in his memoirs: North Korea was a Soviet project, making Soviet intervention more likely than a Chinese one; and any Chinese intervention meant Soviet intervention—a probable sign that Moscow was moving toward global war. Acheson told the Senate Foreign Relations Committee that "the Russians are behind all these movements" and willing to "undertake risks . . . which might lead . . . to the possibility of general war." Yet he shared the JCS's view that Chinese intervention was not conclusive proof of a Soviet intention to launch global war. The JCS were committed to limited war, encouraged pursuit of a political solution, and proposed no change in the instructions to the UN commander. But they recommended that the United States should develop its plans on the basis that the risk of global war was increasing.[131] Official Washington viewed the situation through the wrong prism, seeing Soviet moves as decisive, failing to recognize the entirely understandable Chinese concerns about the arrival of major forces at their border, and dismissing their willingness to launch a serious military response.

Meanwhile, the lull in Chinese action on the battlefield seemed to reduce the perils of confrontation, and so MacArthur was allowed to bomb the Yalu River bridges, while South Korean and U.S. forces advanced to the Yalu. This produced a wave of optimism at MacArthur's headquarters and in the American press, but Acheson was more circumspect.[132] At a conference on 15 November he stressed the need to remove any misunderstandings held by the Chinese. At the same meeting, assistant secretary Dean Rusk admitted the administration did not know why the Chinese had intervened.[133] But the momentum lay with MacArthur. On 21 November the NSC agreed that MacArthur's offensive should proceed, though Acheson expressed concern at MacArthur's decision to divide his forces with the US 8th Army to the west and X Corps to the east. The NSC's only concession to diplomacy was to agree that Acheson should contact the Chinese, which he tried and failed to do.[134] The secretary's support for the UN offensive was undoubtedly influenced by domestic pressure. The Republicans made major gains in the congressional elections of 7 November, reducing the Democrats' majorities in the senate from 12 to 2 and in the House from 92 to 35, on the basis of sharp and sometimes vicious attacks on Acheson and his Asian policies.[135] Even some Democrats blamed him for the failures in Korea. Neither Truman nor Acheson wanted to be charged with denying MacArthur victory. So MacArthur launched a new offensive on 24 November. Within days UN forces were overwhelmed by over 300,000 organized Chinese forces. MacArthur declared, "We face an entirely new war."[136]

The initial reaction of Acheson and Truman to this disturbing news was a mixture of tough talk and reassurances to Americans and international allies. On 29 November Acheson addressed the National Council of Churches of Christ in Cleveland. He spoke of the situation in grand terms, declaring that the "nation's peril is our challenge." He placed the ultimate responsibility for aggression in Korea on the Soviet Union. This evoked concern in London about escalation,[137] but what really unsettled the British government was Truman's press conference on the morning of 30 November. After the president declared that the United States was ready to deploy "every weapon we have," a reporter asked if this meant there was active consideration of the use of the atomic bomb. Truman replied: "There has always been active consideration of its use." The president also said that the "military commander in the field will have charge of the use of the weapons."[138] Ambassador Franks tried to reassure London, saying that Truman had issued a clarification, which "makes absolutely clear that no new action is under consideration and that there has been no change in the general situation in regard to the atomic bomb."[139] Before Franks's telegram arrived, the British parliament held an anguished debate, putting the prime minister under pressure to act. Attlee told an emergency cabinet meeting on the evening of the 30th that "urgent action was necessary to allay public anxiety."[140] He quickly arranged to meet Truman in Washington between 4 and 8 December.[141] The French government was also deeply worried: prime minister Pleven and foreign minister Schuman traveled to London for talks with Attlee and Bevin and backed the British desire to avoid escalation and any use of atomic weapons.[142]

Disquiet among allies added to the atmosphere of anxiety in Washington. For all Acheson's and Truman's tough talk, the American capital was in turmoil. The massive Chinese intervention produced vociferous denunciations from the usual Republican critics. Acheson had faced assaults since 1946 from Senators Taft and Wherry, whom he later described as his two most implacable opponents until McCarthy began his attacks. Criticisms had first surfaced in August when UN forces were retreating and senator Wherry had talked of the "blood of our boys" being on Acheson's shoulders.[143] In December Republicans in Congress voted unanimously in the House and by 20 to 5 in the Senate declaring a lack of confidence in Acheson, who was stoutly defended by the president.[144] Attacks also came from less partisan, more respected sources. The distinguished journalist Walter Lippmann urged Acheson to step down as secretary because he had lost the support of Congress. Lippmann heard from the *New York Times* journalist, James Reston, how Acheson had dismissed a peace offer by the Chinese proposing a cease-fire, saying it was merely a Soviet device to prevent NATO from completing its new military command structures. It prompted him to write a column on 14 December calling for Acheson's resignation, since his policies were a "disaster abroad," brought "disunity at home," and failed to "command general support in Congress." In a personal letter he explained how he disliked helping the attacks of the McCarthyites, but he did not see how Acheson could hope to be effective if he "does not have the substantial confidence of the country."[145]

Amid this negative onslaught, American policymakers engaged in anguished debate about the meaning of Chinese actions and the best response. Charles Bohlen, a Soviet expert who was minister at the Paris embassy, became concerned that "there was no major official in the administration experienced in dealing with Soviet affairs." He contacted the other leading State Department authority on the Soviets, George Kennan, who was in Princeton on leave, and "urged him to go to Washington and impress on Marshall and Secretary Acheson the underlying reasons for the turn of events in Korea." Acheson "enthusiastically accepted his offer of temporary help."[146] Kennan's arrival at the State Department on Sunday 3 December brought a voice of restraint among the "jittery reactions and wild counsels." He was pleased to observe Acheson's "characteristic spirit and wit, which no crisis and no weariness seemed to extinguish." He told the secretary that he regarded the prospects as poor: if the UN forces were not to appear weak and have any chance of negotiating a ceasefire, then they would need to demonstrate their ability to stabilize the front.[147] The next day he wrote to Acheson urging him to be candid in government discussions and with the American public about this major failure and disaster. This need not result in the loss of US self-confidence or the country's bargaining power. The letter so impressed Acheson that he read it to his State Department advisers, and quoted its entire text in his memoirs, describing it as "so wise and inspiriting."[148]

Talks between Attlee and Truman were held from 4 to 8 December. They covered a number of issues: arrangements for European defense, Britain's rearmament program and the need for help with supplies of raw materials, and British proposals for improved liaison. In each of these areas the British and Americans had a meeting of minds, though Acheson bemoaned Attlee's elusiveness on Germany and European defense. The main topic was Korea and its implications for the general situation in the Far East. Attlee and his team agreed with Truman and Acheson on the need to remain in Korea, to localize the conflict, and to seek a ceasefire. But the British were skeptical about the application of economic sanctions and pursuit of subversive activities against Mao's China. They were also ready to accept an armistice in Korea as part of a wider settlement in the region. [149] For Acheson this was a step too far. As the secretary told Franks, he and the president "were not reconciled to the concessions which would be necessary to make a negotiated settlement possible." [150] The other important issue in the discussions was the atomic bomb; indeed, fear of its use had triggered Attlee's visit. Despite the prime minister's best efforts, the talks witnessed a further watering down of British influence. Attlee skillfully led Truman to declare that they were partners on this matter and he would not use the weapon without consulting Britain. Acheson intervened, took the president aside and explained that constitutionally he could not do this. So the agreed text spoke only of keeping Britain informed: "The President told the Prime Minister that it was also his desire to keep the Prime Minister at all times informed of developments which might bring about a change in the situation." [151]

A few days after the discussions with Attlee, Acheson traveled to Brussels for a meeting of the North Atlantic Council, where he pressed forcefully for a substantial strengthening of Western defenses. The Americans were already setting an example by tripling their planned military budget for fiscal year 1951 to $48.2 billion. [152] Acheson's advocacy worked. In the course of little more than a year military expenditure by European members of NATO rose from approximately $5.3 billion to $8.2 billion. [153] The Council also agreed to establish a unified force, supplemented by further US forces, and to create the position of NATO supreme commander. Acheson declared American willingness to appoint to the post Dwight D. Eisenhower, who had led the invasion of Western Europe in 1944.

There was only limited progress on German rearmament. The French retained their opposition to German troops in a NATO force, preferring them to be part of what they now called the European Defense Community. Paris did at least concede that the unit for the German contribution should be, not a battalion, but a regimental combat team of approximately 6,000 men. As a temporary expedient that would sustain the momentum, Acheson authorized a compromise: the two approaches would be pursued in tandem. [154] But he grew increasingly frustrated at the failure to find a way forward: the remainder of his secretaryship witnessed repeated failure to make progress.

THE GREAT DEBATE AND GENERAL MACARTHUR

Truman's announcement on 19 December of the decisions to appoint Eisenhower and commit further US forces finally unleashed what came to be called the "great debate," which had been simmering since the Chinese intervention. On 20 December the former president, Herbert Hoover, argued that the United States should not send any more money or troops until the Europeans had organized their armies to provide a "sure dam against the red flood." Acheson called this "quivering in a storm cellar." The highpoint of the first phase of the debate came with senator Taft's 10,000-word speech on 5 January 1951. Taft declared that the Soviets did not want war and Washington should not provoke them unnecessarily. The United States should build up its air force and navy, rather than its army. Meanwhile, it should honor its commitment to NATO but only with a token force, and, in any case, Truman could not send American forces abroad without congressional approval.[155] Wherry tabled a resolution embodying this idea. The debate rumbled on until the senate adopted an amended version of the Wherry resolution in April by a vote of 69 to 21. It granted Eisenhower four US divisions in Europe but required the president to ask Congress for any additional forces. Taft felt obliged to support it, since it included the requirement on the president to seek congressional sanction for further force deployments. As James Patterson says of this phase of the great debate, it ended "with the administration in tenuous command of its policy."[156]

If strengthening of European defense was one strand of Acheson's pugnacious response to collapse in Korea, strong words at the UN was another. For all his frequent declarations that actions mattered more than words, he became firmly attached to the idea of a UN resolution condemning the Chinese communists for their aggression. Attlee and the Canadians counseled against such a step but their reticence only delayed the Americans, who introduced their draft on 20 January 1951. Over the course of the next ten days, Acheson wore down British and Canadian opposition and they eventually agreed to support an amended resolution which offered a less automatic route to sanctions. The resolution passed on 1 February.[157]

By this time the military situation in Korea had improved, thanks to the arrival of General Matthew B. Ridgway as the new commander of the 8th Army after the death of General Walton Walker on 23 December. Ridgway showed vigorous, courageous, and thoughtful leadership as he launched a successful new offensive in late January. By adept use of intelligence he identified major Chinese concentrations of forces and subjected them to devastating air and artillery attacks and broke their offensive capabilities. He followed this up with driving assaults by UN forces, which brought a series of victories culminating in the recapture of Seoul in March 1951. Ridgway disproved MacArthur's pessimistic reports on the military situation. As

Acheson observed, while MacArthur was fighting Washington, Ridgway was fighting the war.[158] Chastened by the Chinese intervention, Acheson told the British ambassador that the Americans did not want to extend hostilities; and that, despite his expansive rhetoric, MacArthur was receiving instructions from Washington urging restraint in the use of UN forces.[159]

MacArthur was unable to accept such restrictions. At the height of the crisis on 6 December, Truman had sent the UN commander a clear order not to speak publicly about the war. As early as August 1950, MacArthur had shown his inability to follow guidance from the JCS and shown little respect for Truman as commander-in-chief. The series of victories up to late November had protected him; and, although the defeats by the Chinese had made him vulnerable, he had avoided presidential censure. Ridgway's successes in spring 1951 seemed to encourage MacArthur to become reckless and arrogant once more. He overstepped the mark and triggered the second phase in the great debate. The imminence of a presidential statement on the possibility of a ceasefire led him to make his views public. On 24 March the general issued his own declaration demanding that China begin talks with the UN Command or face the destruction of its ports and cities. This was clearly designed to undermine the prospects for discussions, win support from the American public, and compel Truman and Acheson to accept his plan for what he called total victory.[160] Although the president displayed what Acheson described as a mixture of "disbelief and controlled fury," Truman did not immediately dismiss the general. By 5 April the president had decided MacArthur must go; and this was confirmed when the Republican minority leader in the House, Joseph W. Martin, read a personal letter from the general saying "we must win. There is no substitute for victory."[161] On 11 April MacArthur was relieved of all his commands. Ridgway succeeded him.[162]

What followed was an astonishing public outcry, which brought the great debate to a crescendo. Richard Rovere and Arthur Schlesinger speak of a "violent discharge of political passion."[163] The British diplomat, Paul Gore-Booth, reported that MacArthur's removal "has let loose a flood of nastiness in this country such as I have never seen before."[164] MacArthur returned to the United States and received a hero's welcome, while Truman and Acheson faced public outrage: effigies of the president and the secretary were burned in public.[165] On 19 April MacArthur addressed a joint session of Congress. The Republicans then secured a congressional hearing into the general's dismissal. MacArthur testified for three days, Marshall and Bradley each spoke for six days, and Acheson faced questioning for eight days. The proceedings produced over two million words on the record. Smith describes the published *Hearings* as "one of the richest single sources for an understanding of Acheson's style, his manner with Congress, and thoughts on foreign policy." The secretary "spoke clearly, calmly, and sometimes from notes as he presented Asian policy since the Second World War."[166] He offered an authoritative commentary on the central purposes of American foreign policy since 1945 and the seriousness of the Soviet challenge. He also addressed the hazards involved in expanding the war into China. This might bring in the Soviet Union, risk escalation to a third world war, and would weaken relations with some allies. Furthermore, he enumerated the sequence of difficulties with MacArthur. Acheson's presentation was commanding and impressed even his opponents.[167] But the testimony of Marshall, Bradley, and the JCS proved the decisive contribution: it took the sting out of MacArthur's argument. They all disagreed with his strategy; Bradley aptly and succinctly said it would "involve us in the wrong war, at the wrong place, at the wrong time, and with the wrong enemy."[168] Although it was not immediately clear at the time, the undermining of MacArthur's case for a wider war at the hearings helped to strengthen Truman's and Acheson's case for a limited war.

As the MacArthur affair flared and then subsided, the new UN commander, Matthew Ridgway, shared the Truman administration's readiness to pursue ceasefire talks. Secret discussions took place between George Kennan of the State Department and Jakob Malik, Soviet ambassador to the UN. On 8 July liaison officers met at Kaesong. Two days later formal talks began.[169]

The stabilization of the front and the opening of armistice talks offered Acheson a respite from the avalanche of criticisms. For all his resilience, he was a politically battered figure. The domestic attacks and the Korean War had reinforced his "situations of strength" rhetoric, his urging of the need for greater military strength. But there was always more to his outlook than tough talk and military might. In February 1951 he wrote a reply to the father of a corporal in the US Marines, who had expressed his bewilderment at having to fight in Korea. He showed a parent's appreciation of how the son's military service had dashed the promises of youth. He placed the issue in a larger framework, saying the problem was the age-old one of good versus evil, the need to resist threats to liberty. But he also emphasized that it was a new difficulty—the Soviet challenge to American efforts to build a peaceful postwar order. He declared "we are standing with one foot in the world of our hopes for a future world order among nations, and the other foot in the world of power" so as to resist Soviet attempts at "extending their rule over the entire world." In answer to the son's doubts about the value of losses of life in Korea, he replied that the sacrifices showed that those who loved freedom and believed in the UN were willing to fight for them. By standing firm they were trying to avoid taking the road to another world war. He closed by saying what was important was not that the young Marine felt that he and the administration were right on a particular issue but that he retained his faith in the ideals on which this nation was founded.[170]

Acheson had experienced the most intense, geographically wide-ranging, and challenging period of his career. He and Truman were proud of their defense of South Korea but had seriously misjudged the Chinese. Although they had weathered the storm in the winter of 1950–1951, Korea was in stalemate. Acheson would have been wiser to have adopted the same approach to the French in Indochina as the one he deployed toward the Dutch East Indies and pressured them to leave. On the positive side, he had brokered an agreement to restrict arms supplies to the Middle East; and had bolstered NATO defenses, though he had failed to resolve the involvement of German forces. As he entered the final phase of his secretaryship, he faced problems across the globe—from the French fight in Indochina and the making of a peace settlement with Japan in Asia to German rearmament and building up NATO in Europe to the rise of new difficulties in the Middle East.

NOTES

1. Smith, *Acheson*, 167–168; *Congressional Record*, vol. 96, 81st Congress, 2nd Session, 1338–1340 (McMahon), 1473–1478 [Tydings], 2 February 1950. *Present at Creation*, 377–378.

2. Acheson, "Peace Goal Demands Firm Resolve," *DOSB* 22:555 (20 February 1950), 272–274; Acheson, "'Total Diplomacy' to Strengthen US Leadership for Human Freedom," *DOSB* 22:559 (20 March 1950), 427–429; *Present at Creation*, 378–379.

3. L of C, Jessup Papers, box I:140, M-L McCarran Committee, McCarthy Charges 1951 folder, Department of State Press Release, 9 August 1951, containing these quotations; also at *DOSB* 25:634 (20 August 1951), 314–315.

4. NARA, RG 59, State Department, General Records of the Office of the Executive Secretariat, Summaries of Daily Meetings, 1949–1952, box 1, Summary of Daily Meeting with the Secretary, 13 February, 21 February, and 8 March 1950.

5. Truman to Tydings, 3 April 1950, available at www.presidency.ucsb.edu (viewed 13 August 2014). See also Smith, *Acheson*, note at 439.

6. L of C, Jessup Papers, box I:140, Subject File, 1924–1959, M-L McCarthy Hearings Misc. March 1950 folder, Joseph P. Kamp, *America Betrayed* (New York: Constitutional Education League, 1950), 31, 34.

7. James T. Patterson, *Mr. Republican* (Boston, 1972), 445–449; idem., *Grand Expectations: The United States, 1945–1974* (New York: Oxford University Press, 1996), 202–203.

8. Yale, Acheson Private Papers, box 6, folder 78, reel 5, p. 0240, Clifford to Acheson, 21 March 1950.

9. Stimson letter, *New York Times* (27 March 1950), 22; Herblock cartoon "Somebody Around Here Is Helping the Communists!" *New York Times* (26 March 1950).

10. TNA, FO 371/81644, AU10511/3, Franks to Bevin, 25 April 1950.

11. TNA, FO 371/81615, AU1016/10G, FO to Washington, telegram 1586, 24 March 1950, FO 115/4478, Franks to FO, telegram 1006, 28 March 1950.

12. TNA FO 371/81611, AU1013/12, Franks to FO, dispatch 159(S), 18 March 1950. See also, James Reston, "Acheson and Congress: A Delicate Situation," *New York Times* (5 March 1950): Acheson "won so little support from his friends" in Congress over his remarks on Hiss.

13. *Present at Creation*, 373.

14. Truman, "Annual Budget Message to Congress: Fiscal 1951," 9 January 1950, available at www.presidency.ucsb.edu (viewed 15 August 2014); Michael J. Hogan, *A Cross of Iron: Harry S. Truman and the Origins of the National Security State, 1945–1954* (Cambridge: Cambridge University Press, 1998), 285, 303–304.

15. *FRUS 1950* I, 234–290, NSC 68, 14 April 1950. For evaluations of NSC 68, see Ernest R. May, ed., *American Cold War Strategy: Interpreting NSC-68* (Boston: Bedford Books/St.

Martin's Press, 1993), Steven L. Rearden, "Frustrating the Kremlin Design: Acheson and NSC 68," in Douglas Brinkley, ed., *Dean Acheson and the Making of US Foreign Policy* (Basingstoke: Macmillan, 1993), 159–175.

16. Interview with Nitze, in Isaacson and Thomas, *Wise Men*, 499.

17. Hogan, *A Cross of Iron*, 303–304; McMahon, *Acheson*, 110.

18. HSTL, Oral History Interview with Edward W. Barrett, 9 July 1971, p. 71, available at www.trumanlibrary.org/oralhist/barrette.htm (viewed 20 January 2017); Edward W. Barratt, *Truth is Our Weapon* (New York: Funk & Wagnalls, 1953); Truman address to American Society of Newspaper Editors, 20 April 1950, available at www.presidency.ucsb.edu (viewed 28 August 2014). The files for this campaign are at NARA, RG 306, USIA, Press and Publication Service/Publication Division, Master File Copies of Pamphlets and Leaflets, 1953–1984, box 4, "Campaign of Truth" folder.

19. Roosevelt famously said that France had controled Indochina "for nearly a hundred years but the people are worse off than they were at the beginning"; *FRUS Conferences at Cairo and Tehran*, 872–873, FDR memorandum for Hull, January 24, 1944.

20. Mark Atwood Lawrence, *Assuming the Burden: Europe and the American Commitment to War in Vietnam* (Berkeley: University of California Press, 2005), 68–69, 74–75.

21. *FRUS 1946* VIII, 77–78; Lawrence, *Assuming the Burden*, 173, 176.

22. Robert McMahon, *The Limits of Empire* (New York: Columbia University Press, 1999), 32–33; McMahon, *Acheson*, 120; *FRUS 1949* IV, 258–261, memorandum of conversation, 31 March 1949.

23. Senate Foreign Relations Committee, *Reviews of World Situation, 1949–1950*, 90 (Acheson testimony 12 October 1949).

24. NARA, RG59 State Department, Lot 53D444, Records of Executive Secretariat, Records of Dean Acheson, box 13, Memorandums of Conversation, 1947–1952, September 1949 folder, memorandum of conversation, 15 September 1949. See also *FRUS 1949* IV, Part 1, 654–661. *FRUS 1950* VI, 711, editorial note.

25. See *FRUS 1949* VII, Part 2, 736–737, secretary of state to certain diplomatic offices, 8 May 1949; and Acheson's testimony of 10 January 1950 in Senate Foreign Relations Committee, *Reviews of World Situation, 1949–1950*, 152–154.

26. Roger Buckley, *Occupation Diplomacy* (Cambridge: Cambridge University Press, 1982), 162 (September 1949 British pressure for a draft Japanese treaty, which was produced on 13 October 1949); Lawrence, *Assuming the Burden*, 227–229.

27. *FRUS 1949* VII, Part 2, 1215–1220, NSC 48/2, "The Position of the United States with respect to Asia," 30 December 1949.

28. *DOSB* 22:555 (20 February 1950), 291–292.

29. See, for example, *FRUS 1949* VII, Part 1, 105–110, Bruce to Acheson, 11 December 1949 , and *FRUS 1950* VI, 730–733, memorandum of conversation, 16 February 1950.

30. *FRUS 1950* VI, 711–715, Problem Paper: Military Aid for Indochina, 1 February 1950.

31. See Senate Foreign Relations Committee, *Reviews of World Situation, 1949–1950*, 268 (Jessup's testimony, 29 March 1950), 266 (Acheson's testimony, 29 March 1950); Lawrence, *Assuming the Burden*, 266–267.

32. HSTL, Acheson Memoranda of Conversation, memorandum of conversation, 9 March 1950, available at www.trumanlibrary.org/whistlestop/study_collections/achesonmemos/view.php?documentid=66-6_19&documentYear=1950&documentVersion=both (viewed January 2017).

33. *FRUS 1950*, 744–747, NSC 64, 27 February 1950.

34. *FRUS 1950* III, 1007–1013, secretary of state to acting secretary of state, 8 May 1950.

35. *FRUS 1950* III, 1038, US Delegation to Webb, 11 May 1950.

36. Senate Foreign Relations Committee, *Reviews of World Situation, 1949–1950*, 268 (Jessup's testimony, 29 March 1950), 293 (Acheson's testimony 1 May 1950), 267 (Acheson's testimony, 29 March 1950).

37. McMahon, *Limits of Empire*, 62.

38. Kennan to Acheson, 23 August 1950, available at www.trumanlibrary.org/whistlestop/study_collections/achesonmemos/view.php?documentid=ki-14-7&documentYear=1950&doc-

umentVersion=both (viewed 20 January 2017); see also Miscamble, *Kennan*, 277, and Smith, *Acheson*, 316.

39. 82nd Congress, 1st Session, Senate Armed Services Committee and the Foreign Relations Committee, *Hearings To Conduct An Inquiry into the Military Situation in the Far East and the Facts Surrounding the Relief of General of the Army Douglas MacArthur from His Assignment in that Area, Part 3* [3 parts] (Washington, DC: USGPO, 1951) [hereafter *MacArthur Hearings*], 1772 (Acheson testimony, 2 June 1951).

40. *FRUS 1952–1954* XII, Part 1, 69–75, NSC meeting, 5 March 1952; Smith, *Acheson*, 324.

41. NARA, RG 59, State Department, General Records of the Office of the Executive Secretariat, Summaries of Daily Meetings, 1949–1952, box 2, Secretary's Daily Meeting, 8 February 1952.

42. *FRUS 1952–1954* XIII, Part 1, 141–144, memorandum of conversation, 12 May 1952; *FRUS 1952–1954* XII, Part 1, 127–134, NSC 124/2, "United States Objectives and Course of Action With Respect to Southeast Asia," 25 June 1952. *FRUS 1952–1954* XIII, Part 1, 210–213; Smith, *Acheson*, 326–328.

43. *FRUS 1952–1954* XIII, Part 1, 323–325, memorandum of conversation by secretary of state, 22 December 1952.

44. "Mr Acheson answers some questions," *New York Times Book Review* (12 October 1969).

45. George C. Herring, *America's Longest War: The United States and Vietnam, 1945–1975* (New York: McGraw-Hill, 1996), 24–25.

46. NARA, RG 59, State Department, General Records of the Office of the Executive Secretariat, Summaries of Daily Meetings, 1949–1952, box 1, Summary of Daily Meeting with the Secretary, 7 March 1950.

47. Acheson, *Sketches*, 41–46 covers Acheson's being told, Bevin's response to Acheson and talks between Acheson, Bevin, and Schuman about the announcement.

48. *DBPO*, 2nd, I, No. 2, pp. 2–5, note from French ambassador in London to Mr. Bevin, 9 May 1950.

49. Acheson, *Sketches*, 44.

50. Acheson, *Sketches*, 45. Bevin's biographer says this argument might have worked rhetorically for Acheson but it was not accurate, for the French were annoyed by the way devaluation was handled; Alan Bullock, *Ernest Bevin: Foreign Secretary* (New York: W. W. Norton, 1983), 720–722.

51. *Present at Creation*, 385.

52. *DBPO*, 2nd, I, 105–106 (Franks to Bevin, Tel. No. 1547, 29 May 1950), 259–260 (Franks to Makins, 14 July 1950).

53. *DBPO*, 2nd, II, 70, Brief for the UK Delegation, 21 April 1950.

54. *FRUS 1950* III, 869–881, "Essential Elements of US-UK Relations," 19 April 1950.

55. L of C, Harriman Papers, container 270, Country File: U.K., Douglas to Paris, Cable No. 791, 7 May 1950.

56. *DBPO*, 2nd, II, 242–244 (Agreed Anglo-American Report: Continued Consultation and Coordination of Policy), 293 (Acheson's remarks at 10 May 1950 meeting); *Princeton Seminars*, microfilm, roll 3, frames 832–837, 10 October 1953; *Present at Creation*, 387–388. See also Lawrence S. Kaplan, "Dean Acheson and the Atlantic Community," in Brinkley, ed., *Acheson and Making of US Foreign Policy*, 32.

57. *DBPO* 2nd II, 6–7, Record of meeting, 10 May 1950.

58. *FRUS 1950* III, 94–125, which contains US proposals for improving organization and building up defense forces, and the agreement reached; *DBPO*, 2nd, II, 379–381, containing CAB 129/40, CP(50) 118, 26 May 1950.

59. Rudy Abramson, *Spanning the Century: The Life of W. Averell Harriman* (New York: William Morrow, 1992), 440.

60. *House of Commons Debates*, Vol. 433, cols. 433, 985–989.

61. *FRUS 1947* V, 1049.

62. John Acacia, *Clark Clifford: The Wise Man of Washington* (Lexington: University Press of Kentucky, 2009), 104–109; *FRUS 1948* V, [972–978], 975; Clifford, *Counsel*, 9–15.

63. *FRUS 1949* VI, 876–878, Pinkerton to Acheson, 28 March 1950.

64. *FRUS 1949* VI, 944–947, memorandum of conversation, 26 April 1950.

65. *FRUS 1949* VI, 957, Truman to Ethridge, 29 April 1950.

66. John B. Judis, *Genesis: Truman, American Jews and the Origins of the Arab-Israeli Conflict* (New York: Farrar, Straus and Giroux, 2014), 343.

67. *FRUS 1949* VI, 1060–1063 (acting secretary to the president, 27 May 1949), 1072–1074 (acting secretary to embassy in Israel, 28 May 1949).

68. NARA, RG 59, State Department, General Records of the Office of the Executive Secretariat, Summaries of Daily Meetings, 1949–1952, box 1, Summary of Secretary's Daily Meeting, 15 April 1949. *FRUS 1950* VI, 1339, (NSC 47/1, 1 September 1949), 1430–1440 (NSC 47/2, 17 October 1949, which recommended both US assistance in the task of reconciling Israeli-Arab differences, and collaboration with Britain so as to achieve a stable Middle East). *FRUS 1950* VI, 1455–1456 (the possibility of a $20 million credit for Israel).

69. Peter L. Hahn, *The United States, Great Britain and Egypt, 1945–1956* (Chapel Hill: University of North Carolina Press, 1991), 82–83, 97–102; *FRUS 1950* III, 1129; *DBPO* 2nd II, 284–286, 289–290; *FRUS 1950* V, 167–168; *DOSB* 22:570 (5 June 1950), 886; Shlomo Slonim. "Origins of the 1950 tripartite declaration on the Middle East," *Middle Eastern Studies* 23:2 (1987), 135–149.

70. *Present at Creation*, 337.

71. Princeton, John Foster Dulles Papers, box 47, Acheson, Dean 1950 folder, Dulles to Acheson, 29 March 1950, Acheson to Dulles, 30 April 1950.

72. "Mr. Acheson Answers Some Questions," *New York Times* (12 October 1969).

73. Princeton, Dulles Papers, box 47, Acheson, Dean 1950 folder, Vandenberg to Acheson, 31 March 1950. Bentley Historical Library, Ann Arbor, Michigan, Arthur H. Vandenberg Papers, box 3, microfilm roll 5, Acheson to Vandenberg, 10 April 1950; NARA, RG 59, State Department, General Records of the Office of the Executive Secretariat, Summaries of Daily Meetings, 1949–1952, box 1, Secretary's Daily Meeting, 8 August 1949; James Reston, "Dulles Named US Adviser to Renew Bipartisan Policy," *New York Times* (7 April 1950), 1; Chace, *Acheson*, 260–262.

74. *Present at Creation*, 410–411; Isaacson and Thomas, *Wise Men*, 509–510; Abramson, *Harriman*, 445–446.

75. *Princeton Seminars*, roll 4 [reel 3, track 1, p. 9], 13 February 1954.

76. For a detailed account of the events of 25–30 June, see Acheson, *The Korean War* (New York: W. W. Norton, 1971), 15–31, which gathers together, in slightly revised form, the separate sections on the war in *Present at the Creation*. See also, Truman, *Years of Trial and Hope*, 377–391.

77. *FRUS 1950* VII, 155–156, text of resolution.

78. *FRUS 1950* VII, 157–161, Blair House meeting, 25 June 1950.

79. Frank Costigliola, ed., *The George Kennan Diaries* (New York: W. W. Norton, 2014), 250 (26 June 1950 entry).

80. *FRUS 1950* VII, 178–183, Blair House meeting 26 June 1950.

81. *FRUS 1950* VII, 186–187 (draft text of statement), 200–202 (meeting with congressional leaders, 27 June 1950), 202–203 (text of statement), 211 (text of resolution).

82. TNA, CAB 128/17, CM 39(50), 27 June 1950; TNA, FO 371/84057, FK 1015/40, FO to Washington, Tel. No. 2904, 27 June 1950, and Franks to FO, Tel. Nos. 1771 and 1772, 27 June 1950; PREM 8/1405 Part I, Franks to FO, Tel. No. 1773, 27 June 1950; *FRUS 1950* VII, 187 note 3, 207 (decision to adopt resolution, 27 June 1950).

83. William Stueck, *Rethinking the Korean War* (Princeton, NJ: Princeton University Press, 2002), 222.

84. They were Australia, Belgium, Canada, Colombia, Ethiopia, France, Great Britain, Greece, Luxembourg, the Netherlands, New Zealand, the Philippines, Thailand, and Turkey.

85. *FRUS 1950* VII, 255 (editorial note); Truman, *Years of Trial and Hope*, 390–391; *Present at Creation*, 412.

86. *Present at Creation*, 413.

87. *FRUS 1950* VII, 286–291; *Present at Creation*, 414.

88. *Present at Creation*, 414.

89. *Present at Creation*, 415; Chace, *Acheson*, 288; *Princeton Seminars*, roll 4, reel 3, track 1, 13 February 1954.

90. Department of State Memorandum, "Authority of the President to repel the Attack in Korea," 3 July 1950, *DOSB* 23:578 (31 July 1950), 173–178.

91. *Princeton Seminars*, roll 4, [reel 3, track 1], 13 February 1954; Walter LaFeber, *The American Age: US Foreign Policy at Home and Abroad, 1750 to the Present*, 2nd ed. (New York: W. W. Norton, 1994), 515.

92. Acheson to Ambassador Kirk, 28 June 1950, quoted in Stueck, *Rethinking the Korean War*, 81; Warren I. Cohen, *The Cambridge History of American Foreign Relations. Volume IV: America in the Age of Soviet Power, 1941–1991* (Cambridge: Cambridge University Press, 1993), 68.

93. Truman press conference, 29 June 1950, available at www.presidency.ucsb.edu (viewed 28 February 2012); Dean Acheson, "Act of Aggression in Korea," *DOSB* 23:575 (10 July 1950), 46.

94. Costigliola, ed., *Kennan Diaries*, 251 (entry for 27 June), 253–254 (entry for 28 June); *FRUS 1950* VII, 217, draft policy statement prepared by secretary of state, 28 June 1950.

95. NARA, RG 59, Lot 53D444, State Department, Records of Executive Secretariat, Records of Dean Acheson, box 13, Memorandums of Conversation, 1947–1952, June–August 1950 folder.

96. Acheson Memoranda of Conversation, memorandum of conversation with Morgenstierne, 30 June 1950, available at www.trumanlibrary.org/whistlestop/study_collections/achesonmemos/view.php?documentid=67-02_46&documentYear=1950&documentVersion=both (viewed 20 January 2017); *FRUS 1950* VII, 180 [178–183], memorandum of conversation, 26 June 1950.

97. *FRUS 1950* VII, 239, memorandum by Merchant, 29 June 1950; *Present at Creation*, 411–412, Truman, *Years of Trial and Hope*, 389–390.

98. Truman's special message to Congress, 19 July 1950, available at www.presidency.ucsb.edu (viewed 3 October 2014).

99. *Present at Creation*, 415.

100. *FRUS 1950* VII, 329, 333n; *DOSB* 23:576 (17 July 1950), 83.

101. William Stueck, *The Korean War: An International History* (Princeton, NJ: Princeton University Press, 1995), 65–66; *Present at Creation*, 424.

102. *Present at Creation*, 423–424, Truman, *Years of Trial and Hope*, 404–408.

103. *FRUS 1950* I, 344–345, memorandum of conversation, 14 July 1950.

104. Truman's special message to Congress, 19 July 1950, available at www.presidency.ucsb.edu (viewed 3 October 2014).

105. *FRUS 1950* I, Report to NSC, 30 September 1950. For the claim that NSC 68 would have been implemented without the Korean War, see Rearden, "Frustrating the Kremlin Design," 171

106. *FRUS 1950* III, 138.

107. TNA, CAB 129/41, CP(50) 181, Cripps, "Defence Requirement and United States Assistance," 31 July 1950; CAB 128/18, CM 52(50), 1 August 1950.

108. NARA, RG 59, Lot File 54D224, box 24, Perkins to Acheson, 31 August 1950; RG 59, State Department Central Decimal Files 1950–1954, 795.00/8–3150, box 4268, Memorandum of Conversation, 31 August 1950; TNA, CAB 128/18, CM 55(50), 4 September 1950.

109. Senate Foreign Relations Committee, *Reviews of World Situation, 1949–1950*, 291 (Acheson testimony, 1 May 1950).

110. *FRUS 1950* III, 130–132 (Douglas to Acheson, 12 July 1950), 157–158 [51–159] (Bruce to Acheson, 28 July 1950 on German rearmament but only as part of European effort), 180–183 (McCloy to Acheson, 3 August 1950 also advocating Germans as part of European army); cited in McMahon, *Acheson*, 136.

111. *DBPO* 2nd III, No. 3i [microfiche], Defence Committee, 1 September 1950.

112. *FRUS 1950* III, 287–288 [285–288] (Acheson-Schuman conversation, 12 September 1950), 299–300 [293–301] (Acheson, Schuman, and Bevin conversation, 14 September 1950), 301–302 (Acheson to Truman, 14 September 1950); McMahon, *Acheson*, 137–140. Acheson later observed that the Department of Defense had insisted on the "one package." He thought it

"wiser to establish the united command, leaving it to the logic of mathematics to convince everyone that no plan would be tenable without Germany"; Acheson, *Korean War*, 55n.

113. *FRUS 1950* III, 316–320, Acheson to Webb, 17 September 1950.

114. Senate Foreign Relations Committee, *Reviews of World Situation, 1949–1950*, 376–378.

115. James F. Schnabel, *The United States Army and the Korean War: Policy and Direction: The First Year* (Washington, DC: USGPO, 1972), 173–177.

116. *FRUS 1950* VII, 721–722, Acheson to Truman, 11 September 1950; Truman, *Years of Trial and Hope*, 410; Collum A. MacDonald, Korea: The War Before Vietnam (New York: Free Press), 38.

117. TNA, FO 371/84059, FK 1015/86G, Franks to FO, Tel. No. 1859, 4 July 1950.

118. Elsey to executive secretary of NSC, 12 July 1950, quoted in Doris M. Condit, *The Test of War, 1950–1953* (Washington, DC: Historian's Office, Office of the Secretary of Defense, 1988), 62.

119. *FRUS 1950* VII, 410, 712–721 (NSC 81/1), 712n (Truman's approval).

120. *DBPO*, 2nd, IV, 144–148; TNA, CAB 128/19, CM 61(50), 26 September 1950; *DBPO*, 2nd, IV, 176; *FRUS 1950* VII, 807–808, 826–828.

121. *DBPO*, 2nd, IV, 146–148 (Nye [New Delhi] to Commonwealth Relations Office, 23 September 1950), 165–167 (Hutchinson [Peking] to FO, 3 October 1950).

122. TNA, FO 800/462, FE/50/38, Bevin to Acheson, 4 October 1950.

123. Text of Wake Island meeting, in Richard H. Rovere and Arthur M. Schlesinger, *The General and the President and the Future of American Foreign Policy* (New York: Farrar, Straus and Young, 1951), 253–262, quotation at 258. Acheson asked to be excused from attending, saying MacArthur had many of the attributes of a foreign sovereign but he did not think it wise to recognize him as one; Acheson, *Korean War*, 60.

124. *DBPO*, 2nd, IV, 188–190, Franks to FO, Tel. No. 2950, 1 November 1950; Schnabel, *Policy and Direction: First Year*, 233–237.

125. Ferrell, ed., *Off the Record*, 191–193 (entry for 14 September 1950); Abramson, *Harriman*, 456–457.

126. *Present at Creation*, 441; Condit, *Test of War*, 35.

127. Acheson, *Korean War*, 64–65; Truman, *Years of Trial and Hope*, 426–427; Smith, *Acheson*, 212–213.

128. Acheson, *Korean War*, 67; Omar N. Bradley and Clay Blair, *A General's Life* (London: Sidgwick & Jackson, 1983), 584–590.

129. Stueck, *Korean War*, 112.

130. TNA, CAB 128/18, CM 73(50), 13 November 1950; *DBPO*, 2nd, IV, 202–204, Bevin to Franks, 14 November 1950. On the buffer zone proposal see Peter N. Farrar, "Britain's Proposal for a Buffer Zone in November 1950: Was it a Neglected Opportunity to End the Fighting in Korea?," *Journal of Contemporary History*, 18:2 (April 1983), 327–351; Franks to FO, 15 November 1950, quoted in Anthony Farrar-Hockley, *The British Part in the Korean War* 1 (London: HMSO, 1990), 300.

131. Bradley, *General's Life*, 564; Senate Foreign Relations Committee, *Reviews of World Situation, 1949–1950*, 370–371 (testimony, 28 November 1950); *FRUS 1950* VII, 1117–1121, JCS memorandum to secretary of defense, 9 November 1950.

132. Thomas J. Hamilton, "US Troops Reach Frontier of Manchuria in Northeast; Chinese Held Demoralized; UN Fire Power Is Believed Too Much for Reds," *New York Times* (21 November 1950); Smith, *Acheson*, 213–214.

133. Walter H. Waggoner, "Acheson Hints at Readiness for Peiping Talks on Korea," *New York Times* (16 November 1950), Acheson, "United States Foreign Policy," *DOSB* (27 November 1950), 853–855; Smith, *Acheson*, 214–215.

134. *FRUS 1950* VII, 1204–1208, memorandum of conversation by Jessup, 21 November 1950.

135. "Truman Loses," *New York Times* (12 November 1950).

136. *FRUS 1950* VII, 1237, MacArthur to Joint Chiefs of Staff, 28 November 1950.

137. Acheson, "The Strategy of Freedom," *DOSB* 23:598 (18 December 1950), 962–967. TNA, FO 371/84120, FK1023/202, Franks to FO, Tel. No. 3220, 30 November 1950.

138. *FRUS 1950* VII, 1261–1262.

139. *DBPO*, 2nd, IV, 222–223 which contains at note 2 the quotation from Franks's telegram.

140. TNA, CAB 128/18, CM 80(50), 30 November 1950, 6:45pm.

141. *DBPO*, 2nd, IV, 224, FO to Franks, 30 November 1950 and Franks reply at note 3.

142. TNA, FO 371/83019, F1027/6G, record of a meeting, 2 December 1950. On French thinking, see Alfred Grosser, *La IVe République at sa politique extérieure* (Paris: Armand Colin, 1972), 280–281.

143. *Present at Creation*, 365; William S. White, "Wherry Says Blood of G.I.'s in Korean War is on Acheson," *New York Times* (17 August 1950), 14. Such was the antipathy between Wherry and Acheson that, when the senator had jabbed his finger at him, the secretary had to be restrained from punching him; Isaacson and Thomas, *Wise Men*, 530, Acheson, *Sketches*, 128–130.

144. Isaacson and Thomas, *Wise Men*, 545; Truman, *Years of Trial and Hope*, 484–486.

145. Ronald Steel, *Walter Lippmann and the American Century* (Boston: Little, Brown, 1980), 473–475. Although a supporter of a firm stance against the Soviet Union, Lippmann had criticized various initiatives from the Truman Doctrine to the American commitment to Chiang Kai-shek. Lippmann's comments clearly rankled Acheson, who later described him as "that ambivalent Jeremiah"; *Present at Creation*, 223.

146. Bohlen, *Witness to History*, 294–295.

147. George F. Kennan, *Memoirs, 1950–1963* (New York: Pantheon Books, 1972), 30–31; *Present at Creation*, 476–477; *FRUS 1950* VII, 1335–1336; Princeton, George F. Kennan Papers, box 29, 1950 folder, Kennan to Bohlen, 5 December 1950.

148. *Present at Creation*, 476.

149. See *FRUS 1950* III, 1720–1723, 1739–1758 and *FRUS 1950* VII, 1361–1377, 1382–1386, 1790–1408, 1435–1442, 1449–1465, 1468–1479 for the US records; and PREM 8/1200 for British records.

150. *DBPO*, 2nd, IV, 240, Franks to Bevin, Tel. No. 3282, 4 December 1950.

151. *FRUS 1950* VII, 1479, Final Communiqué, 8 December 1950; Dean Acheson, "No yearning to be loved—Dean Acheson talks to Kenneth Harris," *Listener* (8 April 1971), 442–444.

152. Condit, *Test of War*, 240.

153. TNA, CAB 128/19, CM 7(51) and CM 8(51), 25 January 1951; Leffler, *Preponderance of Power*, 412.

154. *FRUS 1950* III, 585–595 (US minutes of first meeting of sixth session of North Atlantic Treaty Council with defense ministers, 18 December 1950), 595–604 (minutes of second meeting, 19 December 1950); Acheson, "United Action for Defense of the Free World," *DOSB* 24:600 (1 January 1951), 3–6; *Present at Creation*, 486.

155. *Present at Creation*, 486–493; *Congressional Record*, 82nd Congress, 1st Session, vol. 97, part 1, 57–64, Taft speech; Kenneth Scott Latourette, *The American Record in the Far East, 1945–1951* (New York: Macmillan, 1952), 189–190; Patterson, *Mr. Republican*, 477.

156. Patterson, *Mr. Republican*, 481.

157. *FRUS 1951* VII, 115–116 (draft resolution, 20 January 1951), 150–151 (final text, 1 February 1951). On Canadian reticence about the advance to the Yalu and the condemnatory resolution, see Lester Pearson, *Memoirs II: 1948–1957: International Years* (London: Victor Gollancz, 1974), 166–171, 279–314.

158. MacDonald, *Korea*, 95; Jonathan M. Sofer, *General Matthew B. Ridgway: From Progressivism to Reaganism, 1895–1993* (Westport, CT: Praeger, 1998), 117; Michael Schaller, *Douglas MacArthur: Far Eastern General* (New York: Oxford University Press, 1989), 228.

159. *FRUS 1951* VII, 296, Memorandum of Conversation, 5 April 1951.

160. Douglas MacArthur, *Reminiscences* (New York: McGraw-Hill, 1965), 441–442; MacDonald, *Korea*, 95; MacDonald, *Britain and the Korean War*, 47–49; *Present at Creation*, 519.

161. *FRUS 1951* VII, Part 1, 299, MacArthur to Martin, 20 March 1951.

162. Text of Truman address, 11 April 1951, in Rovere and Schlesinger, *General and President*, 263–268.

163. Rovere and Schlesinger, *General and President*, 5.

164. Bodleian Library, Oxford, Paul Gore-Booth Papers, Ms.Eng.c.4518, P. Gore-Booth to M. A. Hamilton, 17 April 1951. A later British evaluation noted the American "predilection for

emotional outbursts" but emphasized that it was "important to contrast the violence of the convulsion with the damage it actually did." It quoted Acheson's claim that it was a form of "national thinking aloud"; TNA, FO 371/97579, AU1011/1, Washington Embassy Annual Report for 1950 and 1951, 23 May 1952.

165. Rovere and Schlesinger, *General and President*, 12.
166. Smith, *Acheson*, 274.
167. *MacArthur Hearings Part 3*, Acheson testimony 1–2, 4–9 June 1951.
168. Bradley, *General's Life*, 639–640; Rovere and Schlesinger, *General and President*, 176; *MacArthur Hearings Part 2*, 732 (Bradley testimony 15 May 1951).
169. *FRUS 1951* VII, Pt 1, 460–462, 483–486, 507–511 (Kennan-Malik talks, May–June 1951), 636 (liaison meeting, 8 July 1951), 649–656 (record of first meeting, 10 July 1951), 848–850 (communists called off talks, 23 August 1950); *Present at Creation*, 533–534.
170. Acheson to Moullette, 23 February 1951 was published in a pamphlet, "*It has fallen to us*" (Washington, DC: State Department, 1951).

Chapter Six

Global Challenges, 1951–1953

In the last twenty months of the Truman administration Acheson confronted a global array of challenges. New pressing concerns emerged over the Middle East, where the rise of nationalism, Britain's declining power and difficulties with Egypt and Iran led policymakers in Washington to explore a more direct role. In Asia there was a continuing stalemate on the battlefield in Korea and the frustrations of peace talks at Panmunjom; the growing problems of the French in Indochina; and worries about the role of communist China in the region. These concerns helped to hasten efforts to secure a peace treaty with Japan and to devise defense arrangements with Australia and New Zealand. In Europe there were efforts to improve the machinery of NATO and relations between the different allies; and, especially, the continuing intractability of Germany's place in European defense. Latin America had never been a particular interest for Acheson, but even here there was a revolution in Bolivia and the beginnings of difficulties in Guatemala.

THE MIDDLE EAST

In the spring and early summer of 1951 Acheson's attention shifted from Korea, where the battlefield stabilized and peace talks began, to the Middle East (broadly defined as the area from Egypt to Iran). American policymakers after 1945 had regarded the Middle East as the primary responsibility of the British.[1] But following the outbreak of the Korean War in June 1950 officials in the State Department became concerned about Soviet expansion in the region and favored a more direct involvement. On 26 July Truman observed that the Soviets were likely to initiate trouble in the area.[2] Officials in the State Department did not foresee a direct attack. Rather, they were anxious about instability giving Moscow the opportunity to intervene. Although Truman's warning did not lead to any specific action, in early 1951 problems in the region resurfaced and Washington gave them more attention, as the crisis following Chinese intervention in Korea had eased. The difficulties arose in two countries where the British played a major role—Egypt and Iran.

The British had occupied Egypt since 1882 and greatly increased their forces during the Second World War. In October 1946 British foreign secretary Ernest Bevin and Egyptian prime minister Ismael Sidky reached agreement: British forces would quit Cairo and Alexandria by March 1947 and leave the Suez Canal base by September 1949, while the Egyptians promised to join a defense board that would meet if war broke out in the region. The deal soon unraveled, as the Egyptians claimed that the British accepted Sudan as part of Egypt while London maintained that the section of the agreement on Sudan left the status of the territory unchanged, and therefore not an integral part of Egypt. British troops departed from the two towns but remained at the Suez base, while protracted talks were held to try and find a solution. They became deadlocked in September 1950 and the stalemate deepened in the following months, leading Bevin to consider concessions. The situation worsened when ill health forced Bevin to resign in March 1951 and his successor as foreign secretary, Herbert Morrison, showed little readiness to make concessions.[3] Morrison was a talented politician who was one of the guiding lights in the reforming program of the Labour government. Unfortunately, he was not well suited to his new post, possessing neither a detailed grasp of international affairs nor a feel for how to tackle such issues. As a result, Acheson enjoyed a far less smooth relationship with the new British foreign secretary.

Acheson wanted the British both to retain their leading role in the region and to reach an accord with the Egyptians, but each of these goals seemed in jeopardy. British military and financial strength were in decline. And, in Washington's view, London had little appreciation of the significance of growing nationalism in the region. Acheson and his officials concluded that the British position in Egypt and American support for Israel inflamed Arab nationalism and encouraged neutralism. Egyptian discontent was evident when its representative abstained in the UN Security Council's vote of 27 June that called for collective action in Korea. Given these circumstances, the Americans tried to press the British to reach an accommodation with Cairo.[4]

American worries deepened in the spring of 1951 when a full-blown crisis arose between the Iranians and the British-owned Anglo-Iranian Oil Company (AIOC). The already strong nationalist feeling in Egypt intensified. George McGhee, assistant secretary of state for Near Eastern, South Asian, and African affairs, assumed a leading role in trying to prevent Egyptian neutralism. On a visit to London, he urged the British to make concessions.[5] A 21 May American aide-memoire to the British embassy suggested that the British should "reach a mutually satisfactory agreement which takes into account . . . Egyptian national aspirations." Morrison reported this request to the cabinet and endorsed the desire to avoid a rupture, though he noted that the "wide divergency" between them and the Egyptians meant there was "little prospect of agreement." The tone of his memorandum revealed his pessimism about the prospects for an agreement.[6] As Peter Hahn points out, "Even before it became clear that American pressure on Egypt and Britain would fail to elicit concessions from both powers . . . McGhee embarked on a determined campaign to make the United States responsible for Middle Eastern security as a way to resolve the Anglo-Egyptian impasse, curb the slide toward neutralism, and promote Western strategic interests."[7] He had advocated this approach as early as October 1950 in talks with Pentagon officials; and by January 1951 Acheson was persuaded. In a message to Secretary of Defense Marshall he recommended "more affirmative United States action . . . to safeguard our vital security interests in the Middle East."[8]

In May 1951 the British proposed the creation of a Middle Eastern Command (MEC). This initiative sought to solve Anglo-American disagreement on the JCS's desire to create a western Mediterranean naval command as part of NATO. Since an American admiral, Robert B. Carney, was in charge of the Atlantic Naval Command, London wanted a single Mediterranean naval command under a British admiral. The British ambassador, Sir Oliver Franks, and the head of the British Joint Services Mission in Washington, Air Chief Marshal William Elliot, presented the idea on 16 May.[9] The State Department immediately agreed to the proposal, and McGhee was especially enthusiastic, for they saw its potential to solve the Anglo-Egyptian base dispute. By August the British embraced this idea. Acheson spoke of how "some form of internationalization of the Suez Canal bases under M E Command arrangements might draw Egypt into the picture in a special position."[10]

There was an obstacle to this scheme—the insistence of both the British and Americans for unrestricted access to the Suez Canal, which took the form of seeking a Security Council resolution condemning Egyptian failure to agree. The Egyptians did not want to end their blockade of oil to the British refinery in Haifa, which they regarded as a matter of national security. The British Labour government was under pressure from the Conservatives to be tougher on Egypt, even to the extent of using force. On 1 September the Security Council passed the British resolution 8–0, with abstentions by the Soviet Union, China, and India. The Egyptians resented this vote. Meanwhile the British and Americans accelerated their efforts at creating a MEC, although it took nearly a month of talks with interested parties before the Americans launched the scheme on 10 October.

The MEC aimed to secure the region from the Soviets and to bring Arab states into partnership with the West, and it would be located in Cairo, which the Americans felt would also help in solving the Anglo-Egyptian dispute over the military base at Suez. Israel was not included. The United States and Britain persuaded France and Turkey to be cosponsors. This overture failed, as the Egyptians immediately rejected the invitation and passed legislation abrogating their defense treaty of 1936 with Britain, insisting that all British troops should quit Egypt. The United States and Britain then invited other Arab states to join but all refused because their populations agreed with the Egyptian government's position.[11]

The rejection of the MEC and the abrogation of the 1936 treaty were the products of escalating nationalist anger with the British. Even though the 1946 Bevin-Sidki agreement had not been ratified by the Egyptian parliament, the British honored the commitment to depart from Egyptian towns by March 1947. But they stayed at the Suez base and increased its garrison from the 10,000 allowed by the Anglo-Egyptian treaty of 1936 to nearly 38,000. This angered Egyptian opinion, which was already inflamed by the Mufti of Jerusalem, who blamed the British for allowing the creation of the state of Israel, and by the Islamic fundamentalists, the Muslim Brotherhood, who urged Egyptians to launch a holy war against the Jews. Egyptians then blamed their defeat by Israel on the poor equipment given to its army by Britain. When Nahas Pasha of the nationalist Wafd Party became prime minister in 1950, he demanded that Britain reduce its forces to a strength of 10,000. This campaign escalated after October 1951 just as the new Conservative Party government took office with Winston Churchill as prime minister and Anthony Eden as foreign secretary. Both men were determined to show firmness in the face of Egyptian demands. Nahas responded to London's refusal by cutting off supplies of fresh food to the base and moving its 40,000 civilian workers to Cairo.

Tensions peaked in January 1952 when the village of Kafr Abdou was destroyed after it launched an attack on a British filtration plant. After two Britons were killed, British forces moved against Ismailia's auxiliary police station on 25 January. When the policemen refused (on orders from Cairo) to surrender, the British attacked and killed forty-two Egyptian policemen. This sparked riots in Cairo, which Britain suppressed. Although Acheson sympathized with the British position, he made it clear that the United States would not endorse such action; and so Eden decided that the soldiers should not intervene.[12]

Acheson, who had previously left matters to McGhee, became increasingly involved, as he began to worry about reports that communists had helped to organize the riots in Cairo. This coincided with the first indications of a more pliable British attitude toward the MEC. Acheson and his officials wanted to persuade the Egyptians to accept an amended MEC, but London, and Churchill especially, were opposed. When Acheson found an ally in Eden, a joint American-British scheme, the Middle East Defense Organization (MEDO), was presented in June 1952 to the Egyptians. By calling it a planning board rather than a command they hoped to demonstrate a greater sense of equality between the indigenous members and the Western partners. But Egypt remained unenthusiastic. Its government had been fatally weakened by its ostensible inability to prevent the riots in Cairo. A military coup followed on 23 July and a new regime emerged—the "Free Officers" led by General Mohammed Naguib, though it soon became clear that Colonel Gamal Abdel Nasser was the real leader. Acheson and State Department experts worried at first about the new regime's land reforms and the cancellation of elections, but they were pleased that the government had stabilized the situation in Cairo and removed the danger of communism. They hoped that Naguib could be a moderate leader who might work with the West. In September 1952 Acheson approved the idea of the extension of military assistance. On 6 October he agreed to Naguib's request for military equipment, endorsing a military assistance grant of $10 million. The secretary told Harriman that he regarded Naguib as "our best chance to establish a relationship of confidence between his country and the West." However, Truman rejected Acheson's proposal in January 1953 after being persuaded by Israeli opposition. He did approve the sale of $11 million of defense equipment, though this did not include jet aircraft, and $10 million of economic aid. [13]

In explaining the failure to find any effective way forward, Hahn concludes that "Egyptian nationalism and British stubbornness prevented the United States from promoting an Anglo-Egyptian settlement acceptable to the Egyptians." [14] The Egyptians opposed any defense arrangement before the British left the Suez base. Sudan was the major stumbling block in a deal between the British and Egyptians on Suez. Even though the end of 1952 saw some small movement between the British and the Egyptians on both the Suez base and Sudan, Acheson's outlook had changed. Responding to the advice of Henry Byroade, who succeeded McGhee in April 1952, Acheson adopted a less optimistic view of the British and a growing belief in the need for a more prominent US role. [15] He agreed with a State Department assessment: "it is no longer safe to assume, automatically, that Britain can and should be considered the principal protector of western interests in the Middle East." [16] He authorized an aide-memoire to the British embassy on 5 November, stating the United States would be willing to take an active part in negotiations with Egypt. [17] He also endorsed the view in the Department of Defense that the Americans now "had the responsibility in the Middle East and had to do something about it," even if "there would be great resentment on the part of the British." [18]

IRAN

Acheson's frustrations over Egypt were dwarfed by his anxieties over a more serious crisis that developed when the new government in Iran nationalized the British-owned Anglo-Iranian Oil Company (AIOC) in the spring of 1951. The crisis in Iran combined strategic concerns about Soviet influence in the region with the growing importance of oil. In 1950–1951 about 70 percent of Western Europe's oil came from the Middle East; and Iranian oil constituted about 40 percent of Middle Eastern oil. In consequence, there was a real fear that disruption to Iranian supplies would result in shortages.[19] Although some warned of possible direct military action by the Soviets, Acheson was more concerned about how the crisis might spread instability and offer an opening to Soviet assistance to Iranian communists. He sympathized with the British position but was anxious that stern British action might lead to economic collapse followed by a communist coup or even direct Soviet military action in the north (a resurrection of their pressure in 1946).[20]

Ranged against these considerations was Acheson's recognition that Iranian action threatened a vital British asset. AIOC possessed the world's largest oil refinery at Abadan, and it was Britain's greatest single overseas investment, valued at $448 million in 1946. The estimated replacement cost of AIOC assets in Iran was $1.4 billion. It provided energy to the British economy and substantial dollar earnings, calculated at more than $400 million per year.[21] Moreover, the British government held 51 percent of the shares in AIOC. Yet it allowed the company to determine its response to the Iranians.

AIOC was founded as the Anglo-Persian Oil Company in 1909, changing its name to the Anglo-Iranian Oil Company in 1935. It had reached a new agreement in 1933 which gave Iran a royalty plus 20 percent of the company's worldwide profits. Although this was a better deal than those offered by other oil companies, AIOC came under pressure to improve the terms of the agreement. This led to the Supplemental Agreement of 1949, which substantially increased the royalties and provided a large lump sum. The deal only came before the Iranian parliament, the majlis, in June 1950, by which time the Korean War had broken out and generated a major increase in demand. This, in turn put AIOC under pressure to offer still better terms.[22]

By this time there had been a revolution in the nature of agreements between oil companies and host countries. In May 1943 Standard Oil of New Jersey and Shell had reached a 50:50 deal in Venezuela: various payments to the Venezuelan government would be raised to match the net profits of the oil companies in the country. Although this was seen as a product of the exigencies of war, the Venezuelan government enshrined the arrangement in a new tax law in 1948. Saudi Arabia sought a similar deal with the American company, ARAMCO. The company reached agreement in December 1950, once it became clear that it could deduct half its payments to the Saudis from its taxes to the United States government. Given these contracts, AIOC leaders knew they must offer more to Iran. So they proposed a 50:50 deal, but by early 1951 this was not sufficient to satisfy the majlis. There was growing pressure to nationalize AIOC. On 7 March the prime minister, Ali Razmara, who tried to find a deal with the company, was assassinated and in an atmosphere of rising tension the leading nationalist and critic of AIOC, Mohammed Mossadeq was appointed as premier. He promptly nationalized AIOC, which the Shah approved on 1 May.[23]

Acheson understood the importance of AIOC to Britain and valued the British as strategic allies in the region, but believed that London should recognize the need to adjust to changed circumstances. The secretary and McGhee sought to convince British officials. The two men had reason to be hopeful: Acheson enjoyed an extraordinary level of confidential consultation and trust with the British ambassador, Sir Oliver Franks, who had been McGhee's moral tutor when he had been a Rhodes Scholar at Oxford in the 1930s. Cabinet ministers and officials in London were less ready to concede the American point. The new British foreign secretary, Herbert Morrison, was especially difficult. His deputy, Minister of State Kenneth Younger, noted in his diary: "He has not yet got down to the job. His handling of it, though fairly adroit, has been thoroughly superficial, and even the House has begun to notice how ignorant he is every time he answers questions."[24] London's outlook was greatly influenced by the reporting of the ambassador in Tehran, Sir Francis Shepherd, who declared: "I think we should fight for [the] retention by the Anglo-Iranian Oil Company, as far as possible, of the control of the industry they have built up. . . . The disappearance of the A.I.O.C. and its replacement by [an] international consortium would be a considerable blow to our prestige in this country."[25]

The ever-astute Franks recognized that such attitudes were unwise. He cabled London: "I must record that I see little chance, within my present instructions, of finding a solution, however it may be presented, which will induce the Americans to lend us their active support in any negotiations with the Persians."[26] Such was Franks's disquiet that he telephoned the Foreign Office and "pleaded for as much imaginative latitude as possible in the instructions he was expecting to receive." In particular, he shared the American belief that "we should make a bow in the direction of nationalisation."[27]

At their meeting on 17 April Franks told McGhee that AIOC proposed Iranian representatives on its Board of Governors, equal sharing of profits, and the creation of a separate Iranian-owned firm to handle internal distribution of petroleum products. Although he appreciated these suggestions, McGhee felt more was required to placate Iranian political forces demanding nationalization.[28] When they met again the next day, McGhee strongly urged that the British offer "at least some facade of nationalization." Although Franks was sympathetic to McGhee's point, the assistant secretary incurred the ambassador's stern disapproval when he seemed to suggest that American support depended on such gestures. McGhee accepted that Britain had made real concessions and would enjoy American "benevolent neutrality, although we could not lend support in the face of strong reaction."[29] By persuading the Foreign Office to ease its stance, Franks could note that "the Americans have moved considerably from their original disapproval and are now anxious to help out."[30] McGhee gave his assessment of the situation to Acheson on 20 April. He believed that the British did not feel the pressure for nationalization was as great as the State Department considered it, and, consequently, "the British believe that they can get by with fewer concessions than we think possible."[31]

Acheson met Franks on 27 April and warned against a tough British line, since this risked the issue "being captured by the U.S.S.R."[32] Franks was a consummate professional, fully understanding the need to carry out his instructions, but he also shared much of the American perspective on this question. He observed: "The real trouble with A. I. O. C. is they have not got far enough past the stage of Victorian paternalism."[33] He believed that the "Kipling type of technique" was inappropriate to the current Middle East.[34]

Acheson and McGhee were proven correct and AIOC was nationalized on 1 May, which triggered British cabinet discussion of possible military intervention. Acheson made clear to Franks on 11 May that the United States had "grave misgivings with respect to the use of force," unless there was danger to British citizens requiring their evacuation, Soviet intervention, or a communist seizure of power. At the same time Acheson was conciliatory to the British, saying that they would inform the Iranians that American companies would not agree to operate AIOC properties. The secretary wanted to counter the British suspicion that American reluctance to back AIOC was due to competition between American and British oil companies.[35] As British plans for possible military action continued, Acheson again warned that the United States would only support military force if requested by the Iranian government to prevent a communist coup d'état or to rescue British nationals in peril.[36] The State Department issued a statement the next day that combined sympathy for the Iranian wish to secure a larger share of income from their oil and a warning about "the serious effects of any unilateral cancellation of clear contractual relationships."[37] Any tendency to be too easy on the British was tempered by the regular advice of the United States ambassador in Tehran, Henry Grady, who disparaged AIOC and advised Washington to extend a credit to the Iranians. Grady wanted the proposed $75 million loan by the American Export-Import Bank increased to $100 million, but the majlis still rejected the offer.[38] Acheson was concerned about the situation, whose seriousness he stressed to the NSC on 16 May. In June he made this clear to the embassy in Tehran, encapsulating a new NSC paper, NSC 107/2, which concluded that it was imperative that Iran remained aligned to the West: the "loss" of Iran would seriously endanger the entire Middle Eastern area, Pakistan, and India. It would also damage Western economic and military interests because of Western Europe's dependence on Middle Eastern oil.[39]

Meanwhile the situation in Iran deteriorated. A delegation from AIOC visited Iran but confronted what the State Department described as a "position not only completely unreasonable but designed to remove all hope negots [sic] with Brit [sic] except on terms [of] complete capitulation to Iran nationalization demands."[40] Morrison sought an injunction against Iran at the International Court of Justice. The Iranians refused to recognize the court's jurisdiction and gave the AIOC manager at Abadan, A.E.C. Drake, and his British workers a week to choose whether to work for the new National Iranian Oil Company or leave. The Cabinet on 21 June considered military and naval action at Abadan, while AIOC threatened to close down its refinery because of a new Iranian anti-sabotage law. The cruiser HMS *Mauritius* was moved to the waters near Abadan.[41]

On 4 July Acheson spoke to Franks, who had just returned from consultations in London, in a meeting at the home of Averell Harriman, special assistant on national security affairs to Truman. McGhee and deputy under secretary H. Freeman Matthews also attended. The ambassador conveyed the considerable anger felt in London at the "insolent defiance of decency, legality and reason by a group of wild men in Iran." But he agreed with Acheson that military action was inadvisable. The secretary then proposed that Harriman should visit Tehran and try to renew the negotiations. Franks urged his government to accept the offer. He argued that Acheson and the State Department wanted to help Britain but were constrained by American public opinion which regarded the British as adopting an imperialist attitude to Iran. If Harriman failed because of Iranian intransigence, then the Americans might be ready to support Britain. If his mission succeeded in restarting talks, then they would have avoided a disaster.[42]

Harriman arrived in Tehran on 15 July and was greeted by 10,000 demonstrators. There followed two weeks of intense but fruitless talks with Mossadeq. Harriman considered the Iranian leader a demagogue who lacked any real understanding of the oil industry, and was responding to considerable pressure from Muslim extremists who rejected any dealings with foreigners. Harriman was initially "greatly concerned over his [Mossadeq's] adamant and rigid position." Although he described the discussions as "Alice in Wonderland," he found Mossadeq personally agreeable and decided a deal might be possible. It is clear that Harriman was also sympathetic to the Iranian case: he described AIOC's "[r]igidity against modification or adjustment of concession," and its "[a]utocratic attitude." On 27 July he flew to London and urged the British government to send a personal envoy of cabinet level. He hoped that his friend Hugh Gaitskell, chancellor of the exchequer, could lead a British mission.[43] He had to accept a lesser figure, the Lord Privy Seal, Richard Stokes.[44] When Acheson saw Franks on 2 August, the ambassador spoke approvingly of Harriman's efforts, pronouncing them a "God send." But he was unenthusiastic about Stokes, whom he described as "a bluff, genial, open and hearty man, not accustomed to dealing with the Iranian mentality." He feared Stokes and Mossadeq would find it "difficult to find a common language."[45]

Franks's assessment proved all too accurate. The Stokes mission of 4–22 August drew up an eight-point proposal, which Harriman thought reasonable, but, contrary to guidance, Stokes revealed the proposal to the press. The Iranians rejected the proposal and negotiations were suspended. In his memoirs Acheson judged the Harriman mission successful in "turning back Britain and Iran from the brink of hostilities" but a failure in its attempt to find a long-term solution to the oil dispute.[46] Both Acheson and Harriman counseled British restraint as matters escalated in September. On the 25th the Iranian government announced that British employees at Abadan would be given a week's warning to leave the country. Two days later the Cabinet met to consider a military seizure of the refinery. Morrison maintained that the government should not allow the expulsion of the British workers, but prime minister Clement Attlee stressed how the United States had consistently opposed the use of force. The Cabinet agreed that they could not afford to break with the Americans over Iran. On 4 October the British staff left Abadan.[47] Much to Acheson's regret, the British sought a resolution of the UN Security Council to compel Iran to abide by the International Court of Justice's interim injunction to freeze the case until the court had debated its jurisdiction in the case, an injunction Tehran had ignored. The resolution failed to secure sufficient support in a floor debate in October.[48] It did briefly raise the prospect of a possible deal when Mossadeq visited the United States for the debate and then for medical consultations in November. He appeared open to an agreement whereby another "neutral" company might operate the Abadan refinery and AIOC could sell Iranian oil on the now accepted 50:50 share of profits. Acheson took Mossadeq's proposal seriously but it went nowhere partly because the British were unenthusiastic and partly because McGhee, and Paul Nitze, director of the PPS, believed it remained too vague about the price per barrel Iran wanted for its oil.[49]

On 25 October the Conservatives won the British general election and Churchill returned as prime minister, while Anthony Eden succeeded Morrison as foreign secretary. In rhetoric at least, Churchill adopted Morrison's more belligerent approach. On a visit to Washington in January 1952 he told Truman and Acheson that he would not have let the Iranians eject AIOC if he had been in office, even if this required a "splutter of musketry."[50] Eden was a better interlocutor than Morrison, but Acheson never really struck up an effective relationship with him. In his memoirs he called Eden's arrival "a great and signal improvement, except on Iran. In that area Eden continued to take advice from the same sources which had, I thought, poisoned the judgment of the Labour Party—the bureaucracy of the Anglo-Iranian Oil Company, the Ministry of Fuel and Power, and the Treasury."[51]

Acheson sought a way forward in 1952 but the issue remained stalemated for the rest of the Truman administration. Franks encapsulated the situation: "The Americans are convinced that we ought to show ourselves ready to negotiate with Musaddiq as long as he is there, realising that on all grounds a settlement must be reached fairly soon and that this settlement must include the complete disappearance of A. I. O. C. in any shape or form from Persia itself."[52] Acheson encouraged the vice president of the International Bank for Reconstruction and Development (the World Bank) to explore a possible settlement with Camille Gutt, Mossadeq's financial adviser and former head of the International Monetary Fund. Churchill launched an initiative during Eden's absence from the Foreign Office through illness; Truman encouraged an attempt in the last weeks of the administration; but all failed to find formulas that would satisfy both Britain and Iran.[53]

The monthly economic report of 9 December 1952 from the US embassy in Tehran captured the economic conditions in the country at the end of the Truman administration. It noted the departure of British embassy staff from the country on 1 November and the growth of rumors that the Americans might actively intervene and provide a solution, but hopes of this faded by the end of the month.[54]

Acheson came to the end of his term with a sterner view of cooperation with Britain on Iranian oil. He reported to Truman that efforts had foundered and continued failure meant economic and political collapse in Iran. He asked for, and received, presidential approval for the advance of $100 million to Iran against future oil deliveries and authorization of the involvement of American oil companies in Iran. This decision found expression in an NSC paper—NSC 136/1. United States policy would entail "full consultation" with the British and aim to "avoid unnecessarily sacrificing legitimate" British interests or "unnecessarily impairing Anglo-American relations." But the Americans were not willing to let the British veto any initiatives it deemed necessary to US policy toward Iran.[55] This was a foreshadowing of the eventual settlement under the Eisenhower administration when American oil companies took the lead in a new agreement, which became possible following a CIA-led coup to overthrow Mossadeq in August 1953.

Henry Grady criticized Acheson's approach to the Iranian problem, accusing him of deferring to British wishes. In his memoirs he said "we joined the British and supported them in their policy rather than insisting they follow ours." He described the British government's decision not to interfere with AIOC policies as "an untenable position and ridiculous." The editor of Grady's memoirs, John T. McNay, claims that Acheson "clung to Anglo-American partnership and to his effort to preserve British imperial power even at the expense of U.S. interests in Iran." Acheson had indulged in a "conflation of British and U.S. interests." McNay's narrative makes Grady the heroic opponent of this foolish policy. Grady was right about the rigidities of AIOC and the strange reluctance of the majority shareholder to exert any pressure but McNay is mistaken in assuming that Acheson's approach was dominated by a readiness to meet British concerns. McGhee, who was closer to American policymaking than Grady, provides a more balanced account, revealing Acheson's wish to work with the main Western power in the region and highlighting American pressure on London and the concessions made by AIOC, which had accepted the 50:50 principle by April 1951. Moreover, by the end of 1952 Acheson was close to advocating independent action by the United States.[56]

The failure of a deal meant oil stopped flowing from Iran. In response, the Truman administration invoked the Defense Production Act of 1950 and, by giving anti-trust exemptions to nineteen oil companies, got them to create a voluntary committee to coordinate and pool supplies and facilities. As a result there was no shortfall in supplies. In 1950 global oil production was 10.9 billion barrels per day, with Iran contributing 666,000 barrels per day. By 1952 global production reached 13 billion barrels per day, while Iranian production was reduced to 20,000 barrels per day.[57]

ASIAN SECURITY: THE JAPANESE PEACE TREATY AND THE ANZUS TREATY

Both the difficulties in the Middle East and the continuing problems in Korea hastened American interest in drawing up a peace treaty with Japan. Serious work on a treaty began in early 1950. Acheson worked closely with Walton Butterworth, assistant secretary for Far Eastern Affairs. Butterworth encountered considerable criticism from opponents of the administration's China policy, leading Acheson to feel he needed a change of team if there was to be progress on a treaty. In an act that earned great respect from Acheson, Dean Rusk, deputy undersecretary for substantive matters, volunteered in March 1950 to take a demotion and assume Butterworth's post. This proved a shrewd move, for Rusk enjoyed good relations with Republican senators Alexander Smith (New Jersey), Bourke Hickenlooper (Iowa), and William Knowland (California); and was a close friend of John Foster Dulles.[58] Acheson sought to initiate negotiations as soon as possible and to conduct them through diplomatic channels rather than a multilateral conference and thereby ensure that they followed "a constructive American lead." He heeded the advice of Rusk and Butterworth that Dulles should take the leading role in these talks, since he had "no prior contaminating contact" with the issue.[59]

Dulles assumed his duties on 18 May and immediately began to work closely with John M. Allison, director of the Office of Northeast Asian Affairs. Allison later described Dulles as "a hard but fair taskmaster, man of great vision, imagination, and above all, energy."[60] Dulles wanted to pursue a treaty that was not a victor's peace. He had been a member of the US delegation at Versailles and shared the popular view that a harsh treaty with Germany had sown the seeds of future aggression.[61] To foster momentum for a treaty and to forestall any delaying tactics by Defense Secretary Johnson and chairman of the JCS Bradley, who had just announced their imminent tour of Pacific bases, Acheson arranged for Dulles and Allison to visit Tokyo in June. They met General Douglas MacArthur, Supreme Commander Allied Powers (SCAP), who shared their view of the need to press ahead with a non-punitive treaty. The Pentagon, however, was cautious about ending the occupation. Japanese security was suddenly even more important, because their trip was only a few days old when an attack by North Korean forces precipitated the outbreak of the Korean War. Progress was not helped by an unsuccessful meeting between Dulles and the Japanese prime minister, Shigeru Yoshida, who was in Allison's words, "cautious, seemingly evasive." Dulles became extremely agitated by this meeting and had to be calmed down by Allison and William Sebald, political advisor to MacArthur.[62]

When he returned to the United States Dulles urged the case for action on a peace treaty with Japan.[63] He wanted, in particular, to overcome the Pentagon's anxiety about security in the region. The State Department produced a short draft treaty, which included a clause that would involve the presence of American forces in Japan after signature of the treaty. Dulles and departmental officials appreciated that this was inconsistent with a commitment to treating Japan as a sovereign state once the treaty came into effect. So a Defense-State Department committee worked on finding a formula that encompassed both Japanese sovereignty and a continued US military presence. Washington would accede to a Japanese request for military aid; and security arrangements between the two countries would be settled in a separate bilateral agreement. On 7 September 1950 Acheson and Defense Secretary Louis Johnson signed a memorandum, which was approved the next day by the president. Dulles would lead negotiations, under the guidance of Acheson.[64] The memorandum contained concessions to the Department of Defense that Acheson was skeptical about—he later noted that they "proved utterly unworkable." But he regarded them as a price worth paying, because the agreement achieved his two primary aims: it sanctioned the start of serious negotiations and accepted that these would be pursued through bilateral diplomacy rather than a multilateral peace conference.[65]

Dulles and Allison took advantage of the next session of the UN in New York to speak to members of the Far Eastern Commission, the various countries which had fought against Japan. They provided them with a draft peace treaty. Although the covering note stressed that the draft was "suggestive and tentative," some countries thought it was "our idea of a complete treaty, and their reaction was vigorous to say the least." Allison said of the Australian ambassador, Percy Spender: "I thought he would burst a blood vessel." Other delegations had reservations but Dulles and Allison believed they had sufficient agreement to pursue a first draft treaty. Only the Soviets reserved their judgment. On 4 December 1950 the State Department publicly announced its general principles for a peace treaty with Japan. [66]

Meanwhile, Acheson succeeded in maintaining the momentum. This owed a good deal to Johnson's departure as secretary of defense and the arrival of George Marshall as his successor. On 13 December Acheson wrote to Marshall suggesting they seek an early settlement and ignore the stipulation in the September memorandum that they await a favorable outcome of the situation in Korea. At the same time, he demonstrated his affinity for the Pentagon's security concerns by saying that the United States should retain a substantial military presence in Japan and explore a security pact with the Pacific island nations (Australia, New Zealand, the Philippines, Japan, and possibly Indonesia). Finally, he hoped Marshall would agree that Dulles should lead a presidential mission to Japan. [67] The secretary's advocacy worked. Despite the wariness of the JCS about an early peace with Japan, Marshall met Acheson on 8 January 1951 and agreed on guidance for Dulles's visit to Japan, which Truman endorsed on the 10th. It included the aim to achieve a peace settlement without awaiting a favorable resolution of the military situation in Korea. [68] Dulles undertook his second visit to Japan in January–February. He talked to the Japanese Prime Minister Yoshida Shigeru, who accepted the basic American terms for a peace treaty, though he expressed his desire to "go very slowly with any possible rearmament of Japan." [69]

Acheson and Dulles now wanted to finalize the text of a treaty as soon as possible. Dulles saw the British ambassador, Oliver Franks, and suggested they produce a joint draft treaty. [70] This was partly a device for encouraging action by Britain, the other major belligerent in the war against Japan. Dulles might have underestimated the differences between the two countries but he succeeded in giving the British a sense of purpose. An American draft was sent to the British on 23 March and a British draft was dispatched on 7 April. [71] There were clear differences between the Americans and the British, leading Dulles to observe that "he had come to feel we were drifting seriously apart." He was particularly uneasy about London's wish to invite the communist Chinese to participate in the talks on a treaty. Franks played an important part in facilitating progress. He suggested discussions between each country's specialists.[72] They met in Washington in April–May, with the British following Franks's injunction to seek the maximum area of agreement on the text of the treaty before addressing more troublesome procedural questions such as the involvement of communist China.[73] At the end of the talks Franks reported that they had narrowed though not eliminated the areas of disagreement.[74] Dulles's attitude seemed more auspicious: "His tone was calm and he showed understanding of our difficulties, though not disposed to minimise his own."[75] A joint draft treaty was produced on 3 May.[76]

As the Anglo-American draft was being prepared, the relations between MacArthur and the president over the Korean War reached the breaking point, leading to the president's dismissal of the general. Conscious of MacArthur's standing in Japan and the potential damage his removal might cause, Acheson called Dulles to a late night meeting at his home in Georgetown on 10 April to warn him of the president's move. Although Dulles was dismayed at the decision, he agreed to travel to Tokyo where he succeeded in reassuring Yoshida and his government.[77]

Dulles then visited London in June for further talks, which resulted in an Anglo-American draft treaty of 14 June that resolved nearly all the remaining disagreements. It delivered all that Acheson and Dulles wanted. On the question of Japan's future attitude toward communist China Morrison conceded a compromise arrangement whereby Japan would be free, after signature of the treaty, to decide which Chinese regime to recognize.[78] Following some minor amendments, the Anglo-American draft was circulated, on 13 August, to all the allied governments. A handful of minor issues were settled bilaterally between each government and the United States before they assembled for the peace conference in San Francisco.[79]

Fifty-two nations attended the San Francisco Conference of 4–8 September, including the Soviet Union, which had not contributed to the August draft but promised to bring its own proposals to the meeting. This opened the prospect of multilateral negotiations, and the attendant risk of Moscow using them to obstruct a settlement, something Acheson had been determined to avoid ever since he had initiated serious work on a settlement in spring 1950. But he was not diverted. As the State Department briefing made clear, it was "a signing conference, not a negotiating conference."[80] In the first plenary session Acheson displayed considerable aplomb in establishing procedures that ensured delegates agreed to the draft text and preventing the leader of the Soviet delegation, Andrei Gromyko, from thwarting this plan.

As Acheson, in his role as temporary president, set about securing acceptance by the assembled delegates of the conference rules, Gromyko interrupted to request that the government of the People's Republic of China be invited. Acheson responded that, as the matter before the conference was the adoption of rules, which had been moved and seconded, he ruled the Soviet proposal as out of order. Thereupon Gertruda Sekaninova, delegate from

Czechoslovakia, intervened to second Gromyko's motion. When Acheson stated that he had already ruled that this motion was out of order, Gromyko countered that the rules had not been adopted yet, so the temporary president could not rule against the proposal. Acheson replied by calling for a vote by the whole conference on whether it wished to sustain the chair and its ruling. He requested a show of hands. Gromyko protested. Acheson then said he would allow Stefan Wierblowski, the Polish delegate, to speak for five minutes, followed by someone who supported the ruling. As Kenneth Younger (senior British representative until Foreign Secretary Herbert Morrison arrived) came to speak in favor of the chair, the Polish delegate continued beyond his allotted five minutes. Acheson urged him to resume his seat, but when this failed, Acheson began approaching the Polish delegate so as to escort him back to his seat. Eventually Younger spoke. The vote then followed and sustained Acheson by 35 votes to 3.[81]

Acheson later explained how his actions at the conference greatly benefited from his apprenticeship under Speaker Sam Rayburn of the House of Representatives and its Rules Committee. In the matter of rules governing the consideration of a bill, there was an "open rule," which allowed amendments to a bill; and a "closed rule," which permitted no amendments. His performance was all the more impressive, for he was ill with ptomaine poisoning: "If I have ever felt worse, the memory of it mercifully escapes me," he noted in his memoirs.[82] Dean Rusk might have been Acheson's aide in achieving this coup over the Soviets but his memoirs accept the deviousness of Acheson's behavior. He said he did not blame the Soviets for walking out: "Those rules of procedure were outrageous, and I blush to think of my own role in those parliamentary manoeuvres."[83]

Once Acheson overcame this hurdle, the conference proceeded to accept the August draft. Only the Soviet Union, Poland and Czechoslovakia refused to sign.[84] This outcome was possible because Acheson had taken the trouble, before the conference, to talk to key figures from a large number of the countries sending delegations to San Francisco. He soothed French chagrin at their lack of a contribution to the draft treaty. The Philippines, Australia, and New Zealand were reassured by security agreements with Washington. In particular, he and Dulles coached Yoshida to remain quiet about the security agreement with the United States and to reassure its former enemies that Japan would be willing after the conference to hold negotiations about reparations.[85]

Acheson's handling of the Soviet intervention proved a national sensation. Defense Secretary Robert Lovett was stopped in his car in Long Island by a mechanic who suggested he join a group of TV viewers who were cheering Acheson, who seemed about "to take a swing at a Pole." The conference proceedings attracted an audience of 45 million Americans. The whole incident made a television star of the secretary, who was praised for his magisterial handling of Soviet blocking tactics. The British embassy reported how handling of the conference gave him a personal triumph with the American public and, in particular, with the West Coast public. He was greeted with spontaneous applause on his return to Washington. Even one of his archcritics, Senator William Knowland (R-California), praised his efforts. [86]

At the same time as the treaty was being completed, Acheson and Dulles concluded a number of security agreements. A separate United States–Japanese Security Treaty was signed, as prefigured in the September 1950 memorandum. Acheson had broached the possibility of a general Pacific security agreement, which was incorporated into the January 1951 guidance to Dulles. But Dulles soon discovered that Australia, the Philippines, and New Zealand did not want to join a defense system that included Japan. There was also the danger that the system might mushroom in size, when the British proposed the addition of Malaya and Hong Kong, the Dutch put forward Indonesia, and the French suggested Indochina. So Acheson settled on two agreements: the Philippines Mutual Defense Treaty, which was signed on 30 August and came into effect in August 1952; and the Australia–New Zealand Treaty (ANZUS), which was signed on 1 September and came into operation in April 1952. [87] Acheson did not seek these security agreements but regarded them "as a reasonable price for the Japanese peace treaty." Indeed, he believed they were unnecessary. On the other hand, Dulles, who led the negotiations, wanted to extend the system and developed the Southeast Asia Treaty Organization (SEATO) in 1954. [88]

Acheson's next task was to ensure that the peace treaty and the security agreements were ratified by Congress. Acceptance of the Japanese settlement soon came to hinge on Tokyo's attitude toward China. Fifty-six senators announced their refusal to support the treaty if the Japanese government decided to recognize the Beijing government. [89] To forestall this problem, Dulles traveled to Japan with Senators Sparkman and Smith, the ranking Democratic and Republican members of the Far Eastern subcommittee of the Senate Foreign Relations Committee, and secured a letter from Yoshida promising that his government would open relations with Chiang's government in Taiwan and not the communists in Beijing. [90]

The British objected to Dulles's efforts to elicit a Japanese commitment before the treaty became effective, contending that this was a violation of the June Dulles-Morrison compromise. [91] Still, the Foreign Office must have expected the Japanese would recognize the Taiwan government. After all, Franks had suggested as early as February that the "Americans are almost certain to encourage . . . the making of an agreement between the Japanese and the Chinese Nationalists." [92] The issue caused discord between London and Washington. Eden believed that there should be no Japanese commitment until after the peace treaty came into effect. During the Washington visit of Churchill and Eden in January 1952, Acheson and Dulles explained that the Americans had received a message from Yoshida, saying the Japanese government would establish diplomatic relations with Taiwan, and that it would probably be necessary to use it during the Senate's consideration of the Japanese Peace Treaty. When Eden replied by saying he would have preferred to see nothing done or said until Japan gained full sovereignty but did not want to make a major issue of this, Acheson could reasonably have concluded that Eden was saying that they still disagreed but accepted that the American would go ahead.[93]

But then things unraveled. Eden returned to London on 15 January and the Yoshida letter was published on the 16th. The foreign secretary was distressed by this. Such was his dismay that he complained to Washington about not being given advance notice of the intention to publish and the American failure to show a copy of the letter to him or the British ambassador.[94] Although he had grounds for complaint about the intention to publish and the way in which this was done, he was wrong about the text of the letter. Dulles showed the letter to Franks on 9 January.[95] In addition, both the British and American records of the Acheson-Dulles-Eden meeting on the 10th make clear that Eden could have had no doubt about the purpose of the Yoshida letter and its intended use by the Americans. When this was confirmed in an investigation by Foreign Office officials, Eden honestly admitted: "I don't remember this; my fault no doubt." The episode soured his view of Dulles, noting (on another matter) on 6 February: "Dulles is so tricky that I wonder whether he may not try to use this, like he did showing the Yoshida letter to H. M. Ambassador + [sic] taking it away again."[96] When Franks saw Acheson on 16 January, he was asked to convey his strong regret at what had happened. Acheson was apologetic about the manner in which matters had been handled. In his memoirs he called it "an inexcusable bungle."[97]

Acheson now concentrated on the congressional hearings. In testimony to the Senate Foreign Relations Committee on Monday 21 January 1952, he gave a brief outline of the successful completion of the Japanese Peace Treaty before handing over to Dulles for a more detailed summary.[98] He wisely left the handling of the treaty in the full Senate to William Knowland, "whose ideological credentials handcuffed the conservatives."[99] Acheson intervened only on particular issues. On 29 January 1952 Senator Alexander Wiley (R-Wisconsin) wrote to Acheson expressing his concern that the Soviet Union and Communist China, who had not signed the Japanese Peace Treaty, might claim the right to send forces to Japan. Acheson's reply of 5 February made clear that they had no such legal entitlement, because the 26 July 1945 Potsdam surrender terms did not give allied powers the right individually to occupy Japan. It sanctioned an allied occupation, but Acheson felt that the risk of Soviet or Chinese action was not affected by purely legal considerations. Moscow would be motivated, rather, by its assessment of its interests.[100]

As the hearings proceeded Acheson had to address the issue of the department's Loyalty Security Board's investigation of Edmund Clubb, director of the Office of Chinese Affairs, in a press conference on 5 March. Acheson reversed the board's finding that Clubb was a security risk on the advice of a "trusted" Foreign Service officer, who had reviewed the case. The incident revealed Acheson's determination not to succumb to what he called the "witch hunt for supposed subversives." Clubb was then offered a more junior post. As the *Washington Post* observed, he "was 'cleared' and irremediably crippled." He decided to retire.[101] This dust-up did not derail the ratification process. On 20 March the Senate approved the treaty 66–10; the Security Treaty between the United States and Japan was endorsed 58–9. Acheson took the occasion to pay tribute to the "brilliant and devoted role" of Dulles, whose service was "an outstanding example of bipartisan foreign policy at its most effective."[102] Dulles thanked Acheson for his complete support, the trust and confidence he and the president had placed in him, and the "devoted and sacrificial service" of officials in the State Department. Acheson replied by saying it had been a "joy to work with you" and praised his grasp of problems, resourcefulness, and dedication.[103] Truman signed both agreements on 15 April and they went into effect on 28 April.

The ratification of the treaties marked Acheson's last major achievement during his secretaryship. Scholars rightly praise Dulles for his skill in negotiating the peace treaty. Richard Immermann calls it a "masterful feat," delivering full independence to Japan, US bases in Japan and Okinawa, Japanese recognition of Taiwan, and the exclusion of the Soviets. Robert McMahon notes how Dulles demonstrated a "shrewd eye for the fundamental needs of his interlocutors and for what could be compromised—and what could not."[104] All this is true, but Acheson deserves more credit than is often recognized. He initiated serious work on a treaty, recognized the need to utilize Dulles to secure a bipartisan approach in Asia where there were bitter party divisions, pressed for action on what he identified as key issues, and maintained the momentum toward a settlement. He provided the broad framework in which Dulles should work—in particular the avoidance of a multilateral peace conference. This offered an ideal combination, for Acheson's oversight, general guidance, and wider vision of American foreign policy and of Japan's place in Asia complemented Dulles's strengths. As Townsend Hoopes observes, Dulles was better suited to focusing on single problems; he was more of a tactician than a strategist; he lacked the managerial talent for developing orderly and comprehensive plans; and he was insensitive to the interdependence of problems.[105]

THE COLD WAR AND ANTI-COMMUNISM AT HOME: THE
JESSUP NOMINATION

The Japanese Peace Treaty and the Pacific defense agreements demonstrated that there could be bipartisanship on Asia. But the treaty had barely been signed before there was a fresh wave of Republican assaults on the administration over the nomination of Philip Jessup as an American representative at the UN. It marked the predictable revival of Senator McCarthy's attacks on Jessup's "affinity for Communist causes," which had begun in spring 1950. It also involved the more respected ranks of the Republican Party when Senator Robert Taft indicated he was likely to oppose the nomination. [106]

Truman sent nominations to the Senate on 13 September 1951 of ten people to represent the United States at the sixth session of the UN that would meet in Paris on 3 November. The nominations were considered by a subcommittee (chaired by Senator John J. Sparkman, D-Alabama) of the Senate Foreign Relations Committee, which reviewed the suitability of the candidates and chose to hold extensive hearings on one of them, Acheson's ambassador-at-large, Philip Jessup. Such was the atmosphere of the time that Jessup, who had been nominated and confirmed for this position on three previous occasions, was subjected to searching scrutiny. In the course of nine days of testimony the senators explored various allegations about Jessup's associations with organizations with communist connections. These hearings coincided with those of Senator Pat McCarran's (D-Nevada) subcommittee on internal security of the Judiciary Committee, which was investigating the Institute of Pacific Relations and its alleged influence on Far Eastern policy toward communist goals. McCarran suggested the subcommittee should examine Jessup's senior role in the IPR. [107]

The overriding concern of Sparkman's subcommittee was the administration's Asian policy. Acheson found himself under pressure to prove his strong anti-communist credentials; and, in particular, his seeming readiness to reach an accommodation with the communist government in Beijing. In a letter to the subcommittee on 5 October 1951 Acheson assured Congress that the United States would resolutely oppose giving Mao's government control of Taiwan and a seat in the UN as the price of peace in Korea. Acheson's letter answered the request of Senator Alexander H. Smith (R-New Jersey), ranking GOP member of the subcommittee, for a restatement of State Department views on communist China. Acheson said Smith must have misinterpreted a 1949 conversation with Jessup from which Smith inferred that the department was planning to follow Britain in recognizing the communist regime in China. [108]

Jessup faced two main charges, which were aimed at Acheson as much as the nominee. The first, from McCarthy, was a repetition of his continuing claim that Jessup was affiliated to subversive organizations. In detailed testimony, Jessup systematically rebutted these allegations. The second was from Harold E. Stassen, president of the University of Pennsylvania and former Republican governor of Minnesota, who testified on Thursday 8 October. He repeated his claim (made to the McCarran committee) that the late senator Vandenberg told him of a meeting with Jessup and Acheson and their abortive proposal to cut off arms to Chiang's nationalists. He did so, even though the State Department had explained that Jessup did not attend the 5 February 1949 meeting and that the recommendation to deny further weapons was made by Major General David S. Barr, the senior US military representative in China. Stassen also spoke of his participation in a round table discussion at the State Department in 1949 on Far Eastern policy at which Jessup presided, and how most of the members favored recognizing the communist government.[109] On 11 October the State Department released the transcript of the round table discussion. It included a comment by Stassen on 6 October that was not in keeping with his outlook in 1951: "In my mind the pluses are very large on the side of saying we want to watch this picture for a couple of years before we recognize the Communist Government of China."[110]

In this atmosphere, it is entirely understandable why Acheson and Jessup needed to present a clear-cut case for the administration's consistent opposition to recognition of the communist government in China. This was, unfortunately, not the occasion to expatiate on the complex realities of international affairs. Yet, in the immediate aftermath of Mao's victory, Acheson and his advisers did show an openness to some kind of relationship and even possible recognition of Beijing. This was not something he wanted to speak about in October 1951, or perhaps believed was his outlook in late 1949 to early 1950.[111]

The subcommittee reported favorably on nine of Truman's nominations but did not endorse Jessup, rejecting him by a vote of three to two. The full committee then took no action on the nine nominees. By a motion on 19 October the committee was discharged from further examination of these nine appointments and the Senate gave its advice and consent to their appointment.[112] The liberal journalist Elmer Davis exposed the unconvincing nature of the subcommittee's decision. He noted that two of the three nay votes came from senators Brewster and Gillette, who had been absent for a good deal of the time when Jessup was testifying. The third opponent, Senator Smith, said he respected Jessup's ability, integrity, and loyalty but voted against him because he was a symbol of the group attitude toward Asia which seemed completely unsound.[113] Truman was determined not to be denied, invoking his constitutional right to make appointments when the Senate was in recess. He declared that he found "no reason in the record of the hearings to change my high opinion of Mr Jessup's qualifications for this post."[114]

THE KOREAN WAR: BATTLEFIELD STALEMATE AND THE
FRUSTRATIONS OF ARMISTICE NEGOTIATIONS

Truman might have circumvented the obstruction to Jessup's appointment but pressure on the administration did not ease. In particular, lack of progress in Korea brought criticisms from the Republicans. These resonated with the American public, which saw its soldiers continue to die and the battlefield remain stalemated, while the armistice talks made no headway. It was small comfort to see the casualties were much lower than in the first year of the war: 21,300 Americans died between June 1950 and June 1951, while there were 12,300 deaths in the next two years.[115] In his last year in office Acheson faced stalemate on the battlefield and in armistice negotiations, determined communist propaganda campaigns, and problems in maintaining a united front with Western allies, particularly the British. At home Senator Taft continued his attacks, while Dulles, released from his Japanese Peace Treaty duties and advisory role at the State Department, delivered partisan assaults on the timidity of American strategy in a presidential election year.

While the war had settled into a battle of position roughly around the 38th parallel, truce talks made no progress. The main obstacle concerned prisoners of war. Article 118 of the Geneva Convention of 1949 stipulated that POWs should be automatically repatriated when a war ended. But the situation in Korea was more complex. Many North Korean and communist Chinese prisoners in American captivity wanted asylum in South Korea or Taiwan. Acheson's advisors debated the issue, which was decided when Truman declared, "We will not buy an armistice by turning over human beings for slaughter or slavery."[116] As a way forward, the Americans developed the idea of voluntary repatriation but it was rejected by the communist negotiators when it was tabled at Panmunjom. The Chinese proposed that POWs should be screened to establish who wished to be repatriated. Developments in the main prison camp on Koje-do Island complicated this task. POWs were allowed to create separate nationalist and communist compounds. Before the screening started, anti-communist leaders in their compounds secured a majority in favor of repatriation by a campaign of intimidation; and the communists prevented screening from taking place among their prisoners. Then communist POWs abducted the commandant of the camp and, in return for his release, extracted a public statement that seemed to suggest the authorities had not treated prisoners in a humane way. Only 31,000 of the 116,000 prisoners demanded repatriation, which grew to 70,000 (later raised to 80,000–85,000) when those in the unscreened communist compounds were added. As a result, the communists rejected the process and armistice negotiations remained deadlocked. [117]

Given the stalemate, the talks became a prolonged opportunity for propaganda by the communists, much to Acheson's irritation. In March 1952 he had to respond to allegations by the Chinese that UN forces in Korea had used biological weapons. He vigorously rejected the charges and recommended to the president that they invite Paul Ruegger, president of the International Committee of the Red Cross, to investigate the claims, a suggestion that Truman endorsed. Ruegger promptly contacted the two sides in the Korean War, saying the Red Cross would begin an inquiry, provided both sides agreed. Acheson then replied, on behalf of the United States government for the Unified Command, fully accepting the Red Cross plans.[118] China, North Korea, and the Soviet Union also accused the UN forces of brutal treatment of prisoners. The declaration of martial law in South Korea, as of midnight on 24 May, did not lead Americans to believe they were achieving stability in the country.[119] This "vituperative propaganda of the communists" at the armistice talks led Acheson to advise the president that it might be necessary to halt or in some way suspend them.[120]

Meanwhile, General Mark Clark, who replaced Ridgway as UN commander in May 1952, advocated the use of military pressure to break the deadlock. Acheson agreed, even though departmental officials were dubious about its likely effectiveness. Truman promptly endorsed air attacks, which began on 23 June and targeted hydro-electric plants in North Korea. This action was doubly irritating to the British: it jeopardized their attempts through India, and its contacts with China, to break the impasse in truce talks; and they resented that they were not consulted or given prior knowledge of Truman's decision. Eden's deputy at the Foreign Office, Minister of State Selwyn Lloyd, expressed his "considerable concern" about this to State Department officials.[121] The British were careful to convey their anger in private, while publicly maintaining their support for American actions. Acheson, who traveled to London on 22 June (as part of a European trip) and faced British complaints firsthand, acknowledged his regret at the misunderstanding.[122] This produced, in turn, concern from Senator Knowland about what Acheson had said to British members of parliament.[123] British sensitivities were eased by Acheson's words and by the decision to appoint a British deputy to General Clark.

As the next session of the UN approached, Acheson explored different options. The secretary and his officials consulted Britain, France, Canada, Australia, and New Zealand but failed to persuade them to join a total embargo of China.[124] He wanted a tough line at Panmunjom and backed the American negotiators' decision to call a recess in the truce talks on 4 October.[125] Worried about communist efforts to win over the Arab-Asian bloc in the UN, he also tried to demonstrate more sympathy toward colonial issues. For example, despite French protests, he backed the request to include Tunisia and Morocco on the general assembly's agenda. When he spoke to the general assembly, he adopted a conciliatory tone, reiterated the US desire to play a moderating role on colonial issues, and stressed American interest in the economic development of undeveloped countries.[126] Eight days later, the secretary delivered a four-hour speech presenting a resolution calling on China to accept an armistice based on voluntary repatriation.[127]

Although Acheson enjoyed the support of Britain and Canada, they had doubts in private about his inflexibility on repatriation and were receptive to the possibility of an alternative resolution from the Indian representative, Krishna Menon. On 29 October Acheson held talks with Selwyn Lloyd, who outlined Menon's planned resolution. The secretary "strongly opposed" what he regarded as a vague resolution that would undermine the principle of no forced repatriation, and Lloyd agreed. British doubts about Menon's draft seemed to be confirmed when Eden told Acheson that he found it "too confusing and unmanageable." But the British desire to see progress led them to produce, after discussions with the Indians, a draft resolution that David Bruce, who had succeeded Webb as under secretary in April, described as contemplating the ultimate abandonment of no forced repatriation.[128] Acheson became extremely agitated. When he met Eden and Lloyd on 19 November, he harangued them for more than an hour, arguing that they had not been honorable on the issue.[129]

Eisenhower's victory in the presidential election of 4 November only added to Acheson's anxieties and irritability. In a speech on 24 October Eisenhower had said that, if elected, he would go to Korea before January. Acheson was infuriated by the suggestion in the speech that his January 1950 address excluding Korea from the American defensive perimeter had encouraged the communists to attack. But his greater concern was whether the firm line at Panmunjom would be maintained. He secured Truman's approval of a draft statement supporting no forced repatriation that Eisenhower might use during his planned visit to Korea. The president-elect did not respond to Acheson's message.[130]

The Eisenhower episode signaled that Acheson's role in shaping Korea policy was effectively over. The Menon resolution was adopted by the UN General Assembly on 3 December,[131] and the administration left office with little public optimism about its policies on Korea.[132] Although the Chinese and North Koreans rejected the Menon plan, it proved to be the basis for a solution of the POW problem. A breakthrough came when Stalin died on 5 March 1953 and those vying for his succession were ready to lessen tensions, which led the Chinese and North Koreans to adopt a more constructive attitude. Talks began on 8 April and produced an armistice agreement on 27 July 1953.[133]

EUROPEAN SECURITY

Acheson's last year and a half also brought frustrations over Europe. If his main difficulties over Korea had come from the British, the French posed the main impediment on European security. Acheson had made real progress in early 1951. He had secured congressional approval of Eisenhower's appointment as NATO supreme commander, with a substantial American military presence of four divisions in Europe. He had argued that Europe also needed a German contribution, and had presented a proposal to include a German contingent in NATO. Under American pressure the French had suggested that the Germans should form part of a European Defense Community (EDC). In an effort to maintain the impetus, Acheson had agreed in December 1950 that the two schemes should be pursued simultaneously.

Six months later, no solution was at hand. So Acheson decided in July 1951 to abandon the simultaneous approach and commit the United States to EDC, in the hope that this would stimulate action. He stressed the urgency of adding German forces to strengthen Western security, while recognizing that this could only be achieved if they could reach an agreement that satisfied French fears about German power and met the West German desire for equality of treatment. He also accepted London's reluctance to join the scheme: he agreed that Britain, like the United States, should be outside EDC but deeply involved in it through NATO.[134] If he was disappointed by French inaction on EDC, he was heartened by the ratification in April of the European Coal and Steel Community, which suggested to him that there could be agreement between France and Germany. He met Marshall and his senior officials at the Department of Defense on 16 July, persuading them of the need not just to achieve effective European defense and German rearmament but also the "restoration of German sovereignty." The two departments put their case to Truman, who immediately backed the proposal.[135]

Acheson pursued his plan with vigor and determination. In September he spoke to the French foreign minister, Robert Schuman, explaining that there was a danger that Congress might halt military aid to Europe if they did not find a way of achieving German rearmament. At the NATO Council meeting in Ottawa (15–20 September) he pressed his case but without success. It seemed to Anthony Eden as if EDC was doomed to failure. But Acheson did not relent. West German Chancellor Konrad Adenauer visited Paris in November and held his first talks with Acheson, Eden, and Schuman. They did not find a solution to the question of German rearmament, but Acheson was able to achieve a major step forward. He told Adenauer that the United States regarded West Germany as a partner; any decisions of importance to the Germans would be made together. A further NATO Council meeting in Rome (24–28 November) did not achieve a breakthrough, leading Acheson to vent his frustrations to Truman. The next NATO meeting, he declared, would be the final chance to settle the issue.[136] Yet, for all his ire, Acheson's reassurances to Adenauer had lessened one of the two obstacles he had identified in his July memorandum. He now needed to find a way of allaying French fears.

An opportunity arose when he traveled to London to represent the president at the funeral of King George VI in February 1952. He held talks with Eden and Schuman and then Adenauer joined the discussion. They reached agreement on the constitutional relations between NATO and EDC and the level of expenditure and limitations on the types of arms that Germany could produce. On the issue of restricting production of certain types of arms in a forward area, which included Germany, they found a formula that met the French wish to impose limitations on Germany and the German desire not to concede major constraints to its sovereignty.[137]

The next NATO Council met in Lisbon between 20 and 26 February and endorsed these agreements, but not without last-minute difficulties that Acheson proved adept in tackling. In a marathon session, which involved staying up until 4:00am, he obtained authority to lead from Schuman and then Eden before they went to bed, and doggedly pressed French and British officials toward solutions. They reached agreement on the economic burdens of defense. Acheson recognized that the United States was much better placed to increase defense spending than the West Europeans, who voiced concerns about the strains caused by rises in military expenditure since the outbreak of the Korean War. The Mutual Security Agency, created in October 1951 to supersede the Economic Cooperation Administration, would offer assistance toward defense costs. The Ottawa meeting in September 1951 had created the Temporary Council Committee of all twelve NATO members, with an inner group—the wise men—of Harriman, Edwin Plowden for Britain, and Jean Monnet for France, to investigate defense burden sharing. Its report proposed a coordinated European approach, which ensured a more equitable distribution of efforts. It also offered evidence that the Europeans were making a fair contribution to NATO's defense, something that should answer congressional claims that the Europeans were leaving things to the United States. The Council approved the report, including its recommendation to create the post of NATO Secretary-General.[138]

Lisbon also welcomed two new NATO members—Greece and Turkey. Acheson had opposed their exclusion in the original treaty in 1949 but had changed his mind, partly because of the Korean War, and backed their associate membership in September 1950. By 1951 he shared their desire for full membership and took the lead in persuading and pressuring hesitant Europeans to support their case. The Ottawa Council in September invited Greece and Turkey and they signed a protocol in October. The senate ratified this in February 1952 and the two countries were formally admitted in time to attend the Lisbon meeting.[139]

A challenge to NATO unity came with the Soviet diplomatic note of 10 March 1952, which tried to undermine the unity of the Western allies by offering the prospect of a deal leading to a united Germany. It did not halt progress toward an agreement on EDC, though Acheson needed to travel to Paris and Bonn to help to resolve remaining minor issues, such as the wording of British and American guarantees to EDC. On 27 May an EDC treaty and a protocol delineating the relationship between EDC and NATO were signed in Paris. Acheson, Eden, and Schuman also signed contractual agreements with West Germany effectively ending the occupation. Acheson soon discovered the precarious nature of the EDC scheme. In talks on 28 May the French president, Vincent Auriol, attacked EDC and declared the Germans not the Soviets were the main threat in Europe.[140] When Acheson left office in January 1953 the French National Assembly had not ratified the EDC treaty; and, indeed, rejected it in August 1954. Eden brokered a deal that saw West Germany join NATO in 1955, which France accepted when the United States and Britain strengthened their occupation forces in Germany.

LATIN AMERICA

Evidence of the truly global nature of Acheson's concerns in the final phase of his secretaryship came with the emergence of issues affecting Latin America. Africa was the only region to receive less of the secretary's attention in his first two years. The scale of American aid testified to the low importance of the region to the United States: $79 million went to its twenty republics between 1949 and 1952. In the same period, the rest of the world received $18 billion of US assistance.[141] Developments in 1951–1952 required greater engagement, and Acheson offered some astute responses.

Acheson recognized the United States' significant economic ties with Latin America, since the region attracted a quarter of US exports and more than a third of US foreign investment in 1945; and he understood the strategic importance of the Panama Canal. But he harbored no anxieties about the region, sharing the widespread belief that Franklin Roosevelt's good neighbor policies had been a stabilizing influence. Washington did offer military aid and signed the Rio Treaty of Reciprocal Assistance in September 1947 with the American republics. The principal aim was to reassure Latin American governments, since the United States did not see a major security threat or consider the region an arena in the Cold War. Acheson showed limited interest in the history, politics, and culture of the area and regarded it as far less significant than Europe, Asia, and the Middle East. Indeed, he made only one visit to South America between 1945 and 1953. The July 1952 trip to Brazil consisted mainly of rest and recuperation after the hectic round of talks in Europe in May and June. It involved largely ceremonial activities and no discussion of substantive issues. In his memoirs he summed up the region: "An explosive population, stagnant economy, archaic society, primitive politics, massive ignorance, illiteracy, and poverty—all had contributed generously to the creation of many local crises." He added that the area's needed foreign investment produced an ambivalent response: a welcome escape from peonage but the accompanying threat of United States exploitation and "perpetuation of domestic control by the small reactionary class."[142] On his return, he wrote to Frankfurter about the "undisciplined . . . administratively hopeless" country. In seeming contradiction, the great exponent of orderly processes also noted the "amazing greatness of Brazil. . . I am in love with it. And it almost killed me with kindness."[143]

Acheson left the daily work of diplomacy with the region in the capable hands of the Spanish-speaking assistant secretary Edward G. Miller, whose bustling energy brought a sense of purpose to the bureau for inter-American affairs—"[h]is animation left the secretary of state free to be inattentive."[144] It was at Miller's urging that he made his only notable engagement in his first two years, his speech of 19 September 1949 in New York. Acheson might have called it ritualistic,[145] but, as one of his biographers notes, it reveals him as "sympathetic, condescending, paternalistic." When he described the countries of the region as part of a family, the clear implication was that the United States was its father.[146] The speech also displayed complacency toward Latin American needs. In response to their appeals for economic aid, something resembling the Marshall Plan, he offered little, suggesting that they should seek assistance through Point 4 (Truman's commitment in his January 1949 inaugural to assist developing countries), the Export-Import Bank, and the World Bank.

Such attitudes disappeared after the outbreak of the Korean War. Acheson needed to enlist Latin American support in the conflict and to secure everlarger supplies of their commodities. In December 1950 he called for a meeting of the American republics in Washington, which was held in March–April 1951. He urged them to join the struggle against the Soviet threat. As the talks ended, Acheson tried to coax them with flattering remarks about the "cooperative and brotherly way" they had worked together on problems, and of their "great ability and . . . great skill." He received polite responses but little concrete action.[147]

The increased need for raw materials during the Korean War caused other US agencies to object to the raised prices but Acheson backed generous deals with the Latin American producing nations. In March 1952 he approved an agreement with Venezuela.[148] His intervention on Bolivia was even more striking. In 1951, as the Reconstruction Finance Corporation negotiated a price for tin, Acheson shared the view of his officials that they should not insist on a price that would cause economic troubles, and thereby risk political upheaval, and warned that halting purchases of Bolivian tin as a bargaining tactic would bring explosive consequences. [149]

In 1952 he was even ready to accept a left-leaning revolution and nationalization of the tin mines in Bolivia. Victor Paz Estenssoro won election as president in April with the help of the Nationalist Revolutionary Movement (MNR). The army opposed the new government but it survived thanks to the workers from the tin mines going onto the streets. In return Paz nationalized the three largest tin companies and initiated land reform, actions likely to prompt calls for action in Washington. But Acheson followed Miller's advice, which favored recognition, saying the MNR was popular and wished to distance itself from its earlier communism. The secretary chose to work with the new regime, believing the Bolivian revolution was not "communist oriented." In June Truman recognized Paz's government. When a Bolivian official on a visit to Washington informed Acheson of his government's intention to nationalize the tin mines, the secretary declared that such decisions were the concern of the Bolivian government provided it compensated the owners. He added that nationalization might be harmful, as it could jeopardize continued foreign investment and recruitment of experienced personnel. Talks were held to reach a deal on compensation, though it took until July 1953 to complete the agreement. Meanwhile, Bolivia received aid from the United States that amounted to $100 million by the end of 1953. [150]

Guatemala also emerged as a focus of Acheson's attention in 1952. The Arévalo government of 1944–1950 pursued a reformist agenda of improving workers' conditions and wanted, in particular, to act against the American-owned United Fruit Company. Colonel Jacobo Arbenz Guzman was a prominent member of this government and was elected president in November 1950, taking office in March 1951. Concerned about the threat to American companies, the CIA wanted to act against Arbenz. Truman was sympathetic, but it appears that Acheson remained unaware of this. Acheson adopted tough diplomacy by cutting US aid when it became clear that Arbenz was intent on radical action. In June 1952 Arbenz issued Decree 900 which would compel United Fruit to yield huge swathes of unused land, and in February 1953 the Guatemalan government confiscated a quarter of a million acres, valuing it at $1.2 million. The State Department suggested that $16.5 million was a more appropriate figure. Even before this confiscation, the CIA was planning intervention, but the department refused an export license in July 1952 for a shipment of arms to Arbenz's opponents. [151]

Truman, however, approved action by the CIA, which worked on a scheme in August and September. Guatemalan exiles and Nicaragua's leader, Somoza, would be brought by United Fruit vessels to overthrow Arbenz. By early October Acheson learned of these plans and opposed them. He later observed that Somoza's talk about cleaning out communism in Guatemala was frightening the daylights out of him. According to his biographer, under secretary David Bruce persuaded Acheson to convince the president that the CIA's plan to use force was illegitimate and should be canceled. When Frank Wisner and J. C. King of the CIA met Bruce and Miller on 8 October they heard how the State Department approved the raising of funds but opposed the movements of arms. There is no record of Acheson's conversation with Truman but King was clear that "all of the action planned in support of the opposition was off."[152]

It is certainly true that Acheson "contributed nothing memorable to the history of US–Latin American relations."[153] His priorities lay elsewhere. Yet when he did act, he showed a better touch than the next administration. He shared their patronizing attitudes but, when framing policy, he was more willing to consider the consequences for these countries, and not just American interests. In particular, he eschewed intervention.

END OF A SECRETARYSHIP

Acheson's term as secretary and the Truman administration ended in a wave of unpopularity. Throughout his period of office there had been articles assailing his record. One by Felix Wittmer was reprinted and used by the Republicans in the presidential election campaign.[154] In December 1952, 32 percent approved Truman's performance, while 56 percent disapproved.[155] After twelve years of nearly continuous service, Acheson was physically tired; and even more exhausted emotionally by the assaults on him and his policies and by his frustration at the failure to find a plan for German rearmament and to reach a settlement on Egypt and Iran. He was also dissatisfied with the arrangements for supporting the French in Indochina. On the other hand, his response to Latin American challenges demonstrated sound judgment in avoiding problems but was hardly a notable accomplishment. He could only point to the Japanese Peace Treaty and the Pacific security pacts as real achievements in his last two years. Yet, for all this sense of disappointment about particular issues in 1952, Acheson was certain that his tenure had produced important results—from the consolidation of the European economy to the creation of NATO to the defense of Korea to the integration of the former enemy powers of Germany and Japan into the Western camp. Moreover, he and the president had made a significant longer term contribution. They had worked together to produce a radical rethinking of America's place in the world. They had confronted global challenges and embraced the obligations that they believed the country's great power thrust upon its leaders.

NOTES

1. NARA, RG 59 State Department, Central Decimal File, 1950–1954, box 2915, 641.80/ 8-152, Report, "The British Position in the Middle East," 1 August 1952: "Much of our past and present policy in the Middle East is based on the assumption Britain can and should be primarily responsible for maintaining basic western interests in the area."

2. Truman's conversation with George Elsey, 26 July 1950, quoted in Donovan, *Tumultuous Years*, 204–205; Peter L. Hahn, *The United States, Great Britain and Egypt, 1945–1956* (Chapel Hill: University of North Carolina Press, 1991), 102.

3. *FRUS 1946* VI, 69–78; Hahn, *US, GB and Egypt*, 34, 104; William Roger Louis, *The British Empire in the Middle East 1945–1951* (Oxford: Clarendon Press, 1984), 125.

4. *FRUS 1950* V, 330–332 (Stabler to McGhee, 14 December 1950), 271–278 (State Department Policy Statement, 28 December 1950); *FRUS 1950* VII, 233 (Caffery to Acheson, 29 June 1950), 261 (Caffery to Acheson, 30 June 1950); Hahn, *US, GB and Egypt*, 102–107.

5. Hahn, *US, GB and Egypt*, 107–109; *FRUS 1951* V, 104–109 (Informal US-UK Discussions, 2 April 1951), 113–120 (State Department draft minutes of State-JCS Staff Meeting, 2 May 1951, extract), 356–361 (informal US-UK discussions, 10 April 1951).

6. Hahn, *US, GB and Egypt*, 108–109; *FRUS 1951* V, 366–367, State Department to British embassy, aide-memoire, 21 May 1951. TNA, CAB 129/45 CP(51) 140, Morrison, "Egypt- Defence Negotiations," 28 May 1951; George C. McGhee, *Envoy to the Middle World* (New York: Harper & Row, 1983), 366–383.

7. Hahn, *US, GB and Egypt*, 109.

8. *FRUS 1951* V, 21–23, Acheson to Marshall, 27 January 1951; *Present at Creation*, 362, McGhee, *Envoy to Middle World*, 23.

9. *FRUS 1951* III, 520–522 (British aide-memoire, 15 May 1951), 522–524 (note about US-British talks, 16–24 May 1951).

10. *FRUS 1951* V, 372–376 (Morrison to Acheson, 15 August 1951), 381–382 (Acheson to Morrison, 30 August 1951—quotation at 381); Hahn, *US, GB and Egypt*, 112–116.

11. See *FRUS 1951* V, 200–211 for discussions on MEC and the Egyptian response; Hahn, *US, GB and Egypt*, 116–128; Peter L. Hahn, *Crisis and Crossfire: The United States and the Middle East since 1945* (Washington, DC: Potomac Books, 2005), 15.

12. Hahn, *US, GB and Egypt*, 132–139; Louis, *British Empire in Middle East*, 715–734.

13. Hahn, *US, GB and Egypt*, 140, 144–152; HSTL, Acheson Papers, box 67a, memorandum of conversation with Harriman, 31 December 1952.

14. Hahn, *US, GB and Egypt*, 131.

15. *FRUS 1952–1954* IX, Part 2, 1838–1843, memorandum by Byroade, 21 July 1952: "time has come when we ought to make greater use of our position in Egypt" to aid the British and Egyptians reach a deal. See also the advice of another departmental specialist, *FRUS 1952–1954* IX, Part 1, 256–262, memorandum by Hoskins, 25 July 1952, which declared the "growing need for increased US leadership."

16. NARA, RG 59 State Department, Central Decimal File, 1950–1954, box 2915, 641.80/ 8-152, Report, "The British Position in the Middle East," 1 August 1952; Hahn, *Crisis and Crossfire*, 15.

17. *FRUS 1952–1954* IX, Part 1, 311–313, aide-memoire to British embassy, 5 November 1952.

18. HSTL, Acheson Papers, Acheson Memoranda of Conversation, memorandum of Acheson-Lovett telephone conversation, 6 November 1952, available at www.trumanlibrary.org/ whistlestop/study_collections/achesonmemos/view.php?documentid=71-3_05&documentYear=1952&documentVersion=both (viewed 23 January 2017).

19. McMahon, *Acheson*, 157; Daniel Yergin, *The Prize: the Epic Quest for Oil, Money and Power* (London: Simon & Schuster, 1991), 454, 464; *FRUS 1951* V, 268–276 (National Intelligence Estimate NIE-14, "The Importance of Iranian and Middle Eastern Oil in Western Europe Under Peacetime Conditions," 8 January 1951).

20. David S. Painter, *Oil and the American Century: The Political Economy of US Foreign Oil Policy, 1941–1954* (Baltimore: Johns Hopkins University Press, 1986), 172–174. *FRUS 1951* V, 21–27 (Acheson to Marshall, 27 January 1951), 50–76 (agreed conclusions of Middle

East chiefs of mission conference, 14–21 February 1951), 257–264 (draft NSC study, 27 December 1951), 309–315 (memorandum of conversation, 14 May 1951); *FRUS 1952–1954* X, 21–23, NSC 107, 14 March 1951. *Present at Creation*, 505–507, McGhee, *Envoy to Middle World*, 331–332.

21. W. R. Louis, "Musaddiq and the dilemma of British imperialism," in James A. Bill and W. R. Louis, eds, *Iranian Nationalism and Oil* (London: I. B. Taurus, 1988), 229; Painter, *Oil and American Century*, 174.

22. Yergin, *The Prize*, 453–454; Ronald W. Ferrier, "The Anglo-Iranian Oil Dispute: A Triangular Relationship," in Bill and Louis, eds., *Iranian Nationalism and Oil*, 164–203.

23. Yergin, *The Prize*, 434–436, 445–447, 453–455, Painter, *Oil and American Century*, 173.

24. Kenneth Younger Diary, 13 May 1951.

25. Quoted in Louis, *British Empire in Middle East*, 654.

26. TNA, FO 371/91470, EP1023/18, Franks to FO, Tel. No. 1081, 10 April 1951.

27. TNA, FO 371/91471, EP1023/32, minute by R. Makins of telephone call, 12 April 1951.

28. *FRUS 1952–1954* X, 30–35, memorandum of conversation, 17 April 1951. For his dealings with Franks in April, see also McGhee, *Envoy to Middle World*, 334–336.

29. *FRUS 1952–1954* X, 37–42, memorandum of conversation, 18 April 1951.

30. TNA, FO 371/91471, EP1023/39, Franks to FO, Tel. No. 1194, 18 April 1951.

31. *FRUS 1952–1954* X. 42n.

32. Painter, *Oil and American Century*, 175, McLellan, *Acheson*, 387; HSTL, Acheson Papers, box 66, memorandum of conversation, 27 April 1951.

33. TNA, FO 371/91529, EP1531/241, Franks to Strang, 21 April 1951.

34. HSTL, Acheson Papers, box 66, memorandum of conversation, 27 April 1951. Gaddis Smith mistakenly attributes this remark to Acheson; Smith, *Acheson*, 339.

35. *FRUS 1952–1954* X, 51–54, Acheson to Embassy in Iran, 11 May 1951; TNA, FO 371/91533, EP1531/308, Franks to FO, Tel. No. 1488, 12 May 1951. TNA, CAB 128/19, CM 35(51), 10 May 1951.

36. Painter, *Oil and American Century*, 175, citing *Present at Creation*, 506.

37. State Department statement, "US Position on Iranian Oil Situation," *DOSB* 24:621 (28 May 1951), 851.

38. On Grady, see John T. McNay, *Acheson and Empire: The British Accent in American Foreign Policy* (Columbia: University of Missouri Press, 2001), 129–157 and John T. McNay, ed., *The Memoirs of Ambassador Henry F. Grady* (Columbia: University of Missouri Press, 2009), 158–174. *Present at Creation*, 502.

39. *FRUS 1952–1954* X, 50–51 (Acheson to embassy in Iran, 27 June 1951), 71–76 (NSC 107/2, 27 June 1951); McMahon, *Acheson*, 159.

40. *FRUS 1952–1954* X, 66 editorial note.

41. Kenneth O. Morgan, *Labour in Power* (Oxford: Clarendon Press, 1984), 468–469; *Present at Creation*, 506–507.

42. TNA, FO 371/91555, EP1531/864, Franks to FO, Tel. No. 2060, 4 July 1951 and Tel. No. 2068, 5 July 1951.

43. L of C, Harriman Papers, box 292, Iran Diary and Notes 1951 folder. McMahon, *Acheson*, 159–160; Yergin, *The Prize*, 459–461.

44. *FRUS 1952–1954* X, 92, editorial note; *Present at the Creation*, 508–509.

45. HSTL, Acheson Papers, box 66, memorandum of conversation, 2 August 1951. The permanent under secretary at the Foreign Office, Sir William Strang, also doubted the wisdom of choosing Stokes, who "has never been really tested in international negotiation" and who "is impulsive and at times indiscreet"; FO 800/653, Pe/51/22, Strang minute for Morrison, 25 July 1951.

46. *Present at Creation*, 508.

47. *FRUS 1952–1954* X, 130; *Present at Creation*, 509–510; Louis, *British Empire in Middle East*, 686–689; TNA, CAB 128/20, CM 60(51), 27 September 1951.

48. *Present at Creation*, 510; Mary Ann Heiss, *Empire and Nationhood: the United States, Great Britain and Iranian Oil, 1950–1954* (New York: Columbia University Press, 1997), 79, 97–99.

49. *Present at Creation,* 510–511; Heiss, *Empire and Nationhood,* 100–105.

50. *FRUS 1952–1954* VI, Part 1, 742–746, memorandum of conversation at British embassy, 6 January 1952, quotation at 745.

51. *Present at Creation,* 511.

52. TNA, FO 371/91596, EP1531/1770, Franks to FO, Tel. No. 3223, 5 October 1951.

53. *FRUS 1952–1954* X, 445–447, Churchill initiative, 18 August 1952; *Present at Creation,* 679–685; Heiss, *Empire and Nationhood,* 107–166.

54. NARA, RG 59, State Department, Central Decimal File, 1950–1954, box 5490, 888.00/12-952, monthly economic survey, Iran, November 1952.

55. *FRUS 1952–1954* X, 518–521 (Acheson to Truman, 7 November 1952), 529–534 (NSC 136/1, 20 November 1952); Heiss, *Empire and Nationhood,* 154–155.

56. McNay, ed., *Memoirs of Grady,* 161, 167, McNay, *Acheson and Empire,* 152, 148; McGhee, *Envoy to Middle World,* 318–344. *FRUS 1952–1954* I Part 1, 22–29, memorandum by Acheson of meeting at the White House between the president and General Eisenhower, 18 November 1952. Conveying considerable frustration, Acheson declared that both the British and Iranians had been unreasonable; and that the administration was considering what the United States alone might do to solve the problem.

57. Yergin, *The Prize,* 464.

58. "Acheson shifts Aides," *New York Times* (28 March 1950); Rusk, *As I Saw It,* 160–161, 177.

59. *Present at Creation,* 432, 434–435.

60. See his account in John M. Allison, *Ambassador from the Prairie or Allison in Wonderland* (Boston: Houghton Mifflin, 1973), 140–172, quotation at 140.

61. Frederick S. Dunn, *Peace-making and the Settlement with Japan* (Princeton, NJ: Princeton University Press, 1963), 98–99.

62. *FRUS 1950* VI, 1229–1230 (memorandum by Dulles, 30 June 1950), 1230–1237 (summary report by Dulles, 3 July 1950); *Present at Creation,* 432; Allison, *Ambassador from Prairie,* 148.

63. "Statement by John Foster Dulles," 1 July 1950, in *DOSB* 23:575 (10 July 1950), 49–50.

64. *FRUS 1950* VI, 1290–1293 (Allison memorandum to Acheson, 4 September 1950), 1293–1296 (Acheson and Johnson joint memorandum for the President, 7 September 1950); it was approved by Truman on 8 September as NSC 60/1; Allison, *Ambassador from Prairie,* 145–151; *Present at Creation,* 431–434; Dunn, *Peace-making and Japan,* 105–108.

65. *Present at Creation,* 434–435.

66. *FRUS 1951* VI, 1296–1303, State Department memorandum, 11 September 1950, attaching draft of peace treaty with Japan; Allison, *Ambassador from Prairie,* 151; "US Sets Forth Principles for Japanese Peace Treaty," 24 November 1950, in *DOSB* 23:596 (4 December 1950), 881.

67. *FRUS 1950* VI, 1363–1367, Acheson to Marshall, 13 December 1950. Acheson was following the recommendations of Dulles and Allison, who stressed that there should be "prompt action to commit Japan, spiritually and politically, to the cause of the free world," but he did not use Dulles's form of words; *FRUS 1950* VI, 1359–1360, memorandum by Dulles and Allison, 8 December 1950. Acheson, *Present at Creation,* 434–435.

68. *FRUS 1951* VI, Part 1, 787–789, Acheson to Marshall, 9 January 1950, enclosing memorandum to president and draft letter to Dulles. No record of the Acheson-Marshall meeting was located by the FRUS editors.

69. For records of the visit, see *FRUS 1951* VI, Part 1, 827–873 passim, quotation at 829. See *FRUS 1951* VI, Part 1, 818–822, memorandum of conversation, 27 January 1951 for MacArthur's views; and *FRUS 1951* VI, Part 1, 827–829, memorandum of conversation, 29 January 1951 for Yoshida's views. Dulles, "Laying Foundations for a Pacific Peace: Report on Work of Presidential Mission to Japan," [broadcast of 1 March 1951] *DOSB* 24:610 (12 March 1951), 403–407.

70. TNA, FO 371/92532, FJ1022/100, Franks to FO, Tel. No. 606, 28 February 1951.

71. *FRUS 1951* VI, Part 1, 944–950, Provisional United States Draft of a Japanese Peace Treaty, 23 March 1951.

72. TNA, FO 371/92539, FJ1022/227, Franks to FO, Tel. No. 1030, 6 April 1951. See also R. Buckley, "Joining the Club: The Japanese Question and Anglo-American Peace Diplomacy," *Modern Asian Studies* 19:2 (1985), 308.

73. See TNA, FO 371/92545, FJ1022/336 and 342, FO 371/92546, FJ1022/357, and FO 371/92547, FJ1022/366 for British minutes of the meetings, 25 April to 4 May. TNA, FO 371/92540, FJ1022/265, Franks to FO, Tel. No. 1163, 16 April 1951. There do not appear to be any American minutes; *FRUS 1951* VI, 1021–1022, editorial note.

74. TNA, FO 371/92547, FJ1022/366, Franks to FO, Tel. No. 1381, 4 May 1951.

75. TNA, FO 371/92546, FJ1022/361, Franks to FO, Tel. No. 1362, 3 May 1951.

76. *FRUS 1951* VI, Part 1, 1024–1037, Joint United States–United Kingdom Draft Peace Treaty, 3 May 1951. See also "Draft Peace Treaty with Japan and Japanese Statements," [Statement by Ambassador Dulles," 11 July 1951, p. 132] in *DOSB* 25:630 (23 July 1951), 132–145.

77. *Present at Creation*, 540, *FRUS 1951* VI, Part 1, 972–976, memorandum by Dulles, 12 April 1951.

78. *FRUS 1951* VI, Part 1, 1105–1110, 1118–1133. For the British records, see TNA, FO 371/92553, FJ1022/498, FO 371/92554, FJ1022/513–516, 518, FO 371/92556, FJ1022/546–549, 562–563. An agreed communiqué on the compromise was, at Dulles's request, never published: TNA, FO 371/99402, FJ1026/3.

79. "Text of Proposed Treaty," *DOSB* 25:635 (27 August 1951), 349–357.

80. State Department, "Background: Japanese Peace Conference, San Francisco, September 1951," 1.

81. State Department, *Conference for the Conclusion and Signature of the Treaty of Peace with Japan, San Francisco, 1951*, document 11: first plenary session, 5 September 1951, 10:00am, pp. 3–11. The pagination of this volume is not consecutive; each document is separately paginated. *Present at Creation*, 544–545.

82. *Present at Creation*, 542, 544; *Princeton Seminars*, roll 4, frames 1478–1527, 14 March 1954.

83. Rusk, *As I Saw It*, 177.

84. State Department, *Conference for Treaty of Peace with Japan, San Francisco, 1951*. See also, TNA, FO 371/92594, FJ1022/1343, 1354 and FO 371/92595, FJ1022/1361, 1366 for British records.

85. Smith, *Acheson*, 295; *Princeton Seminars*, roll 4, frames 1514–1516, 14 March 1954. *Present at Creation*, 541–542, 544–545.

86. *Present at Creation*, 546. William S. White, "Acheson Superb at Treaty Parley, Says Senate Critic," *New York Times* (11 September 1951), 1; "Acheson's Triumph," *Washington Post* (12 September 1951), 14; Richard L. Strout, "GOP Praise for Acheson Follows Treaty Victory," *Christian Science Monitor* (11 September 1951), 1.

87. See *FRUS 1951* VI Part 1, 132–265 for talks on ANZUS and treaty with the Philippines; "US, Australia, New Zealand Negotiate Security Treaty," *DOSB* 25:630 (23 July 1951), 147–149. Text of US-Japanese Security Treaty, 8 September 1951, in *DOSB* 25:638 (17 September 1951), 464–465.

88. Smith, *Acheson*, 300, 304.

89. "56 in Senate Bar Tokyo-Peiping Ties," *New York Times* (14 September 1951), 3.

90. *FRUS 1951* VI, Part 1, 1466–1467, Yoshida to Dulles, 24 December 1951.

91. *FRUS 1951* VI, Part 1, 1467–1470, Dulles memorandum for Acheson, 26 December 1951.

92. TNA, FO 371/92531, FJ1022/75, Franks to FO, Tel. No. 449, 13 February 1951; Roger Buckley, *Occupation Diplomacy: Britain, the United States and Japan 1945–1952* (Cambridge: Cambridge University Press, 1982), 176–177.

93. *FRUS 1952–1954* XIV, Part 2, 1077–1080, memorandum of conversation, 10 January 1952; TNA, FO 800/781, FE/52/5, conversation between Eden and Acheson, 10 January 1952; TNA, FO 371/99403, FJ10310/4, Franks to FO, Tel. No. 107, 10 January 1952. See also FO 371/97593, AU1051/25, Eden-Pearson conversation, 13 January 1952, when Eden reported that he and Acheson agreed to disagree.

94. TNA, FO 371/99403, FJ10310/8, FO to Washington, Tel No 313, 16 January 1952.

95. *FRUS 1952–1954* XIV, Part 2, 1075–1077, memorandum of conversation, 9 January 1952; *Present at Creation,* 604.

96. TNA, FO 371/99404, FJ10310/42 and 43.

97. TNA, FO 371/99403, FJ10310/10, Franks to FO, Tel. No. 186, 16 January 1952; HSTL, Acheson Papers, box 67, memorandum of conversation, 16 January 1952. Acheson wrote to Lester Pearson of Canada: "I think we were at fault in not being more explicit"; Acheson, *Present at Creation,* 604.

98. 82nd Congress, 2nd Session, Hearings before the Senate Committee on Foreign Relations, *Japanese Peace Treaty and Other Treaties Relating to Security in the Pacific* (Washington, DC: USGPO, 1951), 1–4, statement by Acheson, 21 January 1952.

99. Beisner, *Acheson,* 480.

100. Senate Foreign Relations Committee, *Japanese Peace Treaty and Other Treaties Relating to Security in the Pacific,* 63–64, Acheson to Wiley, 5 February 1952.

101. NARA, RG 59, State Department, Special Files Japan 1947–1956 Lot Files (Lot 54 D 423, 57 D 149, 58 D 118, 58 D 637), microfilm roll 1, pp. 00132, 00134–00142; E. J. Kahn, *The China Hands: America's Foreign Service Officers and What Befell Them* (New York: Penguin, 1976), 228–231, 240–243; *Present at Creation,* 633. Executive order 9835 of 22 March 1947 established Loyalty Boards in each government agency, following recommendations by the Temporary Commission on Employee Loyalty (set up by Truman in November 1946). It adopted a similar approach to the attorney general's list of 1942.

102. Acheson statement, 21 March 1952 in *DOSB* 26:666 (31 March 1952), 491.

103. NARA, RG 59, State Department, Special Files Japan 1947–1956 Lot Files (Lot 54 D 423, 57 D 149, 58 D 118, 58 D 637), microfilm roll 1, p. 00145, Dulles to Acheson, 21 March 1952 and Acheson to Dulles, 24 March 1952 in State Department Press Release, 25 March 1952.

104. Richard Immerman, *John Foster Dulles: Piety, Pragmatism, and Power in U.S. Foreign Policy* (Wilmington, DE: Scholarly Resources, 1999), 37; McMahon, *Acheson,* 154.

105. Townsend Hoopes, *The Devil and John Foster Dulles* (Boston: Little, Brown, 1973), 110, 488.

106. William S. White, "Jessup Denounces M'Carthy Charges As Danger to U.S.," *New York Times* (21 March 1950), 1, 25; "Taft Implies Fight On Jessup, Bowles," *New York Times* (14 September 1951), 4.

107. 82nd Congress, 1st Session, Hearings Before a Subcommittee of the Senate Foreign Relations Committee, *The Nomination of Philip C. Jessup,* 27 September, 2–5, 8, 15, 17–18 October 1951 (Washington, DC: USGPO, 1951). Acheson, *Present at Creation,* 573–574. L of C, Jessup Papers, box 144, McCarthyism M-l, October 1951 folder [series of folders all titled October 1951], "L'Affaire Jessup and the evidence," *America: National Catholic Weekly Review* 86:4 (27 October 1951), 89.

108. L of C, Jessup Papers, box 1:144, McCarthyism M-l, October 1951 folder [series of folders all titled October 1951]; "We Won't Buy Korea Peace, Acheson Says," *Washington Post* (6 October 1951).

109. *The Nomination of Jessup,* 610, 682, 686–704, 742–743. L of C, Jessup Papers, box 1:144, McCarthyism M-l, October 1951 folder [series of folders all titled October 1951]; Don Irwin, "Stassen Calls Testimony of Jessup False," *New York Herald Tribune* (9 October 1951).

110. L of C, Jessup Papers, 1:145, McCarthyism, 1950–1954, Policy toward China, 1951 folder, transcript of round table discussion of Far Eastern Policy, 6–8 October 1949.

111. See chapter 4.

112. L of C, Jessup Papers, box 1:137, M-L 1951, Hearings—Fall of 1951—Miscellaneous Background Papers (Mostly Press Releases) folder, Statement by the President, 22 October 1951, Elmer Davis to Mrs. Jessup, 19 October 1951.

113. L of Congress, Jessup Papers, box 1:138, M-L 1951, Hearings—Fall of 1951—Misc. folder [multiple folders with this designation]; and box 1:137, M-L 1951, Hearings—Fall of 1951—Miscellaneous Background Papers (Mostly Press Releases) folder, Elmer Davis to Mrs. Jessup, 19 October 1951.

114. L of C, Jessup Papers, box 1:137, M-L 1951, Hearings—Fall of 1951—Miscellaneous Background Papers (Mostly Press Releases) folder, Statement by the President, 22 October 1951.

115. Acheson, *Korean War*, 129.

116. Statement of 7 May 1952, quoted in Truman, *Years of Trial and Hope*, 521.

117. *FRUS 1952–1954* XV Part 1, 195n, 223–224, secretary's daily meeting 22 May 1952. Stueck, *Korean War*, 266, 271–272, 276; MacDonald, *Korea*, 134–153.

118. *FRUS 1952–1954* XV Part 1; 73–74 (memorandum of conversation, 3 March 1952), 79–80 (Secretary of State to the President, 11 March 1952); Acheson correspondence with ICRC, 11–13 March 1952, in *DOSB* 26:665 (24 March 1952), 452–453. See also *FRUS 1952–1954* XV, Part 1; 343–344, editorial note; Ernest R. Gross, "The Soviet Germ Warfare Campaign: The Strategy of the Big Lie," [Statement of 1 July 1952] *DOSB* 27:683 (28 July 1952), 153–159.

119. *FRUS 1952–1954* XV Part 1, 242n.

120. *FRUS 1952–1954* XV Part 1, 226–227, memorandum of conversation, 22 May 1952.

121. *FRUS 1952–1954* XV Part 1, 351–352, editorial note, 352–354 (acting secretary of state to embassy in London, 24 June 1952); NARA, RG 59, State Department, Central Decimal File, 1950–1954, box 4281, 795.00/6–2352, discussions with Selwyn Lloyd, 23 June 1952; NARA, RG 59, State Department, Central Decimal File, 1950–1954, box 4281, 795.00/6-2552, discussions with Selwyn Lloyd (on 24 June), 25 June 1952.

122. Acheson, *Korean War*, 135–136.

123. NARA, RG 59, State Department, Central Decimal File, 1950–1954, box 4281, 795.00/6-2752, memorandum of conversation, 27 June 1950; NARA, RG 59, State Department, Central Decimal File, 1950–1954, box 4281, 795.00/6-2752, Jack K. McFall to Senator Knowland, 30 June 1952 (enclosing comments by Secretary of State Acheson on 26 [*sic*] June 1952 before informal meeting of Members of Parliament in London).

124. *FRUS 1952–1954* XV Part 1, 551–553, Hickerson to Acheson, 2 October 1952.

125. *FRUS 1952–1954* XV Part 1, 554–556, Clark to JCS, 8 October 1952; Acheson statement, 8 October 1952, in *DOSB* 27:695 (20 October 1952), 600.

126. *FRUS 1952–1954* III, 32–34. Thomas J. Hamilton, "Acheson Urges U.N. to Fight in Korea Until a Just Peace," *New York Times* (17 October 1952), 1, 9. Stueck, *Korean War*, 291, 293.

127. *FRUS 1952–1954* XV Part 1, 563, editorial note; *Present at Creation*, 765–767, Acheson, *Korean War*, 138–141; Acheson speech in *DOSB* 27:697 (3 November 1952), 679–692, and *DOSB* 27:699 (10 November 1952), 744–751.

128. *FRUS 1952–1954* XV Part 1, 566–568 (memorandum of conversation by Acheson, 29 October 1952), 607–610 (secretary of state to Department of State, 12 November 1952), 614–615 (Bruce to Truman, 13 November 1952).

129. Churchill College, Cambridge, Selwyn Lloyd Papers, SELO 4/28, Diary, 13 and 19 November 1952; Evelyn Shuckburgh, *Descent to Suez: Diaries 1951–56* (London: Weidenfeld & Nicolson, 1986), 53–54. Acheson's account conveys no sense of his irascible behavior; Acheson, *Korean War*, 145.

130. Eisenhower speech, 24 October 1952, available at https://eisenhower.archives.gov/research/online_documents/korean_war/I_Shall_Go_To_Korea_1952_10_24.pdf (viewed 23 January 2017); *FRUS 1952–1954* XV Part 1, 578, memorandum of conversation by Acheson, 5 November 1952; NARA, RG 59 State Department, Central Decimal File, 1950–1954, box 4284, 795.00/11-652, Acheson memorandum to Truman, 6 November 1952. Acheson, *Korean War*, 144–145. Eisenhower does not mention this in his memoirs; Dwight D. Eisenhower, *Mandate for Change* (London: Heinemann, 1963), 72, 93–95.

131. *FRUS 1952–1954* XV Part 1, 702–705.

132. See S. L. A. Marshall, "Korean Stalemate—the War of 'Where Do We Go From Here,'" *Reporter* (11 November 1952); reprinted in *The Reporter, The Political Yearbook 1952* (New York: Fortnightly Publishing Company, 1953), 38–41.

133. *FRUS 1952–1954* XV Part 1, 902–1151 and *FRUS 1952–1954* XV Part 2, 1153–1445.

134. *FRUS 1951* III Part 1, 813–819, Acheson memorandum, 6 July 1951.

135. *FRUS 1951* III Part 1, 836–838 (memorandum by secretary of state, 16 July 1951), 849–852 (memorandum by Acheson and Lovett to Truman, 30 July 1951), 847–849 (editorial note).

136. Acheson, *Sketches*, 49–51, 167–168; Anthony Eden, *Full Circle* (London: Cassell, 1960), 33–34; *FRUS 1951* III Part 1, 652–692 (proceedings at Ottawa) 714–743 (proceedings at Rome), 747–751 (Acheson to Truman, 30 November 1951).

137. *Present at Creation*, 615–621; Eden, *Full Circle*, 40–41.

138. *FRUS 1952–1954* V, Part 1, 107–174 (proceedings), 177–179 (final communiqué, 26 February 1952), 175–176 (Acheson to Truman, 26 February 1952); *Princeton Seminars*, roll 4, frames 1527–1533, 14 March 1954; Acheson, *Present at Creation*, 625–626; Acheson, *Sketches*, 52–55, 105–118; Edwin Plowden, *An Industrialist in the Treasury: The Post-War Years* (London: Andre Deutsch, 1989), 125–132.

139. *Present at Creation*, 569–570; *FRUS 1952–1954* V, Part 1, 23, Acheson to Schuman, 4 February 1952.

140. *FRUS 1952–1954* V, Part 1, 292–301; *Present at Creation*, 643–646; Acheson, *Sketches*, 57–58.

141. Smith, *Acheson*, 357.

142. *Present at Creation*, 257–258. On the Truman administration's approach to the region, see David Green, "The Cold War Comes to Latin America," in Barton J. Bernstein, *The Politics and Policies of the Truman Administration* (Chicago: Quadrangle Books, 1970), 149–195; Alan M. McPherson, *Intimate Ties, Bitter Struggles: The United States and Latin America since 1945* (Washington, DC: Potomac Books, 2006), 18–25; and Richard Immerman, *The CIA in Guatemala: The Foreign Policy of Intervention* (Austin: University of Texas Press, 1982), 9–13.

143. L of C, Frankfurter Papers, box 19, reel 11, Acheson to Frankfurter, 10 July 1952.

144. Beisner, *Acheson*, 569.

145. Acheson, "Waging Peace in the Americas," *DOSB* 21:445 (26 September 1949), 462–466; *Present at Creation*, 330.

146. Smith, *Acheson*, 356.

147. *FRUS 1951* II, 925–927 (memorandum by Miller, 15 December 1950), 928–929 (Acheson to Diplomatic Offices in American Republics, 16 December 1950), 960–961 (editorial note), 969 (notes of under secretary's meeting, 6 April 1951); "Fourth Meeting of Consultation of Ministers of Foreign Affairs of American Republics," *DOSB* 24:615 (16 April 1951), 606–615, Acheson, "Outstanding Achievements," *DOSB* 24:615 (16 April 1951), 616–617.

148. *FRUS 1952–1954* IV, 1600–1613; Truman approved Acheson's recommendations on 17 March 1952.

149. *FRUS 1951* II, 1157–1159 (memorandum of conversation, 9 July 1951), 1164–1166 (memorandum of conversation by Miller, 9 November 1951); Smith, *Acheson*, 359. Glenn J. Dorn, "Pushing Tin: U.S.-Bolivian Relations and the Coming of the National Revolution," *Diplomatic History* 35:2 (April 2011), 203–228.

150. *FRUS 1952–1954* IV, 502–503, Acheson to Embassy in Bolivia, 8 September 1952. NARA, RG 59, State Department Central Decimal File 1950–1954, box 4608, 824.054/9-2452, Miller to Embassy in Bolivia, 25 September 1952; 824.2544/1-2452, Mills, "Strategic Importance of Tin," 24 January 1950; 824.2544/1-2552, Acheson memorandum for president, 3 January 1952; 824.2544/11-2152, aide memoire by Bolivian embassy, 21 November 1952. Smith, *Acheson*, 360; Beisner, *Acheson*, 575–576; McPherson, *Intimate Ties, Bitter Struggles*, 31–32.

151. *FRUS 1951* II, 1436–1444 (Miller, "Current relations with Guatemala," 12 June 1951), 1446–1448 (memorandum of conversation by Clark, 15 November 1951); *FRUS 1952–1954: Guatemala*, document 10 (CIA telegram, 25 June 1952), document 12 (CIA memorandum, 9 July 1952; available at https://history.state.gov/historicaldocuments/frus1952-54Guat/comp1 (viewed 23 January 2017). Beisner, *Acheson*, 576–581.

152. *FRUS 1952–1954: Guatemala*, document 23 (CIA memorandum, 8 October 1952), document 24 (CIA memorandum, 8 October 1952); available at https://history.state.gov/historicaldocuments/frus1952-54Guat/comp1 (viewed 23 January 2017). *FRUS 1952–1954* IV, 1041–1042, Mann to Acheson, 12 October 1952. *Princeton Seminars*, 22 July 1953, roll 3,

frames 516–616. Beisner, *Acheson*, 583; Nelson D. Lankford, *The Last American Aristocrat: The Biography of David K. E. Bruce* (Boston: Little, Brown, 1996), 249; Immerman, *CIA in Guatemala*, 121; Nick Cullather, *Secret History: The CIA's Classified Account of Its Operations in Guatemala, 1952–1954*, 2nd ed. (Stanford, CA: Stanford University Press, 2006), 29–31.

153. Smith, *Acheson*, 360.

154. "In the Mercury's Opinion: The Apotheosis of Acheson and Marshall," *American Mercury* LXXIV (February 1952), 3–7; "Acheson's list of stupidities could fill this magazine" (5). Felix Wittmer, "Freedom's Case Against Dean Acheson," *American Mercury* LXXIV (April 1952), 3–17; "Acheson's record of disservice to the cause of freedom begins nineteen years ago when he became one of Stalin's paid American lawyers" (5).

155. Roper Center Public Opinion Archives, Truman Presidential Approval Poll, 11–16 December 1952; available at https://presidential.roper.center (viewed 23 January 2017).

Chapter Seven

Afterlife of a Secretary

Acheson left the State Department for the last time on 16 January 1953, receiving a farewell from a crowd of several hundred, testament to the high esteem in which he was held by the department. He received his cabinet chair as a parting gift. Clearly moved by the demonstration of admiration and warm regard, he offered some brief remarks, observing that he felt very close to a previous secretary, John Quincy Adams, whom he described as "a peppery old fellow" but one with a keen sense of public service.[1] The next day, the *New York Times* devoted an editorial to him. It noted that he served at a time when the United States graduated from one of the major powers to leadership of half the world. "This was a sudden coming of age in a stormy period with an enemy just about as powerful and determined as we were." He formulated policies for this new era and if those policies merit praise, then Acheson should also be praised. He faced "a degree and ferocity of abuse that was rare even in our outspoken history" but met it "without a murmur and with unfailing dignity." It concluded that "here was a man of a stature commensurate with the role he was given to play." At his final press conference on the 14th he had delivered his goodbyes in an understated elegiac tone.[2]

On 19 January Acheson made his fiftieth and final appearance before the Senate Foreign Relations Committee, giving a characteristically confident performance. The report on the closed session by the chairman, Senator Alexander Wiley (R-Wisconsin), revealed that Acheson had taken a much more optimistic view of Western Europe than his successor-designate, John Foster Dulles, who had spoken of the dimming prospects for the region when he had addressed the committee the previous week.[3]

When Acheson stepped down as secretary of state, he was eighty-one days short of his sixtieth birthday: he never held high office again in the remaining eighteen years and nine months of his life. Acheson's last two decades fall neatly into two phases. First, there were the two terms of the Eisenhower presidency. He returned to his old law firm, Covington and Burling, and accepted J. Robert Oppenheimer's invitation to join a seminar of former officials at Princeton to examine in considerable detail the policies he pursued as secretary of state. In addition, he gave a number of oral history interviews for the Truman presidential library. During these years, he reflected a great deal on politics and foreign policy in particular, defended his record, delivered lectures and talks, wrote three books and many articles offering a critique of Eisenhower and his secretary of state, John Foster Dulles; became a leading adviser to the Democratic Party; and engaged in a bitter dispute with George Kennan over Germany.

The second period saw him more directly involved in shaping national policy when a Democratic president returned to the White House in January 1961. John F. Kennedy solicited his advice about the appointment of the secretary of state and the broad patterns of the US relationship with its NATO allies. In the course of the presidency, Acheson also gave his views on key problems, most prominently on Berlin in 1961 and Cuba in 1962. After Kennedy's assassination, the new president, Lyndon B. Johnson, also consulted the former secretary, particularly on the growing crisis over Vietnam. Somewhat surprisingly, given his sharp criticisms of Acheson during the 1952 presidential election, Richard Nixon also sought Acheson's counsel in 1969–1971.

REFLECTING AND WRITING ABOUT BEING SECRETARY OF STATE, 1953–1960

By January 1953 Acheson was tired emotionally and physically following nearly continuous service at the State Department since February 1941. After the heavy workload, he and Alice took a much-needed two-month holiday in Antigua with Archibald and Ada MacLeish. The Achesons' close friends, John and Betty Cowles, also joined them. The publisher of the *Minneapolis Star and Tribune* and the former secretary enjoyed each other's company and regularly discussed domestic and international politics. Acheson described life in Antigua as "too pleasant, easy and lazy to be in any remote way moral."[4] He distanced himself from events: the *New York Times* arrived a week or so late and was "thrust upon me by kind friends, against my will." He swam, allowed himself "some moderate use of alcoholic beverages," but, above all, indulged in the luxury of reading. He read G. M. Young's biography of Stanley Baldwin, Thomas's life of Lincoln, the correspondence of John Adams and Thomas Jefferson, the Holmes-Laski letters, Henry David Thoreau, and the mysteries of Josephine Tey.[5] He told Jeffrey Kitchen, who had served as his executive assistant at the State Department: "My real life is in that hazy realm where the well being of the animal merges into the life of the mind created by books so that one feels detached from person, or time or place and lives several lives—all inconsistent all at the same time."[6]

He returned to the United States in late March and spent April on his farm at Sandy Spring in Maryland, celebrating his sixtieth birthday on the 11th, "painting the porch furniture, plowing the garden, wheel barrowing manure for her [Alice's] roses, building a new wood fence and taking the grandchildren down to the next farm to see horses, cattle, pigs, and puppies." He told Truman that he was "also getting pretty steamed up about the way the pupils whom you had to teach so carefully are really fouling things up." There was "a terrible retrogression . . . in the processes of government. Ike is presiding over something which is corruptive on a really grand scale." He especially lamented the sacking of Paul Nitze, who had been director of the Policy Planning Staff at the State Department.[7]

Although he recharged his batteries and returned to his law practice at Covington and Burling on Monday 4 May, Acheson did not adjust easily to the new circumstances. The daily activities of a lawyer were less appealing than being at the center of politics and international affairs. As he explained to John J. McCloy on 30 July 1953: "I still cannot get used to the feeling—and I know you have experienced it too—of being so completely cut off from events with which one has lived for so long."[8] Nor did the law prove as lucrative as might have been expected—Republican-inclined executives were often reticent about employing the services of such a high-profile Democrat.

At the same time, Acheson became involved in various forms of reflection on his time in office. He agreed to the suggestion by Robert Oppenheimer, former director of the Manhattan Project to build the atomic bomb and now head of the Institute of Advanced Studies at Princeton, that he join a number of other former officials from the Truman administration to discuss his time as secretary. The resultant "Princeton Seminars" took place in July, October, and December 1953 and February, March, and May 1954.[9] Although initially doubtful about their utility, Acheson took the sessions very seriously, showing a desire not just to record what happened but also to probe the issues. In his 17 February 1954 memorandum to members of the seminar Acheson considered the upcoming topics and how they might be explored. He noted how, up to that point, they had concentrated on the narrative and hoped that they might devote attention to problems and purposes in their final sessions in March. He gave particular attention to the weakness and instability of France. The second area he suggested was what Chester Bowles, an ardent liberal who had served as US ambassador to India, 1951–1952, called the "uncommitted areas" of Southeast and South Asia, the Middle East, and Africa. He also raised Latin America: "They and we expect

too much of each other and often talk foolishly. But our relations are important both ways." And he favored discussion (with Dean Rusk and Philip
Jessup present) of American involvement in the UN, saying they should
consider Philip Jessup's belief that the futility of working with the UN was
mainly due to the international situation and not the institution. [10]

Acheson also gave extensive oral testimony to the Truman Library. Indeed, he played an important part in the fundraising efforts for the presidential library. [11] He gave five interviews over the course of three days in February 1955 to Truman's main aides in his memoirs project—the journalist
William Hillman, who had written a study of Truman in 1952, [12] David
Noyes, and the academic Francis Heller. Acheson later told Truman that he
and Alice had delighted in their visit to Kansas City and "[E]ven when the
three man jury had me under examination I was reliving days which were the
best and fullest I have ever lived." [13] Acheson went further by offering detailed commentaries on the texts of the president's two volumes of memoirs.
He admonished Truman for deploying the phrase "striped pants boys in the
State Department," saying not only that it was a tiresome cliché but that it
"gives quite the wrong impression of the tremendous support you gave to the
career service." He agreed that James Byrnes had failed to consult the president adequately at the Moscow Council of Foreign Ministers in December
1945 but defended the former secretary's handling of the arrangements for
Bulgaria and Romania. Byrnes had not, as the draft memoirs suggested,
allowed the Soviets to have their way. He put in place arrangements that the
Soviets did not honor. Acheson also urged Truman to be much tougher in his
account of MacArthur's behavior in 1950–1951. All these suggestions were
adopted. [14] Finally, Acheson advised the former president on several
speeches. [15]

In addition to these oral testimonies, he defended his time in office more
explicitly, both publicly and in private correspondence. The journalist David
Lawrence criticized Acheson's writing for enflaming partisanship over
foreign policy, Alger Hiss, and communists in government. In an article for
Harper's magazine, Acheson declared that his party handled foreign affairs
better than the Republicans, whose preoccupation with domestic communism
he bemoaned. [16] Republicans bridled at Acheson's strictures and accused him
of working in consort with Hiss, who had written an article for *Pocketbook*
magazine defending the Yalta conference. They further accused Acheson and
Hiss of jointly working to elect a left-wing Democratic presidential candidate. [17]

Acheson also entered debates through correspondence on his term as
secretary. On 6 August 1956 he wrote:

> We need the most rigorous sort of thinking to guide us to lines of action for
> dealing with events and problems rushing at us. But, hard as this is, I suspect it

is the easiest part of the task. Infinitely harder in a democracy is to produce leadership with the necessary character to do what brains direct; and a people with the necessary self-discipline to do what it dislikes. Perhaps it is impossible. Perhaps we shall not be able to save ourselves unless we become "hopped up" as "true believers." Somehow, I can't believe it. If I am wrong, "I tremble for my country," as Jefferson said, "when I reflect that God is just."[18]

Acheson's thoughts on his time in office developed into reflections on the office of secretary of state and the making of American foreign policy, and, in particular, the relationship between the secretary and the president and between the secretary and the State Department. His ideas appeared in a number of articles and contributions to books and were an important part of his first book, *A Democrat Looks at His Party.*[19]

Acheson argued that the final responsibility for decision in foreign policy resided with the president acting on behalf of the whole people, and without this presidential direction, policy drift ensued. Different presidents had reached decisions by different means. Jefferson, Lincoln, and Wilson pursued it by solitary reflection and study, while Truman was determined to stick to channels. However he decided to work, Acheson contended, the president "must be free to choose the methods most suited to him. He cannot be confined by law."[20] Although the president directed foreign policy, the secretary must be privy to all the president's thoughts and have the last chance to give advice before action is taken.[21] The relationship between the president and the secretary entailed two mutual obligations: the secretary's duty to keep the president fully informed and the president's responsibility to reach decisions clearly and to support them in a strong way so that action could easily follow. There needed to be an effective partnership between the two men, one that necessarily turned on their individual personalities, experience, and training, and on the political exigencies and circumstances of the times. To achieve all this, they needed to spend a good deal of time together and to have confidence in each other. The secretary should be the "principal adviser and executive agent in foreign affairs and the trusted confidant of all his [the president's] thoughts and plans."[22]

The secretary would only succeed in this if he harnessed the skills of the State Department with its wealth of knowledge about the complex world beyond American shores. Acheson stressed that departmental officials were the "originators, as well as the executors of foreign policy." It was the duty of these officials and the secretary in particular to address the difficult task of seeing beyond immediate issues to emerging problems.[23] Foreign affairs was an area of special competence: people who had spent their lives studying foreign nations knew more about them than those who had not. The Department of State should be the principal, unifying, and final source of advice on foreign affairs. It was the secretary's task to draw from the department in usable form its full knowledge and wisdom.[24]

The secretary's advice should not come only from his knowledge or that of his closest aides: the "formulation of judgment as to facts, probabilities, policy, and actions calls for institutional effort, for which there is at the Secretary's hand one of the most effective instruments in the world—the Department of State." Issues so complex and interrelated required specialized knowledge and demanded levels of synthesis that no single individual or small group could provide. The officials, he added in a clear jibe at Dulles's approach to the department, should be free to express their thoughts: "This freedom cannot exist in an atmosphere of bullying, suspicion, intimidation, or officially prescribed values and attitudes." Finally, he explained the need to avoid being dominated by pressing day-to-day concerns: "Today's problems crowd out tomorrow's, next month's, next year's." "The press of daily work leads to the continuance of courses of action after the reasons which called them into being have ceased to exist." When he was secretary, George Marshall had created the Policy Planning Staff to tackle these difficulties.[25]

Acheson stressed the episodic way foreign issues arose for both government and people and the need to "seduce his fellow citizens to leave their own problems, pleasures, or rest" and consider these external concerns. He also emphasized the importance of power and securing consent if American foreign policies were to be effective. Americans understood and practiced this in domestic politics but "have been insulated from these truths in our international life by our long sheltered position behind two oceans." Indeed, "we have actually been misled by the experience of our dramatic sorties into the larger world. It seemed to us that it is our role to intervene in world affairs with sporadic and violent bursts of energy and with decisive and definitive effect." But this experience had brought disillusionment when those assisted did not remain appealing, were not grateful, and became demanding. Acheson urged his readers to recognize that Americans needed to adjust to "continuing responsibility" in the new Cold War era.[26]

REFLECTING AND WRITING ABOUT AMERICA AND THE WORLD, 1953–1960

These thoughts about the secretary, the president, and foreign policy shaded into growing criticisms of the Eisenhower administration and the new secretary of state, John Foster Dulles. Neither Truman nor Acheson had warmed to Eisenhower after their experience of his campaign and their encounters with him in the transition period from November 1952 to January 1953. But Acheson's strongest strictures involved Dulles, whose moralism and preaching had always repelled him. Although he respected Dulles's role in negotiating the Japanese Peace Treaty and helping to secure its passage through Congress, he soon became dismayed with Dulles as secretary. His early reaction to the new administration was characteristically sharp and partisan. In March 1953, he told Archibald MacLeish:

> The political atmosphere in Washington is unbelievable. The gentlemen of the press, who still faun in print, tell you privately that it has taken sheer genius to get things as backed up in two months as our new masters have done. Ike, they say, has enough prestige to save the day if he will realize what is going on—i.e. that he is caught in an ice floe moving to the right; on one side is McCarthy who has no limit, only infinity; on the other side is Taft, Ike's protector, whose limit is not yet in sight. Whether this is true or not I do not know. The smart boys + girls are talking this way.[27]

In August he told Lucius Battle that "Dulles' people seem to be like Cossacks quartered in a grand old city hall, burning the panelling to cook with."[28]

If Acheson disdained the general way that Dulles failed to utilize the talents of State Department officials, he was appalled by the new secretary's treatment of John Carter Vincent, who had served as director of the State Department's Bureau of Far Eastern Affairs and faced accusations of communist sympathies. On 12 December 1952 the federal Loyalty Review Board concluded by a 3-to-2 vote that Vincent's loyalty was suspect. The circumstances of the decision and the board's reasoning were odd. The original three-man panel voted 2-to-1 in favor of Vincent but then the chairman, Hiram Bingham, added two members, who voted against him. In explaining their recommendation the board wrote that it had taken into account one individual's testimony, even though they neither accepted nor rejected it. Walter Surrey, Vincent's lawyer, approached Acheson, who was at the end of his term in office and thereby limited in what he could do. By this time, Acheson had realized that he was not compelled to sack someone on the basis of the Loyalty Board's recommendation—something he regretted having done with Foreign Service officer John Service in 1951. He expressed his misgivings about the board's ruling to Truman and secured the president's agreement to reexamine Vincent's case. He then asked Adrian Fisher, his departmental legal adviser, to contact the distinguished judge, Learned Hand, to convene another five-member committee to examine Vincent's case. Hand, of course, would have to report to the new secretary, Dulles. Acheson met Dulles as part of the transition of administrations on 24 December and explained the intention to have Hand investigate. Acheson declared: "It seemed to me that the opinion of the Loyalty Board had passed judgment not on Mr Vincent's loyalty but on the soundness of the policy recommendations he made. If disagreements on policy were to be equated with disloyalty, the Foreign Service would be destroyed."[29]

As the Eisenhower administration took office on 20 January, Hand wrote to Dulles to ask whether he and his committee should continue their work, but Dulles replied on the 29th saying that they did not need to proceed, for he would deal with the matter himself. Dulles gave his verdict on 4 March: Vincent was not guilty of disloyalty and was not a security risk but he could not remain in the State Department. Dulles maintained Vincent failed "to meet the standard which is demanded of a Foreign Service officer," but did not define that standard. He gave him a choice of being dismissed or volunteering to retire.[30] Dulles's biographer has defended him by saying that Vincent's association with the failure of policy to China had made him a liability. Therefore, Dulles was seeking a compromise—he overturned the Loyalty Board's "reasonable doubt" about Vincent's loyalty but had conceded that Vincent had to go. "The Secretary's decision was a compromise between principle and political demands in an attempt to protect not only his own position but also that of the department and Service and foreign policy generally."[31] Acheson was less understanding, noting that six previous secretaries had not found Vincent's counsel as sub-standard. The case served to confirm his low opinion of Dulles.[32]

Acheson remarked on the "inordinately stupid way my successor is alienating people on whom he will have to rely."[33] He lamented to Oliver Franks that Washington, DC, was a tomb—"ideas do not live here anymore."[34] He was also highly critical of Eisenhower's and Dulles's new policies. He attacked the "new look" strategy that sought to reverse the major rearmament program envisaged in NSC 68 and endorsed by the NATO meeting in Lisbon in 1952. He staunchly contested the emphasis on cost-cutting for conventional forces and a reliance on nuclear forces. Dulles's theories of massive retaliation and limited nuclear war were anathema to him.

Doubts about the president and secretary, about the institutional procedures and the key policies appeared initially in Acheson's private correspondence. In October 1953 he took advantage of a major address to air his views publicly, as he received the Woodrow Wilson Award. His lecture on "Post-War Foreign Policy Second Phase" offered a clear, if indirect, critique of Eisenhower and John Foster Dulles. The "leadership of a coalition of free peoples requires that the purposes and policies put forward are broad enough to embrace the interest of the whole group," it "cannot be personal or narrow." Any leader who "insults or denigrates our allies" and regards the United States as "the sole repository of wisdom and resistance to tyranny" damages our alliance.[35]

Acheson expanded his attack on the policy of instant retaliation in a *New York Times* article. He lamented how the current administration undermined good relations with allies: a preoccupation with the threat of domestic communism and the presence of communist parties in allied countries led Eisenhower and Dulles to have doubts about allies. Even more worrying was the policy of instant atomic retaliation. This should only be contemplated as the nation's declared response to a major assault on a vital interest and deter the enemy from launching such an attack because of its suicidal consequences. Korea taught that this threat would not deter local aggressions, which should be met, not with instant retaliation, but with a conventional response by the United States and its allies. This meant America should cultivate and not antagonize its allies.[36] He wrote to Truman saying he had become "too worked up over the fraud of the New Look." International affairs could not so easily be reduced to such "slick talk."[37] In a letter to John Cowles of the *Star and Tribune* of Minneapolis he challenged Cowles's support for the Eisenhower administration's strategic idea of drawing a clear line and launching a major assault if that line were to be crossed. Such an approach posed a genuine risk of allowing an escalation to World War III. Acheson also repudiated Cowles's claim that that was the policy pursued by Truman and Acheson when in office. On the contrary, their policy toward Berlin, the Greek-Turkish crisis, and Korea was to avoid enlarging the conflict into general war.[38] In an article in *Harper's* in November 1955, Acheson lambasted Dulles's policy of massive atomic retaliation, calling it "a classic illustration of the way a leader among free nations should not proceed."[39]

Truman disappointed Acheson by his readiness to understand Eisenhower's and Dulles's policies. The former president drafted a speech in 1953 regretting the way matters were drifting and how there was a weakening of the defense program, but he hesitated to attack Eisenhower. Acheson and Harriman suggested the speech went too far in claiming that the new administration was carrying out Truman's foreign policy. Acheson was sharper in his criticism three and a half years later when he expressed dismay that Truman had written an article for the *New York Times* that "cut a good deal of ground" from Acheson's critique of the administration's foreign policy. Truman argued that Congress had little choice but to accept Eisenhower's program. Acheson crisply responded: "If this is so, then I spent four useless hours before the Foreign Affairs Committee and a good many useless days of work in devising what I thought an excellent alternative." In 1958 he admonished the former president: "you have encouraged very grave error." He disagreed with Truman's unconditional backing of the administration's support for the Taiwan regime's control of the offshore islands of Quemoy and Matsu. It risked escalation over an issue of no great importance to the United States.[40]

Robert McMahon has deftly judged Acheson's elegantly written and well-argued claims. Acheson identified real policy differences from abandonment of NSC 68 to adoption of massive retaliation to raising the risks of confrontation with the Soviet Union to evoking anxieties among allies. But there were more continuities than Acheson seemed ready to concede—from recognition of the scale of the Soviet threat to a commitment to a powerful

Western military stance to counteract that threat and resist communist expansion. "Acheson's partisan inclinations—and it bears emphasizing that he *always* saw himself as a loyal Democrat—led him to accentuate deliberately all policy disagreements."[41] Moreover, he overstated Dulles's flaws. For all his many failings, he was not the complete disaster of Acheson's portrait. Dulles might have been "a dogmatic and uncompromising anticommunist" in public but was "generally patient and flexible in the behind-the-scenes diplomacy."[42]

Despite its potency, Acheson's critique of Eisenhower's foreign policies did not persuade senior Democrats to enlist his support in the presidential campaign in 1956. Adlai Stevenson, who had unsuccessfully run against Eisenhower in 1952, was once again the Democratic Party's candidate. Born into a wealthy family and educated at Choate School and Princeton University, he was embraced by the liberal wing of the party but had very similar views to Eisenhower. He opposed "socialized medicine," condemned McCarthy but approved the removal of teachers who were communists, and believed the states should tackle civil rights. Despite such attitudes, liberals warmed to his internationalism and to his polished speech-making.[43]

Acheson endorsed Stevenson in 1952 and did so again 1956, even though it meant not supporting his friend Averell Harriman. Indeed, he hoped Harriman might curb Stevenson's excesses—preventing him from deploying phrases like "the relentless pursuit of peace." But Acheson sensed the candidate did not warm to his advice: "My impression was that my line of thought seemed to him not what the customers are asking for now-a-days."[44] Perhaps Stevenson's tepid response helped prompt Acheson's opinion that "Adlai has a third-rate mind that he can't make up."[45] Nevertheless, Acheson lent his aid to Stevenson: he and Paul Nitze, who had helped to bring Acheson back into Democratic Party circles, collected speech material on various foreign policy issues that might arise during the campaign.[46] On 26 September 1956 Acheson delivered a powerful assault on the policies of Eisenhower and Dulles, describing them as "playing Russian roulette with an atomic pistol." Such policies left US allies "scared to death." The Eisenhower administration had entered office believing that the country was all-powerful and could accomplish anything it willed, while setbacks were due to irresolute allies or to disloyal people within the United States. Acheson argued that this was not the best way forward. The country should, instead, renew and refresh relations with friends and allies, which was only possible if the administration genuinely believed that it needed these allies as much as they needed the United States.[47]

For all Acheson's efforts, Eisenhower once again defeated Stevenson and by a wider margin than in 1952—the president's share of the popular rose from 55 to 57.5 percent, while his opponent's fell from 44.5 to 42 percent. Acheson's assessment of Stevenson's campaign was sharply critical. In a private letter on 11 December he declared that he could not agree that Stevenson fought a good campaign. He added: "He is no leader, but a wordy man. Not a man of words, like Churchill, or Savonarola, or even Hitler or Huey Long, who made words flashing swords in their hands. But like the editorial writer of the *New York Times*, fluent, grammatical, precious, sometimes whimsical, intellectually dapper, and at the same time paunchy, whose words are cold puddings that failed and fell. No, I have had all of that 'leadership' that I can take, and I don't want to hear, or give a hoot, what his views are about anything."[48]

Although senior figures in the party did not share Acheson's critique of Stevenson, they recognized the need to act. On 27 November 1956 the party's National Committee created the Democratic Advisory Council. In June 1957 Acheson agreed to chair its foreign policy committee, and invited Nitze to serve as its vice-chairman.[49] Three interventions by Acheson seem to have contributed to the party's recognition of his considerable assets. In addition to his spirited campaign speeches, there was his critique of Dulles's handling of the Franco-British military intervention to retain control of the Suez Canal. He charged Dulles with being vacillating, devious, and damaging the Western alliance. At the same time, the administration's advocacy of "national liberation" had encouraged rebels in Hungary to expect American assistance but it then failed to help them when they faced Soviet troops in October–November 1956. He told Frank Altschul that "vast damage is being done to the Western alliance." An article in May 1957 castigated Dulles for giving a victory to the Egyptian leader, Nasser.[50] Acheson's third intervention was his detailed testimony to the House Foreign Affairs Committee in January 1957 in response to the president's speech to Congress launching the "Eisenhower Doctrine" in the Middle East. He particularly objected to the idea that the president should be given the authority to commit US military forces to protect states in the region. This was "perilously like another approach to the brink." Congress should authorize the executive to decide whether Soviet action was "intended to be the beginning of the third world war."[51]

The foreign policy committee had twenty-seven members and most were sympathetic to Stevenson's ideas, but Acheson soon emerged as its intellectual driving force. Indeed, he had just published his second book, *A Citizen Looks at Congress*, which reexamined Woodrow Wilson's *Congressional Government* (1885) in the light of his own experience of working with Congress.[52] Acheson challenged Wilson's view that Congress should take the leading role in the formulation and implementation of foreign policy. He maintained, rather, that Congress's responsibilities should be confined to approving or disapproving presidential proposals. The committee divided between Stevenson, Chester Bowles, and William Benton on one side and Acheson and Nitze on the other: between arguments for greater economic aid to underdeveloped countries and those for the construction of greater military power. Bowles and Benton had formed a successful advertising agency and had supported Stevenson for some time. Indeed, Bowles had opposed Truman's nomination as presidential candidate in 1948. [53]

In the next three years Acheson's committee produced a number of reports reflecting his outlook on American foreign policy, such as "America's Present Danger and What We Should Do About It," a rejoinder to Eisenhower's State of the Union speech of January. Acheson also wrote five pamphlets on US foreign and military policy aimed at assisting party members in presenting the Democratic case to the public and media. [54] At the same time he delivered lectures articulating this vision. Acheson gave a speech on "Moralism in Foreign Policy" in April 1957, which was published in *The Reporter*. He observed that "moralistic legalism" was "tragically irrelevant to our real purposes." Believing the United States was pursuing "a crusade or mission" had "led to actions" that were "contrary to our interests." He addressed the theme again in "Morality, Moralism and Diplomacy," at the University of Florida in February 1958. In a direct, if unidentified, attack on Dulles he criticized those who "demand a moral policy": the principles they enunciate are often "closely related to the holder's most deep-seated prejudices and limitations of his experiences." [55]

In seeming contradiction of these critiques, Acheson had often resorted to moral precepts when in office. He castigated the Chinese intervention into the Korean War as revealing their "complete disregard of any kind of morality." He spoke of how "relationships in the world" were "based on moral conviction and moral responsibility." Acheson was even more explicit in using morality in "Shield of Faith" when he stressed how a sense of moral purpose guided American actions in the world: "Our moral purpose is an essential part of the 'wholeness' of our foreign relations." If the United States were to "fulfill the responsibility of leadership in the world," it was "essential that we . . . achieve a union of our moral purpose and our physical power." Such assertions expose Acheson to the charge of hypocrisy. Brinkley suggests that his use of moral language was partly a response to McCarthyite attacks and the need to persuade the American people that he was pursuing a just policy. Brinkley adds that, free from the pressures of office, Acheson could examine moralism more objectively. Yet, he concludes, that an important part of his objections were personal—he deeply disliked Dulles's moralistic approach. One might add that Acheson did not oppose any use of moral vocabulary; rather, he objected to its overt deployment and the idea that it was a means of solving problems. As he explained in his *Yale Review* article, moral precepts could not be separated from international affairs but they offered only "delusive simplicity" and rarely provided the tools to tackle problems. [56]

In August 1957 Acheson delivered the Clayton lectures at Tufts University. They were published the following year as *Power and Diplomacy*. Painting a picture of the collapse of the British-dominated world order and the rise of Soviet power, he emphasized the need for American material strength and political and economic leadership to ensure stability. He also urged caution in an era of nuclear weapons, where their use would be "more dangerous and destructive than the threat posed by the enemy." Good relations with allies that were free from preachments were vital in this task. He particularly stressed that Western Europe, with the largest concentration of skilled workers in the world, substantial natural resources, and an industrial infrastructure second only to that of the United States, was vital to American security in the Cold War confrontation with the Soviet Union. Washington needed to recognize that American assistance was essential for the Europeans who could not resist the Soviets on their own. [57] In a talk at the launch of the book in February 1958 he stressed this central message and the need to be cautious about negotiating with the Soviet Union. The United States should neither fear negotiations, nor approach them naively. [58]

Only three months after his Clayton lectures, Acheson clashed with George Kennan on US support for Western Europe. The former director of the Policy Planning Staff during the secretaryships of Marshall and Acheson delivered the prestigious Reith lectures, which were broadcast by the BBC in Britain. His third talk broached the idea of the withdrawal of British, Soviet, and United States forces from Central Europe and the possibility of a neutral Germany. [59] The suggestion provoked an explosion of angry denunciation from Acheson. The ferocity of Acheson's remarks was partly the product of his deep dismay toward Kennan's proposals but they also reflected a sharpening of Acheson's temperament. In response to a request from a New York organization, the American Council on Germany, he penned "A Reply to Kennan" in January 1958, saying this was Kennan's attempt to resurrect his failed attempt to press this policy in 1949. Acheson condemned Kennan's proposal as dangerous, for it would threaten the survival of the West German state and promote a new phase of isolationism in America. The council then circulated Acheson's two-page statement together with others by Truman, Harriman, Stevenson, and Senator Lyndon Johnson backing Acheson. [60] Acheson conveniently forgot that he had listened sympathetically to Kennan's ideas, known as Program A, in his first months as secretary of state in early 1949, and only rejected them after strong French opposition. [61]

Acheson wrote a fuller rebuttal for the journal *Foreign Affairs*. He penned a warm letter to Kennan on 13 March, enclosing proofs of the article. He noted a Chinese proverb, quoted or invented by a reviewer of the latest volume of Kennan's study of US-Russian relations immediately following the First World War: retired diplomats should write history, but deal with nothing in the last thousand years. "We have differed on this subject too long for it to affect my deep regard and affection for you." He added; "I hope the same is true of you, although I am more accustomed to public controversy and criticism than you are. So you are entitled to a few earthy expletives."[62] Kennan replied on 20 March, saying "I bear no hard feelings." He was disappointed by the way Acheson's statement had been quickly exploited by people "for whose integrity of motive I have not the same respect." He said he would reply in detail to Acheson's article in the same forum where it appeared. But he added that "rarely, if ever, have I seen error so gracefully and respectably clothed. One hates to pluck at such finery."[63]

Many felt that Acheson had been too harsh in his reaction. Philip Jessup was "somewhat startled at the vehemence of your attack." He was bothered that "the policy problem was somewhat buried in a sense of concern about personalities." In addition, Jessup declared that he and others hoped that Acheson did not mean to say that because a proposal was dismissed in 1949 it could not be reexamined in 1958. Acheson replied in robust style. He recognized that the "brawl causes pain to mutual friends. George always engenders more solicitude in others than he shows to others." He added: "I was not writing for our friends . . . I was writing for the Germans to destroy as effectively as I could the corroding effect of what he had said and that he was a seer in these matters." Acheson concluded that he had it on "high authority in Germany, at least, what I have said has been effective."[64] Kennan's biographer concedes that Acheson was right on the issue at the time. However illogical, it worked, for "few people anywhere—not even most Germans were seeking to overturn it." But Gaddis argues that by the 1980s Kennan's prediction was coming true, as Germany's division was crumbling.[65]

Although Acheson's primary concern in these years was foreign policy and the continued success of the Atlantic alliance, he also became involved in an important domestic issue. The civil rights of black Americans became a pressing concern by the mid-1950s. In 1954 the Supreme Court ruled against "separate but equal" provisions for education in southern states in the *Brown versus Board of Education* case. In 1956 it ordered the desegregation of buses in Columbia, South Carolina, and Montgomery, Alabama. The 18 February 1957 cover of *Time* magazine featured the black civil rights campaigner, Dr. Martin Luther King Jr. The ambitious senator for Texas, Lyndon Baines Johnson, took up the issue, partly because he favored better treatment of African Americans but mainly as a means of enhancing his political standing and making him a serious contender in the 1960 presidential election. Eisenhower displayed little enthusiasm for civil rights but recognized the wave of change. He sent troops to Little Rock, Arkansas, to ensure the Brown ruling was upheld and supported a House of Representatives bill in 1956 to extend the voting rights of black Americans. Indeed, he saw the political benefits of such action, as the Republicans attracted more African

American votes in the 1956 presidential election. This transfer of voters away from the Democratic Party was another reason why Johnson wished to act.

As the 1956 bill was reintroduced in January 1957 Johnson saw his opportunity. The House again passed the bill but everyone expected it to fail again in the Senate. They underestimated Johnson's talents as a political operator. He enlisted the help of Acheson, who advised him to abandon Part III, which extended federal authority over states. Keeping this part of the bill, he told Johnson, "would be hopeless confusion—just madness," as it would antagonize southern Democrats; by contrast, its removal would save the government "from the vain attempt to enforce two Reconstruction statutes which no majority of the Supreme Court has been able to interpret." Johnson secured the omission of Part III. The original bill envisaged its enforcement by federal judges. Southern senators objected to this, seeking jury trials for cases both of civil contempt (where a judge seeks to ensure a court order is carried out) and criminal contempt (where a judge punishes someone for violating an injunction). Acheson helped in the drafting of a compromise: there would be jury trials for criminal contempt cases but not for civil contempt cases. The bill passed the Senate on 7 August by 72 votes to 18. But the House would not accept the amended bill and inserted a clause granting a qualified right to jury trials. A judge could try criminal contempt cases but if the sentence exceeded $300 in fines or 45 days in jail, the defendant could have a retrial by jury. The bill passed both houses on 29 August and Eisenhower signed it into law on 9 September.[66]

Acheson applauded the outcome in person to Johnson; and, demonstrating he was no slouch as a political operator, agreed to lay out the substance of these remarks in a letter to Johnson on 13 August, which might be used to persuade northern liberal critics. He could not understand why there was hesitancy in recognizing that it was "among the great achievements since the war." "Can't we for once be proud of ourselves when we do the right thing?"[67] The act did not lead to an increase in the number of black voters. But it marked a significant precedent: for the first time in eighty-two years a civil rights measure was passed and not talked out.[68]

As the Eisenhower presidency came to a close and with it the first phase of Acheson's life after office, two very different journalists offered their appraisal. Cabell Phillips wrote a laudatory profile of Acheson, which spoke of the "incisiveness and clarity of his critiques" of contemporary policies, and of his "meticulous dissection of the Dulles and Eisenhower foreign policy." In the same year, Walter Lippmann, often the critic at the feast, penned an article that lamented the habits of Acheson and other similarly rigid types who were "like old soldiers trying to relive the battles in which they won their fame and glory." "Their preoccupation with their own past history" kept them "from dealing with the new phase of the Cold War."[69]

ADVISING JOHN F. KENNEDY, 1961–1963

John F. Kennedy won the presidential election of November 1960 with Lyndon Johnson as his running mate. Acheson knew Johnson much better than Kennedy, partly because of his involvement with the Civil Rights Act of 1957. He was impressed by LBJ, calling him "the one man in the Democratic Party whose rare gifts of leadership . . . make possible the solution of this seemingly impossible problem [of racial divisions]." In a letter to Truman he described Johnson as "the ablest man in public life today. He has thousands of faults [but] . . . he is a giant among pygmies."[70] Moreover, Acheson had clashed with Kennedy over the latter's July 1957 speech in the Senate advocating independence for the French territory of Algeria.[71] Acheson, however, came to know Kennedy better after the senator joined the Democratic Advisory Council in 1959 and by 1960 concluded he would make the better candidate in the presidential election. He told Truman in April 1960: "Maybe we should all give Jack a run for his money—or rather Joe's." By June, when Nixon was the Republican nominee, he told the former president, "We have got to beat Nixon. We shall probably have to do it with Kennedy." In assessing the Democratic National Convention that nominated Kennedy, Acheson concluded that Johnson had "retrograded" since 1956, while "Jack and his team were the only 'pros.'"[72]

Immediately following his narrow victory in November, Kennedy turned to Acheson for advice, despite the reservations of Arthur Schlesinger Jr., the distinguished historian of the FDR administration and appointee as White House special assistant. In a letter to the president-elect, Schlesinger observed: "I wonder whether, with all his superb qualities, he is not too consumed in vanity and bitterness to have gone past the point of usability." He had spoken to Acheson in early October and his "remarks to me at that time led me to urge you to consider the matter very carefully before you confide any important responsibilities to him."[73] Kennedy, however, was keen to enlist the support of senior establishment figures like Acheson (and Harriman); and was impressed by the former secretary's intellectual command of issues. They met at Acheson's Georgetown home on 28 November 1960 to discuss who should become secretary of state. Acheson suggested David Bruce, under secretary of state in the last months of the Truman administration, for an interim period while grooming Paul Nitze for the job. In the meantime Nitze could serve as under secretary. When Kennedy said he needed to choose a Democrat for the job of secretary of state, Acheson suggested Dean Rusk. Acheson praised Rusk's loyalty and efficiency, though he wondered whether he would be as effective "when the whole responsibility was put on him." Kennedy also asked Acheson to consider serving as US ambassador to NATO but he politely declined the offer.[74] Acheson was "impressed by his air of calmness, of authority, of seriousness, and of modesty." He also believed that Kennedy "would be decisive."[75]

It seems probable from a letter he wrote to Dirk Stikker, the Dutch diplomat who was NATO secretary-general from 1961 to 1964, explaining why JFK would not be able to make him secretary of state, that Acheson harbored a faint hope of being called to be secretary. But Kennedy never seriously considered this option. He made his views clear in an interview with the journalist Theodore White, who was writing a profile of Rusk: "Acheson—a brilliant advocate, sarcastic but too bitter. I couldn't have worked with so bitter a man."[76] In any case, Acheson had reservations about what was rumored to be the framework for foreign policy in the new administration. He warned: "A President can't [*sic*] be his own Secretary of State in the mid-twentieth century. The phrase was used of F.D.R. but it wasn't [*sic*] true. The job was simply not done. This would happen again if it were tried again. Then we should have another investigation to devise new machinery which we don't need. But we do need to use what we have and man it properly."[77] So began the slightly stiff relationship between Acheson and Kennedy. Acheson later observed: "I would not say in any way we were friends, we were acquaintances—and he was extremely deferential to me."[78]

Within a month of entering office, Kennedy sought Acheson's counsel on NATO policy. During his first weeks in office as secretary Rusk requested and received Acheson's advice. He tried to persuade his former boss to serve as US ambassador to NATO but Acheson again refused. Rusk then told him that the president wanted him to lead a task force on NATO, which Acheson agreed to undertake but made clear he would do so only as an unpaid consultant, thereby allowing him to continue his work as a lawyer. The president formally announced the appointment on 8 February. Acheson worked hard over the next six weeks with State Department, Department of Defense, and NATO officials to produce an assessment that the captured political, economic, and military dimensions of American involvement with NATO. As the report was taking shape, he held discussions with Kennedy, meaning the president possessed a clear sense of its main ideas when Acheson submitted the report in March. It stressed that the connection between the United States and Western Europe was the foundation of the nation's foreign policy and the connection's coherence and strength should be maintained. In particular, American conventional forces in Europe should be augmented. The president largely endorsed Acheson's ideas, resulting in a policy directive in April 1961 that included only minor alterations to the task force draft.[79]

Overlapping with the US-NATO relationship was the continuing problem of Berlin, which Acheson also reviewed at Kennedy's request. The Soviet leader, Nikita Khrushchev, had issued an ultimatum in November 1958 warning the other three occupying powers that, if they did not reach an understanding within six months, he would conclude a peace treaty with East

Germany. Such a treaty would have placed access routes to West Berlin under East German supervision and raised the prospect of a confrontation, since the Western powers did not recognize the East German regime. Khrushchev suspended his ultimatum as the four powers met at a Foreign Ministers Conference in July 1959, when he accepted Eisenhower's invitation and traveled to the United States in September 1959, and during a summit meeting in Paris in May 1960. But the Soviets' shooting down and capture of an American U-2 spy plane caused the summit to collapse and renewed tensions over Berlin, which remained unresolved when Kennedy assumed the presidency.

Acheson had aired his robust view of how to respond to Moscow soon after Khrushchev's ultimatum. In a contribution to the *New York Times Magazine* in April 1959 he explained that the Soviets "negotiate by acts, not debate, offer and counteroffer. Their purpose may be to separate allies, or to undermine governments with their own people, or to win over uncommitted peoples." The United States should be wary of any understanding with Moscow that undermines the security of Western Europe.[80] He also broached these ideas in a lecture about summit meetings. He doubted the value of such meetings, saying that "in the last twelve years the international conference has ceased to be an instrument for ending conflict and has become one for continuing it."[81] He developed his ideas on Berlin in a March 1959 article for the *Saturday Evening Post*, where he emphasized that Khrushchev's note constituted a challenge that should be met by America's cool steadfastness and the use of conventional forces rather than the threat of a nuclear attack.[82]

Acheson submitted his review of the Berlin question to the president on 3 April 1961, and summarized his thinking to a meeting on 5 April that Kennedy held with the British prime minister, Harold Macmillan, who was visiting Washington. Acheson declared that Berlin was of supreme importance and that was why the Soviets were pressing the issue. "If the West funks Germany will become unhooked from the Alliance." This was a crucial test of will. An economic and political response was insufficient. Meeting this test in the air would not work because the Soviets could shoot down the planes. There had to be a test on the ground with a division. This would demonstrate that "it was not worthwhile to resist a really stout Western response." If there were a major Soviet retaliation, then the United States would gain a clear strategic perspective. Kennedy welcomed Acheson's report but made clear that he had not yet decided on what to do.[83]

Meanwhile, Kennedy met Khrushchev in Vienna in June in a bruising exchange that led to a renewal of the six month ultimatum on Berlin. Kennedy adopted a tough but more nuanced response than Acheson advised. At a coordinating committee on 16 June and in a memorandum on 28 June Acheson again stressed that Berlin was a test of will "involving deeply the prestige of the United States," and offering any concessions would convey "an appearance of weakness." The United States needed to convince the Soviets that it was "in earnest about defending Berlin"—even including a readiness to risk use of nuclear weapons.[84] At a meeting of the National Security Council on 29 June Acheson again dominated discussion as he offered a commanding recitation of his position. This was the highpoint of his influence. His views alarmed Harriman, the president's other senior external advisor. When the NSC met again on 13 July, it adopted a less aggressive stance, rejecting Acheson's suggestion that the president declare a national emergency.[85] Disappointed at this outcome, Acheson told Truman that there was too much focus on "image" at the expense of "the most vigorous leadership."[86] Still, on 25 July the president demonstrated the resolute demeanor that Acheson advised when he gave a radio and television address, recalled reservists to active service, and announced a 25 percent increase in defense expenditure.[87] Acheson delivered a final Berlin report on 1 August and left for a holiday in Martha's Vineyard. He told Truman how he planned to "phase out" his work for the administration, saying that "work for this crowd is strangely depressing. Nothing seems to get decided."[88] Acheson had not properly grasped what Robert Dallek calls JFK's "reflective temperament."[89] Meanwhile, Khrushchev did not act on his ultimatum. Instead, East German forces began building a wall on 12 August that divided East and West Berlin. This action halted the movement of refugees to the West, which had always been the main worry of the East Germans and the Soviets. Kennedy did not respond immediately, and, after reflection, decided not to deploy the large force Acheson favored. He dispatched a battle group of 1,500 men, who passed unhindered by Soviet and East German border guards. Content that Western access routes were secure, the Americans accepted the new situation.

For over a year Acheson remained uninvolved with the administration and with foreign affairs. Although Kennedy retained his high regard for Acheson's talents, relations had cooled after the former secretary's cutting remarks about him reached the president, who was characterized as a tyro performer with a boomerang that returned to hit him.[90] Acheson traveled a great deal, especially in Europe. He also resumed his work as a lawyer, representing Cambodia at the International Court of Justice at The Hague in a dispute with Thailand over territory that contained a ninth-century temple. After his victory, Cambodia awarded him the Grand Cross of the Royal Cambodian Order.[91]

When a truly serious crisis arose over Cuba in October 1962, he was recalled to offer his counsel. Cuba had become an issue for Eisenhower after Fidel Castro overthrew the Fulgencio Batista regime in 1959, seized $1 billion of American assets on the island, and turned to the Soviets for aid. Fears of the spread of communism in the hemisphere led to pressure to act against Castro. During his presidential campaign, Kennedy had asked Acheson about

Cuba, worried that it might be a base for communist action in Latin America. The former secretary later observed that he had advised Kennedy to "stop talking about Cuba," since he "was likely to get himself hooked into positions which would be difficult afterwards."[92] At some point in March 1961 Kennedy told Acheson about the plans for a CIA-run invasion of Cuba by exiled opponents of the Castro regime. Acheson was wholly opposed: it was not necessary "to call in Price Waterhouse to discover that 1,500 Cubans weren't as good as 25,000 Cubans . . . this was a disastrous idea."[93] Nevertheless, the incursion took place at the Bay of Pigs in April and proved the disaster that Acheson predicted. He expressed incredulity at this "asinine" action, saying that he and Truman had "turned down similar suggestions for Iran and Guatemala."[94] On 8 October 1962 he told Truman: "Cuba is a problem that I am glad I don't have to deal with. Two Presidents have pretty well messed it up."[95] Within a week, Cuba became the epicenter of the most serious crisis of the Cold War era.

On 14 October 1962 American aerial reconnaissance discovered the construction of missile sites on Cuba. Kennedy assembled various experts, including Acheson, to advise him.[96] On 16 October a special group, the Executive Committee of the National Security Council, known as ExComm, was established. Rusk asked Acheson to join the group, which he attended for the first time on 17 October. The meeting explored three perspectives on developments. First, was the belief that the discovery of the missile sites did not constitute a significant development and therefore no action was required. This point of view was soon discounted. Acheson shared the outlook of a second group which argued that the missile sites were likely to become an acute danger and military action should be taken to prevent their becoming operational. Under secretary George Ball was the sole advocate of a third approach that sought a diplomatic way forward. He suggested that military action would amount to a second Pearl Harbor. Acheson vigorously condemned the reference to Pearl Harbor, arguing that the unprovoked and unannounced Japanese attack on Hawaii, which was thousands of miles distant from Japan, was not the same as the Soviets placing nuclear missiles just ninety miles from the United States and then denying it. Moreover, he added, they knew it violated the long-standing American commitment to upholding the Monroe Doctrine that precluded a European power securing a strategic foothold in the Western Hemisphere.[97]

Acheson presented his case for military action to the president on the next day. He later observed that Kennedy, as always, listened to him with "courtesy and close attention and examined my reasons and premises thoroughly." He came away unsure of the impact of his arguments.[98] On 19 October ExComm explored in separate groups the two choices before it—the diplomatic and the military—and the actions each approach would entail. Although Acheson joined the group pressing for an air strike, he did not remain in the meeting for long, arguing that he was not a member of the government and should not be deciding on such momentous matters. Notwithstanding his formal explanation, it is clear that he found the work of the group unsatisfactory. He described it as "leaderless, repetitive and a waste of time."[99] With the exception of Ball, all the president's advisors, including his brother, Attorney General Robert Kennedy, backed an air strike. But the president decided against their advice and opted to pursue a naval blockade. Kennedy asked Acheson to travel to Europe to brief the French president, Charles de Gaulle, and the NATO Council. Acheson left on Sunday 21 October and returned on Wednesday 25 October.[100]

When Acheson returned on the 25th tensions seemed to have eased. Acheson, keen to evade ExComm, reported to Rusk, saying that although things appeared calm, the missiles were still there and time was running out. He once again proposed that they launch an air strike. There followed two messages from Khrushchev on 26 October. The first was rather shapeless, emotional, and confused. It acknowledged the missile sites and proposed that an American undertaking not to invade Cuba might lead to the removal of missiles. Khrushchev's second message was more formal and direct, stating that missiles would only be removed if US missiles were taken out of Turkey. On Saturday 27 October the tension mounted considerably when a U-2 plane was shot down over Cuba. ExComm now recommended that preparations be made for a military strike. But the president decided on one more effort of diplomacy. Partly on the advice of his brother, they sent a message to Khrushchev, replying positively to the first letter and awaited his response. Khrushchev accepted these terms, when Kennedy also said that American missiles would be removed from Turkey but would not be announced as part of any deal.

Acheson praised the president's performance in the crisis. He wrote to Kennedy on 28 October commending his "leadership, firmness and judgment over the past patchy week." On 30 November he spoke of JFK's "wisely conceived and vigorously executed" response. But his admiration was restrained: a wrong-headed policy had succeeded only because the president had been "phenomenally lucky."[101]

Two months after the crisis Acheson provoked Anglo-American strains over his view of Britain's place in the world. He exposed British sensitivities about their global status at the very moment when there were doubts about their ability to maintain their nuclear capability with an effective missile system. On 5 December he delivered a speech at West Point that depicted, with characteristic epigrammatic sharpness, Britain's diminished global standing:

> Great Britain has lost an Empire and has not yet found a role. The attempt to
> play a separate power role—that is, a role apart from Europe, a role based on a

"special relationship" with the United States, a role based on being head of a "Commonwealth" . . . is about to be played out.

Great Britain, attempting to work alone and be a broker between the United States and Russia, has seemed to conduct a policy as weak as its military power.

Acheson's words exposed a raw nerve in Britain about the country's international status. The popular press was predictably outraged but even Prime Minister Macmillan's reaction was overwrought. He observed to a colleague that Acheson had committed the same error as Philip of Spain, Louis XIV, the Kaiser, and Hitler in underestimating Britain.[102] Undaunted by the uproar, Acheson nonchalantly closed a letter to Truman with the salutation: "warm greetings from British Public Enemy No. 1."[103] Acheson played no further significant role in the Kennedy administration, which came to an abrupt and shocking end with the assassination of the president on 22 November 1963. Vice President Johnson assumed the presidency.

ADVISING LYNDON JOHNSON, 1963–1968

Relations between Johnson and Acheson had become strained after Acheson backed JFK in 1960. The journalist Joseph Alsop observed that their relationship had "rusted." He added: "Johnson felt Acheson had snubbed him, while Acheson thought that Johnson was not so much an astute politician as a garrulous political operator."[104] Acheson appreciated how effectively Johnson had assumed command after the assassination. He observed: "With sensitivity and talk he led the nation in proper but not mawkish mourning. When the funeral was ended, he assumed charge of headquarters." But the former secretary had also developed a significant number of doubts about Johnson, not least his "foul mouth and double dealings."[105] In his first meeting with the new president he discovered, or confirmed, another unsatisfactory character trait. As he sought to explore with Johnson the contents of his memorandum urging no reductions in the US military presence in Europe, he found the president completely obsessed by the Soviet refusal to allow an American theater group to perform *Hello Dolly!* in Moscow. Johnson sought Acheson's advice and received the crisp reply: "I don't care what the Russians think about *Hello Dolly!* And neither should you." This briefly led to consideration of Acheson's memorandum but it was clear that Johnson was still focused on *Hello Dolly!*[106]

This episode revealed some of Johnson's ambivalence toward senior figures like Acheson in the foreign policy establishment. He eagerly sought their counsel, hoping to obtain their loyalty and respect. Yet he was frequently suspicious of them for what he believed was their inclination to take the credit for achievements. He made disparaging remarks about diplomats and ridiculed Acheson before journalists by imitating his grand manner.[107] Rusk later observed that Johnson was a "natural ham actor." "His impersonations of Dean Acheson testifying before Congress were outrageously funny. He acted out the full, patrician, immaculately dressed figure of Dean Acheson with his bristling mustache, entering a Senate committee room, with his nose in the air and twitching as though he were smelling a skunk."[108]

David Bruce captured Acheson's personality and outlook at this time in his diary entry for 21 December 1964. Bruce was at a dinner in Washington where Acheson did a lot of talking:

> Dean was attractive, amusing, but devastating in criticism of almost every leading politician in the Atlantic Community. He is reputed to be a close advisor of President Johnson. He has fully achieved the ultimate of independence, to do and say whatever he likes. Whoever is flailed by him will long remain sore.[109]

Despite such attitudes and behavior, and recognizing that he lacked any detailed grasp of foreign affairs, Johnson turned for advice to the establishment's foreign policy elders, and to Acheson in particular. The first major issue involving Acheson came in early 1964 with the crisis over the former British-controlled island of Cyprus in the eastern Mediterranean. Britain had granted independence in 1960, once it had secured two sovereign military bases on the island. The constitution of the new republic was designed to safeguard the interests of both the Greek and Turkish populations. The Greek Cypriots comprised about 80 percent of the population and the country's first president was a Greek, Archbishop Makarios. But Makarios resented the near veto held by Turkish Cypriots. In November 1963 he proposed constitutional amendments designed to remove the protected position for the Turkish Cypriots. Within a month, the island was embroiled in civil war. British forces on the island and then a UN peacemaking force failed to quell the violence. As the situation worsened, the Johnson administration became increasingly concerned, fearful of a growth in communist influence, since Makarios had skillfully played up the threat from the Cypriot communist party on the island as a means of coaxing financial assistance from Washington.[110] Under secretary of state George Ball assumed responsibility for Cyprus and suggested to the president that Acheson be asked to serve as mediator. It was felt that Acheson's involvement with the Truman Doctrine in 1947 made him someone both Greeks and Turks would regard as sympathetic to their interests.[111]

Following the failure of talks between the two sides in Washington, Acheson traveled to Geneva in July. After overcoming the initial opposition of U Thant, the UN secretary-general, to his role of mediator, he held several weeks of talks with the two sides. He devised an elaborate partition plan that

would have left most of the island under Greek Cypriot control while granting two or three "cantons" to Turkish local authority and affording the Turks
a military base in Cyprus. The Turks were willing to consider the scheme but
the Greeks resolutely rejected the plan.[112]

Acheson left Geneva frustrated at his failure. He reported to Ball that the
Greek prime minister, George Papandreou, "has not made one attempt toward the agreement he could have and which would give him nine-tenths of
all he hoped for."[113] In another cable to Washington he observed: "Makarios
was like a mad man whom the Greeks could not stop."[114] Acheson's correspondence with friends captured his mixed feelings. He told his former classmate at Yale, Ranald MacDonald, that his efforts at mediation constituted
"the worst rat race I have ever been in—trying to deny Greeks and Turks
their historic recreation of killing one another."[115] He wrote to MacLeish:
"You know nothing of the deeper frustration of life until you spend two
months keeping Greeks and Turks from killing one another while hoping all
the time, not only that they would do just that, but make a pretty thorough job
of it."[116] On the other hand, he told his former executive assistant at the State
Department, Lucius Battle, in December that "the negotiating role which I
had in Geneva this summer "was great fun," his "Turkish and Greek colleagues became friends, if not to one another, at least of mine," and "we
came close to an understanding which might have cropped the Archbishop's
whiskers and solved the idiotic problem of Cyprus." But Papandreou was "a
garrulous, senile, windbag without power of decision or resolution," who
"gave away our plans at critical moments to Makarios, who released them to
the Greek press."[117] He delivered his more considered thoughts in a speech
to the Chicago Bar Association in March 1965. He spoke of the Turkish
readiness to make concessions but in doing so "they would be negotiating
with themselves," because of Makarios's "daily denunciation of any settlement but unconditional surrender."[118]

By this time, a larger problem had arisen in Vietnam. Since the end of
French colonial power and the division of the country in 1954 successive
American administrations had provided aid to the South Vietnamese government. In the first half of 1965 Johnson committed ground troops to ensure the
survival of the South Vietnamese government against the onslaught of Viet
Cong guerrillas and the North Vietnamese army. Soon, his generals sought
ever-larger numbers of soldiers. Under Secretary of State George Ball was
disturbed by the escalation and devised a peace plan. He contacted Acheson
and enlisted his support. They had first met in Washington in the 1930s but
they began fuller contact during Acheson's time as chairman of the Democratic Party's foreign policy committee in the late 1950s and continued during the Kennedy and Johnson administrations. These two lawyer-diplomats
were convinced Atlanticists and held each other in high regard, even though
Ball did not share Acheson's emphasis on military strength in American

foreign policy. They presented a plan in discussions with the president, Rusk, and defense secretary Robert McNamara. It proposed a ceasefire, amnesty for any Viet Cong who stopped fighting, the development of an all-Vietnam constitutional government, formed in elections where the Viet Cong could vote, and withdrawal of US forces. But the plan went nowhere because the Saigon government rejected a proposal that did not guarantee them a role in negotiations.[119]

For all his embrace of Ball's ideas, Acheson advocated a vigorous approach when he joined a group of distinguished former officials, called to the White House by Johnson on 8 July. The "wise men," as they came to be known, discussed Europe, Latin America, and Vietnam in separate panels. When they gathered in plenary session, Vietnam dominated. Acheson joined Omar Bradley, former chairman of the JCS; John J. McCloy, who had served as the first US High Commissioner for Germany; Robert Lovett, former defense secretary; and Arthur Dean, John Foster Dulles's former law partner, in agreeing that the president should expand the war as the generals suggested. In his account of the three-hour meeting Acheson noted how they were all "disturbed by a long complaint [by LBJ] about how mean everything and everybody was to him." Acheson believed Johnson should stop "fighting the problem," an allusion to George Marshall's apothegm—do not fight the problem, decide it. "Finally I blew my top and told him that he was wholly right in the Dominican Republic," where LBJ had sent troops to defeat a leftist coup, and in Vietnam, where "he had no choice but to press on."[120]

Acheson's successively contradictory positions on Vietnam need explaining. Isaacson and Thomas argue that his advocacy of a firm line arose from a mixture of ingredients: his "penchant for action, impatience with self-doubt," and the belief that fighting in Vietnam in 1965 was just as necessary as in Korea in 1950. Furthermore, it would have been a betrayal of the soldiers dying in Vietnam not to support the president's strategy.[121] One should add that Acheson's doubts about the strategic importance of Vietnam did not rest, at this stage, on a detailed grasp of the issues and were easily trumped by his instinctive response to a problem—the need to demonstrate American resolve. It seems clear from his explosion in the meeting with the president that he wanted Johnson to act decisively, just as Truman had done during his administration.

Acheson made clear in the 8 July meeting that the president's principal concern should not be Vietnam but, rather, the United States' relations with its European allies, where American leadership had been lacking. He was especially anxious to minimize the disruptive behavior of French president Charles de Gaulle, whom he admired personally, while worrying about French pursuit of an independent line that led to the recognition of China and to exploration of improved Franco-Soviet relations. Acheson feared that French policy might encourage a wider European trend, and, in particular, that West Germany's desire to establish closer ties with France might loosen its NATO commitment. Acheson displayed great confidence in his ability to achieve these goals—if only Johnson would allow him to act. He was given little opportunity in 1965. He told Noel Annan, the Cambridge academic, that he was attempting to persuade LBJ to abandon his "fixation on Alabama and Vietnam and back on to the even more—or, at least, equally important problem of leadership in Europe." He asked Johnson's permission to undertake another review of NATO, like the one he had completed for Kennedy, but the president remained vague. In a letter to Anthony Eden, Acheson noted the president's tendency to "concentrate where the most noise is coming from."[122]

It was not until 1966 that he became directly involved—and only after a surprising decision by de Gaulle. Thanks to being well-briefed by Charles Bohlen, the US ambassador in Paris, Acheson was aware that the French military was exploring changes to its arrangements for American bases in France. In a November 1965 talk he predicted that Paris was likely to demand French control of all NATO forces in France. De Gaulle's 7 March 1966 message to Johnson was altogether bolder: he declared that the French military would quit the NATO integrated command and all foreign forces would have to leave France. Acheson was given the task of conducting an inquiry into the implications of de Gaulle's decision and provided with an office on the department's seventh floor and a staff of middle-ranking officials. He advised a restrained response to the French decision and predicted that it would not have a significant impact on NATO. Johnson followed this advice and was careful not to attack de Gaulle on the issue. Acheson was less circumspect, launching a blunt critique of the French president on television, in the press, and in testimony to Congress. Yet he also showed his creative side to a House subcommittee, saying that NATO was not merely an anti-Soviet alliance; it was an innovative organization capable of pursuing conciliation with Eastern Europe.[123]

Later in the year Acheson expressed his frustration with the work on de Gaulle and NATO: "I have just finished a four months' stint of volunteer work in the State Department . . . rarely have I been so frustrated. There must be an easier way of doing things than this presently in vogue in Washington." Two months later he told Truman of his "unrequited toil" and went on to speak critically of Rusk. "He had been a good assistant to me, loyal and capable. But as number one he has been no good at all. For some reason unknown to me, he will not disclose his mind to anyone. The Department is totally at a loss to know what he wants done or what he thinks." He was also critical of the president: "He too hates to decide matters, is a worse postponer than FDR. The phrase for now is 'to preserve all one's options.' That means to drift and let decisions be made by default. It passes for statesmanship in our town to-day." In addition, Acheson concluded that Johnson could not tackle more than a few matters at once, which meant that Vietnam crowded out Europe. He lamented that Johnson "would rather be devious than straightforward." While Acheson was advising him on NATO, LBJ "was circulating rumors to the press that my views were not his." Yet Acheson recognized the president's qualities: "He could be so much better than he is. He creates distrust by being too smart. He is never candid. He is both mean and generous, but the meanness too often predominates. He yields to petty impulses."[124]

Meanwhile, Vietnam was coming to dominate the administration. American involvement had deepened massively since the summer of 1965. Johnson accepted the judgments of the military commanders that the war was going well and yielded to their escalating requests for additional US forces in the country, which had reached over 500,000 by late 1967. In the United States there was a growing anti-war movement, especially among college students. As Dallek says, "For Johnson, the question at the end of 1967 was . . . how to convince Americans that the war was going well and would be won if only they continued to back the boys in the field."[125] Johnson summoned another meeting of the "wise men." Acheson attended alongside George Ball, Omar Bradley, and Arthur Dean from the July 1965 gathering. John McCloy and Robert Lovett chose not to answer the call. The group was augmented by the presence of Clark Clifford, the president's most intimate private advisor; Abe Fortas, Supreme Court Justice and close confidante of LBJ; McGeorge Bundy, former national security advisor; Robert Murphy, former assistant secretary in the State Department; Douglas Dillon, former Treasury secretary; General Maxwell Taylor; and Henry Cabot Lodge, former ambassador to Vietnam.

They met in the State Department on 1 November and received a briefing from General Earle Wheeler, chairman of the JCS, who presented a determinedly optimistic account of progress in the war. Secretary of State Rusk endorsed this verdict. When the group met the president the next day, Acheson seemed persuaded by Wheeler's presentation. He told Johnson: "I got the impression that this is a matter we can and will win," although he did not believe that bombing would force Hanoi to negotiate. His belligerent tone was evident in his declaration: "We want less Goddamn analysis and more fighting spirit." Drawing a parallel with Korea, he concluded that the communists would give up once they learned they could not win—"This is the way it was in Korea. This is the way Communists operate." In a letter to John Cowles, he observed: "The more I watch this war the more the parallels I see to Korea and the more I admire my Chief [Truman]."[126] Only George Ball argued against the continuation of the existing policy. As they departed, Ball remarked to Acheson, McCloy, and John Cowles: "I've been watching across the table. You're like a flock of old buzzards sitting on a fence, sending young men off to be killed. You ought to be ashamed of yourselves."[127]

Averell Harriman, who wanted to pursue a negotiated peace, was disappointed by what he heard of Acheson's contribution to the November discussion. He was even more concerned by Acheson's comments in an interview in December, when the former secretary argued that the United States should continue the existing strategy until North Vietnam capitulated, just as had been done in Korea. So Harriman met Acheson on 12 December and bluntly declared that Acheson's outlook was too inflexible and wedded to the past. Vietnam was not like Korea. The Soviet Union and China were no longer allied. The war in Vietnam was different from that in Korea—it was a guerrilla and not a conventional conflict. The tactics of attrition deployed in Korea would not work against the Viet Cong. Acheson surprised Harriman by being willing to hear these strictures and voiced his suspicions of the military. The optimistic predictions of the generals were one constant between Korea and Vietnam. Harriman asked Acheson to speak to LBJ but the former secretary doubted he had much influence left with the president. [128] Although Harriman probably imagined his advocacy was influencing Acheson to rethink his outlook, Acheson was already having doubts, which were reinforced when he discovered from McNamara that they had run out of bombing targets. [129]

Just as Acheson's misgivings were deepening, the war in Vietnam reached a turning point in early 1968. The communist forces launched a massive assault on all the major cities in the south during the Tet holiday in January. It was a devastating attack that contradicted all the talk by the administration and the military about how they were winning the war. The American forces did succeed in defeating the Tet offensive but its psychological effect on American opinion was profound. The country was also beginning to feel the economic consequences of the war. Johnson once again asked the "wise men" to give their counsel. If Acheson's commitment to the continued fight had weakened that winter, he certainly was not going to talk about disengagement in the middle of the Tet offensive.

On 27 February Johnson called Acheson to see him. Their forty-five minute meeting went badly. Acheson could not tolerate Johnson's long whine about his troubles and simply quit the meeting to return to his law office. National security advisor Walt Rostow telephoned Acheson, who declared: "You can tell the president—and you can tell him in precisely these words—that he can take Vietnam and stick it up his ass." The president then spoke to Acheson and persuaded him to return to the White House. When they met Johnson agreed that Acheson should conduct a full investigation of the war and with complete access to people and classified documents. [130]

Acheson undertook his inquiry amid growing social and economic turmoil and a national mood encapsulated in the title of Arthur Schlesinger's 1969 book, *The Crisis of Confidence*. [131] Acheson could hardly fail to notice the precipitate decline in public backing for the war and in the president's popularity. His close examination of classified materials and conversations with officials in the State Department and the Department of Defense revealed the growing disquiet about the effectiveness of American strategy. Riots in major cities over the past several years provided evidence of a worrying growth in racial tensions. At the same time, the country experienced the economic effects of the conflict. By 1968 the war was costing $3.6 billion a year, adding to a worsening balance of payments deficit and to a decline in the value of the dollar. In November 1967 the British had devalued the pound, which led to huge losses from the gold pool. By 14 March 1968 the United States reached crisis point, having lost nearly $400 million in gold trading on the 13th alone. Acheson told John Cowles that, in the face of the gold crisis, Washington was "in an atmosphere of crisis."[132]

Johnson invited Acheson to lunch on 14 March to discuss both Vietnam and the gold crisis. Acheson made clear his concerns about the quality of military advice: "Mr. President, you are being led down the garden path." They agreed that the time was right for another meeting of the wise men.[133] When the group gathered at the State Department on the evening of 25 March, Acheson was joined by Ball, Bundy, Dillon, Fortas, Lodge, Murphy, and Generals Bradley, Ridgway, and Taylor. Clark Clifford also attended in his new role as secretary of defense. They heard a number of presentations on the war. During dinner Clifford suggested that there were three possible options: "muddling along" with the current policy, reducing the bombing campaign, and ending the ground operations. Acheson and the other advisors listened carefully to the briefings and gave their verdict at a meeting on the afternoon of the 26th. A minority wanted to continue and even escalate if necessary. Acheson summed up the majority view: "we can no longer do the job we set out to do in the time we have left and we must begin steps to disengage." Fortas countered by saying they never sought a military victory; rather, they wanted some kind of settlement between North and South Vietnam. In the official record Acheson responded by saying that they could not achieve by military means the goal of keeping the North Vietnamese from attacking the South Vietnamese. When General Wheeler had made (at a 1:00pm meeting) the same point as Fortas, Acheson had been much blunter: "Then what in the name of God are five hundred thousand men doing out there? Chasing girls?"[134]

Johnson was shocked and angered by the advice of the wise men but grudgingly recognized the force of their views. He gave a major speech on 31 March and announced a halt to the bombing of North Vietnam and his decision not to seek a second term as president. He asked Harriman to open talks with the North Vietnamese. Acheson hoped they had found a better way forward but he was soon disappointed. He observed to Harriman: "I thought for a while we had him [LBJ] on course. But I gather Bunker and Westmoreland have fed him some new meat. I do not envy you a negotiation without a goal. Perhaps the Viet Minh will think you are being inscrutable, a well known Western characteristic."[135]

REFLECTING ON HIS LIFE

Throughout this period of intense scrutiny of US-Vietnam policy, Acheson consciously drew on his experience in the Korean War. Indeed, it was at the forefront of his mind because he was writing his memoirs of his time at the State Department between 1941 and 1953. In the 1950s Acheson had written three studies on politics. In the 1960s he wrote three books of memoirs. In May 1961, just as the Kennedy presidency began, he released *Sketches from Life of Men I Have Known*, dedicated to his wife. It contained deft portraits of Bevin, Schuman, Adenauer, and Churchill; Marshall and Vandenberg; Molotov and Vyshinsky; and the Lisbon 1952 conference and a state visit to Austria in 1952.[136] In 1965 he completed an affecting memoir of episodes in his life: his early years in Middletown, Connecticut, his work on a Canadian railroad, his time as a law clerk at the Supreme Court and as a lawyer in the interwar years, and his brief service in the FDR administration. *Morning and Noon*, dedicated to Felix Frankfurter, stops in February 1941 when he joined the State Department.[137] His time at the State Department between 1941 and 1953 was the subject of his 350,000-word memoir, *Present at the Creation*.

After leaving office in January 1953 Acheson gathered his thoughts and considered but later dropped the idea of writing a memoir. As the Eisenhower presidency came to an end there were reassessments of Acheson's time in office. In 1959 the *New York Times* published a positive verdict.[138] But Acheson faced a more critical scrutiny from scholars. First there was William Appleman Williams's *The Tragedy of American Foreign Policy*, which suggested that American policy toward the Soviet Union was less a reaction to Moscow's aggression or even provocative policies than the product of an aggressive American pursuit of economic expansion. There followed a series of what came to be known as revisionist indictments of the whole course of US foreign policy since 1945 from, among others, David Horowitz, Ronald Steel, and Richard Barnet.[139]

Acheson's son, David, recalled urging his father to produce his own account or these revisionist interpretations would dominate. We lack evidence of Acheson's thinking at this time. But his interview in June 1969 seems to support his son's recollection. He observed how he had hesitated to write a memoir of these years because he felt he could not be objective. He had now decided to put aside detachment in favor of speaking out. Acheson also feared that Adolf Berle might publish an account. Henry Kissinger played an important role in Acheson's decision to resurrect the book: he arranged for his research assistant, Marina Finkelstein, to assist in collating materials. Acheson began writing in 1966 and continued for the next two years, at Harewood or in the West Indies, between periods of work for the Johnson administration.[140] *Present at the Creation* was published in September 1969. Given its huge scale—778 pages—it is a great source of information. It contains vivid and perceptive portraits of key figures. Above all it possesses literary grace. Isaacson and Thomas praise its "great sweep and rolling thunder."[141] It proved a huge success, with sales soon reaching about 75,000 copies.[142] It also gathered much praise from discerning critics and went on to win the Pulitzer Prize in 1970. Arthur Schlesinger wrote to Acheson praising the book: it was "a distinguished contribution to the history of our times—but few historians, alas, can write with such fascination and wit." Acheson's reply revealed he still possessed a gentler (and self-deprecatory) quality to his wit: "If I ever come to believe the book is as good as my friends tell me it is, I shall be insufferable, but there are some who think I am already."[143]

Present at the Creation has greatly influenced studies of Acheson and the foreign policy of the Truman administration ever since. Anxious to defend containment against the charges of the revisionists, the memoirs offer a logical/cogent account of developments and rationale for containment that overstates the consistency and coherence of the administration's foreign policy. Examination of contemporary documents reveals a more complicated picture of Acheson's outlook and responses. If a tough attitude characterized the years 1950–1952, the period 1945–1949 saw a greater readiness to find solutions to problems than either his critics or Acheson's memoirs suggest.

SOUTHERN AFRICA

Acheson's Atlanticist credentials lay at the center of his memoirs. But it would be a mistake to think that he was unconcerned with regions of the world other than Europe. He saw these areas as less important in geopolitical terms but did not regard them as being insignificant. He was always interested in Latin America—it regularly featured on any list he compiled of regions meriting the attention of policymakers. He had strongly endorsed Johnson's intervention in the Dominican Republic in 1965. But he became particularly interested in southern Africa. In 1965 a crisis arose over the British colony of Southern Rhodesia, which had been virtually self-governing since 1923. The British government tried to negotiate a constitution for an independent Rhodesia but the white government of Ian Smith refused to grant voting rights to black Rhodesians and declared itself independent of British rule. The UN would not recognize Rhodesia and Britain imposed sanctions, which were endorsed by the United States. Acheson attacked the British government, the UN, and the Johnson administration in a number of newspaper articles. His address to the American Bar Association in 1968 condemned "arrogant" international lawyers, who justified interfering in Rhodesian domestic affairs. Acheson cited legal precedent to support his case against the legality of intervention. This elicited a strong response from his friend and former colleague, Philip Jessup, who charged Acheson with citing a judicial decision that "you obviously did not take the trouble to study."[144] Acheson's testimony to the subcommittee on Africa of the House of Representatives Foreign Affairs Committee repeated his case against interfering in internal affairs, maintained the sanctions would not work, and warned of the economic and strategic harm they would bring.[145]

Douglas Brinkley observes that Acheson's position was "rooted in a cluster of prejudices and attitudes that were beyond the reach of rational opposition. He would never try to appreciate the aspirations for political freedom of the peoples of the third world."[146] This judgment is sound but needs qualification. Acheson spoke disparagingly of how "many of the blacks are still in a state of Neolithic culture," while southern African whites were "competent, highly-developed people." When his various articles were collected and distributed by the Rhodesian government he gave the appearance of being an apologist for the Rhodesian government.[147] Acheson was, indeed, rigid on Rhodesia and on many other issues. Yet he had spoken approvingly of nationalist aspirations in a number of speeches.[148] It is one of the paradoxes of his last years that his convictions too often overrode his analyses. Moreover, the impetus for his engagement with the issue was his concern for order in international relations rather than his racial attitudes.

ADVISING RICHARD NIXON, 1969–1971

Richard Nixon's victory in the 1968 presidential election led to Acheson's final and most improbable partnership with a president. Their previous encounters hardly suggested grounds for fruitful collaboration. During the 1952 presidential campaign Nixon, who ran as the vice presidential candidate, had strongly criticized Acheson. He attacked the Democratic candidate, Adlai Stevenson, by describing him as a graduate of Acheson's "Cowardly College of Communist Containment." Nixon admitted in his memoirs that Acheson was too irresistible a target: "his clipped moustache, his British tweeds, and his haughty manner made him the perfect foil for my attacks on the snobbish kind of Foreign Service personality and mentality that had been taken in hook, line, and sinker by the Communists." By 1969 Nixon regretted "the intensity of those attacks," though he still believed that Acheson was wrong on Asia.[149] After the Republicans won in 1952, Acheson had been excoriating in his comments on the Eisenhower administration. Acheson publicly aired his low opinion of Nixon as late as December 1967: "I have no respect for him at all. And I would be sad indeed if he became President of the United States."[150]

Yet Acheson became an advisor to the new administration. This was largely the result of his relationship with Henry Kissinger, who assumed the role of national security advisor. They first met in 1953 when Kissinger was a graduate student at Harvard.[151] They also found common ground in their opposition to Kennan's support for disengagement in Europe in his 1957 Reith lectures. Kissinger wanted Nixon to enlist Acheson's advice. Acheson responded partly because he continued to crave a place at the center of power, partly because he succumbed to flattery, but also because he believed that the new administration might well pursue the vital goal of disengaging from Vietnam. Nixon indicated that he was receptive to the idea, but Acheson made the first move by offering his services to the president at the annual Gridiron dinner in Washington in March 1969.[152] There quickly followed a meeting at the White House.

Acheson met Nixon, with Kissinger in silent attendance, on 19 March 1969, with the president determined to set a positive tone by speaking of the Marshall Plan as one of the "great acts of statesmanship in American history." Nixon then addressed his main concern—what to do about Vietnam. Acheson discovered that they had broadly similar views. He observed: "American policy had been very sensible until the Johnson decision in '65 to put in substantial troops. Although I had supported this, I now thought I had been wrong. Here the President interjected that he had also supported it and also thought that we had been wrong." Nixon also asked Acheson's advice on whether they might open negotiations with the Soviets. Acheson thought they might never achieve a North-South agreement. In any case, the real negotiation was on the ground: to demonstrate that the communists could not win, just as Ridgway had done in Korea. Acheson concluded: "I did not think it was a good time to negotiate." Nixon's biographer, Stephen Ambrose, tartly but aptly observed that "in Acheson's view, it was never a good time."[153]

Acheson related his favorable impressions of the meeting to a number of friends. He reported how the hour-long talk continued without interruption, unlike in the LBJ years when "people were running in and out of the room." He added: "I got a feeling of orderliness and concentration rather than a Napoleonic drive and scattered attention." Alice Acheson asked him whether he had changed his opinion of Nixon and he replied that he had moved to a more favorable one, from "abusive hostility to respect with a dash of flattery."[154] To another correspondent, he declared that Nixon "impressed me favorably; and our talk was relaxed, serious and informative both ways."[155] In another letter he maintained that "Nixon is a definite relief from L.B.J., not out of definable positive virtues, but from the absence of a swinish, bullying boorishness which made his last years unbearable." [156] He felt the administration "was made up on the whole of pretty good men, intelligent, high-minded, conservative, but wholly inexperienced in government and—so it seems to me—naive beyond words."[157] He seemed to prefer the more orderly and calmer atmosphere of the early years of the Nixon White House as compared with the more frenetic and anguished latter period of Johnson's presidency. Stephen Ambrose suggests: "Acheson was more impressed by Nixon than the other way around."[158]

Acheson was unimpressed by Nixon's secretary of state, William Rogers. Acheson's son-in-law, William Bundy, reported that the State Department "has never been so bewildered and leaderless as it is now."[159] The situation was made worse by the way Kissinger had extended his position as Nixon's principal foreign policy advisor, prompting a letter of concern by Dean Rusk to Acheson: "Kissinger is gutting the role and responsibilities of Bill Rogers." Rusk wondered whether he and Acheson should speak to Rogers about this. Although he shared Rusk's concern, Acheson did not think speaking to Rogers would help. He added: "Bill Rogers' difficulties, including his inability to speak effectively to foreign governments which you mention, spring from his own inadequacies and not from Henry Kissinger or anyone else. One conclusion I hold after some experience is that a quiet word with Bill Rogers is not only a waste of time, but is far better left unspoken." Jussi Hanhimäki rightly notes that it was "too late to rescue Secretary of State Rogers from growing irrelevancy. Kissinger had already outmaneuvered Rogers, with Nixon's apparent approval, at almost every turn."[160] Acheson wrote an article about the issue that was remarkably restrained from such a forceful advocate of the secretary's role. Perhaps his friendship with Kissinger influenced his judgment. He suggested that White House advisers came to play greater roles because they delivered "what is not being done anywhere to the satisfaction of the man responsible, the President." He added, "Why, one may ask, is not the proper remedy to find a Secretary who will do or have done what is necessary? The answer unhappily is that such men are not easy to come by or bring in."[161]

Not only did Acheson show understanding of Kissinger's growing influence, he rallied to Nixon's defense in late 1969 as anger at the administration reached a peak. On 7 October David Broder wrote in the *Washington Post*: "It is becoming more obvious with every passing day that the men and the movement that broke Lyndon Johnson's authority in 1968 are out to break Richard Nixon in 1969. The likelihood is great that they will succeed."[162] A few days later Dean Acheson warned against "the attempt being made from many sources to destroy Nixon." In an exclusive interview in the *New York Times* he said, "I think we're going to have a major constitutional crisis if we make a habit of destroying Presidents." He added that "Nixon isn't going to do anything bad. If he does, impeach, throw him out."[163]

Acheson told Nixon that he should do more to explain the administration's goals in Vietnam to the American people. Nixon called Acheson to a meeting at the White House on 27 October and asked whether he should announce additional withdrawals of US forces and outline a timetable for this. Acheson resolutely opposed this idea, saying that producing a timetable would "indicate weakness and yielding to pressure." It would not "appease those who criticized him or reassure the great mass of people that he was in command of the situation and was operating under a definitive plan." Acheson declared the president's approach as "sound, but that he has great trouble communicating with the great majority who really agree with him."[164] In November 1969 Nixon sifted advice about how to proceed in the talks on Vietnam. Acheson counseled that "any announcement of withdrawal schedules would put us at a disadvantage."[165] In his speech of 3 November 1969 Nixon declared that the United States would maintain its commitment in Vietnam, it would keep "fighting until the Communists agreed to negotiate a fair and honourable peace or until the South Vietnamese were able to defend themselves." At the same time, there would be disengagement along the lines of the Nixon Doctrine, which prescribed that departures of US forces would be "linked to the progress of Vietnamization, the level of enemy activity, and developments on the negotiating front" and not by demonstrations in America.[166]

If Nixon heeded Acheson's advice on Vietnam, the administration's secret incursion into Cambodia in 1970 provoked the former secretary's wrath. Acheson was unconvinced that the strategy would work: "it is easier to send our troops in than it is to get them out." He now "declined to attend a meeting at the White House . . . since I disagree strongly with policy," describing the intervention as "a new dive into Southeast Asia's quagmire." He was frustrated that the administration was taking initiatives that added to domestic turmoil. Perhaps he was also uneasy about American aggression against a country that had recently honored him for his successful legal advocacy in their case before the International Court of Justice.[167] The events in Cambodia were symptomatic of how little Acheson was told about the administration's policies and, in particular, its use of threats as a diplomatic method.[168]

Meanwhile, Acheson responded to Nixon's call for assistance in defeating Senate majority leader Mike Mansfield's amendment, which sought to reduce American forces in Europe by half to 150,000. Acheson proposed that they assemble a group of former secretaries of state, secretaries of defense, high commissioners for Germany, NATO commanders, and chairmen of the JCS, who would embody the bipartisanship of postwar foreign policy, and who would release a statement opposing the amendment. He also was highly effective in cajoling these figures to agree when they gathered in the White House on 13 May 1971. He assumed the lead in talking to the press about their statement, delivering remarks in his usual forthright style: it would be "asinine," "sheer nonsense" to cut forces without cuts by the Soviets. He told John Cowles that it "has been great fun," even if the "liberals will excommunicate me." Another letter spoke of "my mad Democratic friends," and how he had "urged a battle royal with no quarter asked or given."[169]

Acheson offered his counsel to Nixon right up to the last weeks of his life. But, by 1971, he was privately scathing toward the administration: "My sad, current conclusion is that the present Administration is the most incompetent and undirected group I have seen in charge of the U.S. government since the closing days of the Wilson Administration. No one is evil, whatever some may think of Agnew, just plain ignorant and incompetent."[170] He sympathized with those dismayed by the release of the Pentagon Papers, which constituted the detailed confidential history of American engagement in Vietnam. In an article for the *New York Times*, he referred to the "purloined papers."[171] In his final undated letter, written to Archibald MacLeish sometime in September or early October 1971, he spoke approvingly of Nixon's measures on floating the dollar: "I think so far he has gone at it the right way and is on the right course. I fear that his greatest troubles lie ahead. And I wish him—as I told him three days ago—all the luck (and he needs luck) in the world."[172]

Acheson in the final two decades of his life appeared less flexible, more assertive and acerbic in personal terms, and more of an advocate of aggressive policy options. This was less a radical departure than a shift in scale. He had been sharp tongued throughout his adult life and had advocated, at least since early 1950, a firm stand backed with military power. However, for all the continuing command of the issues and sophistication of his analysis, his policy advice in these years was cruder, as were his observations about people and events. This was partly the product of age and a more rigid outlook, while heart, thyroid, and stomach problems heightened his inclination to be irritable. Douglas Brinkley suggests another influence: "The 'attack of the primitives' clearly had scarred Acheson, leading him to coarsen his method of foreign policy analysis and turning him into a caustic, and at times vengeful, man."[173] By the 1960s he faced a new type of criticism from revisionist historians who asserted that the Truman administration had pursued a reckless foreign policy. For all his robust character, these assaults affected him.

Acheson's behavior was also influenced by the circumstances in which he was operating. When he was out of office, and even when he was advising Kennedy and Johnson, he was less informed, lacking continuous access to the wealth of cable traffic that provided detailed information on countries and developments around the world. He was also not subject to the same daily discipline of debating the issues with experts in the State Department. Liberated from the responsibilities of office, he did not need to temper his views to the practicalities of power. He was free to give full expression to his opinions without the need to adjust his position in the light of domestic and international circumstances. In responding to revisionist critiques, he sometimes defended his and Truman's policies by misremembering or producing neater versions of the sequence of events. And he gave policy prescriptions that were not tied to his actual experience. He was not in office when Marshall agreed to an airlift as a response to the Berlin blockade in 1948. Indeed, when he became secretary in January 1949 he initiated talks that led to a negotiated settlement. Yet in 1961 he advocated the very high risk military response that had been rejected in 1948.

He might have been out of office and more rigid, but Acheson did have an impact in this period. In the late 1950s he played a significant role in restoring confidence to the Democratic Party and articulating a convincing foreign policy outlook. After 1961, he commanded the considerable respect of Kennedy, Johnson, and Nixon, who eagerly sought his advice. He made an important contribution to keeping an American commitment to the Atlantic alliance, helping to defeat attempts like the Mansfield amendment to reduce that attachment and urging a restrained response to de Gaulle's challenge. It was fortunate that his rash recommendations for a robust action toward Berlin and Cuba did not prevail, but his skillful diplomacy on Cyprus deserved a better outcome. He made his most significant contribution on Vietnam. He backed Ball's peace plan in 1965 but then endorsed military action in 1965–1967. On Vietnam, as on so many other issues in his last decade, the president requested Acheson's advice without providing him with the complete picture. Acheson reflexively adopted the central precept he took as the main lesson of his time as secretary—the need to be decisive and tough in the face of threats. But when he received a full briefing on Vietnam in early 1968, something that was a regular feature of his time in office, he recommended American withdrawal and his wise counsel was heeded, if reluctantly, by Johnson.

Acheson remained intellectually alert, lively, witty, and engaging company to the end and, despite his often unyielding views, continued to display a healthy readiness for self-mockery. His farm at Sandy Spring had increasingly become his retreat, where he relaxed with carpentry, rural chores, and wide reading. It was there that he died of a cerebral hemorrhage on 12 October 1971.

NOTES

1. "Acheson In Farewell to Department Aides," *New York Times* (17 January 1953), 7; "The Secretary's Farewell to His Colleagues," *DOSB* 28:709 (26 January 1953), 161–162.

2. "Acheson Bows Out," *New York Times* (17 January 1953), 34; Acheson's Farewell Press Conference, *DOSB* 28:709 (26 January 1953), 129–130.

3. William S. White, "Acheson Says NATO Can Now Curb Reds in Western Europe," *New York Times* (20 January 1953), 1, 3.

4. L of C, Jessup Papers box II:3, Acheson folder 1, Acheson to Jessup, 17 February 1953.

5. *Affection and Trust: the Personal Correspondence of Harry S. Truman and Dean Acheson, 1953–1971* (New York: Alfred A. Knopf, 2010), 7–8, Acheson to Truman, 21 February 1953; *Among Friends,* 79 (letter to Jeffrey Kitchen, 13 February 1953), 80 (letters to David Acheson, 19 February 1953, and to Patricia Acheson, 22 February 1953), 81–82 (letter to Ned Burling, 8 March 1953); L of C, Jessup Papers box II:3, Acheson folder 1, Acheson to Jessup, 24 February 1953.

6. *Among Friends,* 79, Acheson to Kitchen, 13 February 1953. He later said three months was "all too short"; Houghton Library, Harvard University, Christian A. Herter Papers, A3, Acheson to Herter, 10 November 1960.

7. *Affection and Trust,* 13–14, Acheson to Truman, 14 April 1953.

8. Yale, Acheson Papers, box 21, folder 261, reel 13, frame 0862, Acheson to McCloy, 30 July 1953.

9. For the transcripts, see HSTL, Acheson Papers, boxes 78–81, Princeton Seminars, 1953–1970 File, sessions on 2, 8–9, 15–16, and 22–23 July, 10–11 October and 11–13 December 1953, and 13–14 February and 14 March and 15–16 May 1954; they are also available as a separate microfilm.

10. L of C, Frankfurter Papers, Acheson, Dean G 1953 folder, Acheson to Frankfurter, 10 July 1953; L of C, Herbert Feis Papers, box 10, Acheson seminar folder, Acheson memorandum, 17 February 1954.

11. See *Affection and Trust,* 35 [34–37], Acheson to Truman, 8 October 1953.

12. William Hillman, *Mr. President* (New York: Farrar, Straus and Young, 1952).

13. HSTL, HST Papers, box 641, Post-Presidential Papers, Memoirs Interviews with Associates of President Truman File, Acheson, Dean, Acheson interviews, 16 February, 17 February am, 17 February pm, 18 February am, 18 February pm 1955. *Affection and Trust,* 67, Acheson to Truman, 21 February 1951.

14. *Affection and Trust,* 46–47 (Truman to Acheson, 28 January 1954), 52–54 (Truman to Acheson, 28 May 1954), 76 (Truman to Acheson, 7 June 1955), 77–86 (Acheson to Truman, 21 June 1955), 86–88 (Acheson to Truman, 24 June 1955), 88–91 (Acheson to Truman, 27 June 1955), 91 (Truman to Acheson, 30 June 1955), 96–106 (Acheson to Truman, 18 July 1955), 108–120 (Acheson to Truman, 25 July 1955).

15. *Affection and Trust,* 29 (Truman to Acheson, 18 August 1953), 30 (Truman to Acheson, 2 September 1953), 30–32 (Acheson to Truman, 24 September 1953).

16. Clemson University, Byrnes Papers, box 19, folder 13, David Lawrence, "Acheson and Byrnes Fan the Flames," *Washington Star* (27 October 1955). Lawrence also criticized Byrnes's article, "Stop Shooting the Sentry," *Collier's* (11 November 1955), 46, 50, 54.

17. "G.O.P. Charges Acheson, Hiss Plot Together," *Chicago Tribune* (12 November 1955), 7; Douglas Brinkley, *Dean Acheson: the Cold War Years, 1953–1971* (New Haven, CT: Yale University Press, 1992), 39–40.

18. L of C, Nitze Papers, box 17, folder 3, Acheson to Gary, 6 August 1956.

19. Acheson, *A Democrat Looks at His Party* (New York: Harper and Brothers, 1955).

20. Acheson, "The Responsibility for Decision in Foreign Policy," *Yale Review* XLIV:1 (September 1954), 1–12, quotation at 8.

21. Acheson, "Introduction," Louis J. Halle, *Civilization and Foreign Policy: An Inquiry for Americans* (New York: Harper & Brothers, 1955), xi–xxii.

22. Acheson, "The President and the Secretary," in Don K. Price, ed., *The Secretary of State* (Englewood Cliffs, NJ: Prentice-Hall, 1960), 27–50, quotation at 34.

23. Acheson, "The President and the Secretary," 41.

24. Acheson, "The Responsibility for Decision in Foreign Policy," 10.

25. Acheson, "Introduction," xi–xxii, quotations at xix.

26. Acheson, "Introduction," xvi.

27. L of C, Archibald MacLeish Papers, box 1, Acheson, Dean folder, Acheson to MacLeish, 26 March 1953.

28. HSTL, Lucius D. Battle Papers, box 1, Letters to Battle from Dean Acheson, 1952–56 folder, Acheson to Battle, 6 August 1953.

29. *Present at Creation,* 712.

30. *DOSB* 28:708 (19 January 1953), 121 (Loyalty Board Finding, 12 December 1952), 122–123 (Acheson memorandum to Truman, 3 January 1953); *DOSB* 28:711 (9 February 1953), 241 (Hand to Dulles, 20 January 1953, Dulles to Hand, 29 January 1953); *DOSB* 28:708 (23 March 1953), 454–455, Dulles memorandum on Vincent, 4 March 1953; Kahn, *China Hands*, 11, 250–256; Michael A. Guhin, *John Foster Dulles: A Statesman and His Times* (New York: Columbia University Press, 1972), 198–200; *Present at Creation*, 712.

31. Guhin, *Dulles*, 200.

32. *Present at Creation*, 713. L of C, Jessup Papers, box 1:3, Acheson folder 1, Acheson to Jessup, 17 February 1953.

33. HSTL, Battle Papers, box 1, Letters to Battle from Dean Acheson, 1952–56 folder, Acheson to Battle, 7 April 1953.

34. Yale, Acheson Papers, box 12, folder 150, Acheson to Franks, 28 December 1953.

35. L of C, Nitze Papers, Name File, container 17, folder 2, Acheson, Dean 1949–1955, Acheson speech "Post-War Foreign Policy - Second Phase."

36. Acheson, "Instant Retaliation: The Debate Continued," *New York Times Magazine* (28 March 1954), 13, 77–78 .

37. *Affection & Trust*, 51, Acheson to Truman, 26 March 1954.

38. L of C, Nitze Papers, box 17, folder 2, Acheson, Dean 1949–1955 folder, Acheson to John Cowles, 7 June 1954.

39. Quoted in Brinkley, *Acheson*, 39.

40. *Affection and Trust*, 23 (memorandum of conversation, 23 June 1953), 159–160 (Acheson to Truman, 15 January 1957), 204–205 (Acheson to Truman, 17 September 1958).

41. McMahon, *Acheson*, 180–181.

42. Randall B. Woods, *LBJ: Architect of American Ambition* (New York: Free Press, 2007), 314.

43. James T. Patterson, *Grand Expectations: The United States, 1945–1974* (New York: Oxford University Press, 1996), 252–254, 305, 309.

44. *Among Friends*, 107, Acheson to Annie Burr Lewis, 1 November 1955; *Affection and Trust*, 129–132, Acheson to Truman, 23 November 1955.

45. Interview with Robert Bowie, January 1991, Brinkley, *Acheson*, 47.

46. L of C, Nitze Papers, box 17, folder 3, Nitze to Harlan Cleveland, 10 September 1956.

47. L of C, Nitze Papers, box 17, folder 3, Acheson address, "The Shape of Foreign Policy Issues in 1956," to the Western Suburban Democratic Club of Maryland, Bethesda, Maryland, 26 September 1956. Jay Walz, "Acheson Asserts US Scares Allies," *New York Times* (27 September 1956).

48. L of C, Nitze Papers, box 17, folder 3, Acheson to Charles B. Gary, 11 December 1953.

49. *Affection and Trust*, 170–171, Acheson to Truman, 5 June 1957.

50. *Among Friends*, 116–118, Acheson to Frank Altschul, 4 October 1956; Acheson, "Foreign Policy and Presidential Moralism," *Reporter* (2 May 1957), 11; available at www.unz.org/Pub/Reporter-1957may02-00010 (viewed 6 April 2016).

51. Eisenhower's Special Message to Congress on the Middle East, 5 January 1957, available at http://www.presidency.ucsb.edu (viewed 1 April 2016); "Text of Acheson Statement Before House Hearing on Proposed Middle East Policy," *New York Times* (11 January 1957), 4; McLellan, *Acheson*, 414–415; *Affection and Trust*, 159–160, Acheson to Truman, 15 January 1957.

52. Acheson, *A Citizen Looks at Congress* (New York: Harper & Brothers, 1957); Woodrow Wilson, *Congressional Government: A Study in American Politics* (Gloucester, MA: Peter Smith, 1974 edition).

53. Brinkley, *Acheson*, 54–58; Chace, *Acheson*, 378; McMahon, *Acheson*, 183–184; Howard B. Schaffer, *Chester Bowles : New Dealer in the Cold War* (Cambridge, MA: Harvard University Press, 1993), 9–11, 36, 156; Patterson, *Grand Expectations*, 156.

54. Brinkley, *Acheson*, 60–61.

55. L of C, Nitze Papers, box 17, folder 4, Acheson speech, "Moralism in Foreign Policy," 25 April 1957. Acheson, "Foreign Policy and Presidential Moralism," *Reporter* (2 May 1958), 10–14; available at www.unz.org/Pub/Reporter-1957may02-00010 (viewed 6 April 2016).

Acheson speech, "Morality, Moralism and Diplomacy" at University of Florida, 20 February 1958; printed in *Yale Review* XLVII:4 (June 1958), 481–493, quotation at 483.

56. Acheson, "Strategy of Freedom," *DOSB* (18 December 1950), 962; Acheson, "Plowing a Straight Furrow," *DOSB* (27 November 1950), 840; Acheson, "Shield of Faith," *DOSB* 23:594 (20 November 1950), [799–811], 800, 799; Brinkley, *Acheson*, 25–26.

57. Acheson, *Power and Diplomacy* (Cambridge, MA: Harvard University Press, 1958), 63, 11.

58. L of C, Jessup Papers, box II:3, Acheson folder 1, Acheson remarks, 17 February 1958.

59. George F. Kennan, *Russia, the Atom and the West* (London: Oxford University Press, 1958), chapter III: The Problem of Eastern and Central Europe, 33–50.

60. "Text of Acheson's Reply to Kennan," *New York Times* (12 January 1958), 25; Brinkley, *Acheson*, 79–82; Chace, *Acheson*, 375.

61. *FRUS 1949* III, 102–103, memorandum of conversation, 9 March 1949; John Lewis Gaddis, "The United States and the Question of a Sphere of Influence in Europe, 1945–1949," in Olav Riste, ed., *Western Security: The Formative Years* (Oslo: Norwegian University Press, 1985), 77–78 [60–91].

62. Yale, Acheson Papers, box 17, folder 222, Acheson to Kennan, 13 March 1958; Acheson, "The Illusion of Disengagement," *Foreign Affairs* 36:3 (April 1958), 371–382.

63. Yale, Acheson Papers, box 17, folder 222, Kennan to Acheson, 20 March 1958.

64. L of C, Jessup Papers, box II:3, Acheson folder 1, Jessup to Acheson, 19 March 1958 and Acheson to Jessup, 25 March 1958.

65. John Lewis Gaddis, *George F. Kennan: An American Life* (New York: Penguin Press, 2011), 533–534.

66. Robert Dallek, *Lone Star Rising* (New York: Oxford University Press, 1991), 517–526. *Among Friends*, 128, Acheson to Johnson, 13 August 1957; "Acheson Supports Rights Bill," *New York Times* (8 August 1957), 12; William S. White, "House Passes Rights Bill," *New York Times* (28 August 1957), 1.

67. *Among Friends*, 127–129, Acheson to Johnson, 13 August 1957; *Affection and Trust*, 175–176, Acheson to Truman, 14 August 1957.

68. Brinkley, *Acheson*, 204–205; Yale, Acheson Papers, box 73, folder 1, memorandum of conversation between Acheson and Johnson, 22 July 1957.

69. Cabell Phillips, "Dean Acheson: Ten Years Later," *New York Times* (18 January 1959); Walter Lippmann in *New Republic* (2 November 1959), 3; quoted in Thomas G. Paterson, *Meeting the Communist Threat: Truman to Reagan* (New York: Oxford University Press, 1988), 196.

70. Acheson quoted in Dallek, *Lone Star Rising*, 549; *Affection and Trust*, 226–228, Acheson to Truman, 31 August 1959.

71. Arthur Schlesinger Jr., *Robert Kennedy and His Times* (London: Andre Deutsch, 1978), 199.

72. *Affection and Trust*, 233 (Acheson to Truman, 14 April 1960), 239 (Acheson to Truman, 28 June 1960 [*Among Friends*, 184–185 says 27 June]), 241 (Acheson To Truman, 17 July 1960).

73. Andrew Schlesinger and Stephen Schlesinger, eds., *The Letters of Arthur Schlesinger Jr.* (New York: Random House, 2013), 236–237 [233–237], Schlesinger to Kennedy, 14 November 1960. See Arthur Schlesinger Jr., *Journals, 1952–2000* (New York: Penguin, 2007), 88, 16 October 1960 entry, where Schlesinger recorded how Acheson described the candidates as "schoolkids."

74. John F. Kennedy Library [hereafter JFKL], Oral History Testimony of Dean Acheson, 27 April 1964, pp. 7–8.

75. *Among Friends*, 200 [200–202], Acheson to Stikker, 27 December 1960.

76. Quoted in Michael Beschloss, *The Crisis Years: Kennedy and Khrushchev, 1960–1963* (New York: Edward Burlingame Books, 1991), 356.

77. JFKL, Arthur Schlesinger Jr. Papers, box P8, Dean Acheson folder, Acheson to Isidor Shaffer, 28 November 1960.

78. JFKL, Oral History Testimony of Dean Acheson, 27 April 1964, p. 2.

79. JFKL, John F. Kennedy Presidential Papers, National Security File [hereafter NSF], box 313, Acheson, "Review of North Atlantic Problems for the Future," 24 March 1961; available at http://www.jfkl.org/asset-Viewer/JFKNSF-313-004 (viewed 23 January 2017). *FRUS 1961–1963* XIII, 260–266, document 95 (memorandum of conversation, 21 February 1961): 285–291, document 100 (Policy Directive, "NATO and the Atlantic Nations," 20 April 1961): McMahon, *Acheson*, 189.

80. L of C, Nitze Papers, container 17, folder 5, Acheson address, "Factors Underlying Negotiations with the Russians," Eddie Jacobson Memorial Foundation, Kansas City, Missouri, 15 April 1958; "On Dealing with Russia: An Inside View," *New York Times Magazine* (12 April 1959), 27, 88–89. *Among Friends*, 204–205, 16 February 1961.

81. Acheson, *Meetings at the Summit: A Study in Diplomatic Method* (Durham: University of New Hampshire, 1958), 22 [27pp].

82. L of C, Nitze Papers, box 17, folder 6, Acheson, "Wishing Won't Hold Berlin," *Saturday Evening Post* (7 March 1959), 33, 85–86.

83. *FRUS 1961–1963* XIV, 37 [36–40], memorandum of conversation, 5 April 1961, 3:10pm; Declassified Documents Reference System, 1985, document 2547, Acheson memorandum for president, 3 April 1961; McMahon, *Acheson*, 236n47.

84. *FRUS 1961–1963* XIV, 119–124 (Record of Meeting of the Interdepartmental Coordinating Group on Berlin Contingency Planning, 16 June 1961), 138–154 (Report by Dean Acheson, 28 June 1961).

85. JFKL, Kennedy Presidential Papers, NSF, box 313, NSC meeting, 29 June 1961; available at www.jfklibrary.org/Asset-Viewer/Archives/JFKNSF-313-013 (viewed 23 January 2017); NSC meeting, 13 July 1961, available at www.jfklibrary.org/Asset-Viewer/Archives/JFKNSF-313-014 (viewed 23 January 2017); *FRUS 1961–1963* XIV, 192–194, memorandum of discussion in NSC, 13 July 1961.

86. *Affection and Trust*, 265, Acheson to Truman, 14 July 1961.

87. Kennedy , " Radio and Television Report to the American People on the Berlin Crisis ," 25 July 1961 ; available at www.presidency.ucsb.edu/ws/?pid=8259 (viewed 20 April 2016).

88. *FRUS 1961–1963* XIV, 245–259, Acheson, "Berlin. A Political Program," undated; *Affection and Trust*, 267, Acheson to Truman, 4 August 1961.

89. Robert Dallek, *John F. Kennedy: An Unfinished Life 1917–1963* (London: Allen Lane, 2003), 417.

90. McMahon, *Acheson*, 195.

91. Howard C. Westwood, *Covington & Burling, 1919–1984* (Washington, DC: Covington & Burling, 1986), 142–143; *Affection and Trust*, 275, Acheson to Truman, 3 May 1962.

92. JFKL, Oral History Testimony of Dean Acheson, 27 April 1964, p. 4.

93. JFKL, Oral History Testimony of Dean Acheson, 27 April 1964, p. 13.

94. *Affection and Trust*, 259, Acheson to Truman, 3 May 1961.

95. *Affection and Trust*, 279, Acheson to Truman, 8 October 1962.

96. Acheson, "Dean Acheson's Version of Robert Kennedy's Version of the Cuban Missile Crisis," *Esquire* LXXI (February 1969), 76–78, 94, 96; reprinted as "Homage to Plain Dumb Luck," in Richard A. Divine, ed., *The Cuban Missile Crisis* (Chicago: Quadrangle, 1971), 186–197.

97. *FRUS 1961–1963* XI, 95–100, Memcon, 17 October 1962; Acheson, "Homage to Plain Dumb Luck," 188–190; Sheldon M. Stern, *Averting "The Final Failure": John F. Kennedy and the Secret Cuban Missile Crisis Meetings* (Stanford, CA: Stanford University Press, 2004), 104–108.

98. Acheson, "Homage to Plain Dumb Luck," 192–193.

99. Acheson, "Homage to Plain Dumb Luck," 192.

100. Stern, *Averting "The Final Failure,"* 116–141. Robert F. Kennedy, *Thirteen Days* (New York: W. W. Norton, 1969) gives the misleading impression that he was an opponent of an air strike. *FRUS 1961–1963* XI, 165–167, Paris Embassy to State Department, 22 October 1962: Acheson's report.

101. *Among Friends*, 236 (Acheson to Kennedy, 28 October 1962), 238 (Acheson to Kennedy, 30 November 1962). Acheson, "Homage to Plain Dumb Luck," 187.

102. Dean Acheson speech at West Point, 5 December 1962, in Ian S. McDonald, *Anglo-American Relations Since the Second World War* (London: David & Charles, 1974), 181–182. TNA, PREM 11/4057, Macmillan to Spears, 7 December 1962; editorial, "Alive and Kicking," *Daily Mail* (7 December 1962), 1.

103. *Affection and Trust*, 281, Acheson to Truman, 14 December 1962.

104. Alsop interview, March 1988 in Brinkley, *Acheson*, 206.

105. *Among Friends*, 263, Acheson to Lady Pamela Berry, 20 November 1963; "Thoughts Written to a British Friend on the Assassination of President Kennedy," in Dean Acheson, *Grapes From Thorns* (New York: W. W. Norton, 1972), 81–82; Brinkley, *Acheson*, 206.

106. Brinkley, *Acheson*, 207–208.

107. Isaacson and Thomas, *Wise Men*, 643–644.

108. Dean Rusk, *As I Saw It* (New York: Penguin, 1991), 337.

109. David Bruce Diary, entry for 21 December 1964. I am grateful to Professor John W. Young of the University of Nottingham for this quotation.

110. James E. Miller, *The United States and the Making of Modern Greece* (Chapel Hill: University of North Carolina Press, 2009), 85–95.

111. *FRUS 1964–1968* XVI, 1–166 (Ball missions and meetings in Washington, January–June 1964). Lyndon B. Johnson Library, Austin, Texas, George Ball Oral History, 8 July 1971; available at http://www.lbjlibrary.net/assets/documents/archives/oral_histories/ball_g/ BALL-G1.PDF (viewed 23 January 2017). Lyndon B. Johnson Library, Austin, Texas, George Ball Oral History, 9 July 1971 available at http://www.lbjlibrary.net/assets/documents/ archives/oral_histories/ball_g/BALL-G2.PDF (viewed 23 January 2017). George W. Ball, *The Past Has Another Pattern* (New York: W. W. Norton, 1982), 335–359.

112. *FRUS 1964–1968* XVI, 167–309, Acheson mediation, July–September 1964; Miller, *United States and Greece*, 103–106.

113. *FRUS 1964–1968* XVI, 223–225, Acheson to Ball, 7 August 1964, quotation at 224.

114. *FRUS 1964–1968* XVI, 251–252, Acheson to State Department, 15 August 1964.

115. Yale, Acheson Papers, box 21, folder 264, Acheson to MacDonald, 6 September 1964.

116. L of C, MacLeish papers, box 1, Dean Acheson folder, Acheson to MacLeish, 6 September 1964.

117. *Among Friends*, 264, Acheson to Battle, 7 December 1964.

118. Acheson, "Cyprus: the anatomy of the problem," *Chicago Bar Record* 46:8 (May 1965), 349–356, quotation at 355.

119. *FRUS 1964–1968* II, 627–628 (editorial note), 652–660 (George Ball, "A Plan for a Political Resolution in Viet Nam," 13 May 1965), 665–669 (Notes of a Meeting, 16 May 1965), 674–676 (Taylor and Johnson, "Fundamental Factors in a Solution in South Vietnam," 20 May 1965), 676–679 (Taylor and Johnson, "Questions and Comments relating to 'A Plan for a political resolution in Viet Nam," 20 May 1965); Ball, *Past Has Another Pattern*, 394. David L. DiLeo, *George Ball, Vietnam and the Rethinking of Containment* (Chapel Hill: University of North Carolina Press, 1991), 89–90; James A. Bill, *George Ball: Behind the Scenes in U. S. Foreign Policy* (New Haven, CT: Yale University Press, 1997), 35. Isaacson and Thomas, *Wise Men*, 648–650.

120. *FRUS 1964–1968* III, 137–141, Notes of a Meeting 8 July 1965; *Affection and Trust*, 293–294, Acheson to Truman, 10 July 1965.

121. Isaacson and Thomas, *Wise Men*, 654.

122. *Among Friends*, 238–239 (Acheson to Lady Pamela Berry, 3 December 1962), 242–244 (Acheson to Kurt Birrenbach, 19 February 1963), 265–266 (Acheson to Annan, 15 March 1965, quotation at 266), 267 (Acheson to Eden, no date but probably 1965). Acheson to Johnson, 31 March 1965, in Brinkley, *Acheson*, 226. For Acheson's thinking about NATO at this time, see "Ambivalences of American Foreign Policy," 5 March 1965 lecture to University of Indiana, in Acheson, *This Vast External Realm* (New York: W. W. Norton, 1973), 138–156; and "Foreign Policy of the United States," *Arkansas Law Review and Bar Association Journal* 18:3 (Fall 1964), 225–234, and 230–231 on de Gaulle and NATO.

123. See *FRUS 1964–1968* XIII, 325–453 for coverage of the issue up to August when Acheson departed. Brinkley, *Acheson*, 228–232. L of C, Harriman Papers, box 429, Acheson,

Dean 1961–1968 folder, Acheson statement before Subcommittee on Europe of House Foreign Affairs Committee, 17 May 1966.

124. *Among Friends*, 280, Acheson to Casey, 15 August 1966; *Affection and Trust*, 299–300, Acheson to Truman, 3 October 1966. The comments on Rusk unknowingly echoed those of JFK in an interview with the journalist Theodore White. "He [Rusk] never gives me anything to chew on, never puts it on the line. You never know what he is thinking." He added that Rusk was "calm, wise, thoughtful," an "excellent Secretary if you're not interested in foreign affairs—but I am." White notes in Schlesinger Papers, cited in Michael Beschloss, *The Crisis Years, 1961–1963* (1991), 356–357. *FRUS 1964–1968* XIII, 392, Bruce Diary, 19 May 1966: "It is never difficult to ignite the Acheson powder magazine, and the President's spark set off an explosion. Dean said he resented the president's inferences about his own statements, as well as what he had said about George Ball. Acheson was furious, so was the President."

125. Robert Dallek, *Flawed Giant: Lyndon Johnson and His Times, 1961–1973* (New York: Oxford University Press, 1998), 490.

126. Yale, Acheson Papers, box 7, folder 84, Acheson to Cowles, 21 August 1967; Isaacson and Thomas, *Wise Men*, 677–679.

127. Ball, *Past Has Another Pattern*, 407. For the 1–2 November meetings, see *FRUS 1964–1968* V, 951–970, quotations at 956 and 957.

128. L of C, Harriman Papers, box 429, Acheson, Dean 1961–1968 folder, The Public Broadcast Laboratory, Interview with Dean Acheson, 3 December 1967, and Harriman memorandum, 12 December 1967. Isaacson and Thomas, *Wise Men*, 681–683.

129. Yale, Acheson Papers, box 7, folder 84, Acheson to Cowles, 21 August 1967; box 9, folder 118, Acheson to Eden, 11 December 1967 and Acheson to Eden, 30 December 1967; Isaacson and Thomas, *Wise Men*, 683–684.

130. McMahon, *Acheson*, 203–204; Isaacson and Thomas, *Wise Men*, 687, Brinkley, *Acheson*, 255–258.

131. L of C, Harriman Papers, box 429, Acheson, Dean 1961–1968 folder, Acheson-Harriman telephone call, 7 March 1968.

132. George C. Herring, *America's Longest War: The United States and Vietnam, 1950–1975* 3rd ed. (New York: McGraw-Hill, 1996), 222; Yale, Acheson Papers, box 7, folder 84, Acheson to John Cowles, 14 March 1968. See also *Among Friends*, 292–294, Acheson memorandum on meeting with the president, 14 March 1968.

133. *FRUS 1964–1968* VI, 378–379, memorandum for the record, 14 March 1968; *Among Friends*, 289–291 (Acheson to Cowles, 27 February 1968), 292–294 (meeting with president, 14 March 1968), 295–296 (Acheson to Gould, enclosing Acheson views as of 26 March 1968).

134. *FRUS 1964–1968* VI, 457–458 (editorial note), 466–470 (Notes of Meeting, 26 March 1968 1:15pm), 471–474 (Notes of Meeting, 26 March 1968, 3:15pm), quotations at 471 and 474; Clark Clifford, *Counsel to the President* (New York: Random House, 1991), 517; *Among Friends*, 295–296, Acheson to Gould, enclosing Acheson views as of 26 March 1968.

135. L of C, Harriman Papers, box 429, Acheson, Dean 1961–1968 folder, Acheson to Harriman, 14 April 1968.

136. Acheson, *Sketches from Life of Men I Have Known* (London: Hamish Hamilton, 1961).

137. Acheson, *Morning and Noon*.

138. Cabell Phillips, "Dean Acheson Ten Years Later," *New York Times Magazine* (18 January 1959).

139. Williams, *Tragedy of American Foreign Policy*, Horowitz, *Free World Colossus*, Steel, *Pax Americana*, Richard J. Barnet with Marcus Raskin, *After 20 Years: Alternatives to the Cold War in Europe* (New York: Random House, 1965).

140. Brinkley, *Acheson*, 266, 275–276, interview with David Acheson, April 1988; *Present at Creation*, xv; Beisner, *Acheson*, 636; "Dean Acheson," in Publishers Weekly Editors and Contributors, *The Author Speaks: Selected PW Interviews, 1967–1976* (New York: R. R. Bowker, 1977), 415. Acheson was also responding to Kennan, a "delightful, vain and woozy man," whose memoirs were "driving me crazy"; L of C, MacLeish Papers, box 1, Acheson, Dean folder, Acheson to MacLeish, 13 October 1967.

141. Isaacson and Thomas, *Wise Men*, 720.

142. *Among Friends*, 298, Acheson to Jane Acheson Brown, n.d. but probably late October 1969.
143. Schlesinger and Schlesinger, eds., *Letters of Schlesinger*, 385 (Schlesinger to Acheson, 16 October 1969), 386 (Acheson to Schlesinger, 21 October 1969).
144. Acheson, "The Arrogance of International Lawyers," *International Lawyer* 2:4 (July 1968), 591–600; L of C, Jessup Papers, box II:3, Acheson folder (2 of 2), Jessup to Acheson, 22 July 1968 and Acheson to Jessup, 25 July 1968.
145. US Congress, 91st Congress, 1st Session, Hearings before the Subcommittee on Africa of the House of Representatives Committee on Foreign Affairs, *Rhodesia and United States Foreign Policy* (Washington, DC: USGPO, 1969), 124–169, Acheson testimony, 19 November 1969.
146. Brinkley, *Acheson*, 328.
147. Rhodesian Information Service: *Dean Acheson on the Rhodesian Question* (Washington, DC: Rhodesian Information Service, 1969), 7–9, 22, 27–28. Beisner, *Acheson*, 639.
148. See, for example, his October 1949 speech, "Problems in American Foreign Policy," *DOSB* 21:539 (31 October 1949), 668.
149. Richard M. Nixon, *RN: The Memoirs of Richard Nixon* (London: Sidgwick & Jackson, 1978), 110–111. He also called Acheson the "architect of striped pants confusion" (112).
150. L of C, Harriman Papers, box 429, Acheson, Dean 1961–1968 folder, The Public Broadcast Laboratory, Interview with Dean Acheson, 3 December 1967.
151. Henry Kissinger, *White House Years* (Boston: Little, Brown, 1979), 942.
152. *Among Friends*, 302–304, Acheson to J. H. P. Gould, 21 March 1969.
153. Acheson notes of meeting, Acheson collection, Princeton University; cited in Stephen Ambrose, *Nixon: The Triumph of a Politician, 1962–1972* (New York: Simon and Schuster, 1989), 259–260. *Among Friends*, 302–304, Acheson to J. H. P. Gould, 21 March 1969.
154. *Among Friends*, 302–304, Acheson to J. H. P. Gould, 21 March 1969.
155. *Among Friends*, 305, Acheson to William R. Tyler, 21 March 1969.
156. Yale, Acheson Papers, box 3, folder 33, Acheson to Lady Pamela Berry, 24 June 1969.
157. *Among Friends*, 308, Acheson to Welensky, 28 August 1969.
158. Acheson notes of meeting, Acheson collection, Princeton University; cited in Ambrose, *Nixon, 1962–1972*, 260.
159. *Affection and Trust*, Acheson to Truman, 7 May 1969, 307.
160. Rusk to Acheson, 3 March 1971 and Acheson to Rusk, 10 March 1971, quoted in Jussi Hanhimäki, *The Flawed Architect: Henry Kissinger and American Foreign Policy* (Oxford: Oxford University Press, 2004), 115.
161. Acheson, "The Eclipse of the State Department," *Foreign Affairs* 49:4 (July 1971), 593–606.
162. David S. Broder, "A Risky New Sport: 'The Breaking of the President,'" *Washington Post* (7 October 1969), A19.
163. Nixon, *RN*, 401. Israel Shenker, "Acheson Sees Danger in Attempts to 'Destroy' Nixon," *New York Times* (10 October 1969), 9.
164. Acheson notes of meeting, Acheson collection, Princeton University; cited in Ambrose, *Nixon, 1962–1972*, 307–308.
165. Nixon, *RN*, 408.
166. Nixon, *RN*, 409.
167. *Among Friends*, 314–315 (Acheson to Cowles, 5 May 1970), 315–317 (Acheson to Welensky, 30 June 1970).
168. For an astute analysis of this approach, see William Burr and Jeffrey Kimball, *Nixon's Nuclear Specter: The Secret Alert of 1969, Madman Diplomacy, and the Vietnam War* (Lawrence: University Press of Kansas, 2015).
169. Kissinger, *White House Years*, 938, 943–945. *Among Friends*, 326 (Acheson to Cowles, 21 May 1971), 326–327 (Acheson to Welensky, 2 June 1970).
170. *Among Friends*, 321–322, Acheson to Cowles, 12 January 1971.
171. Acheson, "The Purloined Papers," *New York Times* (7 July 1971), 37; *Among Friends*, 327, Acheson to Cowles, 30 July 1971.

172. L of C, MacLeish Papers, box 1, Acheson, Dean folder, Acheson to MacLeish, n.d. [September–October 1971].
173. Brinkley, *Acheson*, 24.

Conclusion

Acheson's death in October 1971 occasioned obituaries and appreciations of his career that rightly focused on his role in the Cold War.[1] During his service in the Truman administration he became the leading architect of containment, a Cold War policy that prevailed, save for an interlude in the 1970s, right to the end of the conflict in the 1980s. Yet Acheson's career and contribution to American foreign policy and international affairs needs to be seen in a larger context.

His approach to the Soviet Union in the 1940s stemmed from a broader vision of the United States in the world. More than any other secretary of state in the twentieth century, he brought a wide historical perspective (filtered through his experiences) to his thinking. He looked to history for guidance on the strategy the United States should adopt. He sought to make sense of the events as they were unfolding and continued to reflect on them over the years. His outlook was the product of three major ingredients whose combination elicited a distinctive vision. First was his extensive reading in history, giving considerable attention to accounts of Victorian Britain. This has led some writers to suggest he was nostalgic about this lost world and others to claim his attachment to Britain resulted in policies that owed more to British interests than to those of the United States.[2] Certainly, Acheson's upbringing meant he was culturally Anglophile and he developed geopolitical views that were tinged with sympathy for Britain. But he saw faults in the era of *Pax Britannica* and was frequently hardheaded in negotiations with Britain—from Lend-Lease to European integration to policy on China to defense spending. His blunt depiction of Britain having lost an empire and failing to find an alternative role was hardly the mark of a nostalgic Anglophile. His speeches and correspondence might have included many references to British history and literature but contained far more references to

American history. These were the opinions of an American whose enthusiasm for British culture and history never lacked a critical element.

This capacity for critical evaluation constituted the second means by which Acheson developed an understanding of international affairs and devised a view of how the United States should act in the world. As a private citizen, as a public official, and as an unpaid advisor, Acheson analyzed unfolding events, scrutinized new ideas and refined his outlook. But his reading on the past and his careful consideration of current developments were not merely an exercise in intellectual understanding. His approach was instrumental: having the fullest possible grasp of the situation was essential to framing the most effective policies. He was driven to do this by a sense of duty, the third influence on his thinking about the United States' place in global affairs. A sense of personal duty first emerged under the quiet encouragement of his father, while a commitment to public service was consciously cultivated by Endicott Peabody at Groton. As a youth Theodore Roosevelt first stirred Acheson and gave Peabody's general encouragement of public service a more concrete shape: "I thrilled to every bugle call to action blown by the 'Young Turks,' the 'Progressives,' and most of all by 'T.R.'"[3] When he then embraced the cooler, less ebullient vision of Woodrow Wilson and his conception of American leadership, Acheson had moved from the notion of personal commitment to public service to the idea of the nation's duty in the world.

Acheson placed the nineteenth century at the center of his vision, noting how it had witnessed less warfare and more international stability thanks to the *Pax Britannica*—the Royal Navy patrolled the seas, while British finance provided investment around the globe. This resulted in fewer military and political disturbances and allowed "an enormous increase of the human population of this earth and at the same time a standard of living never before thought possible," even if it "contained within it injustices which demanded correction."[4] This system collapsed with the threat from Imperial Germany that led to the First World War. With the decline of British military and financial power and the rise of American power, it seemed obvious to Acheson that the United States should replace the British. But Americans had always wished to stay out of international conflicts beyond the Western Hemisphere. Acheson enthusiastically supported President Woodrow Wilson's decision to intervene in the First World War and was even more enthusiastic about Wilson's commitment of the United States to world leadership. He later observed of Wilson, "If his mistakes were great and tragic, as Maynard Keynes pointed out, great also was his understanding of the new role which his country must play in the realignment of power which the crumbling empires and emergence of new forces necessitated."[5] At the time, Acheson backed involvement in the League of Nations, though his enthusiasm for the international organization ebbed over the next decade.

Acheson was disappointed at the failure of Wilson's project, as the United States entered a period of relative political isolation. From his considerable reading in American history he produced a cyclical interpretation of the nation's responses to the wider world. He talked of national mood periods, describing the country as "perhaps the most moody people in the world." The United States shifted between "manifest destiny" and "introspective depression." He regarded the attitudes adopted in the 1920s and 1930s as "psychopathic," when the country concentrated on its domestic concerns and refused to become involved in foreign disputes.[6]

For Acheson the absence of American leadership posed a real danger with the rise of Nazi Germany and an expansionist Japan. He not only diagnosed the problem, he also campaigned to change American policy, recognizing the need to alter the national mood if there were to be the necessary shifts in policy. He was not alone in urging American engagement but few others were more convincing advocates. With entry into the Second World War in December 1941, the United States wielded the leadership Acheson favored; and it also laid plans for some form of continued engagement at war's end. But continued American engagement was far from certain. Acheson argued for US involvement to avoid postwar chaos. Then the emergence of a further danger to international stability from the Soviet Union led to American commitment and Acheson was the leading shaper of that engagement. His belief in the need to act came partly from his perception of the threat but also from his belief that American power brought an obligation to act. His motivation owed more to a desire for stability than anti-communism. And he believed that American leadership should be in pursuit of important goals, not just the exercise of power—above all, freedom.

These ideas found expression during Acheson's service at the State Department. His actions as assistant secretary in 1941–1945 encapsulated his belief in American engagement: he led the economic measures against Japan in 1941, negotiated a Lend-Lease agreement with Britain, organized the creation of UNRRA and FAO and was the department's senior representative at Bretton Woods. He soon emerged as the most articulate and persuasive advocate of American leadership, showing an adept touch in relations with Congress and a keen grasp of how to appeal to the public and to specialist interests. He understood that US engagement must appeal to both the ideals and interests of Americans. During his term as under secretary in 1945–1947, he favored continued engagement but not because of a threat from a specific power but because of his wider concerns about the state of the world. In characteristic fashion, he painted a picture on a large historical canvas in testimony to Congress in June 1945 of a world that faced a level of upheaval not seen since the eighth century, requiring coordinated action to prevent a descent into chaos. This challenge to the "very foundations, the whole fabric of world organization which we have known in our lifetime and which our fathers and forefathers knew," necessitated taking "the most energetic steps" on "all fronts at the same time."[7] He was ready to work with the Soviets in building this new world. His tough attitudes to Moscow in 1945–1946 were the symptoms of a diplomat who was a hard bargainer, rather than evidence of his identification of a fundamental threat to the international system.

At some point in the winter of 1946–1947, Acheson's viewpoint changed. Certainly by his final months as under secretary in 1947 he used much stronger words about the Soviets and encouraged the strident rhetoric of the Truman Doctrine. Speaking to congressional leaders, he again offered a historical perspective, declaring the need for urgent action because the world faced a confrontation not seen since that between Rome and Carthage.[8] When he returned as secretary in 1949 he was committed to the notion of containment, first coined by Kennan the month after Acheson left office, and became its leading architect. Yet, in his first months in office, he sanctioned the successful negotiations to end the Berlin blockade and further efforts at cooperation on Germany. He also evinced a willingness to find an understanding with Mao's China. By 1950 he placed much greater emphasis on military strength and employed more unyielding rhetoric. He increasingly regarded Stalin's Soviet Union in the same way as he had viewed Hitler's Germany, an outlook that became more pronounced after the outbreak of the Korean War.

Yet he conceived containment as more than an exercise in power politics. It would help preserve liberty and democracy: "the purpose of our foreign policy is to maintain and foster an environment in which our national life and individual freedom can survive and prosper."[9] The recovery of Western Europe, the establishment of democratic governments in West Germany and Japan and the formation of NATO were all designed to secure the realization of these key principles.

If Acheson's activities in office were rooted in his broad vision, their effectiveness turned on his individual talents and his working relations with the president, departmental officials, and with Congress. Success also required productive relations with allies. A vision is of little value without the ability to pursue it effectively. His detailed understanding of the issues, capacity for incisive analysis of problems and commanding presence made him a figure of admiration in the department. He recognized and welcomed the opportunity to utilize the considerable expertise of his officials, whom he encouraged not only to inform him but also to debate the issues with him. He called the State Department "the finest department in the entire government."[10] It is worth noting that two of his most valued advisors were Philip Jessup and Dean Rusk, yet they were much greater enthusiasts for collective security and the UN than Acheson, who emphasized military power. He might have increasingly shared Paul Nitze's similarly power political approach, but his continued high regard for Jessup demonstrates that he never wanted mere yes-men as his closest confidants.

Because American foreign policy is presidential foreign policy, Acheson's relationship with Truman was crucial. Despite their very different backgrounds, they developed what was possibly the most intimate and effective president-secretary relationship in American history. Acheson appreciated that the president was the chief, while Truman trusted his secretary to keep him fully informed and respected his judgment above that of all other advisors. This meant most of Acheson's recommendations were accepted. But his influence was far from being automatically adopted. Truman turned from the Acheson-Lilienthal plan and embraced Baruch's approach to nuclear cooperation with Moscow in 1946, was reticent about the prospects of an opening with Mao's communists in June 1949, resisted the extra spending involved in NSC 68 in 1950 (until the Korean War), and in 1952 sought a more aggressive/interventionist approach to Guatemala than Acheson favored.

Acheson appreciated that American leadership in pursuit of key principles would work only if it was based on cooperation with other countries. The collaboration was more than simply a means to an end. He wanted allies to trust American leaders. "Leadership is accorded where trust has been first given. And trust is dependent on conduct."[11] Other countries would accept the United States' lead if it acted within what Acheson called "a pattern of responsibility," which meant Americans had to act with the "consciousness that our responsibility is to interests that are broader than our immediate American interests."[12] He built up genuinely good relations with Britain's Ernest Bevin and France's Robert Schuman. He wanted them and their peoples to embrace the same values: to see that the United States might be pursuing its own values and interests but this brought benefit to the allies as well. As Robert Beisner notes, "the moral legitimacy of the world's greatest power was intricately connected to its ability to minister to other nations' needs and to exercise restraint in pursuit of its own interests."[13] So persuasive were Acheson's policies and rhetoric that the broad framework that he created in the 1940s remained in place until the end of the Cold War in the 1980s, even if from the 1960s onward there were more European challenges to US leadership, evident in de Gaulle's initiatives and West German *ostpolitik*.

NATO might have been the cornerstone of Acheson's foreign policy strategy but he was never just the "North Atlantic man" depicted by Rusk. Europe was clearly his priority but it was not the only region of importance to him. He was also genuinely concerned about certain parts of Asia. He sought aid for Korea, even contemplating the possibility of assistance to the country under the auspices of the Truman Doctrine. Recognizing the importance of Japan in East Asia, he played a vital role in initiating and maintaining the momentum in pursuit of a peace treaty with Tokyo, appointing a Republican as chief negotiator as the best means of averting partisan opposition. He also recommended the commitment of American resources in support of the French in Indochina. Although this unwise policy arose principally from calculations about French support for German rearmament, it did owe something to his fears of the spread of the communist threat to freedom and democracy in the region.

In the years after 1953 Acheson continued to voice his thoughts about American engagement in the world as both author and, in the last decade of his life, as presidential advisor. These contained a central paradox: he offered sophisticated, nuanced analysis of issues, of individuals and processes, but made crude policy recommendations on Berlin and missiles in Cuba. A speech in 1964 displayed his grasp of the complexities of world politics. He recognized that physical force worked well against a military opponent but was ineffective in imposing compliance on minds not wholly governed by reason or fearful of physical suffering.[14] Acheson's efforts toward a diplomatic solution for Cyprus and his eventual advice on the need for withdrawal from Vietnam show this more thoughtful approach.

The Vietnam recommendations demonstrated a number of precepts by which Acheson tried to live throughout his public career. It was vital to think deeply about issues, however intractable they might appear. The policy maker should meet problems "with the best intelligence" available and not shirk difficult and disagreeable situations. It was "a matter of integrity of character" to avoid the "counsels of discretion and cowardice." It was not possible to avoid all difficulties when tackling a problem. He felt it his duty to "make the best decision you can." Once taken, the decision should be pursued with "courage and determination."[15] Such an approach lay at the heart of Acheson's expectations for his nation, as he encouraged it to accept the obligations of power.

NOTES

1. "Dean Acheson is Dead at 78; Former Secretary of State" and Murrey Marder, "Dean Acheson; Architect of Postwar Activism," *Washington Post* (13 October 1971), A1, A9.
2. McMahon, *Acheson*, 215; McNay, *Acheson and Empire*.
3. Acheson, *Democrat Looks at His Party*, 13.
4. Acheson, "An American Attitude Toward Foreign Affairs," in *Morning and Noon*, 269.
5. Acheson, *Democrat Looks at His Party*, 15.
6. HSTL, Acheson Papers, box 73, speech to War College, 16 September 1948.
7. 79th Congress, 1st Session, Senate Committee on Banking and Currency, *Bretton Woods Agreements Act* (Washington, DC: USGPO, 1945), 19, 21, 49, Acheson testimony, 13 June 1945.
8. Jones, *Fifteen Weeks*, 141.
9. Acheson, "Post-War Foreign Policy," in *Vast External Realm*, 19.
10. Acheson, "Public Service," in *Vast External Realm*, 95.
11. Acheson, *Democrat Looks at His Party*, 96.

12. Acheson, "An Estimate of the Present World Situation," *DOSB* 25:630 (23 July 1951), 123–128, quotation at 128. This phrase was seen as so emblematic of Acheson's approach that it became the title of a compilation of his speeches and other remarks—Bundy, ed., *The Pattern of Responsibility*. See HSTL, Acheson Papers, box 28, B folder, Paul Brooks (editor-in-chief, Houghton Mifflin) to Acheson, 3 July 1951, suggesting the phrase as the book's title.

13. Beisner, *Acheson*, 650.

14. Acheson, "Ambivalences of American Foreign Policy," in *Vast External Realm*, 138–156.

15. HSTL, Acheson Papers, box 73, War College speech, 16 September 1948; *Present at Creation*, 361.

Bibliographical Essay

The starting points for serious study of the life and career of Dean Acheson are two major archival collections. The Dean G. Acheson papers, housed in the Sterling Library, Yale University, comprise eighty-one boxes of material spanning his earliest days to the final months of his life. The abundant correspondence files are especially valuable. Like most members of his generation, Acheson was a regular writer of letters. The Yale collection also includes the texts of speeches and various materials concerning Acheson's books. The 164 boxes of the Dean G. Acheson papers at the Harry S. Truman Library in Independence, Missouri, offer a vital means of charting his activities as under secretary of state and secretary of state, but also contain much useful material on his work as a presidential advisor between 1961 and 1971, as well as the drafts of his books and the texts of his speeches and articles.

The National Archives at College Park, Maryland, hold the files of numerous government agencies involved in Acheson's public career. Most important are the records of the State Department (RG 59). Within these records, the most substantial are the Central Decimal Files, which are subdivided chronologically into 1940–1944, 1945–1949, and 1950–1954. They contain messages in and out of Washington, internal reports, and memoranda. In addition, there are the State Department Lot Files: special files on particular topics or collections of materials of particular individuals. Especially useful for Acheson's time as assistant secretary and as under secretary are the fourteen boxes of Lot 1, while the Executive Secretariat files are a profitable source for Acheson's secretaryship. There are also important documents in the various collections within the records of the Department of the Treasury (RG 56); and in the records of the Foreign Economic Administration (RG 169) and the Office of Alien Property, Foreign Funds Control Committee (RG 131). The *Declassified Documents Reference System*

(DDRS), first published as microfiches and now available through online subscription, provides copies of previously withheld documents but newly released (and sometimes redacted) under the Freedom of Information Act (FOIA).

The various presidential libraries are a wonderful resource for a huge range of topics. The Franklin D. Roosevelt Library in Hyde Park, New York, contains key policymaking materials—especially the President's Secretary's File, which became available online as I completed my research, and the Official File. The President's Secretary's File, the Official File and the Post-Presidential File in the Harry S. Truman Library are similarly rich in documentation. Both libraries also possess numerous private paper collections, which provide a means of deepening our understanding of Acheson as an individual during his public career. Among them, the Adolf Berle and Oscar Cox papers in the Roosevelt Library are most useful in understanding Acheson and economic issues during the Second World War. But even more valuable are the over 700 volumes of the Diary of Treasury secretary Henry Morgenthau. They are not so much a conventional diary as a vast compilation of documents and are a superb means of following important matters because they include letters, memoranda, records of telephone conversations, and minutes of meetings. In the Truman Library the papers of Acheson's executive assistant, Lucius D. Battle, and under secretary James Webb provide details of issues and insights into Acheson's working relationships. The papers of assistant secretary William L. Clayton and those of White House aides Clark Clifford and George Elsey contain much of value.

The Library of Congress is an exceptionally important source of documentation, possessing several dozen collections that are useful. Acheson's correspondence in the papers of Supreme Court justice Felix Frankfurter, Ambassador-at-large Phillip Jessup, and Librarian of Congress Archibald MacLeish are insightful on Acheson's views and personality. The papers of Paul Nitze and Averell Harriman are rich in a range of topics. Both men shared Acheson's foreign policy vision. Yet, if Nitze displayed evidence of his admiration and a growing harmony of outlook on the need for robust policies, Harriman's papers contain several instances of doubt about Acheson's positions on some issues. The papers of Charles Bohlen, Joseph Davies, Herbert Feis, Cordell Hull, and Breckinridge Long all offer important perspectives on the State Department in the 1940s. The Seeley G. Mudd Library, Princeton University, is another valuable archive. Its holdings include the George F. Kennan and David Lilienthal collections, which contain materials relating to their work together but are also revealing about Acheson's personality and views; and the Harry Dexter White papers, covering financial issues during the war. Secretary of State James F. Byrnes's papers and those of his assistant, Walter Brown, at Clemson University, Clemson, South Carolina, are useful but not very extensive. The same is true of the

George C. Marshall papers at the Marshall Foundation, Lexington, Virginia. Chairman of the Senate Foreign Relations Committee Arthur Vandenberg's papers at the Bentley Library, University of Michigan, Ann Arbor, contain some useful correspondence with Acheson. The New York Historical Society possesses the Robert Lovett papers. The University of Virginia holds the Edward Stettinius and Louis Johnson papers.

British government files and private papers are also most helpful in tracking and understanding Acheson's career, given that so many issues touched relations between the two countries and because of the close relationships he established with a number of British figures. The most useful government collection is the Foreign Office's general correspondence (FO 371), which is rich in materials on issues from Lend-Lease and sanctions against Japan to wartime conferences and loan and atomic energy negotiations, from policy on Germany and NATO talks to the Korean War and the Japanese peace treaty. The records of the British embassy in Washington (FO 115), though sparser in documentation, are also very useful in understanding Acheson's diplomacy. These two collections, when combined with Acheson's official memoranda of conversations (now available online through the Truman Library) are a great means of seeing close up the confidential relationship between Acheson and British ambassador Oliver Franks. The memoranda of conversations, of course, are an even more valuable aid to understanding the regular, frank, and close relationship between Acheson and Truman. Among collections of British private papers, the most useful are the Avon (Anthony Eden) papers at Birmingham University Library, the Paul Gore-Booth papers at the Bodleian Library, Oxford, the Lord Strang papers at Churchill College, Cambridge, and the John Maynard Keynes papers and the Fredric Harmer Diary at King's College, Cambridge.

Various official documents are available on microfilm. The most valuable are the 84 reels of the *Harry S. Truman Office Files* (Frederick, Maryland: Microfilm Project of University Publications of America, 1989), which comprise extensive selections from the President's Secretary's File. Others include: *CIA Research Reports Europe 1946–1976* (Frederick, Maryland: University Publications of America, 1983); *Documents of the National Security Council 1947–77* (Washington, DC: Microfilm Project of University Publications of America, 1980); *Records of the Joint Chiefs of Staff, Part 2: 1946–1953. Europe and Nato* (Frederick, Maryland: Microfilm Project of University Publications of America, 1980). Microfilms are increasingly being superseded by digitized records available online or by subscription. The *American Presidency Project* website offers free access to all presidential speeches, statements, and press conferences. The Franklin D. Roosevelt Library now has the President's Secretary's Files and the Morgenthau Diary online, while the Harry S. Truman, John F. Kennedy, and Lyndon B. Johnson libraries also have many documents online.

Numerous printed official documentary collections contain further important materials, such as the records of conferences from UNRRA and Bretton Woods to the San Francisco Conference of September 1951. Above all, there is the *Foreign Relations of the United States* series, which provides a massively detailed record of American diplomacy during Acheson's public career. The series includes more than 100 volumes for his years at the State Department and utilizes not only diplomatic documents but also materials from the Department of Defense, the National Security Council, and various collections of private papers. The British and Canadian equivalent series are also valuable but much less substantial: *Documents on British Policy Overseas*, 1st Series (1945–1950), volumes I–X (London: HMSO, 1984–2014) and the 2nd Series (1950–1955), volumes I–IV (London: HMSO, 1986–1991); and *Documents on Canadian External Relations*, volumes 7–16 [1939 to 1952] (Ottawa: Department of Foreign Affairs and International Trade, 1974–1996).

Congressional hearings provide a vital source for Acheson's views and for capturing his tone and approach in presenting his arguments in public. Together with the debates reported in the *Congressional Record*, they provide important indicators of the political mood in which Acheson had to operate. Acheson made appearances for nomination as under secretary and as secretary and gave testimony to numerous committees on issues from atomic energy to the Truman Doctrine, from NATO to the Korean War (see footnotes for details). The most prominent occasion was his eight days of evidence to the Senate Armed Services Committee and the Foreign Relations Committee in June 1951 after the dismissal of General Douglas MacArthur: *To Conduct An Inquiry into the Military Situation in the Far East and the Facts Surrounding the Relief of General of the Army Douglas MacArthur from His Assignment in that Area* (Washington, DC: USGPO, 1951).

Paramount among the many oral testimonies are *The Princeton Seminars*, a series of confidential discussions between Acheson and prominent officials in 1953 and 1954. Transcripts of the discussions, running to more than 1,700 pages, are available in the Acheson papers at the Truman Library, which has put them on microfilm. Equally valuable is Acheson's detailed testimony, delivered over three days in 1955 and available in Truman's Post-Presidential Papers. In addition, the Truman Library has a very large number of oral histories available online. The John F. Kennedy Library has put online its considerable oral history testimonies, including one by Acheson. Many valuable documents from the President's Secretary's File are also available online through the Kennedy Library. The Lyndon B. Johnson Presidential Library has many oral histories available on its website, including two by George Ball.

The *Department of State Bulletin*, which is available online at many university libraries, is a vital resource for Acheson's (and other senior officials') speeches, for his extemporaneous remarks at press conferences, and for the texts of international agreements. Many of Acheson's speeches and statements were gathered and arranged into a themed volume in his last year as secretary: McGeorge Bundy, ed., *The Pattern of Responsibility* (Boston: Houghton Mifflin, 1952). Two published collections of Acheson's letters provide rich materials for understanding him, his attitudes, and his personal outlook on a range of issues: David S. McLellan and David Acheson, eds., *Among Friends: Personal Letters of Dean Acheson* (New York: Dodd, Mead, 1980); and *Affection and Trust: the Personal Correspondence of Harry S. Truman and Dean Acheson, 1953–1971* (New York: Alfred A. Knopf, 2010).

On leaving office Acheson proved to be a prolific writer of books. In the Eisenhower years there were *A Democrat Looks at His Party* (New York: Harper & Brothers, 1955), *A Citizen Looks at Congress* (New York: Harper & Brothers, 1957), and *Power and Diplomacy* (Cambridge, Massachusetts: Harvard University Press, 1958). In the 1960s he wrote three autobiographical studies: *Sketches from Life of Men I Have Known* (London: Hamish Hamilton, 1961), *Morning and Noon* (Boston: Houghton Mifflin, 1965), and the monumental, Pulitzer Prize–winning *Present at the Creation: My Years in the State Department* (New York: W. W. Norton, 1969). Three volumes of his articles and speeches and occasional pieces were published in the 1970s. *Fragments of My Fleece* (New York: W. W. Norton, 1971) appeared just before he died, while both *Grapes From Thorns* (New York: W. W. Norton, 1972), drafted before his death, and *This Vast External Realm* (New York: W. W. Norton, 1973) were published posthumously. See also the memoir of his son David, *Acheson Country* (New York: W. W. Norton, 1993), which contains much interesting material on Acheson as an individual and as a family man.

A number of published diaries contain useful details of Acheson's personal relations with key individuals and important features of policymaking issues, as well as offering a flavor of how Acheson behaved as assistant secretary, under secretary, and secretary. *Navigating the Rapids 1918–1971: From the Papers of Adolf A. Berle*, edited by Beatrice Bishop Berle and Travis Jacobs (New York: Harcourt Brace Jovanovich, 1973) captures some of the facets of Acheson's wartime work and the often uneasy relations with his fellow assistant secretary. The three volumes of John Morton Blum's *From the Morgenthau Diaries* (Boston: Houghton Mifflin, 1959–1972) are a superb distillation of a rich archive and provide a detailed account of economic affairs. The second volume (1938–1941) and third volume (1941–1945) contain valuable coverage of Acheson's involvement in economic sanctions, Lend-Lease, and the Bretton Woods conference. *The Diaries of Edward R. Stettinius Jr, 1943–1946,* edited by Thomas M. Campbell and George C. Herring (New York: Vantage, 1975) contain some useful entries on Acheson's relations with Stettinius between 1943 and 1945. The entries of Acheson's close friend in *The Journals of David E. Lilienthal* (New York: Harper & Row, 1964) are of great value in understanding Acheson's thinking and temper in the years after 1945. *The Forrestal Diaries*, edited by Walter Millis (New York: Viking Press, 1951) provide a valuable record of the tough attitudes that Acheson initially resisted and the maneuvers the hardliners were using to advance their views.

Among the many useful memoirs, the most important are those of Harry S. Truman: *Year of Decisions, 1945* and *Years of Trial and Hope, 1946–1952* (New York: Signet edition, 1965). Acheson's detailed commentaries on Truman's drafts form part of their correspondence, published in *Affection and Trust*. In addition, there are Truman's more unguarded comments in Robert H. Ferrell, ed., *Off the Record: The Private Papers of Harry S. Truman* (New York: Penguin, 1980). The memoirs of various individuals also add to our understanding of the personal dynamics of policymaking and Acheson's relations with the various officials. Acheson has only a minor role in James F. Byrnes's *Speaking Frankly*, written a few months after leaving office in 1947, and in his later memoir of his whole career, *All in One Lifetime* (New York: Harper, 1958), which reproduces some of the rancor of his break with Truman and Acheson. The following also contain informed and perceptive accounts with useful materials on Acheson's ideas and activities: Charles E. Bohlen, *Witness to History* (New York: W.W. Norton, 1973); Clark Clifford (with Richard Holbrooke), *Counsel to the President: A Memoir* (New York: Random House, 1991); George M. Elsey, *An Unplanned Life* (Columbia: University of Missouri Press, 2005); W. Averell Harriman and Elie Abel, *Special Envoy to Churchill and Stalin 1941–1946* (London: Hutchinson, 1976); George F. Kennan, *Memoirs, 1925–1950* (Boston: Little, Brown, 1967) and *Memoirs, 1950–1963* (Boston: Little, Brown, 1972); and Arthur H. Vandenberg, ed., *The Private Papers of Senator Vandenberg* (Boston: Houghton Mifflin, 1952).

Acheson has been the subject of a number of detailed studies: Gaddis Smith, *Dean Acheson* (New York: Cooper Square Publishers, 1972); David S. McLellan, *Dean Acheson: The State Department Years* ((New York: Dodd, Mead, 1976); Walter Isaacson and Evan Thomas, *The Wise Men: Six Friends and the World They Made* (London: Faber & Faber, 1986); John Lamberton Harper, *American Visions of Europe: Franklin D. Roosevelt, George F. Kennan and Dean G. Acheson* (New York: Cambridge University Press, 1994); James Chace, *Acheson: the Secretary of State who Created the American World* (New York: Simon & Schuster, 1998); Robert J. McMahon, *Dean Acheson and the Creation of the American World Order* (Dulles, Virginia: Potomac Books, 2009); and Robert Beisner, *Dean Acheson: A Life in the Cold War* (New York: Oxford University Press, 2006). Each one of them maintains a high standard in scholarship and percipience. Beisner's masterly study is the most detailed and is based on huge research, but it concentrates on 1945–1953, and, indeed, on 1949–1953 in particular. McMahon's book is a judicious compact assessment.

Acheson's years at the State Department and as presidential advisor are among the most intensively studied periods in American history. Doing justice to this vast literature would require what would be an unwieldy survey. What follows is a highly selective choice of works that have proved most valuable in elucidating issues and aiding an understanding of Acheson.

The best works on the Roosevelt administration are Robert Dallek, *Franklin D. Roosevelt and American Foreign Policy, 1932–1945* (New York: Oxford University Press, 1979, 1995) and David M. Kennedy, *Freedom from Fear: The American People in Depression and War, 1929–1945* (New York: Oxford University Press, 1999). For Acheson's prominent role in sanctions against Japan, see Jonathan Utley, "Upstairs, Downstairs at Foggy Bottom: Oil Exports and Japan, 1940–41," *Prologue*, 8:1 (Spring 1976) and his monograph, *Going to War with Japan, 1937–1941* (Knoxville: University of Tennessee Press, 1985). See also Edward S. Miller, *Bankrupting the Enemy: the US Financial Siege of Japan before Pearl Harbor* (Annapolis, MD: Naval Institute Press, 2007), who maintains Acheson was acting opportunistically. Contrast these verdicts with the earlier studies: William L. Langer and S. Everett Gleason, *The Undeclared War, 1940–1941* (New York: Harper & Brothers, 1953) and Waldo Heinrichs, *Threshold of War: Franklin Roosevelt and American Entry into World War II* (New York: Oxford University Press, 1988). For Acheson's involvement in Lend-Lease and Bretton Woods, see Donald Moggridge, ed., *Collected Writings of John Maynard Keynes volumes XIV–XXVI* (London and New York: Macmillan and Cambridge University Press, 1979–1980), Armand Van Dormael, *Bretton Woods: Birth of a Monetary System* (London: Macmillan, 1978), and Benn Steil, *The Battle of Bretton Woods* (Princeton, NJ: Princeton University Press, 2013).

Acheson's most significant work took place during the Truman presidency. The best study of Truman is Alonzo L. Hamby's *Man of the People: A Life of Harry Truman* (New York: Oxford University Press, 1995), but see also Robert H. Ferrell, *Harry S. Truman: A Life* (Columbia: University of Missouri Press, 1994) and David McCullough, *Truman* (New York: Simon & Schuster, 1992). Robert J. Donovan's detailed studies of Truman's two terms retain their value: *Conflict and Crisis: The Presidency of Harry S. Truman, 1945–1948* (New York: W. W. Norton, 1977) and *Tumultuous Years: The Presidency of Harry S. Truman, 1949–1953* (New York: W. W. Norton, 1982). James T. Patterson, *Grand Expectations: The United States, 1945–1974* (New York: Oxford University Press, 1996) is an astute analysis of the wider domestic context in which Acheson was operating after 1945.

Acheson features prominently in two major studies of the Truman administration's foreign policy: Melvyn P. Leffler, *A Preponderance of Power:*

National Security, the Truman Administration and the Cold War (Stanford, CA: Stanford University Press, 1992) and Arnold A. Offner, *One Such Victory: President Truman and the Cold War, 1945–1953* (Stanford, CA: Stanford University Press, 2002). Both are perceptive and deliver critiques of US policies but Offner is much harsher in his verdicts on both Truman and Acheson. Randall Woods and Howard Jones offer a shrewd assessment in *Dawning of the Cold War: the United States' Quest for Order* (Athens: University of Georgia Press, 1991). See also the studies in Douglas Brinkley, ed., *Dean Acheson and the Making of US Foreign Policy* (Basingstoke: Macmillan, 1993).

The best works on Byrnes are David Robertson, *Sly and Able: A Political Biography of James F. Byrnes* (New York: W. W. Norton, 1994) and Robert L. Messer, *The End of an Alliance: James F. Byrnes, Roosevelt, and the Origins of the Cold War* (Chapel Hill: University of North Carolina Press, 1982). On Marshall, see Forrest C. Pogue, *George C. Marshall: Statesman, 1945–1959* (New York: Viking Penguin, 1991). For Kennan, see John Lewis Gaddis, *George F. Kennan* (New York: Penguin Press, 2011). On the Truman Doctrine and the path to the Marshall Plan, see Joseph M. Jones, *The Fifteen Weeks February 21–June 5, 1947* (New York: Viking Press, 1955). On Germany see Detlef Junker, ed., *The United States and Germany in the Era of the Cold War I: 1945–1968* (Cambridge: Cambridge University Press and German Historical Institute, Washington, DC, 2004). On NATO see Lawrence S. Kaplan, *The United States and NATO: the Formative Years* (Lexington: University Press of Kentucky, 1984). See also, Nicholas Henderson, *The Birth of NATO* (London: Weidenfeld & Nicolson, 1982), a contemporary account published many years later by a British diplomat; and the fully documented study by a Canadian diplomat—Escott Reid, *Time of Fear and Hope: The Making of the North Atlantic Treaty 1947–1949* (Toronto: McClelland and Stewart, 1977). See also, the essays in Olav Riste, ed., *Western Security: The Formative Years* (Oslo: Norwegian University Press, 1985).

Most studies of Acheson concentrate on his European policies. One of the few books on his Asian policies is Ronald McGlothlen, *Controlling the Waves: Dean Acheson and US Foreign Policy in Asia* (New York: W. W. Norton, 1993). For his involvement with China, see State Department, *United States Relations with China with special reference to the period 1944–1949* (Washington, DC: USGPO, 1949), usually known as the *China White Paper*. The Republican Party/China lobby assault on the State Department's China experts is ably covered in E. J. Kahn, *The China Hands: America's Foreign Service Officers and What Befell Them* (New York: Penguin, 1976). On the initial commitments to Indochina, see Mark Atwood Lawrence, *Assuming the Burden: Europe and the American Commitment to War in Vietnam* (Berkeley: University of California Press, 2005) and George

C. Herring, *America's Longest War: The United States and Vietnam, 1945–1975* (New York: McGraw-Hill, 1996). Several books by William Stueck offer insights into Acheson and US policy on Korea: *The Road to Confrontation: American Policy toward China and Korea, 1947–1950* (Chapel Hill: University of North Carolina Press, 1981); *The Korean War: An International History* (Princeton, NJ: Princeton University Press, 1995); and *Rethinking the Korean War* (Princeton, NJ: Princeton University Press, 2002). Chairman of the JCS Omar Bradley's memoir is valuable on both military strategy and civil-military relations during the war: *A General's Life* (London: Sidgwick & Jackson, 1983).

For a fair-minded assessment of MacArthur, see Michael Schaller, *Douglas MacArthur: Far Eastern General* (New York: Oxford University Press, 1989). It might be compared with MacArthur's memoir, which reveals his self-absorbed certainties: *Reminiscences* (New York: McGraw-Hill, 1964). Richard H. Rovere and Arthur M. Schlesinger wrote a lively contemporary critique in *The General and the President and the Future of American Foreign Policy* (New York: Farrar, Straus and Young, 1951).

John M. Allison's memoir, *Ambassador from the Prairie or Allison in Wonderland* (Boston: Houghton Mifflin, 1973), presents a vivid picture of the making of the Japanese peace treaty. Frederick S. Dunn, *Peace-making and the Settlement with Japan* (Princeton, NJ: Princeton University Press, 1963) remains a valuable assessment. See also Michael Schaller, *The American Occupation of Japan: the Origins of the Cold War in Asia* (New York: Oxford University Press, 1985). Both Allison and Schaller outline John Foster Dulles's role in negotiating the treaty and reveals facets of the Acheson-Dulles relationship. Dulles is treated sympathetically in Richard Immerman, *John Foster Dulles: Piety, Pragmatism, and Power in U.S. Foreign Policy* (Wilmington, DE: Scholarly Resources, 1999); and more critically in Townsend Hoopes, *The Devil and John Foster Dulles* (Boston: Little, Brown, 1973).

On the Middle East, see Peter L. Hahn's *The United States, Great Britain and Egypt, 1945–1956* (Chapel Hill: University of North Carolina Press, 1991) and *Crisis and Crossfire: The United States and the Middle East since 1945* (Washington, DC: Potomac Books, 2005); and George C. McGhee's memoir, *Envoy to the Middle World* (New York: Harper & Row, 1983). On the role of oil in American diplomacy, see David S. Painter, *Oil and the American Century: The Political Economy of US Foreign Oil Policy, 1941–1954* (Baltimore: Johns Hopkins University Press, 1986), and Daniel Yergin, *The Prize: the Epic Quest for Oil, Money and Power* (London: Simon & Schuster, 1991). James A. Bill and W. R. Louis, eds., *Iranian Nationalism and Oil* (London: I. B. Taurus, 1988) and Mary Ann Heiss, *Empire and Nationhood: the United States, Great Britain and Iranian Oil, 1950–1954* (New York: Columbia University Press, 1997) are adept studies of the Iranian oil crisis of 1951–1953. On Latin America, see Alan M. McPherson, *Intimate Ties, Bitter Struggles: The United States and Latin America since 1945* (Washington, DC: Potomac Books, 2006) and Richard Immerman, *The CIA in Guatemala: The Foreign Policy of Intervention* (Austin: University of Texas Press, 1982).

The fullest account of the final phase of Acheson's life is the marvelous pioneering work: Douglas Brinkley, *Dean Acheson: the Cold War Years, 1953–1971* (New Haven, CT: Yale University Press, 1992). On Kennedy, see Robert Dallek, *John F. Kennedy: An Unfinished Life 1917–1963* (London: Allen Lane, 2003) and Michael Beschloss, *The Crisis Years: Kennedy and Khrushchev, 1960–1963* (New York: Edward Burlingame Books, 1991). On the Cuban missile crisis, see Sheldon M. Stern, *Averting "The Final Failure": John F. Kennedy and the Secret Cuban Missile Crisis Meetings* (Stanford, CA: Stanford University Press, 2004). Acheson's perspective is available in "Homage to Plain Dumb Luck," in Richard A. Divine, ed., *The Cuban Missile Crisis* (Chicago: Quadrangle, 1971). The best books on Lyndon Johnson are Robert Dallek's two-volume study, *Lone Star Rising* and *Flawed Giant: Lyndon Johnson and His Times, 1961–1973* (New York: Oxford University Press, 1991–1998); and Randall B. Woods, *LBJ: Architect of American Ambition* (New York: Free Press, 2007). On Vietnam see George W. Ball, *The Past Has Another Pattern* (New York: W. W. Norton, 1982) and Clark Clifford's *Counsel to the President*. For the Nixon administration, see Richard M. Nixon, *RN: The Memoirs of Richard Nixon* (London: Sidgwick & Jackson, 1978) and Henry Kissinger, *White House Years* (Boston: Little, Brown, 1979). Good studies of Nixon and Kissinger are Stephen Ambrose, *Nixon: The Triumph of a Politician, 1962–1972* (New York: Simon and Schuster, 1989); and Jussi Hanhimäki, *The Flawed Architect: Henry Kissinger and American Foreign Policy* (Oxford: Oxford University Press, 2004).

Acheson's public career coincided with a golden age in American journalism, a period when national policies received detailed coverage, when issues were extensively debated, when the print media provided the principal source of knowledge and main forum for discussion. Newspapers, especially the *New York Times* but also the *Washington Post*, and magazines such as *Time*, *Newsweek*, and *US News and World Report*, are invaluable sources of information, contemporary analysis, and indicators of trends in political opinion for Acheson's life from the 1930s to the 1970s.

Index

Abadan, 181
Acheson, David (son), 2, 240
Acheson, Dean. *See specific topics*
Acheson, Edward (brother), 1
Acheson, Edward Campion (father), 1–2
Acheson, Jane (daughter), 2
Acheson, Margaret (sister), 1
Acheson, Mary (daughter), 2, 57
Acheson-Lilienthal Plan, 65–66, 261
Achilles, Theodore, 60
Adenauer, Konrad, 110, 197
AEC. *See* American Atomic Energy
    Commission
Agricultural Adjustment Board, 6
AIOC. *See* Anglo-Iranian Oil Company
Allison, John M., 185
Alsop, Joseph, 232
Altschul, Frank, 221
Ambrose, Stephen, 243
America Betrayed (Kamp), 136
American Atomic Energy Commission
    (AEC), 68, 118
American Forum of the Air, 38
"The American Forum of the Air", 13
Anderson, John, 64
Anglo-American Financial Agreement, 69,
    70
Anglo-American nuclear cooperation:
    hydrogen bomb with, 119; *modus
    vivendi* of, 119; revival attempts of, 120

Anglo-Americans: Iran relation with,
    183–184; Palestine question for, 145;
    relationship views of, 231
Anglo-Iranian Oil Company (AIOC), 179;
    Franks on, 180; Iran crisis with, 174,
    178–179; McGhee on, 179–180;
    nationalization of, 178; Stokes mission
    of, 182; Tehran negotiations of,
    180–182
Annan, Noel, 236
ANZUS. *See* Australia–New Zealand
    Treaty
Arab war, 146
ARAMCO, 178–179
Armstrong, Hamilton Fish, 38
Asia: "revulsion against foreign
    domination" of, 123; Secretary of State
    on, 111–115; UN aggression in, 123;
    US and, 70, 123
Assistant Secretary of State, 17–18; at
    Bretton Woods, 40–42; Dumbarton
    Oaks for, 42–44; positions of, 47–48;
    sanctions against Japan while, 23–30;
    under Secretary Hull, 20–23; State
    Department changes with, 39;
    Stettinius, congressional relations and,
    44–45; Truman and, 45–47; on
    UNRRA, 36–38. *See also* Lend-Lease
    agreement
Atlantic alliance, 247

275

Atlantic Charter, 34. See also Lend-Lease
    agreement
Atlantic Council, 142–145
atomic bomb, 63–64, 135
atomic energy: British anxieties of, 64,
    119; CFM information exchange of,
    64–65; Congress protection of, 66–67;
    international control for, 65; issue of,
    63; Stimson on, 63; Under Secretary of
    State on, 63–65
Attlee, Clement, 61, 64, 156; on Byrnes,
    67; Truman talks with, 160–161
August crises, 75–77
Australia–New Zealand Treaty (ANZUS),
    184–191
Axis powers, 25

Ball, George, 230, 237–238, 247
Bao Dai regime, 140
Barkley, Alben, 23
Barratt, Edward W., 139
Baruch, Bernard, 66
Battle, Lucius, 147, 217, 234
Bay of Pigs, 230
Beard, Charles, x
Beijing, 124–125
Beisner, Robert, xii
Bendiner, Robert, x
Berle, Adolf, Jr., 21, 98, 240
Berlin, 228–229
Berlin blockade, 107–110
Bevin, Ernest, 109, 121, 147, 174, 261
Bevin-Sidki agreement, 176
Bidault, Georges, 84
biographies, xii–xiii
bipartisanship, 147–148
Blair House, 150
Bloom, Sol, 45, 48
Bohlen, Charles, 61, 74, 77, 104–105, 156
Bolivia, 200–201
Bolles, Blair, 39
Bonnet, Henri, 105, 140
Bradley, Omar N., 149, 152, 158
Brand, Robert, 32
Brandeis, Louis, 2–3
Bretton Woods, 40–42, 259
Brinkley, Douglas, xii, 222, 246
Britain: atomic energy anxieties of, 64,
    119; bipartisan support assistance for,

9; Egypt and, 174; financial crisis of,
    120; global standing of, 231–232;
    Indochina meetings in, 142–145; loan
    to, 68–70; opinion of, 232; postwar
    deficits of, 68; Rhodesia rule by,
    241–242; for Schuman Plan, 143–144;
    US armament agreement with, 12;
    World War II aid for, 22
British imperial preference, 31
Broder, David, 244
Brown versus Board of Education, 224
Bruce, David, 202, 233
Brune, Lester H., 30
Brussels Treaty of Self-Defense, 102
Bundy, McGeorge, x
Bundy, William (son-in-law), 244
Burling, Edward, 47
Burns, James, 138
Butler, Robert, 86
Butterworth, Walton, 184
Byrnes, James F., 46, 57, 89n45–90n46;
    Acheson, Dean, with, 61–63; Attlee on,
    67; August crises response of, 76–77;
    Byrnes Package Deal of, 61; early life
    of, 59–60; Halifax on, 60; lines of
    command with, 78; Long opinion of,
    60; opinion of, 61; resignation of,
    77–79; as Secretary of State, 59–63;
    time abroad for, 60; Truman problems
    with, 62; Truman time with, 60
Byrnes Package Deal, 61
Byroade, Henry, 177

Cambodia, 229, 245
Canadian Department of External Affairs,
    104
capitalist economic agenda, x
Casey, R. G., 27
Castro, Fidel, 229. See also Cuba
CCP. See Chinese communist party
CEEC. See Committee of European
    Economic Co-operation
Center for International Understanding, 44
Central Intelligence Agency (CIA), 201
Century Group, 9
CFM. See Council of Foreign Ministers
Chace, James, xii
Chiang Kaishek's Kuomintang (KMT),
    117; of China, 101; China port

blockade by, 122; US military aid for, 116; US public opinion of, 125

China: civil war of, 115; Douglas overwhelmed by, 158–159; Japanese removal from, 70; Japan regime recognition for, 187; Korean War intervention of, 157–158; lobby of, 72; Mao regime of, 121–122; Marshall mission to, 70–72; misjudgment of, 165; NSC argument on, 116; NSC contact for, 159; Secretary of State and, 115–117, 156–161, 196; understanding of, 260; US Congressional support for, 71; US military aid for, 71, 117–125

China White Paper (Acheson, Dean), 72, 117

Chinese communist party (CCP), 101, 162

Churchill, Winston: Atlantic Charter of, 34; "iron curtain" phrase of, 74; US armament request of, 10

CIA. *See* Central Intelligence Agency

A Citizen Looks at Congress (Acheson, Dean), x, 221

Citizens' Committee for the Marshall Plan, 85

civil rights, 224–225

Clark, Mark, 195

Clay, Lucius D., 75, 107

Clayton, Will, 58, 68

Clifford, Clark, 77, 137, 145

Clubb, Edmund, 191

Cohen, Benjamin V., 11, 58

Cohen-Acheson opinion, 4–12

Cold War, xi; anti-communism during, 192–193; architect of policy for, 257; attitudes of, 76–77; US foreign policy in, xiii; Western Europe in, 223

Combined Policy Committee (CPC), 67

"Comments on Soviet Compliance with International Agreements Undertaken since January 1941", 77

Committee of European Economic Co-operation (CEEC), 84, 85

Committee of the National Security Council, 230

Committee on Administrative Procedure, 7

Committee on the Marshall Plan to Aid the European Economies, 86

Committee to Defend America by Aiding the Allies, 9

Commonwealth Club, 43

communism, 140; anti-communism in US and, 192–193; tougher attitude toward, 117; view of, 98

Congress: atomic secrets protected by, 66–67; China support from, 71; Korea report to, 151–152; with North Atlantic Treaty, 106; Stettinius relations with, 44–45; support value of, 37; views on, 221

Congressional Government (Wilson, W.), 221

Connally, Tom, 97

Continued Consultation and Co-ordination of Policy, 144

Cooper, John Sherman, 147

Council of Foreign Ministers (CFM): atomic energy information exchange of, 64–65; within Byrnes Package Deal, 61; on Germany, 75; Soviet Union and, 80

Covington, Burling and Rublee, 3, 213

Cox, Oscar, 22

CPC. *See* Combined Policy Committee

The Crisis of Confidence (Schlesinger), 239

Cuba, 229. *See also* Castro, Fidel

Cuban Missile Crisis, 230–231

Cummings, Bruce, 124

Cummings, Homer, 4, 14n15, 52n75

Cypriots, 233–234

Czechoslovak, 91n98–91n99

Davies, John Paton, 112

Defense Production Act, 184

de Gaulle, Charles, 235

Democratic Advisory Council, 221

Democratic People's Republic of Korea, 114. *See also* Korea

A Democrat Looks at His Party (Acheson, Dean), x, 215

Department of Defense, 137–138, 169n112

domestic policy, 147

Donovan, Robert J., xii

Douglas, Lewis, 7, 107, 121, 144

Drake, A.E.C., 181

Draper, William, 113

Dulles, John Foster, 147; criticisms of, 216; at Far Eastern Commission, 186; in Japan, 196; Japanese Peace Treaty role of, 185–186; opinion of, 218; as Secretary of State, 211, 212, 216, 217–223; Vincent verdict of, 218
Dulles-Morrison compromise, 189
Dumbarton Oaks: for Assistant Secretary of State, 42–44; UN at, 43; UN proposed at, 43
Dunn, James, 58
Dutch, 139

East Germany, 227–228
ECEFP. *See* Executive Committee on Foreign Economic Policy
Economic Club of Detroit, "Mutual Advantages of the British Loan" of, 69
Economic Cooperation Act, 86
economic diplomacy, 24, 36–37
economic sanctions, 23–30
economy, 43
EDC. *See* European Defense Community
Eden, Anthony, 182–183
education, 2, 14n3
Egypt, 174
Eisenhower, Dwight D., 78, 162; for civil rights, 224; criticism of, 216, 221; on Korea War, 196; as NATO supreme commander, 161; Stevenson defeated by, 220–221; strategic ideas of, 219; Truman on, 219
ERP. *See* European Recovery Plan
Estenssoro, Victor Paz, 201
Etheridge, Mark, 80, 146
European Cooperation Administration, 86
European Defense Community (EDC): Germany part of, 197; NATO with, 161, 198; rejection of, 199
European funds, 24
European Recovery Plan (ERP), 85–86
ExComm, 230–231
Executive Committee on Foreign Economic Policy (ECEFP), 45
Export Control Administration, 24
Export-Import Bank, 200

family stoic code, 1

FAO. *See* Food and Agriculture Organization
Far Eastern Affairs, 184
Far Eastern Commission, 186
Feis, Herbert, 21
Fleming, D. F., xi
Foley, Edward, 22, 25
Food and Agriculture Organization (FAO), 38
Foreign Affairs, 38
Foreign Exchanges and Foreign Owned Property Committee, 25
Foreign Funds Control Committee, 25, 27
Forrestal, James, 76, 79
France: attitudes on, 121; campaign against Viet Minh, 140. *See also* Paris
Frankfurter, Felix, 2, 7, 32
Franks, Oliver, 84, 179, 186; on AIOC, 180; close relationship with, 103; value of allies through, 120
Fuchs, Klaus, 120

Gaitskell, Hugh, 182
Gardner, Lloyd, xi
General Assembly, 43
George, Walter, 105
Germany, 227–228; CFM on, 75; Department of Defense working with, 169n112; ECEFP for postwar, 45; EDC part for, 197; future of, 106–110; Kennan in, 109; military strength of, 8; NATO on rearmament of, 155–156; rearmament of, 161, 197; Under Secretary of State with, 75; Soviet Union attacked by, 25; Soviet Union blockade for, 107–110; Tripartite Pact, 23; US policy for, 259; zonal authorities of, 75. *See also* Berlin; East Germany; West Germany
gold prices, 4–5
Gooderham, Eleanor (mother), 1
Grady, Henry, 180
Greece: assistance program for, 80–83; Cypriots of, 233–234; for NATO membership, 198; protecting democracy through, 82
Green, Joseph C., 24, 26
Grew, Joseph, 23, 44, 111
Griffin, Allen, 141

Gromyko, Andrei, 187–188
Groton School, 14n3
Groves, Leslie, 64
Groves-Anderson Memorandum, 67
Guatemala, 201
Guzman, Jacobo Arbenz, 201

Hahn, Peter, 175
Halifax (Lord), 34, 35, 60, 69
Hall, Noel, 26
Hand, Learned, 217
Harbutt, Fraser, 74
Harmer, Freddy, 68
Harriman, Averell, 36, 64–68, 144; on
    Mossadeq, 181; valued adviser of, 148;
    on Vietnam, 238
Harvard University, 2
Heinrichs, Waldo, 28
Heller, Francis, 214
Henderson, Nicholas, 103
Hickenlooper, Bourke, 119
Hickerson, John, 149
Hillman, William, 214
Hiss, Alger, 98, 126, 214
Hiss, Donald, 98
Hoffman, Paul, 86
Holmes, Julius, 58
Holmes, Oliver Wendell, 3
Hoopes, Townsend, 191
Hoover, Herbert, 5, 162
Hoover Commission, 86–87
Hopkins, Harry, 17, 19, 32
House Un-American Activities Committee,
    98
Hull, Cordell, 12, 14, 18; Assistant
    Secretary of State under, 20–23;
    Japanese embargo approved by, 30;
    Lend-Lease agreement overseen by, 31;
    as Secretary of State, 19–23; shared
    convictions with, 20
Hurley, Patrick J., 71
hydrogen bomb: AEC for, 118; Anglo-
    American nuclear cooperation for, 119;
    PPS opinion on, 118

Ickes, Harold, 11
IMF. *See* International Monetary Fund
Immermann, Richard, 191
Inchon, 156

Indochina, 139–142, 262; Bao Dai regime
    of, 140; Britain meetings on, 142–145;
    London meetings on, 142–145; military
    strategy of, 141–142; Paris meetings
    on, 142–145; Roosevelt on, 166n19;
    Soviet Union threat against, 141
Institute of Advanced Studies, 213
Institute of Pacific Relations, 192
International Bank for Reconstruction and
    Development, 41. *See also* World Bank
International Court of Justice, 182
international developments, xiii, xiv
international economics, 18, 48
International Ladies Garment Workers
    Union, 8
International Monetary Fund (IMF), 17;
    role in, 41; Soviet Union and, 41, 42
Inverchapel (Lord), 80
Iran: AIOC crisis with, 174, 178–179;
    AIOC negotiations in, 180–182; Anglo-
    American relation with, 183–184;
    approach to, 183–184; economic
    conditions of, 183; Eden with,
    182–183; International Court of Justice
    of, 182; oil production of, 184; US-
    Soviet confrontation of, 74–75. *See also*
    Tehran
"iron curtain", 74
Isaacson, Walter, xii
isolationism, 9–10
Israel: Arab war with, 146; creation of,
    145–146; United States recognition of,
    146
Italy, 23

Jackson, Robert H., 11, 25
Japan: Chinese evacuated from, 70; for
    Chinese regime recognition, 187;
    Dulles in, 196; economic concern for,
    113; expansion of, 23; Foreign Funds
    Control Committee assets freeze of, 27;
    free world cause for, 205n67; freezing
    assets of, 24–25; postwar occupation of,
    111–112; sanctions on, 23–30, 111;
    self-supporting economy of, 113–114;
    Tripartite Pact, 23; US embargo of, 23
Japanese embargo: Hull approval of, 30;
    Japan not dissuaded by, 30; oil exports
    during, 28; tough stance on, 28–29;

Welles on, 29
Japanese Peace Treaty, 184–191, 262;
    completion of, 190–191; drafts of,
    186–187; Dulles-Morrison compromise
    of, 189; Dulles role in, 185–186;
    Gromyko on, 187–188; ratification of,
    191; Rusk role in, 184–185; of San
    Francisco Conference, 187–188
JCS. *See* Joint Chiefs of Staff
Jessup, Philip C., 99; on Kennan clash,
    224; McCarthy attacks on, 192; Stassen
    attacks on, 193; trusted advisor of, 260;
    UN representative nomination of,
    192–193
Johnson, Louis, 118, 132n155, 137
Johnson, Lyndon B., 212; on Acheson,
    Dean, 232–233; advisor (1963–1968)
    for, 232–240; for civil rights, 224–225;
    foreign affairs of, 233; opinion of, 226,
    232, 237; Vietnam and, 234–235,
    237–238, 239
Johnson Act of 1934, 10, 22
Joint Chiefs of Staff (JCS), 114
Jones, Joseph, 81

Kamp, Joseph P., 136
Kee-Connally Act, 61
Kennan, George, 77, 83, 141, 260; clash
    with, 223–224; in Germany, 109; Long
    Telegram and, 74; on Soviet Union, 156
Kennedy, John F., 212; advisor
    (1961–1963) for, 226–232; Bay of Pigs
    and, 230; Cuban Missile Crisis and,
    230–231; foreign policy of, 227
Kennedy, Robert, 231
Keynes, John Maynard, 32–34, 40, 68;
    Lend-Lease agreement negotiator, 32;
    Morgenthau with, 32; trade agreements
    with, 34
Khrushchev, Nikita, 227–228, 231
Kim Il Sung, 114
Kim Ku, 112
King, Mackenzie, 64
King, Martin Luther, Jr., 224
Kissinger, Henry: on Acheson, Dean,
    memoir, 241; with Nixon, 243; of
    Secretary of State gutting, 244
KMT. *See* Chiang Kaishek's Kuomintang
Knowland, William, 189

Knox, Frank, 9
Koje-do Island, 194
Korea: aid for, 70, 114; Congress report of,
    151–152; independent country of, 112;
    military withdrawal from, 115;
    Ridgway in, 162; separate regimes of,
    114; US commitment to, 152. *See also*
    North Korea; South Korea
Korean War, x, 149–154, 156–161;
    armistice negotiations of, 194–196;
    battlefield change in, 156; biological
    weapons allegations in, 195; Bradley
    critical of, 152; breaking deadlock in,
    195; China intervention in, 157–158;
    commitment reinforced with, 141;
    historical significance of, 150; military
    spending for, 154–155; POWs in, 194;
    public outcry of, 163; Soviet Union
    intervention in, 158; stalemate during,
    194–196; UN Security Council for,
    150; US ground troops in, 151; Western
    powers failing in, 159; Yalu River in,
    157
Kuomintang. *See* Chiang Kaishek's
    Kuomintang (KMT)

Latin America: attitudes of, 202; Secretary
    of State and, 199–202; United States
    economic ties with, 199; US
    complacency toward, 200
Lawrence, David, 214
League of Nations, 258
Lee, Raymond, 24
Leffler, Melvyn, xii
legal career: early, 3; return to, 84, 213;
    return to (1933–1929), 6–8
Lend-Lease agreement, 22–23, 31–36, 257,
    259; delays for, 34–35; "discrimination
    clause" of, 34, 35; Hull overseeing, 31;
    Keynes negotiator for, 32; preliminary
    draft of, 33; renegotiation of, 68–69;
    Soviet Union for, 36; State Department
    overseeing, 31; Stettinius reorganizing,
    39
life, reflections of, 240–241
Lilienthal, David, 65, 79, 118
Lippmann, Walter, 160, 171n145, 225
Litvinov, Maxim, 37
Lloyd, Selwyn, 195, 196

Lodge, Henry Cabot, 136
London, 142–145
London Program, 107
Long, Breckinridge, 21, 60
Long Telegram, 74
Lovett, Robert A., 84, 98, 157, 188
Loyalty Review Board, 217
Lucas, Scott, 152
Luhringer, George F., 27

MacArthur, Douglas, 26, 123; Chinese overwhelmed by, 158–159; as SCAP, 185; Secretary of State debate with, 162–165; Truman relationship with, 154, 163; UN forces restrained for, 163; Unified Command supreme commander as, 153–154, 164
MacLeish, Archibald, 2, 62–63, 212
Macmillan, Harold, 228
MacVeagh, Lincoln, 80
Makarios (Archbishop), 233
Makins, Roger, 66
Mansfield, Mike, 245
Mao Zedong, 115, 122
Marines, US, 71
Marshall, George C., 60; admiration for, 79; "chief executive officer" for, 80; China mission by, 71–72; failing health of, 87; Lilienthal on, 79; out of retirement, 157; Policy Planning Staff of, 216; as Secretary of State, 79–80; with Under Secretary of State, 79–80
Marshall, Verne, 13
Marshall Plan, 83–84, 84, 85
Martin, Joseph W., 163
Massigli, René, 143
Matthews, H. Freeman, 181
Maxwell, Russell L., 24
McCarran, Patrick, 7, 116, 192
McCarthy, Joseph R., x; "attack of the primitives" and, 136–137; Clifford against, 137; Jessup attacks of, 192; against State Department, 136
McCloy, John J., 213
McCormack, Alfred, 78
McCormack, John, 23
McCoy, John, 155
McGhee, George, 147, 179–180
McLellan, David, xii

McMahon, Robert, xii, 135, 219–220
McMahon Act, 66–68
McNamara, Robert, 235
McNay, John T., 184
MEC. *See* Middle Eastern Command
MEDO. *See* Middle Eastern Defense Organization
Melby, John, 122
Menon, Krishna, 196
Meon Plan, 196
Middle East, 145–147, 178–179; nationalism growing in, 173; Secretary of State in, 173–177; Soviet expansion in, 173–174
Middle Eastern Command (MEC): MEDO as, 176–177; regional rejection of, 176; Suez Canal under, 175
Middle Eastern Defense Organization (MEDO), 176–177
military, US, 8–9
Miller, Edward G., 200
Miller, Edward S., 24, 29
Miller, John, 136
MNR. *See* Nationalist Revolutionary Movement
Molotov, Vyacheslav, 84
Montreux Convention, 76
Morgenthau, Henry, 4–5, 6, 23, 31, 40; growing approval by, 24; Keynes with, 32; munitions for Soviet Union from, 35–36
Morning and Noon (Acheson, Dean), 240
Morrow, Dwight, 3
Mossadeq, Mohammed, 179, 181
Murphy, Frank, 7, 109
Muslim Brotherhood, 176
Mutual Aid Agreement, 35
Mutual Defense Assistance Program, 106
Mutual Security Agency, 198

Naguib, Mohammed, 177
Nasser, Gamal Abdel, 177
The Nation, 39, 59
National Council of American-Soviet Friendship, "American-Soviet Friendship" speech of, 73
National Defense Appropriation Act of June 1940, 10

Nationalist Revolutionary Movement
(MNR), 201
national policy, 212
National Security Council (NSC), 99;
China argument of, 116; Chinese
contact with, 159; Report 68 of,
137–139; of Soviet Union
expansionism, 138
NATO. *See* North Atlantic Treaty
Organization
NATO supreme commander, 153–154,
161, 164. *See also* North Atlantic
Treaty Organization
Neutrality Acts of 1935, 10, 22, 24
Neutrality Acts of 1937, 10
New Deal, ix
New York Times: on Acheson, Dean, 12;
Cohen-Acheson opinion in, 11;
reevaluation by, x–xi
Nitze, Paul, 74, 118, 213, 260–261
Nixon, Richard, 212; advisor (1969–1971)
for, 242–247; anger at, 244; as early
Acheson critic, 242; Kissinger with,
243; opinion of, 243–244; on Vietnam,
243
Nixon Doctrine, 245
No Foreign War Committee, 13
Noiret, Roger, 107
Nomura, Kichisaburo, 23, 29
North Atlantic Council, 155, 161
North Atlantic Pact, 88
North Atlantic Treaty: article 5 controversy
of, 104–105; Bohlen on, 104–105;
Congress with, 106; formal signature
of, 106; membership questions of, 105;
military actions of, 104; progress of,
103; Secretary of State on, 102–106
North Atlantic Treaty Organization
(NATO), 142; consultant for, 227; de
Gaulle on, 236; EDC with, 161, 198;
European Defense Community of, 161;
foreign policy cornerstone of, 261; on
German rearmament, 155–156; Greece
membership for, 198; political
headquarters of, 145; Turkey
membership for, 198; West Germany
joining of, 199
North Korea: "blatant aggression" of, 152;
Security Council resolution for, 149;

South Korea attack of, 149
North Vietnam: bombing halt in, 239; Viet
Cong guerrillas of, 234. *See also*
Vietnam
Noyes, David, 214
NSC. *See* National Security Council
Nye, Gerald, 10

OEEC. *See* Organization of European Eco-
nomic Cooperation
Office of Chinese Affairs, 191
Office of Far Eastern Affairs, 71
Office of Northeast Asian Affairs, 112
Office of War Mobilization and
Reconversion, 47
Offne, Arnold, xii–xiii
Oliphant, Herman, 5
Oppenheimer, Robert, 118, 212, 213
Organization of European Economic
Cooperation (OEEC), 121

Palestine, 145
Palestine Conciliation Commission, 146
Panama Canal, 199
Panikkar, K. M., 156
Papandreou, George, 234
Paris, 142–145
Pasha, Nahas, 176
Pasvolsky, Leo, 21
The Pattern of Responsibility (Bundy), x
Patterson, James, 162
Patterson, Robert, 67, 114
Pax Britannica, 8, 257
Peabody, Endicott, 258
Peabody code, 6, 14n3
Pearl Harbor, 17
Pearson, Lester B., 150–151
Penrose, E. F., 68
Pentagon Papers, 246
Pepper, Claude, 10
Peurifoy, John E., 98, 136
Philippines, 26
Philippines Mutual Defense Treaty, 189
Phillips, Cabell, 225
Policy Planning Staff (PPS), 83, 112, 118,
216
Porter, Paul A., 80
Potsdam conference, 57

Power and Diplomacy (Acheson, Dean), x, 223
PPS. *See* Policy Planning Staff
Present at the Creation (Acheson, Dean), xi, 240–241
Princeton University, 213
Pulitzer Prize, xii

Quebec Agreement, 67

Rayburn, Sam, 188
Razmara, Ali, 179
Reciprocal Trade Agreements Act, 46
Reconstruction Finance Corporation (RFC), 5–6, 200–201
Reid, Escott, 104
"Report on International Control of Atomic Energy", 66
Republic of Korea. *See* South Korea
reputation, ix–xiii
revisionist historians, xi, 246
RFC. *See* Reconstruction Finance Corporation
Rhee, Syngman, 112
Rhodesia, 241–242
Richard, James P., 83
The Riddle of the State Department (Bendiner), x
Ridgway, Matthew B., 162, 164
Rio Treaty of Reciprocal Assistance, 199
Robertson, Brain, 107
Rogers, William, 244
Roosevelt, Franklin D.: armament agreement by, 12; Atlantic Charter of, 34; campaigning for, 4; evolving opinion of, 7–8; on French controlled Indochina, 166n19; on gold prices, 5; influence with, 63; international developments of, xiv; international economics in, 18; letter from, 12–13; opinions of, 20–21; return to, 12–14; on Stettinius, 44; time in administration, ix; Truman continuing policies of, 46; US foreign policy of, 18–20
Rostow, Walt, 238
Rowe, James H., 87
Royall, Kenneth, 76
Royal Navy, 13
Rublee, George, 47

Ruegger, Paul, 195
Rusk, Dean, 99, 124, 158; comments on, 253n124; critical opinion of, 236; Japanese Peace Treaty role of, 184–185; as Secretary of State, 226; trusted advisor of, 260
Russell, Donald, 78
Russia. *See* Soviet Union

Sandy Spring, 213, 247
San Francisco Conference: Japanese Peace Treaty of, 187–188; Secretary of State at, 187–189; for United Nations Charter, 46
Saudi Arabia, 178–179
Savage, Carlton, 25
SCAP. *See* Supreme Commander Allied Powers
Schlesinger, Arthur, Jr., 5, 226, 239
Schuman, Robert, 109, 143, 261
Schuman Plan, 143–144
SEATO. *See* Southeast Asia Treaty Organization
Secretary of State, 44–45, 97–126, 226, 244; American policies of, 103; appointment as, 87–88; on Asia, 111–115; Asian security by, 184–191; Atlantic Council meetings with, 142–145; bipartisanship restored by, 147–148; call to resign from, 160; China and, 115–117, 156–161; China repatriation resolution by, 195–196; Cold War, anti-communism and, 192–193; end of term as, 202; European security and, 197–199; farewell from, 211; first year as, 125–126; foreign policy responsibility of, 215–216; Indochina and, 139–142; Iran and, 178–184; Korean War and, 149–154, 194–196; Latin America and, 199–202; MacArthur debate with, 162–165; McCarthy and, 136–137; Middle East and, 145–147, 173–177; NBC radio show on, 39; near retirement from, 57–58; nomination of, 97–98; North Atlantic Treaty by, 102–106; NSC report for, 137–139; outlook for, 100–101; problems for, 101–102; reflecting on world 1953–1960,

216–225; reflections on 1953–1960, 212–216; responsibilities as, 21; at San Francisco Conference, 187–189; South America and, 199–200; Soviet Union attitude shift of, 97; staff for, 98–100; sub-committee on, 86; tasks for, 101–102; time in, ix, 48; Truman, State Department and, 98–100; US foreign policy re-evaluated by, 117–126; Western defense built by, 154–156. *See also* Assistant Secretary of State; Byrnes, James F.; Dulles, John Foster; Hull, Cordell; Kissinger, Henry; Marshall, George C.; Rusk, Dean; Stettinius, Edward R.; Under Secretary of State

Security Council, 149

Sekaninova, Gertruda, 187

Senate Committee on Banking and Currency, on Anglo-American Financial Agreement, 69

Senate Foreign Relations Committee, for European defense, 102

SHAPE. *See* supreme head-quarters allied powers in Europe

Shea, Francis M., 24

Shigeru Yoshida, 185, 190

Sidky, Ismael, 174

Sketches from Life of Men I Have Known (Acheson, Dean), x, 240

Smith, Alexander H., 6, 151, 192

Smith, Gaddis, xii

Smith, Ian, 241

Smith, Kingsbury, 108

Snyder, John W., 120

Souers, Sydney, 138

South America, 199–200

South American banks, 29

Southeast Asia Treaty Organization (SEATO), 189

Southern Africa, 241–242

South Korea: North Korea attack on, 149; North Korea border cross of, 156–157; as Republic of Korea, 114; US support for, 150; US troops in, 154. *See also* Korea

South Vietnam, 234. *See also* Vietnam

Soviet diplomats, 37

Soviet Union: advocate for, 73; approach to, 257; atomic bomb for, 63–64; attitude on, 260; avoided war with, 153; Berlin blockade by, 107–110; CFM and, 80; complacency charges toward, 97; cooperation breakdown with, 102; dealings with, 73–75; Germany attack on, 25; IMF and, 41, 42; Indochina threatened by, 141; Kennan on, 156; Korean War intervention of, 158; Lend-Lease agreement for, 36; Middle East expansion of, 173–174; military strength of, 8; munitions for, 35–36; NSC expansionist of, 138; Secretary of State attitude shift toward, 97; Under Secretary of State with, 73; shift in cooperation with, 77; Taft on, 162; threat of, xi; tough line on, 103; US aid to, 35

Spaak, Paul-Henri, 121

Spofford, Charles, 155

Stalin, Joseph, 74

Stanley, Alice (wife), 2

Stassen, Harold E., 193

State Department: changes at, 39; complex issues in, 216; expansion of, 18; foreign affairs in, 215; intelligence shift from, 78; Lend-Lease agreement overseen by, 31; Naguib with, 177; service at, 259

"The State Department Speaks" (NBC radio), 39

State-War-Navy Coordinating Committee (SWNCC), 81, 113, 114

Stettinius, Edward R., 39, 61; of congressional relations, 44–45; Lend-Lease agreement reorganized by, 39; Roosevelt on, 44; as Secretary of State, 44–45

Stevenson, Adlai, 220–221

Stikker, Dirk, 227

Stilwell, Joseph, 70

Stimson, Henry, 9, 12, 63

Stokes, Richard, 182, 204n45

Stone, I. F., 59

Strang, William, on Stokes, 204n45

Strengthening the Forces of Freedom (Acheson, Dean), x

Stuart, John Leighton, 122

Stupak, Ronald, xi

Sudan, 177
Suez Canal, 174, 175
Supreme Commander Allied Powers
(SCAP), 59, 185. *See also* MacArthur,
Douglas
Supreme Court, 2–3
supreme head-quarters allied powers in
Europe (SHAPE), 145
SWNCC. *See* State-War-Navy
Coordinating Committee

Taft, Robert, 124, 136, 162
Taiwan, 123, 153
Tang, James, 123
Tehran, 180–182
Temporary Council Committee, 198. *See
also* North Atlantic Treaty Organization
Thomas, Evan, xii
Thomas Amendment, 5
Time, 39
Tobey, Charles, 40
total diplomacy, 138
totalitarian dictatorships, 8
The Tragedy of American Foreign Policy
(Williams), xi, 240
Treasury, US, 28–29
Tripartite Declaration, 147
Tripartite Pact, 23
Tripartite Washington Declaration, 64,
131n135
Truman, Harry S., ix, 103; Assistant
Secretary of State and, 45–47; Attlee
talks with, 160–161; Byrnes problems
with, 62; Byrnes time with, 60; on
Eisenhower, 219; MacArthur
relationship with, 154, 163; "phase out"
work for, 229; on Quebec Agreement,
67; for Roosevelt polices, 46; on
Taiwan, 123; Zionist pressure on,
146–147
Truman Doctrine, 82, 260; foreign policy
shift with, 83; universally application
of, 113
Truman Library, 214
Turkey: assistance program for, 80–83;
August crises with Yugoslavia and,
75–76; Cypriots of, 233–234; NATO
membership for, 198; protecting
democracy through, 82; Under

Secretary of State working with, 80–83;
US naval task force for, 76
Tydings, Millard, 135

UN. *See* United Nations
Under Secretary at Treasury, ix, 4–6
Under Secretary of State, 57–59; Acheson-
Lilienthal plan of, 65–66; appointment
to, 57–59; atomic energy handled by,
63–65; August crises for, 75–76; British
loan by, 68–70; Byrnes with, 59–63;
Cold War attitudes of, 76–77; Germany
and, 75; Greece working with, 80–83;
Hoover Commission and, 86–87;
leaving office of, 84–86; Marshall, G.,
and, 79–80; Marshall China mission of,
70–72; for Marshall plan, 83–84;
McMahon Act of, 66–68; Soviet Union
and, 73; transition of, 84–85; Turkey
working with, 80–83
UN First Committee, 9–10
UN forces, 163
Unified Command, 153–154
United Fruit Company, 201
United Nations (UN), 17; Asian aggression
through, 123; beginning of, 43; at
Dumbarton Oaks, 43; General
Assembly of, 43; historical framework
of, 46–47; Jessup representative
nomination for, 192–193; stable
economy with, 43; Unified Command
of, 153; wariness of, 47
United Nations Charter, 46
United Nations Food and Agriculture
Organization, 38
United Nations Relief and Rehabilitation
Administration (UNRRA), 36–38, 259;
American Forum of the Air discussion
of, 38; Assistant Secretary of State on,
36–38; early leadership of, 38; launch
of, 37–38
United States (US), 171n164–172n165;
Asia defensive perimeter by, 123; Asia
policy in, 70; Britain armament
agreement with, 12; of British imperial
preference opponents, 31; European
funds frozen by, 24; for Germany
policy, 259; gold crisis of, 239; Israel
recognition of, 146; Japan embargo by,

23; Korea commitment of, 152; Latin
America complacency of, 200; Latin
America economic ties with, 199;
manifest destiny of, 259; military of,
8–9; moral purpose of, 222; postwar
order important for, 164; power role of,
258; Soviet Union aid from, 35;
totalitarian dictatorships response of, 8;
Treasury of, 28–29; Vietnam
commitment of, 245; Western Europe
connection with, 227; World War II
threat to, 22
United States foreign policy, xiii–xiv;
address issues of, 100–101; beginning
in, 13–14; in Cold War, xiii; critiques
of, xi, xiii; influence on, 17; of Johnson,
L., 233; of Kennedy, J., 227; Lawrence
on, 214; NATO cornerstone of, 261;
presidential foreign policy as, 261; reevaluation of, 117–126; revisionist
indictment of, 240; of Roosevelt,
18–20; Secretary of State responsibility
of, 215–216; in State Department, 215;
strategy for, 257; total diplomacy of,
138; tougher rhetoric for, 135; Williams
opinion of, 240
*The United States in World Affairs,
1947–1948*, 123
United States–Japanese Security Treaty,
189
United States military, 71, 117–125
UN representative, 192
UNRRA. *See* United Nations Relief and
Rehabilitation Administration
UN Security Council, 150
US. *See* United States
US-Soviet, 74–75

Vandenberg Resolution, 102
Vanderberg, Arthur, 37, 86, 102
Viet Minh: as communist, 140; Dutch
police action against, 139; French
campaign against, 140
Vietnam: Ball peace plan for, 247;
guerrilla warfare in, 238; Harriman on,
238; Johnson, L., and, 234–235, 239;
military escalation in, 237; Nixon on,
243; Pentagon Papers engagement
history of, 246; presentations on, 239;

recommendations for, 262; Tet
offensive in, 238; US commitment to,
245; war investigation of, 238–239
Vincent, John Carter, 71, 112; Dulles
verdict of, 218; Hand, L., on, 217;
Loyalty Review Board on, 217
Vinson, Fred, 40, 47, 68

Wafd party, 176
Wallace, Henry, 77
Warren, George F., 4–5
wartime diplomacy, 47
Washington, DC, ix, 217
Washington Agreement, 67
Webb, James E., 98–99
Wedemeyer, Albert C., 72
Weizmann, Chaim, 146
Welles, Sumner, 12, 20; on Japanese
embargo, 29; munitions for Soviet
Union, 35–36; resignation of, 39
Western defenses, 154–156
Western Europe, 223, 227
Western powers, 108, 159
West Germany, 143; Basic Law of, 110;
creation of, 107; future of, 109; of
joining NATO, 199; West marks of,
107
Wheeler, Earle, 237
Wherry, Kenneth, 151, 171n143; on
Acheson, Dean, 160; Under Secretary
appointment opposition of, 59
White, Harry Dexter, 40, 41
White, Theodore, 227
Wierblowski, Stefan, 188
Wiley, Alexander, 211
Williams, William Appleman, xi, 240
Willkie, Wendell, 11
Wilson, Edwin, 75
Wilson, Theodore, 33
Wilson, Woodrow, 258
Winant, John, 68
Woodrow Wilson Award, 218
World Bank, 17, 41, 200
World War II, x; Britain aid for, 22; end of,
57; positions throughout, 47–48;
responding (1939–1940) to, 8–10; US
threat of, 22
Wrong, Hume, 125

Yale University, 2
Yalta conference, 45
Yokohama Specie Bank of New York, 29
Younger, Kenneth, 188

Yugoslavia, 75–76

Zhukov, Georgi, 76
Zionists, 146–147

About the Author

Michael Hopkins is senior lecturer in American foreign policy at the University of Liverpool. He is the author of *Oliver Franks and the Truman Administration* (2003, 2016) and *The Cold War* (2011). His edited books include *The Washington Embassy* (2009) and *Cold War Britain* (2003).

Lightning Source UK Ltd.
Milton Keynes UK
UKOW03n0935180517
301409UK00001B/105/P